Integrating Service Level Agreements

Optimizing Your OSS for SLA Delivery

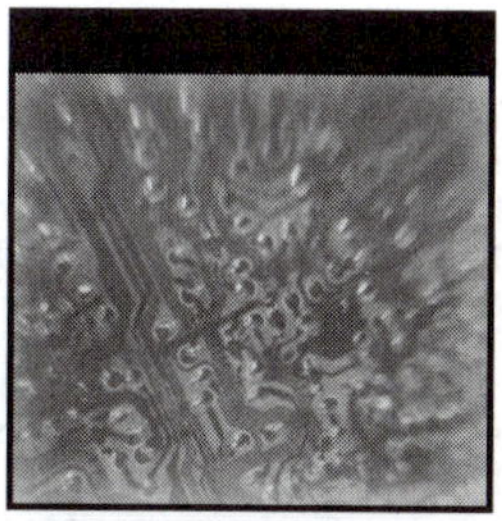

Integrating Service Level Agreements

Optimizing Your OSS for SLA Delivery

John J. Lee
Ron Ben-Natan

Wiley Publishing, Inc.

Publisher: Robert Ipsen
Editor: Margaret Eldridge
Developmental Editor: Kathryn Malm
Managing Editor: Pamela Hanley
New Media Editor: Brian Snapp
Text Design & Composition: Wiley Composition Services

This book is printed on acid-free paper. ♾

Published by Wiley Publishing, Inc., Indianapolis, Indiana
Published simultaneously in Canada

For general information on our other products and services please contact our Customer Care Department within the United States at (800) 762-2974, outside the United States at (317) 572-3993 or fax (317) 572-4002.

Wiley also publishes its books in a variety of electronic formats. Some content that appears in print may not be available in electronic books.

Library of Congress Cataloging-in-Publication Data:

Lee, John (John J.), 1961-

Integrating service level agreements : optimizing your OSS for SLA delivery / John Lee, Ron Ben-Natan.

p. cm.

Includes bibliographical references and index.

ISBN 0-471-21012-9

1. Telecommunication—Quality control. 2. Service-level agreements.
3. Telecommunication—Customer service. 4. Internet service providers.
5. Information technology. I. Ben-Natan, Ron. II. Title.

TK5102.84 .L44 2002
004.6'068—dc21

2002008682

Printed in the United States of America
10 9 8 7 6 5 4 3 2 1

Contents

"There is a wisdom of the head and a wisdom of the heart"

Charles Dickens

To our wives, Becky and Rinat, whose endless dedication and tireless support form the foundation of our success.

About the Authors

John J. Lee is Vice President of Strategy and Business Solutions at ViryaNet, a company that provides wireless workforce solutions. He is an expert in the development of operation and business support systems and a frequent contributor to industry publications.

Ron Ben-Natan is CTO at ViryaNet and has been building distributed systems and applications at companies like Intel, Merrill Lynch, J. P. Morgan, and AT&T Bell Labs for the past 20 years. He has authored several successful books on distributed systems and the application of advanced technologies in business environments.

PART One

The Problem

CHAPTER

1

What Are Service Level Agreements?

In Chapter 1 we will describe SLAs, discuss why they are important, and demonstrate why they are on the way to becoming the driving concept behind all service models.

Service level agreements (SLAs) are about making promises. In the case of telecommunications, these are the promises that underlie all the fiber being laid; all the optics and electronics being developed, bought, installed, and turned up and the exact same promises that drove venture capitalists and investors to back all those telecom businesses that had absolutely no chance—none whatsoever—of ever making a dime.

Definition

In its most basic form, a service level agreement (SLA) is a contract or agreement that formalizes a business relationship, or part of the relationship, between two parties. Most often it takes the form of a negotiated contract made between a service provider and a customer and defines a price paid in exchange for an entitlement to a product or service to be delivered under certain terms, conditions, and with certain financial guarantees.

The TeleManagement Forum's SLA Management Handbook defines an SLA as "[a] formal negotiated agreement between two parties, sometimes called a service level guarantee. As depicted in Figure 1.1, it is a contract (or part of one) that exists between the service provider and the customer, designed to create a common understanding about services, priorities, responsibilities, etc." (GB 917)

Service level agreements emerged in the early 1990s as a way for Information Technology (IT) departments and service providers within private (usually corporate) computer networking environments to measure and manage the *quality of service* (QoS) they were delivering to their internal customers. Service level agreements are the contractual component of QoS and are usually implemented as part of a larger *service level management* (SLM) initiative.

Service level management has been defined by Sturm, Morris, and Jander in *Foundations of Service Level Management* as "the disciplined, proactive methodology and procedures used to ensure that adequate levels of service are delivered to all (IT) users in accordance with business priorities and at acceptable cost" (2000).

Quality of service is defined by the International Telecommunications Union (ITU-T) as "the collective effect of service performances, which determine the degree of satisfaction of a user of the service. Note that the quality of service is characterized by the combined aspects of service support performance, service operability performance, service integrity and other factors specific to each service."

In the last 10 years, SLM and QoS initiatives have routinely been implemented within the IT arena with much success. Originally, much of the SLM data were used to justify procurement and staffing budgets for IT groups that

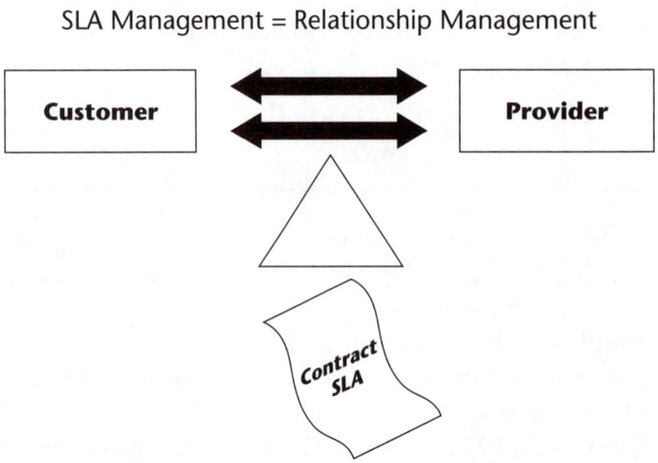

Figure 1.1 Service level agreements as depicted by the TeleManagement Forum in GB 917.

were still considered cost centers and whose real value to the business was not yet fully appreciated. Much of the reporting consisted of QoS data showing customer satisfaction owing to contributions made by IT to user productivity and the bottom line.

Much has changed in the last 10 years. The value of computers in all segments and industries within the business world (as well as in our personal lives) has gone from unproven to absolutely essential. We have entered an era of business specialization, industry consolidation, and realization of large efficiency gains owing largely to technology.

The standardization of hardware, networking, operating system, and many business software standards has made a relative commodity of providing traditional IT department functions such as PC hardware configuration, network connectivity, and email access.

Today the products and services that are routinely contracted for and managed using SLAs seem almost limitless. In the telecommunications space, customers most typically demand financial guarantees on the accurate and timely performance of the network itself, normally measured using statistical indicators such as circuit availability, reliability, and other *key performance indicators* (*KPI*s), as well as service-related activities such as provisioning, installations, trouble response, and fault correction.

Other areas such as responsive customer service, accurate billing, and immediate availability of additional network capacity can also be guaranteed by an SLA. It seems that the main qualifying criteria is that the service be mission-critical and provided by an outside source. SLAs are also used extensively in other industries, most notably in the utility, transportation, and manufacturing fields.

Service Level Agreement Roles and Objectives

Implementing a *service level management (SLM)* program that works for both the service provider and the customer is a very difficult undertaking. Service level agreements are technically complex to pull off from an operational standpoint, but, more important, the perception of the roles that SLAs should play differs greatly for the service provider as compared with the customer. In this chapter we discuss primarily the service provider's point of view; the customer's needs are discussed at length in Chapter 2. The roles most commonly given to SLAs can generally be grouped into six areas, as shown in Figure 1.2:

1. Define roles and accountability
2. Manage expectations
3. Control implementation and execution

4. Provide verification
5. Enable communications
6. Assess return on investment

Defining Roles and Accountability

It is important that both parties to an SLA understand the respective roles and responsibilities defined in the agreement. A number of industry factors have made establishing roles, responsibilities, and performance (and financial) accountability increasingly difficult on both the network and services side of the SLA equation.

Deregulation and the unprecedented growth in technology, customer demand, and new service offerings experienced over the last decade have created a unique environment in which hundreds of service providers depend on their competition to help them to deliver end-to-end services. Since 1984 the "network" and "the cloud" (the worldwide telecom WAN relative to the user's LAN perspective) have become a virtual maze of equipment and capacity owned by a multitude of service providers, including leased lines, *indefeasible rights to use* (*IRUs*), bandwidth swaps, *unbundled network elements* (*UNE*), carrier hotels, collocations, and "meet-me" rooms.

To make it all work, the myriad providers have executed an almost endless number of collocation, interconnection, and capacity leasing agreements with each other, creating a complex web of overlapping business relationships. In the process, networks have become so intertwined and interdependent that many service providers cannot function without the other providers in their competitive space.

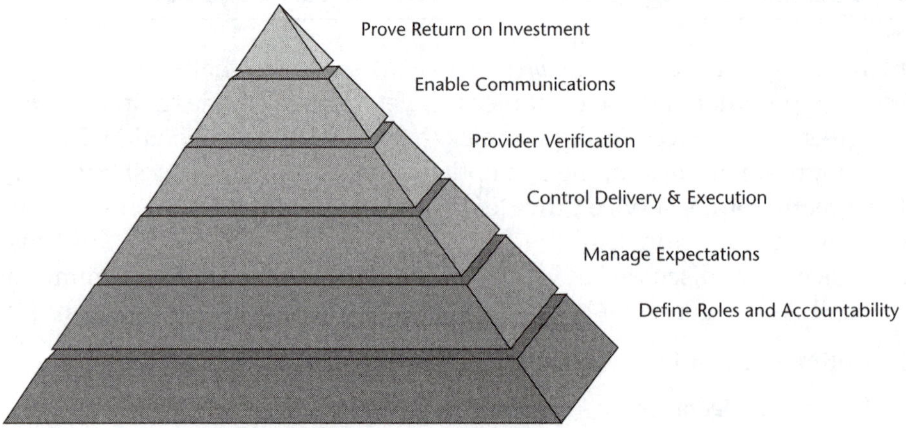

Figure 1.2 The roles played by service level agreements.

Within the industry, the term *coopetition* has been coined to describe this strangely symbiotic situation. The TeleManagement Forum (TMF) has also recognized the phenomenon and the implication for SLAs. The *SLA Management Handbook* uses the term *value chain of service provision* to describe a scenario wherein a number of different service providers are related through a series of SLA relationships that eventually terminate at the end user. A service provider in one SLA can be the customer in another SLA, and vice versa. Today, thousands of different value chains exist—each with any number of service providers (and potential SLAs) imbedded in it. The companies represented in these value chains span the entire cross section of telecommunications, as shown in Figure 1.3.

Other factors, including the increased outsourcing of customer care to large call-center providers, service fulfillment to third-party installers, network monitoring to managed network service providers, and so on, have increasingly blurred the landscape, fragmented the lines of communication, confused end-to-end workflow processes, and made organizational continuity and accountability all but invisible to the customer.

Service level agreements will be used to reestablish the chain of accountability. As outlined by the TMF, each instance of SLA execution will consist of a service provider and a customer. In a well-developed SLA, the roles and responsibilities of each party will be defined as concretely as possible, along with the associated responsibility, liabilities, and recourse available to both parties.

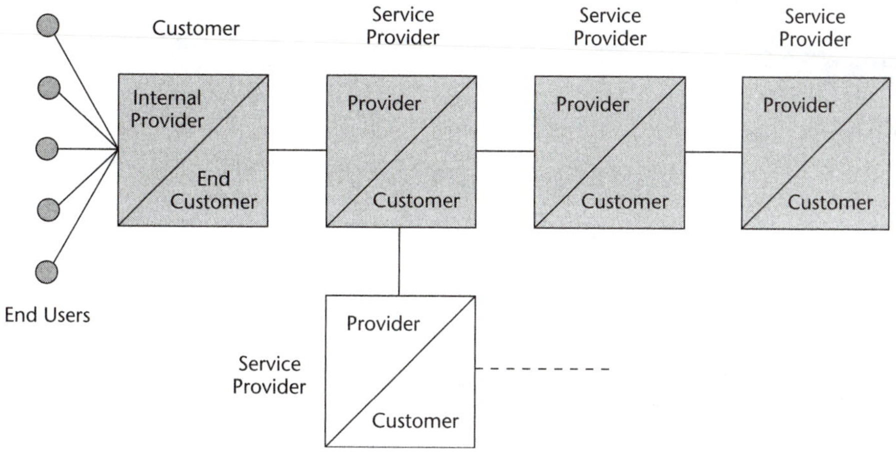

Figure 1.3 TeleManagement Forum's value chain of service provision.

Service level agreements simplify the customer's contractual recourse because the service provider functions as the final guarantor of the end-to-end network. That way, no matter the complexity of the underlying service (multiple service providers, different technologies, and so forth), the customer can hold the service provider solely responsible for delivery to his or her service access point.

To mitigate the associated risks, the service provider (in its role as customer of another service provider) may in turn demand SLAs to cover that relationship. The result is a flow-down effect in which the risks of guaranteeing service to the end customer are spread through multiple SLAs over the end-to-end value chain. An example is shown in Figure 1.4.

Managing Expectations

In general, executing an SLA contractually sets the customer's expectations regarding a product's delivery. Once defined, agreed to, and executed, the terms and conditions that make up the bulk of the SLA contract become the customer's entitlements with respect to the product. This guarantee enables the customer to plan and operate his or her business with a reasonable level of confidence in the availability, performance, or timeframe of a contracted product or service.

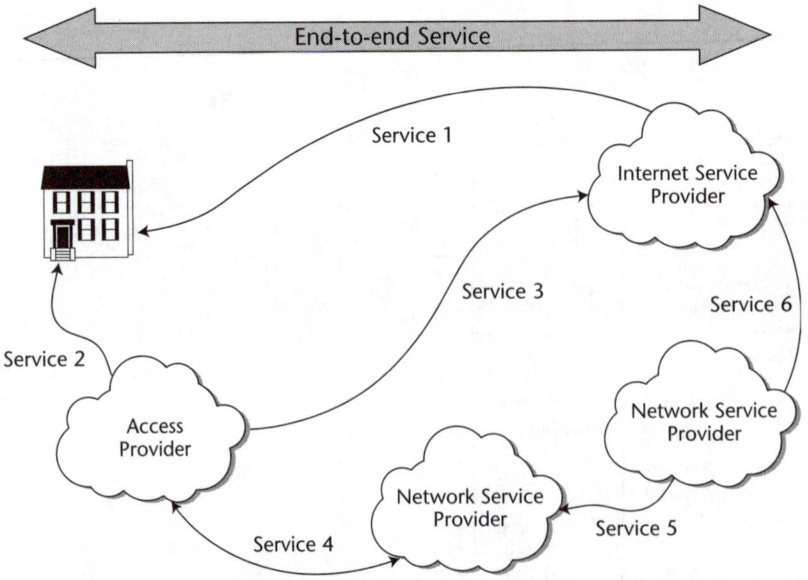

Figure 1.4 TeleManagement Forum's value chain of service provision.

Multiple SLA options (platinum, gold, silver, bronze, and so forth) for the same product or service give the customer the opportunity to weigh competing priorities within his or her own company and understand the relationship of his or her needs to those of other businesses. These options help the customer to allocate financial resources appropriately: He or she may opt for higher levels of availability or quicker response times at additional cost only for the most mission-critical links and decide to settle for a lower level of service for the rest.

Different SLA options and the relationships between the guaranteed level, delivered level, and engineered level are demonstrated in the *SLA Management Handbook*, as shown in Figure 1.5.

Service level agreements also assist the service provider in many ways. By understanding the customer's expectations and the consequences of not meeting them, the service provider's operations managers and other responsible parties can better plan and implement the required infrastructure.

For example, SLA compliance may require that more emphasis be placed on network planning and configuration, collaboration with clients, proactive network management, and renewed emphasis on preventive maintenance, which are all driven by cost containment related to penalty clauses within SLAs. Service level agreement commitments may also demand that personnel or parts be prepositioned at or near the customer's *Service Access Point (SAP)* to ensure adequate response capability or that additional resources such as spare facilities, parts, or backup circuits are put in place to reduce the potential for outages.

Perhaps the greatest advantage of SLAs to both parties is that they set expectations and requirements for the process that will enable successful execution. Every relationship creates dependencies for which the expected results can be attained only if both parties provide the required contribution in a timely manner.

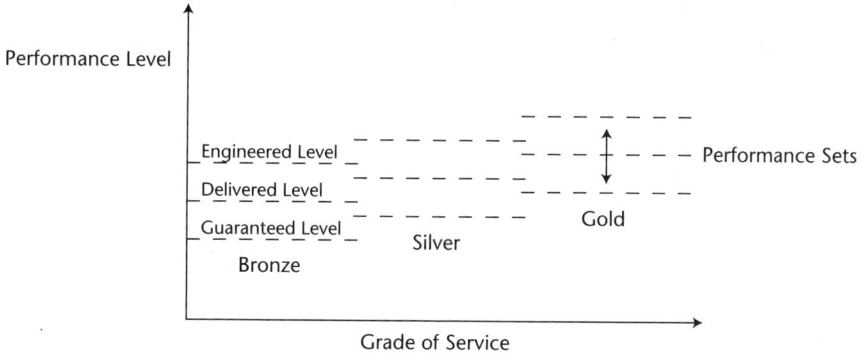

Figure 1.5 The TeleManagement Forum's service level agreement performance levels.

Service level agreements formalize this relationship and, more important, place timeframes, thresholds, and escalation procedures around the execution phase of service fulfillment, assurance, and other areas, such as billing. Both the service provider and the customer are better able to plan because many of the "unknowns" are covered in the SLA, such as volumes, locations, QoS, and costs.

Controlling Implementation and Execution

The SLA is a reference document for managing the execution of the contract and ensuring the timely delivery and continued performance of the product or service within the defined entitlements.

Customers tend to use SLAs to ensure preferential treatment for their particular service needs relative to all the others in the service provider's network. The expectations are clearly set, and during the implementation and execution phases of the contract, the service provider must deliver on these expectations.

For the service provider, delivering the contracted service translates into ensuring that sufficient resources are available to consistently meet or exceed the SLA commitments. The service provider must have an understanding of all the commitments that have been made over the entire customer base and how the requirement for delivering on these commitments affect the supporting organizations.

Service level agreement entitlements have a tendency to affect the service provider's support organization in two ways: (1) They tend to reprioritize the work based on a potential financial impact, and (2) they tend to shorten the time available to perform the work.

Historically, field service organizations have prioritized work based on the impact to the network hardware. Automated network management systems generated much of the fault identification and were usually configured so that fault alarms or outages on the most critical hardware (such as switches) and larger pipes took precedence over those on the smaller, less critical ones. Service orders usually got done after all the trouble tickets were closed. Preventive maintenance was usually relegated to the bottom of the list, as shown below in Figure 1.6.

Although service providers have gone to great lengths to improve fault detection, increase network reliability, and reduce outages that affect service by increasing redundancy and minimizing single points of failure, there will always be critical and even catastrophic failures on the network that require immediate, high-priority response. Along with traditional network priorities, SLAs introduce a new variable into the prioritization formula: financial impact.

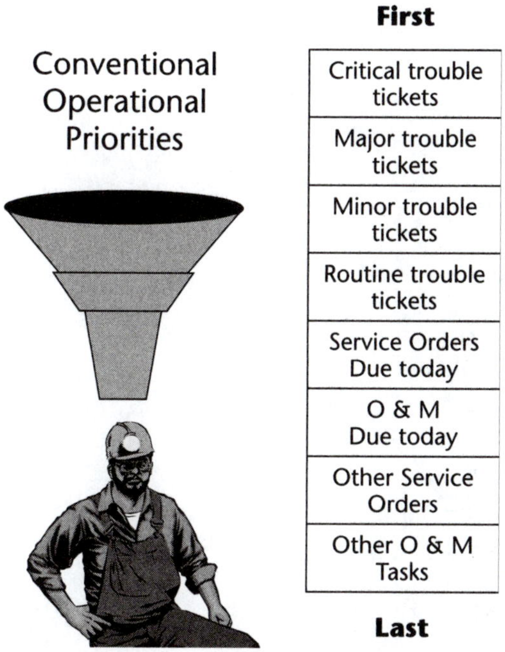

Figure 1.6 Conventional operational priorities.

The growing use of SLAs will force service providers to reprioritize the workload in order to meet the entitlements or risk financial damages. With service providers offering a number of SLA options in order to differentiate their product from the competition's, tasks, circuits, and services are no longer created equal from a prioritization standpoint. Services covered by an SLA will have to go to the front of the line—which, going back to the beginning of this section, is what the customer intended all along. The reprioritized order of work is depicted in Figure 1.7.

Providing Quality of Service Verification

Following (or during) the execution phase, the service provider(s) will be held accountable for performance being in compliance with the agreement. Proof or verification of QoS compliance is a critical component of most SLAs. Many times this has necessitated advanced planning on gathering the data required to provide SLA reporting. This is done as part of implementing an SLA, which is covered later in this chapter.

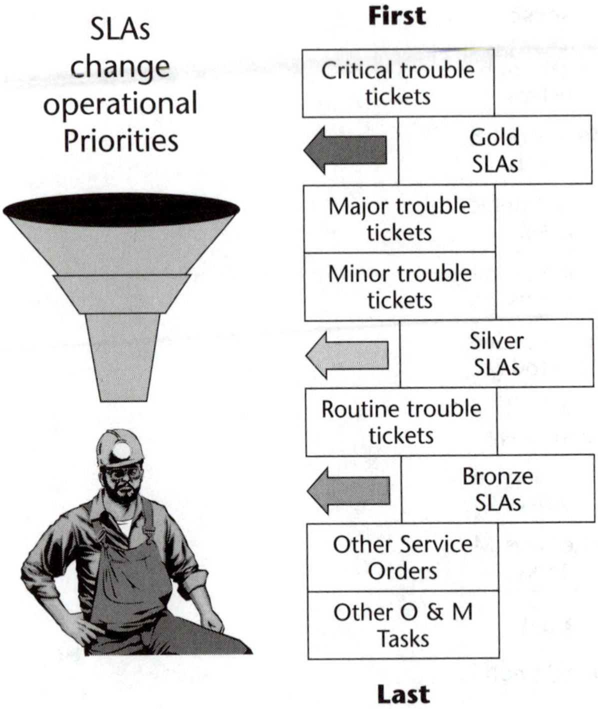

Figure 1.7 Service level agreements change operational priorities.

Making QoS and SLA compliance visible serves the needs of both the customer and the service provider. On the customer side, the customer is able to ascertain that he or she is indeed getting what he or she is paying for. This is especially important to companies that opt for higher levels of QoS (that is, platinum or gold SLAs) who, most often, also happen to be the most important customers.

Good SLA reporting also provides a level of confidence that the QoS is being proactively monitored and that the service provider stands ready to respond to contingencies. Both of these factors contribute to a feeling of security that is an important part of overall customer satisfaction.

For the service provider, good reporting and visibility can provide invaluable information as to the operational effectiveness of the service provider's network and organization in supporting SLA entitlements. The service provider must continually optimize all the solution factors in the SLA equation. Without feedback in the form of QoS reporting, the service provider will be unable to do that. Quality of service performance reports on both the network and activity sides of SLAs can also provide input into the SLA assessment process. The assessment process is covered later in this chapter.

Enabling Communications

Service level agreements provide a framework for both service providers and customers to address their needs, expectations, performance relative to those expectations, and progress on action items that may be undertaken to improve upon either the SLA itself or the service provider's performance.

There are three inherent points in an SLA's life cycle that require good communications between the customer and service provider: (1) during the development of a negotiated SLA, (2) during the implementation and execution of the SLA-covered services, and (3) during customer-focused assessments. These points of the SLA life cycle can generally be mapped to the legal, operational, and financial aspects of the SLA, as shown in Figure 1.8.

Because a single SLA definition or template may cover many individual service instances, communication between service provider and customer is typically on an ongoing, and sometimes event-driven (such as service order or trouble ticket) basis. As we have seen in the previous sections, the SLA determines the roles and expectations of the service provider and the customer and spells out the level of performance that the customer is entitled to. The clearer the definition of all these areas in the SLA, the easier and more concrete the communications will be.

This is especially important during the implementation and execution of SLAs. Event-driven communications are at the heart of SLA operational support. Service level agreements will typically include procedures and timeframes for customer notification, updating, and problem escalation up the service provider's support hierarchy. Similarly, the service provider's support organization must communicate during execution to ensure that compliance is achieved. Of course, in the event of QoS noncompliance, breach of contract, or a disagreement, the SLA will outline the appropriate next steps for correction or other recourse.

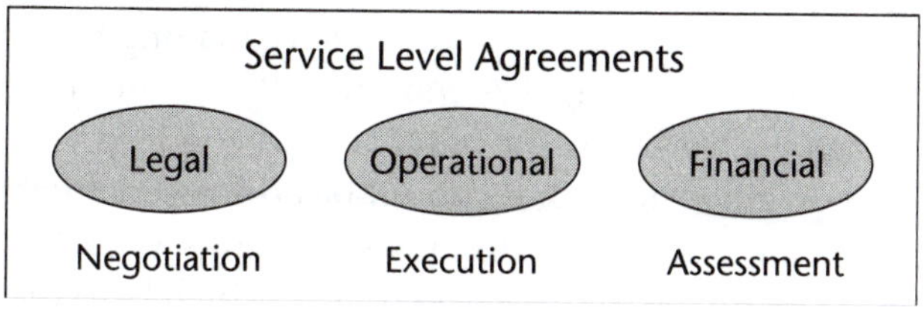

Figure 1.8 Aspects of communication in the service level agreement life cycle.

Assessing Return on Investment

The ability to calculate *return on investment (ROI)* is a key reason that SLAs are becoming more prevalent. As we will be discussing in Chapter 2, the customer uses SLAs to protect his or her business's ability to operate. He or she is even willing to pay extra in order to get a higher level of comfort and security.

The ROI assessment can be considered the financial aspect of verifying that the correct QoS levels were selected for the business. It should be noted that routine verification of QoS differs from a business assessment of ROI in a number of significant ways. Verification is usually ongoing and event driven, concentrating on day-to-day compliance, while ROI assessments are usually more periodic and are intended to measure the impact of the QoS performance (and SLA noncompliance) on the customer's business. It can be said that the verification process is tactical, while the ROI assessment is more strategic to the business.

In most cases, the SLA executor (usually the person responsible for representing the customer in negotiating SLAs) is accountable to his or her management chain for both the costs associated with the services delivered under SLA and the decisions made as to what QoS level is right for a specific application or site. Like the service provider, the SLA executor must provide financial justification and police the QoS for compliance; he or she must then make further decisions on continuance of service under the current SLA or what changes should be made.

The customer could decide that the QoS level he or she is receiving is appropriate, overkill for his or her application, not good enough (which may necessitate upgrading his or her QoS level), or that the service provider's level of compliance is unacceptable. More and more SLAs are providing opt-out clauses for noncompliance, usually with some built-in correction period. If a service provider is unable to come into compliance even after the correction period, the customer can opt out and terminate the contract.

The Service Level Agreement Life Cycle

In order to satisfy the roles and objectives that have already been discussed, the service provider needs to adopt an organized approach to managing SLAs whereby the service provider examines each SLA individually in order to make decisions on deployment, value to the business, terms and conditions to include, and a number of other considerations that should be addressed. Such an approach facilitates comparing the service provider's offerings with the customer's needs and other SLAs available in the marketplace, which help the service provider fit a particular SLA into the overall SLM program or corporate strategy.

In GB917, the TMF has outlined the SLA in order to provide the organized approach needed. We will be using the same phases to describe requirements that should be considered by service providers in integrating SLAs into their product mix. The SLA life cycle consists of the following phases, demonstrated in Figure 1.9:

1. SLA development
2. Negotiation and sales
3. Implementation
4. Execution
5. Assessment

SLA Development

Good business practice drives most service providers to develop a product definition or go through a more extended product development cycle. When they are integrating SLAs into the product mix, service providers must understand and account for the importance of good product definition up front.

A strong product development process should specify, define, test, and cover (or uncover) every aspect of a prospective product or service offering. Strong contract and entitlement development processes are more important for products covered by SLAs. Although SLAs are often treated very much like a product, an SLA is actually a value-added feature of the underlying product or service and should not be thought of in the same context as a product. Product development processes and special considerations for using SLAs as a value-added feature to an underlying product are discussed in further detail in Chapter 2.

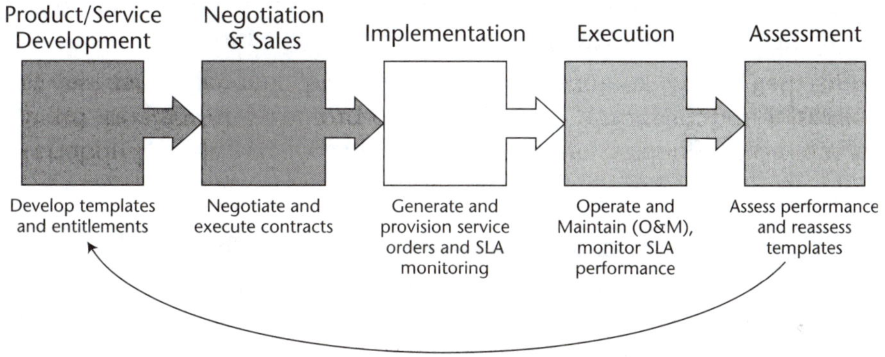

Figure 1.9 The TeleManagement Forum's service level agreement life cycle.

Contrary to common practice, not all products are truly suitable for use with SLAs. Attributes that are specific to service level agreements, such as customer needs, contractual entitlements, terms and conditions, reporting requirements, and SLA pricing may initially be derived from the information accumulated as part of the product development cycle. From that point forward, SLAs differ substantially from products in several ways:

- There may be a one-many relationship among several SLAs and a single product or product bundle. (Note: A single SLA definition may be used across a number of different products, but this does not constitute a one-many relationship between a single SLA and multiple products.) During both contracting and execution, invoking SLA entitlements is presumed to be an event-driven occurrence (service order, trouble ticket, and so forth) usually representative of a single product instance delivered to a single SAP.
- Service level agreements may be bundled with a product, unbundled from the product, or even be selectable, with several optional levels of QoS.
- Service level agreement life cycles do not necessarily run concurrent with the underlying product.

Service providers must take these differences into account when they are developing SLAs. The use of SLAs potentially exposes the service provider to a financial downside (in the form of penalties) beyond the normal risks associated with introducing a new product. Because the potential for sustaining losses greatly exceeds that for making revenues, service providers should give careful consideration to numerous factors when making SLA deployment decisions; for instance, they should understand the impact that introducing a new SLA may have on the profitability and life cycle of the underlying product.

From an accounting perspective, for example, SLA penalties paid out to customers have to come from somewhere. The logical place is the product's monthly recurring charge (MRC), which is normally used for penalty calculation anyway. If excessive QoS penalties make a product unprofitable, does the service provider drop the SLA, the product, or both? When multiyear SLA contracts are in place, is the service provider even able to pursue such an option? These questions must be addresses as part of the service provider's strategy.

On the other hand, a well-thought-out SLA can provide a revenue boost, and a service provider may elect to provide customers with several SLA options for bundling with a product. Service level agreements should include detailed information on the parties involved, the relationship that exists among them, and the products or services that are covered under the SLA. Specific terms and conditions should be defined that detail when and how the services are to be performed or delivered and the responsibilities of the parties; the agreement should also stipulate the exact frequency, locations, and methods through which the performance is to be measured and reported.

Finally, the SLA should provide a framework for taking corrective actions, the time frames for corrective actions, measurement guidelines, formulas for computing penalties, and whether further recourse is available when the SLA's terms are not met. From a purely contractual standpoint, the contract information that should be considered when developing an SLA is illustrated in the framework that follows:

1. Agreement definition
    a) Parties
    b) Contract terms and conditions
    c) Delivery location(s)
        i. Service access point(s)
2. Product definition
    a) Product description
    b) Technical description
    c) Price/cost
        i. Nonrecurring (NRC)
        ii. Monthly recurring (MRC)
        iii. Time and materials (T&M)
        iv. Other charges (MISC)
3. Performance/metric definition
    a) Activity
        i. Service orders
        ii. Trouble tickets
        iii. Routine/preventive maintenance
        iv. Mean Time To Repair(MTTR)
        v. Other metrics
    b) Network
        i. Availability
        ii. Reliability
        iii. Downtime
        iv. Mean Time Between Failures (MTBF)
        v. Other metrics

4. Measurement definition
   a) Start/stop procedures
   b) Points of measurement
   c) Methods of measurement
   d) Frequency of measurement
5. Correction definition
   a) Start/stop procedures
   b) Points of correction
   c) Methods of correction
   d) Time frames for correction
6. Reconciliation definition
   a) Methods of recourse
   b) Penalty/incentive formula(s)
   c) Time frame of recourse
   d) Other actions available

Negotiation and Sales

Once an SLA has been fully developed, it is put on the market with or layered on top of the underlying product. In some instances the SLA may be in a template that has been defined in such a way that it is a *take it or leave it* proposition. This is usually done in the most generic and technically routine service offerings, or when the service provider is developing the *standard* or lowest-level SLA in a multitiered SLA offering.

In most other cases, the customer or service provider may want to modify terms, conditions, or pricing related to the SLA. In some cases, the customer requirements may be so stringent or unique that the SLA is actually developed during negotiations. Many SLA offerings have also been created after the initial SLA development cycle was performed in response to a *request for proposal* (*RFP*) from a potential customer.

The expected outcome of the negotiation and sales phase is an executed agreement. The products and services, terms and conditions, metrics, measurement, and reporting, as well as financial (such as price and penalties) and legal considerations (such as recourse and means to settle disputes, that is, arbitration) should be stated and agreed upon by both parties. These expectations are then carried forward into the implementation and execution phases of the SLA life cycle.

Implementation

Another word for SLA implementation in the telecommunications arena is *provisioning*. During this phase, the services are ordered, activated, and configured for SLA compliance. This may mean that certain baseline measurements are taken, new monitoring capabilities installed, thresholds set, additional reports configured, or almost any number of other possibilities.

While SLAs may be negotiated and agreed to for a large number of products or services, the actual provisioning process usually calls for service to be ordered and turned up individually. This means that implementation is actually on a per instance basis, as opposed to the prior phases of the SLA life cycle. Each instance of the service will normally be tracked by a unique identifier, such as a telephone number, circuit ID, Common-Language Location Identification (CLLI) code, Internet protocol (IP) address, and so forth, and have other discriminating parameters, such as the SAP.

Likewise, each instance may have unique SLA requirements that must be configured, measured, and reported on individually through the execution phase of the service. Like the service itself, the SLA compliance measures taken should be "signed off" on or accepted by the customer before billing for that instance is allowed to begin. Implementation is discussed in detail in Chapters 6 and 11.

Execution

The execution phase is the normal day-to-day operation and associated activities related to the service being delivered. This includes measurement of SLA entitlements on an ongoing basis. Extraordinary events such as circuit degradation, outages, maintenance downtime, and even failure of the capability to measure performance (Operations Support System (OSS) downtime) should be recorded and measured and the impact to the business assessed and reported.

Reconciliation should be performed on those SLAs that have immediate or real-time penalty requirements, while those that have historical or aggregate statistical reporting requirements should be archived for later (periodic) reconciliation. Different functions related to execution are discussed in several of the later chapters.

Assessment

The SLA should be assessed periodically. Assessment is not the same thing as financial reconciliation, which was addressed earlier in the chapter. (Reconciliation on a per instance or per incident basis is part of the execution phase of the SLA.) There are two types of assessments: (1) customer-focused assessments and (2) provider-focused assessments.

Customer-focused Assessments

Customer-focused assessments concentrate on the service provider's performance from the customer's viewpoint. The key metric in this type of review is SLA compliance (primarily availability) and customer satisfaction. The components of customer satisfaction are discussed in Chapter 2 and are contained in the framework that follows:

1. Overall QoS delivered
2. Overall SLA compliance
3. Customer satisfaction
   a) Service level agreements
      i. Contractual performance
      ii. Financial performance
   b) Network performance
      i. Availability
      ii. Other metrics
   c) Operations performance
      i. Call center
      ii. Ordering
      iii. Help desk/Network Operations Center (NOC)
      iv. Field services
      v. Billing
   d) Service level agreement reporting
      i. Notifications
      ii. Metrics
   e) Service level agreement reconciliation
      i. Accuracy
      ii. Timeliness
4. Recommended improvements
5. Other requirements

Provider-focused Assessments

Provider-focused assessments concentrate on the execution of the SLA as a business case within the overall SLA strategy. The intent behind this type of review is to optimize the use of the SLA by the service provider in order to improve profitability through achieving better compliance or reducing penalty exposure by changing the commitment contained within the SLAs. The key metrics in this type of review are delivered QoS, SLA profitability, and recommended improvements. A possible framework for a provider-focused review is outlined below:

1. Overall QoS delivered to all customers
2. Overall SLA compliance to all customers
   a) Service level agreement compliance by network/subnet
      i. Availability
      ii. Other metrics
   b) Service level agreement compliance by organization
      i. Call center
      ii. Ordering
      iii. Help desk/NOC
      iv. Field services
      v. Billing
   c) Service level agreement reporting compliance
      i. Notifications
      ii. Metrics
   d) Service level agreement reconciliation compliance
      i. Accuracy
      ii. Timeliness
3. Overall SLA profitability
4. Service level agreement profitability breakdown
   a. Platinum
      i. Revenues
      ii. Penalties
   b) Gold
      i. Revenues
      ii. Penalties
   c) Silver
      i. Revenues
      ii. Penalties

e) Bronze

i. Revenues

ii. Penalties

5. Recommended improvements

a) Scope

b) Timeline

6. Other requirements

The Outlook for Service Level Agreements

The use of SLA contracts will continue to grow, and eventually SLAs will become the prevailing business model for delivery of a large number of products and services. We've already discussed the dependencies created by coopetition in the telecommunications space. The end result of all this interdependency will be an SLA flow-down effect that will drive many thousands of SLAs as service providers (acting as customers, in turn) to use SLAs to protect their own ability to deliver SLA-based services to their customers. Flow-down SLAs will be addressed in later chapters. There are a number of other reasons for this, but two in particular stand out: the growth in outsourcing and the emergence of pure content providers.

The Growth in Outsourcing

The long-standing trend has been toward corporate outsourcing of many basic IT functions. Reliable connectivity to the outside world via the Internet (primarily in the form of email) and private networks has been the lifeblood of much of the world's financial, commerce, and business markets for years. The emergence of email as a primary business tool, e-commerce, and a dramatic increase in network and data outsourcing have brought more attention to the value of SLAs as a means of ensuring the optimal performance of the network, and, by extension, the associated mission-critical applications. Nothing shuts down office productivity more quickly than email going down (unless it's the power going out!).

Not only are basic IT functions being outsourced, so are many mission-critical functions that were formerly the exclusive domain of internal organizations, including the operation and maintenance of enterprise applications, entire data centers, and even data storage. Figure 1.10 a and b from *Tele.com* magazine as early as May 1997, show the areas that Chief Investment Officers (CIOs) would consider for outsourcing and their priorities.

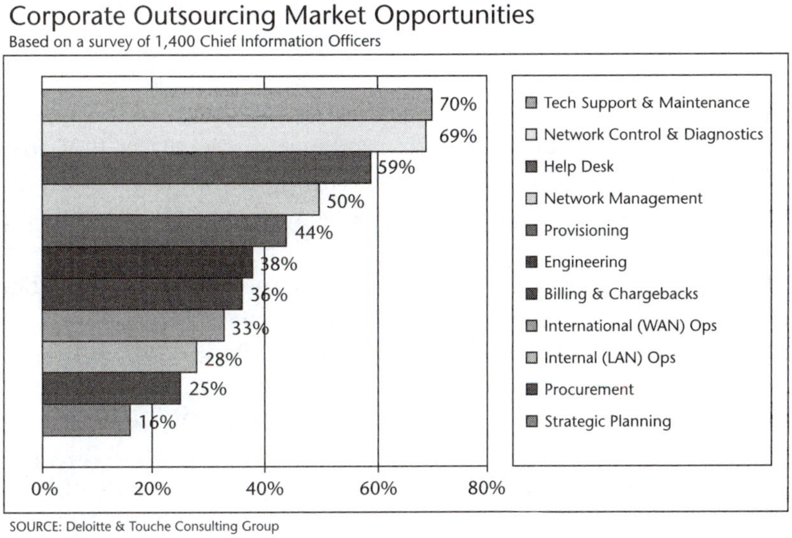

Corporate Outsource Market Opportunities

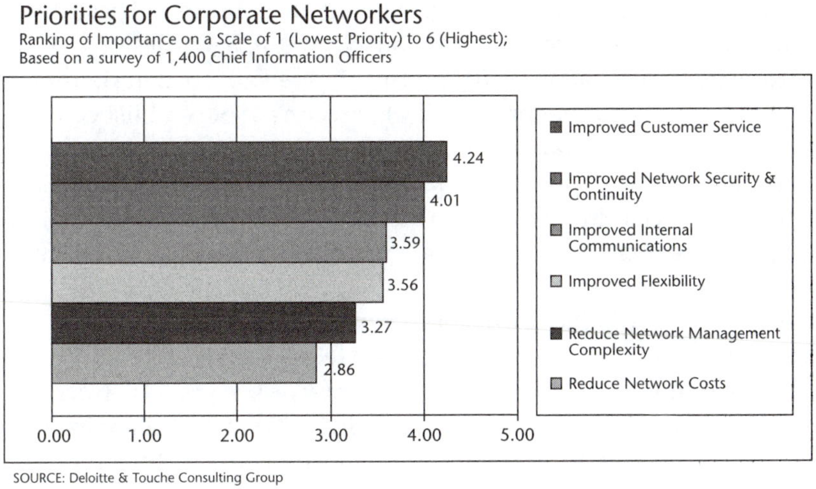

Priorities for Corporate Networkers

Figure 1.10 a and b Outsourcing predictions from *Tele.com.*

Courtesy of Tele.com, copyright 1997.

Especially enlightening is the scope of services that would be considered for outsourcing. In the last 4 years, almost all of the functions identified in *Tele.com* magazine in 1997 have become areas of outsourcing opportunities. As a result, many new business opportunities and new classes of service providers have been created, such as *application service providers* (*ASP*s) and *data storage services* (*DSS*s). These new service providers are, in many cases, emerging content providers.

Some of these outsourced service areas (such as bandwidth availability) are so critical to the continued operation of certain business enterprises that customers are unwilling to accept any service interruptions. The availability of these mission-critical products and services is the primary driver behind using SLAs.

The expectation is one of continued growth. Among the most recent predictions, *Red Herring* quotes Wall Street analysts as saying that revenues seen by data center outsourcers will grow from $3.5 billion in 2000 to $28.5 billion in 2005, a sevenfold increase.

In another example, Red Herring quotes the research firm IDC as projecting a data storage outsourcing resurgence after the business arena's initial rough start. The market is expected to grow from $21 billion in 1999 to $40 billion in 2003.

The Emergence of Pure Content Providers

A new industry is evolving in the form of pure content providers. These high-tech businesses (such as those discussed previously, ISPs, ASPs (Salesforce.com), e-commerce companies (Amazon.com), and even specialized entertainment channels available on the Internet or cable TV) will consist of established companies, startups, and many variations on the two.

New business models will spring up and continue to astound us. For example, according to Cap Gemini, Ernst, & Young, Napster grew to 35 million users in under 2 years. This translated to a compound annual growth rate of over 3,000 percent!

There are many indicators that pure content providers will experience continued strong growth. As an example, Jupiter Media Metrix was quoted in *CEO* magazine as estimating that spending by enterprises just on streaming video technology will explode from $140 million in 2000 to $2.8 billion in 2005.

Whatever business model, industry, or method of inception, the emerging content providers will all have one thing in common—they will be dependent on someone else to get their products to market. These businesses will live or die based on their customers' ability to access their content electronically.

Telecom service providers control this access in the form of bandwidth. Without bandwidth, the content providers have no means to market. Therefore they will want to guarantee that this access is available, reliable, scalable, and robust. They will use SLAs to get those guarantees.

Summary

In this chapter, we have introduced SLAs, explained their relationship to QoS, and examined their place within service level management programs. We have provided the definitions as published by the industry leaders as a starting point for you, the reader, to begin understanding the many aspects of SLAs.

We've explored some of the roles of SLAs in the hopes that you will understand the objectives of the service providers that use them as well as the customers that depend on them. Understanding the relationships, motivations of the various entities involved in SLA development, delivery, and use, and responsibilities of each party is critical to the ability of the reader to make an impact in the SLA arena, whether as a service provider, integrator, or customer.

Examining the roles in SLAs led to our discussion of the SLA life cycle, as reflected in the work done by the TeleManagement Forum. By exploring the technical steps involved in developing, deploying, and analyzing SLA applications, we can understand what makes them work, why sometimes they don't work, and, more important, how to fix them when they don't work the way that you'd like them to.

Finally, we have taken a look at some of the conventional wisdom about the outlook for SLAs. We have explored how the growth of "coopetition", the continued growth of outsourcing, and the emergence of new economy content providers will propel the use of SLAs. The reason for doing this was to better understand why SLAs are important today and why they will grow in importance tomorrow.

Chapter 1 was intended to set a common reference point as to what conventional thinking has been and to discuss some of the reasons behind it. Now that we have done that, we are better equipped to understand how SLAs originated and evolved, what their use is really about, what motivation will drive people to use them, and the factors that make them successful. We will be discussing all these issues in detail in Chapter 2.

CHAPTER

2

The True Intent of Service Level Agreements

In this chapter we provide real examples of what service can look like if SLAs are implemented as they were intended to be. We include a description of business models that can be formed if business-level SLAs become a reality.

Evolution

So what is the true intent of SLAs today? As we stated in Chapter 1, SLAs were originally used by Information Technology (IT) organizations (and adopted by telecommunications providers) to manage the quality of service (QoS) expectations and the perception of their contributions to the company's productivity and bottom-line success. Early goals set for service level management (SLM) initiatives were based on the IT department's (then the service provider) need to validate its existence as an independent entity, justify the budgets being spent, manage (that is, lower) user expectations, prove delivery of services to users, provide a vehicle for ensuring that the scarce IT resources were distributed relatively equally, and provide defensible QoS metrics.

The relative success of SLM in the IT industry has brought about widespread acceptance and adoption of its concepts and methodology, most notably within the telecommunications industry. Over time, the role played by

SLAs has changed substantially since their introduction, as has the perception of IT and telecommunications in the minds of both service providers and customers.

In August 2000 an Internet SLM survey entitled "Service Level Management: North American Survey 2000" was conducted in order to develop best-practices information that would form the basis for an on-line assessment tool. This study, sponsored by Price Waterhouse Coopers, Sun Microsystems, and BMC Software surveyed 182 executive and middle managers regarding their businesses, operations, and SLM implementations (www.nextslm.org).

An especially revealing finding on the business objectives of SLA customers can be inferred by considering the top factors for user satisfaction identified in the survey. The top four factors that accounted for almost 30 percent of the rating variation were:

1. Meeting availability requirements
2. Having an improving or stable availability trend
3. Meeting performance requirements
4. Having short recovery times from unplanned outages

Availability

From the survey results one can deduce that today the true intent of SLAs is to guarantee that a product or service is available when, where, and how the customer needs it. Availability and network performance are reflected in the survey as the overriding factors in customer satisfaction, a finding that confirms what most customers have been saying for years: *Availability of service matters above all else.*

Availability is king. It is strikingly clear that the SLA customer understands that if the product or service is not available, there will be an immediate impact on his or her business. Outages have both tangible and intangible effects (overwhelmingly negative) on the ability of a business to operate. Information technology and telecommunications are now considered so essential to the viability and success of most businesses that outages are no longer acceptable.

The customer mitigates the business risk associated with this dependency in the same way that many of us handle our own risks—through insurance. Insurance, in this case, will come in the form of an extensive use of SLAs. The customer will insist on SLAs from his or her service providers that provide a guaranteed level of service, usually with a fairly substantial financial penalty if the service provider fails to meet the entitlements (that is, availability and other requirements), even if there is a cost premium for the SLA.

Service level agreements have undergone an interesting fundamental change. They have metamorphosed from a defensive mechanism used by a service provider (the IT group) to prove its contribution to the business user (customer) to a defensive mechanism used by the business customer (user) to ensure the availability of an essential product or service delivered by a provider.

It seems that service level agreements originally developed by IT to prove that you've got to have this, even if it costs money, are used today to address the customer's concern that we've got to have this—right here, right now, and as specified, or else... and we are even willing to pay extra to make sure.

Customer Care

A second set of factors was also identified as critical to high levels of user satisfaction. The survey reports, "Customer focus is what separated the solid SLM performers from the stars. Stars distinguished themselves through high-quality communications with their customer-users." The primary factors that drove successful customer care in the survey included:

- The robustness of the SLA
- The sophistication of reporting
- Formal measurement of user satisfaction

So the customer defines superior customer service as robust (enforceable), well-defined SLAs, sophisticated reporting to users, and formalized measurement of customer satisfaction. The customer requires a clear, up-front understanding of the SLA and its role in the delivery environment, as well as the ability to understand how the QoS will be measured and the SLA enforced.

Timely and relevant QoS reporting of the service provider's performance appears to be a mandatory item in order for the customer to feel satisfied that his or her business is protected. Further reassurance also comes from the service provider in the form of a formal customer feedback process followed up with appropriate responses to that feedback.

Which is more important: availability or customer service? The survey states:

> *One of the many questions left unresolved by this baseline study is the causative relationship between the elements. That is, if you attack basic availability issues first, and then address the customer care, are you better off than using the converse strategy or a parallel strategy? The research only suggests that there is a hierarchy of needs that must be met for high satisfaction and that our respondents tend to cluster around stations on that need hierarchy ("Service Level Management: North American Survey 2000," www.nextslm.org, 2001).*

Understanding Need Hierarchies

In order to help answer the question left unanswered by the survey we will now introduce the concept of *need hierarchies*. Since we will use the concept of need hierarchies throughout our examination of SLAs, we should undertake a fundamental understanding of the theory to provide a framework for the discussions that follow in subsequent sections and chapters. Then we can easily adapt the methodology and map our own hierarchy of needs related specifically to SLAs.

Abraham Maslow, an eminent psychologist, is credited with establishing the theory that a hierarchy of needs exists within human motivation. Maslow's theory, the hierarchy of needs, was originally published in *Psychological Review* in 1943 as part of a paper, "A Theory on Human Motivation."

The basic concepts behind Maslow's need hierarchies have long been adapted and used to understand organizational or institutional behaviors. In Edward Hoffman's *The Right to Be Human: A Biography of Abraham Maslow*, Maslow is quoted as saying, "What conditions of work, what kinds of work, what kinds of management, and what kinds of reward or pay will help human stature to grow healthy, to its fuller and fullest stature? Classic economic theory, based as it is on an inadequate theory of human motivation, could be revolutionized by accepting the reality of higher human needs."

Maslow's hierarchy (Figure 2.1) consists of five levels:

1. Physiological (survival needs, that is, food, water, shelter, and so on)
2. Safety (security, protection from harm)
3. Social (belonging, acceptance, friendship, love)
4. Esteem (internal qualities, such as self-respect, autonomy, achievement; and external ones such as status, recognition, attention)
5. Self-actualization (maximizing potential and fulfilling the highest aspirations)

Maslow theorized that lower-order needs such as physiological and security requirements must be satisfied before higher-order needs such as belonging and realizing potential can be addressed. According to Maslow, until lower-order needs are met, those needs will dominate an organism and retard further progress up the hierarchy.

Once lower needs are met, "at once other (and higher) needs emerge, and these, rather than physiological hungers, dominate the organism. And when these in turn are satisfied, again new (and still higher) needs emerge, and so on. As one desire is satisfied, another pops up to take its place." From *Psychological Review* in 1943 as part of Masolw's "A Theory on Human Motivation."

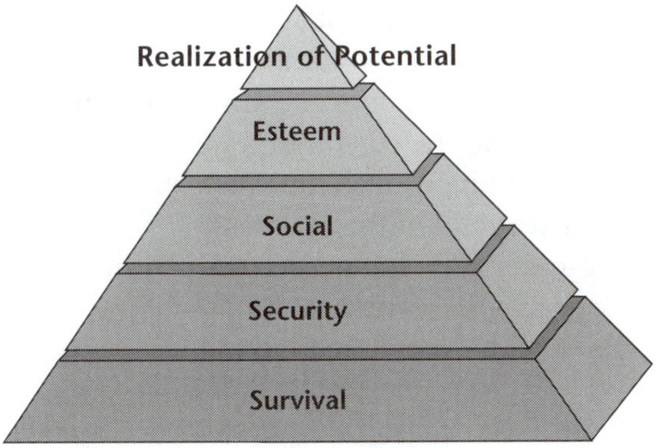

Figure 2.1 Maslow's hierarchy.

The higher on the scale the need, the less necessary it becomes. When an intermediate plateau is reached where the lack of need fulfillment at that level will not allow further upward progress, many times the organism can become accustomed to that state and adapt to the lower standard of expectation, eventually slowing or eliminating growth entirely. Obviously, this is a negative occurrence.

The Service Level Agreement Need Hierarchy

We can map the six main roles for SLAs that we discussed in Chapter 1 into an approximation of Maslow's hierarchy of needs, as shown in Figure 2.2.

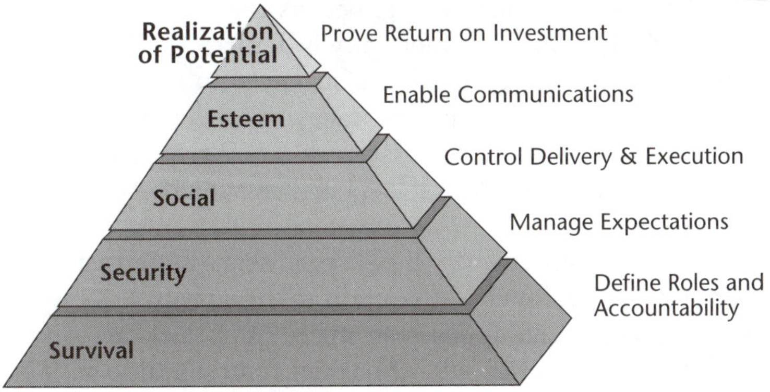

Figure 2.2 Maslow's hierarchy mapped to service level agreement needs.

When we reexamine the roles using this method, it is clear that in most cases, the SLA is used to satisfy primarily lower-order (survival and security) needs of the business customer. In the case of telecommunications, this makes absolute sense. As we have repeatedly stated, the customer's perception of IT and telecommunications services has evolved into one where both are absolutely essential to the viability and survival of the business.

To use Maslow's terminology, these services have become physiological needs to the business organism. Like food and water to a human being, computer systems and connectivity to the outside world are vital to the survival of the business entity.

One of the main reasons that such importance is placed on telecommunications services is that these services enable needs to be fulfilled higher up on the need hierarchy. As we have discussed, email has arguably evolved as the *killer app* for the Internet. Access to the Internet for email is obviously a social need, as is a Web site. It enables a business to participate in the larger community of buyers, sellers, vendors, and partners that make up its industry. Without the foundation of security and survival assured, a business cannot socialize effectively.

The larger, distributed, and more technology-based the business, the more dependent it is on this kind of commerce. In some cases, such as pure e-commerce retailers (Amazon.com), the entire need hierarchy of the business is enabled by the telecommunications technology. What value would Amazon's well-established brand equity (esteem) and innovative business intelligence and billing systems (realization of potential) have to the business if no customers could access the Web site for an extended period of time? Virtually none.

Mapping the results of "Service Level Management: North American Survey 2000" into the roles hierarchy provides some thought-provoking insights into the SLA business model. It would appear that availability, because of its lower-order position (survival and security) within the needs hierarchy, is more important than the customer services defined as important (reporting and customer feedback) in the study. This hierarchy is depicted in Figure 2.3

This assumption is completely in line with the survey's findings and suggests that 100 percent availability with little customer service is more valuable than more mediocre availability with better customer care. Perhaps the question posed as to which problem to attack first has been answered. Availability wins again.

This assertion is given more credibility by the sheer absence of financial reconciliation as a major factor in customer satisfaction in the survey. Relative to preventing outages, the financial compensation made after such an outage seems much less important. No matter what financial remuneration may be made by the service provider following an outage, the customer would prefer that the outage had never happened in the first place. An outage simply causes too much impact on the business.

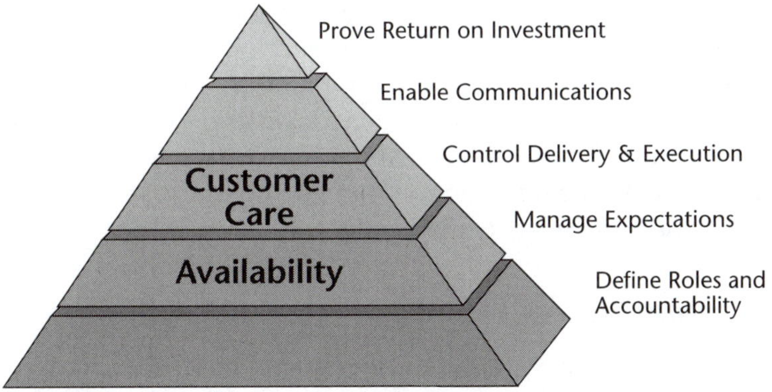

Figure 2.3 Comparison of availability versus customer care needs.

We will be using need hierarchies to understand different facets of SLA integration throughout this book.

The Emergence of the Business Impact Financial Model

Service level agreements and QoS are customer-centric. As integration of IT networking, architecture, dependability, and reliability issues have receded, the actual effects of the technology (as enabling tool sets for the operations of the business) has taken the forefront. Companies in all types of industries that have been affected by the emergence of computer and data networks try to ascertain the positive, negative, or neutral role that IT, the Internet, and telecommunications technologies play within their respective organization.

Policy makers everywhere are looking for profits on their very sizable investments in technology. The technology should make processes more efficient, people more productive, and make interfacing easier for the customers or clients. The primary source of return on investment (ROI) information is QoS reporting, which leads one to the inescapable conclusion that the perception of ROI will become even more customer-centric.

Almost every SLA used today is intended to guarantee the service provider's performance at a predefined QoS level and at a designated *service access point* (SAP). To ensure performance, service provider performance at the SAP is tied to a set of financial penalties. The intent is to *penalize noncompliance in order to provide motivation for service providers to deliver SLA-compliant performance.* We call this the *big stick* approach.

Quality of service has become the standard by which service providers are judged. The focus of QoS has shifted away from the service provider's obsession with the network technology and instead is homing in on the impact of availability on the customer's business. The financial models of SLAs have not kept pace with this evolution. Pricing can be expected to evolve from the current provider-focused penalty formulation methodology to one that is much more aligned to the business impact experienced by the customer.

Provider-Centric Methodology

Current methodology for calculating penalties (the *big stick* approach) is based on the withholding of service revenue from the provider. The financial basis for this is almost always based on monthly service fees, also known as monthly recurring charges (MRC) or one-time installation and start-up fees, known as nonrecurring charges (NRC). Penalty calculations then use a percentage, factor, or multiplier of the MRC or NRC number with entitlement information to arrive at a monetary amount.

EXAMPLE 1: REAL-LIFE SERVICE LEVEL AGREEMENT DEFINITIONS

For Examples 1 and 2, we have provided extracts from actual SLA contracts, leaving out the names of the service providers. For a clearer understanding of penalty calculations, we will go though a more complex calculation scenario in Example 3. The theoretical example used here as Example 3 is also used to explore other aspects of the SLA later in this chapter. See Table 2.1 for SLA Terms and Conditions.

Table 2.1 Service Level Agreement Terms and Conditions

TYPE OF PERFORMANCE REQUIREMENT	FOR EACH	CREDIT EQUALS
Availability	0.10 percent below the performance requirement	1.00 percent of the invoiced service charge for the affected customers of the service, for the given month. Not to exceed 100 percent of the amount that would have been invoiced had there been no credits.
Quality of Service	1.00 percentage point degradation from the performance requirement	1.00 percent of the revenue for the affected customer for the given invoice period. Not to exceed 100 percent of the fixed monthly rate for each month.

EXAMPLE 2: NETWORK PACKET DELIVERY GUARANTEE REMEDY

"If Service Provider fails to meet any network packet delivery guarantee in a calendar month, the customer's account shall be automatically credited for that month for the pro-rated charges for one day of the Service Provider's monthly fee for the service with respect to which a network packet delivery guarantee has not been met."

EXAMPLE 3: CALCULATING SERVICE LEVEL AGREEMENT PENALTY FORMULAS

Let's assume that the penalty calculation formula for the *platinum SLA entitlement covering trouble response and restoral to a DS-3* was defined as twice the monthly recurring charge for each chargeable period (a chargeable period is defined as being of the same duration as the allowable, that is, 1 hour in the case of response and 2 hours in the case of restoral) payable by credit against the next billing cycle. The response period is 1 hour, and the restoral period is 2 hours. This is defined as part of a differentiated SLA strategy implemented by the service provider as shown in Table 2.2.

Table 2.2 Service Level Agreement Penalty Formulas

TYPE OF PERFORMANCE REQUIREMENT	FOR EACH	PLATINUM	GOLD	SILVER	BRONZE	CREDIT EQUALS
Time to Respond	Additional period or fraction thereof	1	2	4	8	Twice the monthly recurring charge (MRC)
Time to Restore	Additional period or fraction thereof	2	4	8	24	Twice the monthly recurring charge (MRC)

For this example, we will assume that trouble ticket 1492 was opened on a circuit covered by this SLA. The ticket was generated by the Customer Care center, was responded to by the Network Operations Center (NOC), and the

(continues)

EXAMPLE 3: CALCULATING SERVICE LEVEL AGREEMENT PENALTY FORMULAS *(Continued)*

circuit was restored by the Operations group. The actual performance on trouble ticket 1492 was reported as follows:

- **Response: 1 hour 55 minutes**
- **Restoral: 3 hours**
- **Downtime: 3 hours**

Let's also add that the monthly recurring charge (MRC) is $1,500 and the SLA required event reconciliation within 30 days. The event reconciliation would reveal that the financial impact of trouble ticket 1492 as incurred by the service provider amounted to $4,260. The breakdown shows that the response was fifty-five minutes late, resulting in a penalty charge of .92 periods.

The restoral was 1 hour late, resulting in a charge of .50 periods. The total event penalty tally would then be 1.42 penalty periods assessed against the service provider multiplied by twice the MRC for a total of $4,260. The exact breakdown and formulas used are detailed later in this chapter (*Reconcilable*).

Business Impact Methodology

The current provider-centric methodology is flawed. As more content-driven business models are developed and brought to market, the SLA contract models will very likely be focused more on the financial damages incurred by the customer as a result of an outage or degradation of service. This new model is called the *business impact* approach.

The intent of a business impact approach is to *mitigate the business risks associated with total dependence on the telecom service provider*, which is obviously much more closely aligned to the true intent of SLAs as used by customers today.

As we said, availability is everything. In the Internet and wireless space, it is not necessary for a circuit to be hard down (or completely inoperative) in order for a content provider to experience a significant business impact. Even simple network congestion can drastically reduce or even totally eliminate the number of hits or transactions that make up the bulk of the revenue for an e-commerce company.

For example, an e-commerce company may contract to lease a frame relay connection with *committed information rates (CIR)* of 768K and an additional 100 percent bursting capability. So a fairly large number of customers can access the e-commerce company's servers simultaneously and experience satisfactory download times for the on-line catalogs.

If the network becomes so congested that the actual throughput of the *Permanent Virtual Circuit (PVC)* is 64K, the company must now support the same number of customers with less than 5 percent of the bandwidth that it formerly had available. Download times for the on-line catalogs could theoretically take ten or even twenty times longer than usual. (The delay time is theoretical because in reality the customer probably will not wait that long for the pages to load; the customer will move on to another site that is accessible in a reasonable timeframe.) The end result may be that most or all of the sales transactions that would have occurred may be lost.

Although some customers may return to the company's Web site after the degradation and complete their transactions, there is no real way to measure the actual business losses that occurred as a direct result of the congestion. What will most likely evolve is the use of different types of historical data and statistical averages for sales transactions to compare the period of congestion with a comparable period. New metrics will allow customers to adapt SLAs based on actual business needs and attributes, as well as adjust requirements based on the dynamics of the business cycle.

Big Stick versus Business Impact

Comparing the two different approaches will reveal a very large disparity in the financial compensation models. The *big stick* approach is entirely provider-centric and punishes the service provider in order to provide motivation, but it bears no relationship to either the actual value of the service to the customer or the business losses the customer could suffer as a result of service being unavailable or impaired.

The *business impact* approach relates the availability of services to both the value of services and potential business losses from the customer's standpoint. With the primary motivation behind SLAs having shifted from proving the service provider's internal return on invested costs to protecting the customer's operational capability and ensuring against losses created by an outage on the part of the service provider, it is logical to assume that the financial models will evolve to support the business impact approach.

It is also logical to assume that the service providers will resist such a change. It will take years and a major revamping of the service provider's mind-set and corporate culture, not to mention Operational Support Systems (OSS) capabilities. Eventually, customer demand will be the determining factor for whether or not these types of changes will take place. We believe that, as we transition to the content provider model, customers will eventually get what they want. Service level agreements driven by the business impact approach will emerge as an unstoppable force in the economics of telecom. We will discuss the business impact model again in Chapter 12.

EXAMPLE 4: POTENTIAL IMPACT TO AN E-COMMERCE SITE

SERVICE LEVEL AGREEMENT DEFINITION

During the negotiation of an SLA, the e-commerce company in the prior example, operating in the retail space, might identify that 70 percent of its daily sales happen between 7:00 p.m. and 2:00 a.m. EST (peak Internet hours). The company may build this peak operating time into the SLA. So each hour during this period is roughly equivalent to 10 percent of that day's revenue stream. The company may also identify that over 50 percent of its annual sales occur between November 15 and December 26. In this case, each week during this period will be seen as contributing 10 percent of the annual revenue, on average.

Let's assume that this company does $50 million in annual revenues. Each week during the holiday season, the company can expect to generate $5 million in on-line sales. Daily sales average out to over $714,000. Each peak hour generates approximately $71,400 in on-line sales.

SERVICE LEVEL AGREEMENT VIOLATION

Now suppose that the network became so congested between 9:00 P.M. and 12:00 P.M. EST (6:00 P.M.–9:00 P.M. PST) from December 10 to December 20 that throughput actually dropped to -384k. (In reality, this would likely be the most vulnerable period for the network to become congested once a certain level of e-commerce is up and running on the network.)

BUSINESS IMPACT

The retailer expects to record revenues of $2.142 million during those 30 hours. But revenue figures for this period reflect just over $1 million ($33,350/hour). Sales data recorded outside the congested hours confirmed the validity of the $71,400 hourly average. It can then be stated that the 50 percent degradation of the guaranteed (CIR) bandwidth caused an approximate $1.14 million potential revenue loss to the company, or 54 percent of projected sales during this period.

Had the business impact approach been used to develop the SLA, the penalty factors and calculations would be as follows:

- Peak hour average revenue $71,400
- Affected hours actual revenue $33,350
- Lost revenue per hour $37,150
- Affected hours per day 3
- Number of days 10

Formula: (Hourly lost revenue × affected hours × days) = business impact

Calculation: ($37,150 × 3 hours × 10 days) = $1,114,500

Service Level Agreement Success Factors

The key to whether an SLA can be considered successful is that it meets most, if not all, of the business objectives of both the service provider and the customer. Service level agreements are only as viable as the service provider's ability to relate the contract entitlements to the service provider's actual performance. While the business imperative may seem obvious, some service providers have marketed SLAs that bear little relation to the product they are selling. Similarly, SLAs have long been offered without a performance measurement component or a way to reconcile the performance.

By reviewing the SLA roles-need hierarchy we developed earlier, it is very apparent that a number of attributes must be present in both the SLA entitlements and the underlying product before an SLA can be deployed successfully. The SLA and underlying service or product must be

- Definable end to end
- Successfully deliverable
- Meaningful in terms of entitlement metrics
- Measurable at the SAP
- Visible
- Financially reconcilable

Understanding the relationship between the roles played by SLAs and the factors that impact success or failure of the underlying product is critical. We have shown this relationship in Figure 2.4.

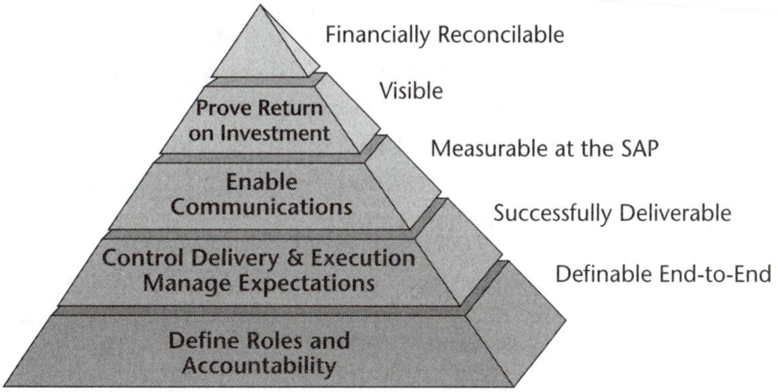

Figure 2.4 The relationship between service level agreement roles and success factors.

The service provider can then develop a framework or checklist that can be used in the product or SLA development cycle to help ensure that all the components necessary for success have been captured, considered, and addressed, prior to releasing the product and/or the SLA into the market. The framework also can be used to help understand deficiencies in existing SLA scenarios and possibly provide a road map for taking corrective actions moving forward. In this section, we have included real-world examples of deficiencies and the theoretical impact of those deficiencies on SLAs.

Definable End-to-End

Because the entitlements within the SLA provide service commitments and technical specifications that can directly impact a product's strategy, pricing, delivery processes, maintenance criteria, and other functional areas, these product attributes should be considered and addressed prior to the sale or introduction of the product into the market. Providers typically perform this analysis as part of the product development or business case cycle, as discussed in Chapter 1.

Unfortunately, many times the entire product definition is only partially done or done piecemeal owing to legacy organizational roles and responsibilities. Product managers many times package the product, branding, and price, using their understanding of the *technology's* (network) capabilities to deliver the product.

Although technical feasibility necessitates that all products and services should have some definitions developed related to the product's technology, features, functions, costs, and other inherent attributes, a more important, and often missed, factor is the *service provider's* (operations') ability to market, deliver, operate, and maintain the product's installed base over the product life cycle.

The product manager or planners must include and account for the service provider's operations capability through the product life cycle because it is truly the operational capability (not the network's capabilities) to support the product that is being guaranteed through SLAs. If the product manager's understanding of the product within the operational delivery environment is flawed, chances are much greater that the SLA portion of the product offering will be unsuccessful.

The operational delivery environment often takes different forms in different organizations and may be called the *provisioning process, delivery model, fulfillment plan*, or something else entirely. Whatever the term used, it is vitally important that the delivery environment be defined in a realistic, executable work flow specific to the product and must consider all parties and functions involved in the end-to-end delivery chain as well as include allowances for contingencies or worst-case scenarios.

Especially important is the need to define the work-flow process from end to end and to identify and consider all the handoffs and touch points among other organizations, systems, work flows, and other business processes. Every party involved in the work flow must continually collaborate with the others in order to execute delivery effectively.

Experience has shown that most departments or organizations do a credible job within their particular sphere of influence. It is when the order or ticket is handed off (or if one party thought it was handed off) to another organization that the potential for delays, nonperformance, miscommunications, or simply losing track of the job is at its highest. The more parties that are involved in the delivery chain, the more complex the work flow becomes—the more complex the work flow, the higher the risk that a bottleneck or breakdown will develop somewhere in the chain. In many cases, multiple points of failure can occur. See Figure 2.5.

Service providers who do not understand and take actions to mitigate complexities in their delivery chain or make unrealistic assumptions based on ideal field conditions in order to make the business case work, risk chaos on the delivery side.

Successfully Deliverable

Successful delivery means more than that the defined product delivery work flow was executed effectively. It also means that the financial goals outlined in the business plan for the product are realizable.

Recent history in the telecommunications arena has shown us that just about anyone with sufficient financial means and relatively little expertise can build a network, bring in customers, and in most cases technically deliver a product or service to market. Nevertheless, as many companies have learned, products must be more than just technically deliverable to be successful.

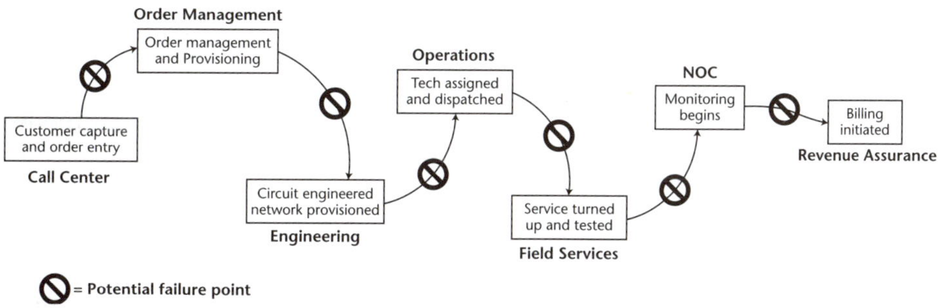

Figure 2.5 Complex work flows create multiple points of failure.

EXAMPLE 5: A REAL-WORLD EXAMPLE: THE OPERATIONAL REALITY OF DSL DELIVERY

Was it realistic for a large service provider to think that initial installations of its newly developed Digital Subscriber Line (DSL) service would be deliverable with a single truck roll? Especially since the last mile was to be leased from the Incumbent Local Exchange Carrier (ILEC). In addition, the service provider had contracted with a third-party installation company to do the installations. What about the idea of drop-shipping the modem to the customer location to save costs? Sounded good, until the technician got on-site and found that the modem was nowhere to be found. Why not? No one had told the customer it was coming, and he refused delivery or sent it back. After all, it didn't have his name on it, just the address.

What about another truck roll? Sometimes it is possible, but not always. Learning quickly, the technician always kept spares in the truck and usually managed to get the hardware installed. Unfortunately, the technician qualified to do the hardware installation was not qualified to install the software. So a second technician was sent out, scheduled to arrive a few hours after the first had left. At least the loop had been qualified... until it had to be requalified as part of field troubleshooting on why the end-to-end test wouldn't work.

What about responsibility for the missing modem? To the field techs, that was a logistics problem that belonged to someone else. If the tech had a modem in the truck, why use drop-shipping? The modem manufacturer simply drop-shipped when and where instructed. The product planner? Those were operational snafus that had to be worked out in Operations.

The end result was indeed chaos. Provisioning times dragged on for months. Actual truck rolls per installation exceeded four times the assumptions. Worse yet, the company actually failed to provide a process for canceling service that included sending someone to retrieve the hardware.

Thousands of modems were stranded on customers' premises. Thousands more were lost as part of the drop-shipping mix-ups. For some period of time, the service provider in question lost or otherwise couldn't account for over 35 percent of the modems it had ordered. The good news is that some of the modems were eventually located—the bad news is they were found on eBay!

It is not enough to have in place the technical means, personnel, processes, and supporting infrastructure to accomplish operational tasks such as ordering, provisioning, network management, and billing. From a business standpoint, it is a reasonable assumption that product delivery at or exceeding a reasonable and achievable volume will positively impact the bottom line.

The key to whether or not a product can be considered deliverable most likely lies in the ability of the service provider to realistically optimize all the costs associated with the delivery of the product or service. The combined costs related to the technical means, personnel, and other infrastructure elements must be recoverable through the sale of the product at the defined level of volume. As we outlined in product definition, all entities, organizations, processes, and touch points within the delivery chain must be identified, accounted for, and bought-in on the role that they will play within the collaborative service delivery work flow.

Furthermore, the costs associated with the end-to-end process flow must be projected, measured, and continually optimized. The efficient execution of the end-to-end work flow is absolutely critical when you are dealing with SLAs. Steep penalties are the price of poor execution.

EXAMPLE 6: THE BUSINESS REALITY OF DSL DELIVERY

Remember the work-flow problems we examined in the earlier DSL example? These types of problems are only the tip of the iceberg. The business side of this example gets much worse. Actual costs associated with just the field operations portion of getting the customer installed, and up and running exceeded the planned dispatch cost by an additional 300 percent. That was primarily owing to a number of factors including the need for additional truck rolls because of poor delivery planning, an uncontrollable logistics chain, untrained personnel, and the premise factor (the premise factor will be discussed in Chapter 3).

Getting back to the example, elsewhere in the service provider's organization, marketing managers waived nonrecurring charges (NRC) for installation in order to gain market share over the competition and increase brand recognition. So, unbeknownst to the managers involved, the cost of acquiring and delivering the customer had more than quadrupled, at the same time that one of every three modems was not delivering service. Meanwhile marketing's strategy for accumulating market share had effectively cut NRC revenue to zero.

The provider then had to rely on the product's monthly recurring charges (MRC) to recoup its costs. After the price of equipment, installation, and other associated costs were factored in, the actual cost of delivering the product to the customer pushed the break-even point to somewhere around 50 months of MRC. So 4 years after installation of a DSL modem in the home, the service company might have a chance to make some money—assuming the customer has not discontined service, moved, or decided to upgrade to a different product.

Needless to say, this particular service provider doesn't do things quite this way anymore. Poor planning cost the company many millions of dollars, both in terms of lost revenue and the cost of bringing a Big 5 integrator in to help the company fix the problems. The financial toll cannot yet be tallied because the many lawsuits that were generated as a result of the service provider's nonperformance may take years to settle. If it were not for the fact that the service provider is very large and has very deep pockets, they might be out of business entirely.

Collaboration in all facets of the business case must be present. The demand and fulfillment chains can no longer afford to be stovepipe hierarchies (stovepipes are organizations and/or systems that exist in relative isolation from most others within the larger enterprise). Gone are the days when Sales throws an order over the fence to Ops. Service providers have yet to come to terms with the financial implications of allowing the stovepipe or noncollaborative organizations and processes to stay in place.

As you can see, the operational reality made the product financially undeliverable as originally laid out. The point being that in order for SLAs to be successful, the underlying product has to be deliverable from every point of view, but especially financially. The bottom line on whether or not a product is successfully deliverable is... the bottom line.

Meaningful Entitlement Metrics

Service level agreements put financial guarantees on the customer's receiving the products or services he or she is contractually entitled to. *Entitlement metrics* are the terms and conditions that make up the contract portion of a product's SLA. The terms and conditions within the entitlements should be clearly defined, outlining the responsibilities of each of the parties; the exact frequency, locations, and methods through which the performance is to be measured, and the corrective actions available, as well as the timeframes, financial penalties or incentives, and other pertinent information.

There are two main types or classifications for SLA metrics. The first type measures the quantity, quality, availability, and level of service delivered by the network infrastructure (network elements). The measurement is based on the ability of the service provider to compile statistics from the network elements themselves using automated reporting generated from the network management function. These measurements are sometimes referred to as *service-dependent* SLA metrics. For simplicity, they will also be referred to as *network* or *device statistics* in this book. Network statistics can include the following:

- Available bit rate
- Available capacity
- Available throughput
- Bit error rate
- Block error ratio
- Committed information rate
- Constant bit rate

- Discarded frames
- Discarded packets
- Errored cell rate
- Network delay
- Nonavailable seconds
- Packet delay
- Packet loss
- PVC throughput
- Resource availability
- Resource utilization
- Severely errored seconds
- Unspecified bit rate
- Utilization rate
- Variable bit rate

The second type of metrics measures the provider's capability to provide resources to deploy, operate, and maintain the services at the level contracted for. The primary focus of this type of metrics is to measure the performance of the service provider's operations infrastructure (technical support) relative to activities that affect the ability of the network to deliver the services. These are sometimes referred to as *service-independent* metrics. Again, for simplicity's sake, this type of metric will be called *activity statistics*. Activity statistics can include the following:

- Escalation guidelines
- Mean time between failures (MTBF)
- Mean time to provision (MTTP)
- Mean time to respond
- Mean time to repair (MTTR)
- Service orders closed
- Service orders opened
- Service orders—on-time rate
- Service orders—overdue rate
- Trouble tickets closed
- Trouble tickets opened
- Trouble tickets—first time fix rate

Although the two entitlement types are overlapping and interdependent on one another, the majority of SLA compliance efforts should be concentrated on activity statistics. The ability of the service provider to model delivery milestones and thresholds related to activities, to measure actual performance, and to optimize the activity statistics determines success or failure in the SLA environment.

Why? The single overriding factor in SLA entitlements is time. Almost all entitlements are based on a time factor in some way, regardless of whether the metrics are network- or activity-based. For example, the network statistic for availability is critical to many customers. It measures the percentage of time that a circuit is up and performing to the specs in the entitlement.

For the downtime to be meaningful, we need to apply a further definition. What starts the clock that measures how long the circuit remains unavailable? The clock could potentially start when signaled by a number of indicators or events including network management alarms, trouble tickets generated by the customer, field tests, or other criteria. When are the availability metrics reported? Monthly, quarterly, and annually are all possible options. When should performance shortfalls be reconciled? Over what time period? Perhaps they will be reconciled each September, covering the prior 12 months.

Once a fault alarm or trouble ticket is received, what happens then, and how soon? The specific response and restoral time criteria should be defined in the SLA as another service entitlement. The entitlement would then be used to drive dispatch prioritization for the service provider's workforce.

Measurable at the Service Access Point

To deliver on SLAs, all facets of the service provider's operational performance must be measured, collected, and analyzed to verify that they comply with the entitlements. Most of the current efforts surrounding SLA management are

EXAMPLE 7: ALLOWABLE DOWNTIME ON A DS-3

On a given DS-3 circuit product, one of the service entitlements may specify that the circuit should be available 99.995 percent of the time.

When the product is not delivering to spec, an activity is generated (usually a trouble ticket) that should result in the performance being brought back into compliance. It is normally the time between problem detection and correction that is measured and compared to the *allowable* downtime specified in the contract.

Calculating the minutes in a year and multiplying by .00005 provides the correct figure: ($525600 \times .00005 = 26.28$). A circuit with 99.995 percent availability is *allowed* about 26.5 minutes of inoperative time (downtime) over the course of a year.

EXAMPLE 8: RESPONSE AND RESTORAL TIMES ON A DS-3

The normal DS-3 service entitlements may specify that the service provider has 2 hours in which to respond and 8 hours in which to restore the circuit to full operation.

The service provider's workforce then responds to the trouble ticket, and reports information regarding the arrival on-site, progress made on restoring service, repairing broken equipment, and closing the job. This information is then compiled and becomes part of the activity statistics.

Take special note that restoring the circuit within the normal DS-3 interval of 8 hours still results in over 7.5 hours of nonallowable or *chargeable* downtime against the availability entitlement. The availability, response, and restoral entitlements are separate line items within the contractual framework.

based on network management technology that is evolving to support SLA-driven statistical thresholds and reporting.

In the SLA environment, the service provider needs much clearer and more comprehensive QoS reporting on a near real-time basis. To serve this market, service providers feel that they must take control of devices end to end as well as manage the connectivity throughout the cloud, which may include measuring performance at numerous points within the network. From the desktop, through the hubs, routers, and on through the wide area network (WAN), new monitoring tools and metrics are being applied to ensure compliance to SLAs.

Yet the great strides made in network management systems, element management tools, and reporting capabilities such as *Simple Network Management Protocol (SNMP),* while vitally important to the service provider, are almost irrelevant to the customer. From the customer's perspective, the only important point of measurement is the one that is contractually defined in the SLA as the *service access point (SAP).*

The service access point, or SAP (also called the *service delivery point*, *point of demarcation*, or *demarc*), is the physical termination point (or device) where the service provider's responsibilities end and those of the customer begin. Delivery to the SAP is the customer's only concern within the entire network. As such, products and services delivered under SLAs must be measurable at the SAP, as shown in Figure 2.6.

While the imperative may seem obvious, measurement has not always been a simple feat to implement in operations. On the device side, the capability to provide the pertinent network statistics is growing at an amazing rate. The more advanced service technology (particularly IP-based networks) is actually easier to manage than are legacy (wireline telephony) networks. With smarter and more manageable devices imbedded in the network and extending into the customer's premises, generating the device statistics at the SAP does not present much of a problem to current network management systems.

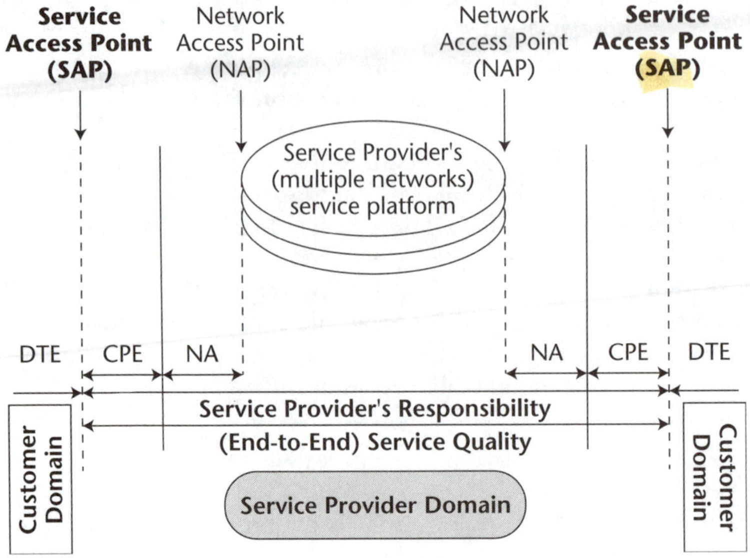

Figure 2.6 Measureable QoS service at the service access point.

Generating and managing meaningful activity-related statistics at the SAP will be more difficult. In the SLA environment, ensuring compliance through proactive management of the time allocated within the contract entitlements is critical. Service orders, trouble tickets, preventive maintenance service (PMS), equipment audits, capacity management, network build-outs, and other normal activities all have the potential to affect service at the SAP.

Experience has shown that it is not unusual for a trouble ticket to be generated for service interruptions caused by service order or preventive maintenance activities. In many cases, it is simply a matter of the right hand not knowing what the left hand is doing. Service level agreement entitlements related to availability and downtime will drive a need for all SAP activity to be captured, managed, and accounted for, since downtime necessitated by excessive routine maintenance has the same customer impact as downtime caused by hardware failure.

The task is made much more complicated by the inherent nature of SLAs. Although performance expectations are clearly defined in contract entitlements, it is really much more important (and valuable) to both the service provider and the customers that the infrastructure be able to proactively avoid broaching an SLA entitlement rather than simply be able to record and reconcile a violation after it has occurred. Therefore the service provider wants to preemptively predict potential violation points so that it can exceed (from a time perspective) the performance outlined in the contractual entitlements.

The service provider must properly prioritize and optimally utilize the human element (workforce) within its support infrastructure. Doing so depends, in large measure, on the capabilities provided by the systems and processes (or lack thereof) that are in place within the service provider's OSS.

Within the larger OSS framework, time utilization of the workforce is normally managed by specific systems, such as provisioning systems for order fulfillment and trouble ticketing systems for service assurance. In addition, operations and maintenance (O&M) tasks (such as preventive maintenance, circuit card revisions, audits, and so on) and engineering tasks (such as network build outs, capacity expansion, and so on) are managed using other tools such as preventive maintenance schedules, project planning tools, and scheduling and dispatch systems.

The current OSS systems and processes are not up to the challenge. To support SLA-related activity reporting at the SAP, these systems will require substantial upgrading in a number of areas. The discrete data found in the separate systems must be consolidated into a single format so that the tasks can be prioritized relative to each other.

Technology must be implemented that will allow for proactive and real-time alarm reporting and task notification (which would imply reporting from the SAP's physical location). Finally, the systems must provide stronger capabilities to provide more detailed and granular activity recording that can support predictive, real-time, and historical activity reporting. We will cover recording and reporting abilities in detail in later chapters.

Visible

Defining entitlement metrics and measuring actual performance against them is only as useful as the parties' capability to apply these metrics to help them accomplish their respective business objectives. Both entitlement and performance information must be readily visible.

An examination of typical service fulfillment and service assurance work flow processes reveals that end-to-end support of service orders and trouble tickets regularly requires the involvement of the customer, the call center, the order management group, engineering, the NOC, field operations, and operations managers. Each of these organizations needs to be able to access the information pertinent to its role in the workflow relative to the SLA entitlements.

In general, visibility and reporting requirements can be divided into two categories: real-time and historical. Of the two, the more important is undoubtedly the real-time visibility and reporting. Real-time visibility and reporting are generally incident-specific, while historical visibility and reporting can be viewed on an incident, functional, geographical, timeframe, or statistical basis.

Real-time visibility of the entitlement is a new requirement that is absolutely mandatory in the SLA environment. As we have already stated, most SLA compliance efforts will be devoted to improving operational effectiveness in operations. In the telecom space, there is a very simple reason for this: Almost all SLAs are intended to keep the contracted bandwidth available. In the manufacturing environment, there is a similar intent: to keep the production line moving. Everything else is secondary.

With SLA terms dictating response, restoral, and provisioning times that may vary according to locations, service types, and even telephone numbers, the service providers will be hard pressed to respond consistently. One of the key factors that will allow them to optimize response times is improving real-time visibility of both entitlement and activity status information for the parties that need it. In many cases, this can include everyone in the workflow, including the customer. Let's examine a realistic example of how this pertains in a relatively simple work-flow scenario.

The visibility of the entitlement must be immediate upon generation of a trouble ticket for this circuit. Once the pertinent information on the problem is gathered, someone (or something if the system is automated) will make an initial determination of the priority of the work to be done relative to other tasks. The decision maker (usually a dispatcher or controller) must have accurate entitlement information readily available to reach the correct conclusion on where the task falls in the workload.

Once the work is prioritized and dispatched to a field technician, the visibility of the entitlement becomes equally critical. The technician must understand that he or she has only 25 percent of the normal time in which to respond to and restore the circuit before penalties start accruing. The escalation timeframes and supporting resources available to the technician must be prepared so that he or she can respond more quickly and potentially have more resources on hand in order to make the entitlement times or, again, risk breaching the SLA.

In our example, it appears that everyone in the work flow performed fairly capably. There were no missed handoffs, logistical problems, or external organizations involved. In summary, this was a best-case scenario. In the normal (non-SLA) response scenario, this response would represent a more than acceptable performance. But closer examination reveals that under platinum SLA entitlements a number of problems existed.

EXAMPLE 9: REVIEW OF THE DS-3 ENTITLEMENTS

Earlier, we outlined a DS-3 circuit, with an availability entitlement of 99.995 percent. As we said, circuits with 99.995 percent availability are *allowed* only about 26.5 minutes of downtime a year. While normal DS-3 service entitlements may specify 2 hours to respond and 8 hours to restore, suppose this particular circuit was covered by a *platinum-level* SLA that entitled the customer to a 1-hour on-site response and a 2-hour restoral.

EXAMPLE 10: OPENING TROUBLE TICKET 1492

Reports show that trouble ticket 1492 was opened on the DS-3 by the customer. It was detected and reported to the call center at 11:50 A.M. The ticket was completed shortly before 12:00 noon. The NOC was able to ascertain that the monitored hardware did show a fault on a multiplexer in a remote switching office that serviced the customer. The NOC classified the trouble ticket as a *major trouble ticket* and, after attempting remote configuration, handed it off to Field Services at 12:25 P.M. This process followed the NOC's general policy of closure or handoff within 30 minutes.

Without entitlement visibility, the NOC prioritized the job based on the element management system's default SNMP level showing the fault as being a *major fault*. The NOC's policy of 30-minute disposition on major trouble tickets applied to all alarms at that level, so following the hand-off from the call center, 40 minutes of the allowable 1-hour response time were used before the hand-off to Field Services.

The 2-hour rule in use throughout Field Services was actually six times longer than the 20 minutes the technician actually had left (after the call center and NOC tasks) to arrive on-site. His arrival on-site was actually 55 minutes late.

Restoral was declared, and the ticket was closed at 2:50 P.M. The 3-hour restoral period exceeded the 2-hour restoral entitlement by 1 hour (50 percent).

Because there was no entitlement visibility, there were no escalation guidelines or procedures that notified anyone in the work flow or management that there were potential SLA violations at several points in the work-flow processes. Consequently, they became actual violations.

EXAMPLE 11: RESTORING TROUBLE TICKET 1492

Field Services routinely responds to *major* trouble tickets by dispatching a technician within 2 hours of notification. In this case, a technician was identified and assigned the ticket at 12:30 P.M. The technician knew the *2-hour rule* and so decided to finish lunch and make one other short stop before making the 30-minute drive to the remote site.

Arriving at the remote site at 1:45 P.M., only 1 hour and 15 minutes after assignment, the technician was able to verify that the DS-3 card was in alarm. He was unable to clear the fault by resetting the card, so he replaced the card with an on-site spare. After internal testing and configuration, he brought the card on-line and verified with the NOC that the alarm had been cleared at 2:38 P.M. The NOC informed the call center that service had been restored at 2:40 P.M. The call center then confirmed this with the customer and closed ticket number 1492 at 2:50 P.M. The total downtime was 3 hours, well under the normal 8 hours.

On the management level, historical reporting becomes more important, but visibility remains crucial to success. While activity statistics such as *mean time to repair* and *first time fix rate* have always been important to field operations managers, the development and introduction of SLA compliance statistics on both the network and activity fronts will drive increased oversight from higher levels of management.

This increased oversight is owing, of course, to the financial component inherent in SLAs and the potential downside implications of poor SLA compliance in the field. Visibility of compliance statistics will be vital to the service provider's ability to optimize his or her support infrastructure in order to reduce or eliminate entitlement violations while maximizing profitability of the SLA offerings.

These reports should also form the feedback loop to the product development process. Good operational reporting will validate the assumptions made during development, provide guidance on needed adjustments, and identify those SLA offerings that are profitable, those that break even, and (with penalty calculations available) those that lose money. This analysis could result in a number of outcomes, including looser entitlements, revamped delivery processes, penalty avoidance strategies, or even removing the SLA offering from the market entirely.

Once the service provider's needs have been addressed, considerable thought should be given to the role of SLA compliance reporting from the customer's standpoint. The customer's priorities and needs are addressed in Chapter 3. If we take into account all the parties involved in the trouble ticket 1492 example, we would see that the community that needed visibility on the SLA at some point in the process was quite large and diverse. This community is shown in Figure 2.7.

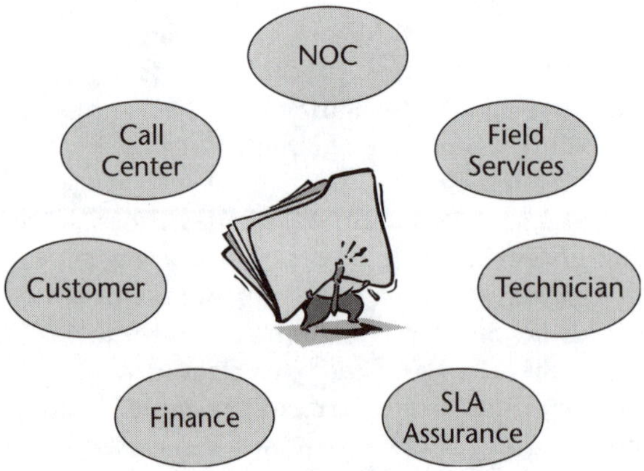

Figure 2.7 Trouble ticket 1492 service level agreement community.

Reconcilable

Finally, the SLA must be reconcilable, no matter how well the service provider has optimized the network, service fulfillment, and assurance processes. Regardless of the improved performance of both the network and personnel performing SLA-related activity, there will still be incidents that will breach the entitlements in the SLA.

At some predefined time, the service provider must provide some form of compensation for the failure to perform as specified. In most cases, SLA reconciliation implies financial compensation. The terms relate to penalty amounts, calculation formulas, minimum or maximum amounts, as well as the frequency, timing, and method of transfer. There should also be legal recourse outlined that one or both parties may undertake should there be disagreement as to the existence, extent, or extenuating circumstances related to a violation, as well as a forum for handling disagreements on the calculation or payment of compensation.

Performance of SLA reconciliation can take a number of forms, but there are two primary types: *one-time* (or event) and *periodic* (or cumulative). Periodic, or historical SLA reconciliations, of course, are driven by the need for reconciling a number of different incidents (trouble tickets) affecting different entitlements over a defined period of time on the same product or service.

EXAMPLE 12: RECONCILING TROUBLE TICKET 1492

In the DS-3 example, we specified an availability entitlement of 99.995 percent or an allowable 26.3 minutes of downtime a year. The normal response and restoral times for DS-3s are 2 hours to respond and 8 hours to restore. The *platinum-level* SLA entitlement defined acceptable response as 1 hour and specified a 2-hour restoral window.

For simplicity, assume that the penalty calculation formula for this SLA was defined as twice the monthly recurring charge for each chargeable period (a *chargeable period* is defined as being of the same duration as the allowable, that is, 1 hour in the case of response and 2 hours in the case of restoral) payable by credit against the next billing cycle.

Let's also add that the *monthly recurring charge* (MRC) is $1,500 and the SLA event reconciliation needs to occur within 30 days of the trouble, and cumulative reconciliation should occur within 14 days of the anniversary of initial service delivery. The measured performance on trouble ticket 1492 was reported as follows:

Response: 1 hour 55 minutes

Restoral: 3 hours

Downtime: 3 hours

The event reconciliation reveals that the financial impact of the trouble ticket 1492 as incurred by the service provider amounted to $4,260. (1) The breakdown shows that the response was 55 minutes late, resulting in a penalty charge of .92 periods. (2) The restoral was 1 hour late, resulting in a charge of .50 periods. (3) The total event penalty tally would then be 1.42 penalty periods assessed against the service provider, multiplied by twice the MRC for a total of $4,260. The breakdown is as follows:

Step 1. Calculate response penalty periods: 55 minutes/60 =.92 periods (1 period = 1 hour)

Step 2. Calculate restoral penalty periods: 60 minutes/120 = .5 periods (1 period = 2 hours)

Step 3. Calculate total penalty: 2 × $1,500 (MRC) × 1.42 = $4,260

The periodic or cumulative reconciliation might occur several months later. During this reconciliation, it is found that trouble ticket 1492 was the only incident of unscheduled downtime during the year (SLA terms will usually exclude routine maintenance from being chargeable, as long as customers are given sufficient notification) downtime during the year.

The financial impact incurred by the service provider against the availability entitlement would be $17,520. The breakdown that follows shows that the downtime of 3 hours results in a penalty charge of 5.84 periods. The total is reached by (1) subtracting the allowable period (in this case 26.3 minutes) from the total downtime and (2) dividing the downtime by penalty periods. Multiplying the penalty periods by twice the MCR would then give us the total amount of the penalty (Step 3). In this case, the total cumulative penalty for the year was $17,520. Here is the breakdown:

Step 1. Calculate chargeable downtime: 180 - 26.3 = 153.7

Step 2. Calculate chargeable periods: 153.7/26.3 = 5.84

Step 3. Calculate total penalty: 2 × 1500 (MRC) × 5.84 = $17,520

Of course, the cumulative total could potentially be much higher if there were several trouble tickets with chargeable downtime. In that case, the total accrued downtime would be computed as part of the penalty formulation.

All told, the total financial impact on the service provider of trouble ticket 1492 is $21,780, broken down as follows:

Event Reconciliation: $4,260

Chargeable response penalty periods = .92

Chargeable restoral penalty periods = .5

Periodic Reconciliation: $17,520

Chargeable downtime penalty periods = 5.84

Total Penalty Reconciliation: $12,780

Summary

To summarize Chapter 2, we have shown that the intent and use of SLAs have changed considerably since they were originally conceived as part of service level management programs by internal IT groups. They have evolved from being a vehicle used to show the value being delivered by IT into a defensive business strategy used by many companies in all industries to protect themselves from depending on critical suppliers.

The round-the-clock availability of communications is now recognized as one of the key enablers of many of today's businesses. Recent surveys indicate that the customer values availability and considers it more important than just about anything else, including customer care. In order to understand the customer's thinking, we examined Maslow's theory on hierarchical needs. We found that businesses perceive communications as a physiological need; without communications a business could not survive.

Following the same line of reasoning, we made a credible case that the customer will continue to focus on (1) ensuring the continued servicing of his or her business needs and (2) taking a more customer-centric approach to how those needs are met. We have already seen that in the marketplace the customer-centric approach will drive SLAs that are based on the actual financial impact of failure of availability on the customer's bottom line rather than on the cost of providing the service. We detailed some of the techniques and methodology of the new approach.

Finally, we conducted a thorough examination of what it will take to make SLAs successful. We established that SLAs must be:

- Definable end-to-end
- Successfully deliverable
- Meaningful entitlement metrics
- Measurable at the SAP
- Visible
- Financially reconcilable

We explored each of these factors in great detail through examples, case studies, and theoretical exercises using sound methodology. What we found was that many real-world problems have been encountered within the industry that may have been prevented if these principles had been adhered to. Understanding the basic principles has prepared us to examine the current state of SLAs within the communications industry at large. We can now try to determine where we are, how we got there, and the further implications of SLAs in the communications industry. The examination of these issues is the focus of Chapter 3.

CHAPTER 3

The Long Ascent to True Service Level Agreement Delivery

In this chapter, we will describe the problems inherent in current approaches to delivering on SLAs. We will explain the background of how we got there, the complexities that make the task of truly delivering on SLAs so difficult, and the organizational issues that must be reckoned with if there is going to be a realistic chance for implementing a solution that works.

Why Delivery Is Important

Everywhere we look, managers at all levels in all kinds of service providers are asking the same questions: What broadband services should I offer? What will differentiate me from the pack? How do I deliver these enhanced services to my customer faster, more reliably, and more profitably than my competitors? How will I know if I am successful? What defines success? Market share? Order volume? Revenue? Cost containment? Customer satisfaction? Margin? Survival?

Yes, survival. The fate of many telecom companies continues to hang in the balance. Although there are various reasons for the recent demise of the competitive local exchange carriers (CLECs), quite a few ran out of money and failed because they couldn't quickly, reliably, and accurately deliver (and bill) for services. Demand is not the problem—it never was. Delivery is the problem.

Just ask the customer. To the customer, SLAs are about guaranteeing delivery. As we stated in Chapter 2, the customer uses SLAs primarily as a means to ensure the availability of the connection. The customer understands the importance of connectivity as the enabler of his or her business. From a need perspective, the availability of telecommunications is a physiological need. Security, socialization, and realization of the business's potential cannot occur if the connectivity need is not satisfied first. The importance of this need is clearly reinforced for the customer every time the email system is down.

Today's customers demand agreements that are very performance-specific, provide clear reporting metrics, and have money-back guarantees or, in many cases, expensive penalties for nonperformance. The customer, like the service provider, has already started to turn away from the external workings of the technologies and look instead to the impact of availability on his or her individual business. As architecture, dependability, and reliability issues have receded, the integration of the IT and telecommunications into business process and policy has taken the forefront.

Through the growing use of SLAs, customers are attempting to link the quality of services (primarily availability) delivered by the service provider's network, fulfillment, and assurance organizations to a financial consequence. As we discussed in Chapter 2, today the financial consequence is based on a provider-centric methodology. We expect this to change. Customer demands will eventually force the financial models behind SLAs to focus on the actual business impact to the customer rather than the cost of providing service. We covered the business impact model in Chapter 2.

Where We've Been

The track record of implementing successful SLAs in the telecommunications industry is, in a single word, terrible. The use of SLAs in telecommunications is not new. Quality of service and performance objectives have been a standard part of service contracts for many years. Service level agreements have been, for the most part, generic, did not outline measurement or metrics, and lacked teeth on both the delivery and the enforcement side. Few SLAs in use, even today, would meet the criteria for success we identified in Chapter 2. In the past (and even today), customers took what they got—which was actually very little in the way of SLA compliance. What alternative did they have? After all, the fox was watching the henhouse.

The Gartner Group predicts that over 80 percent of the SLAs that now exist between service providers and their customers will be breached by 2004. In "Service Level Management: North American Survey 2000," respondents reported that only 25 percent of SLAs in place had penalties for nonperformance. Anyone think that's a coincidence? The Gartner Group goes on to say that SLA compliance is and will continue to be one of the most critical issues facing service providers over the next 5 years.

Although much lip service has been paid to the problem, there is little incentive for the service providers to get serious about fixing it. No one had figured out how to solve the QoS problem—so it was denied, ignored, and almost everyone lived in a state of discontent with the situation, especially the customers. Much of this is purely self-interest on the part of service providers. The huge potential for financial liabilities makes this quality-of-service issue a Pandora's box that few service providers care to open until market conditions force them to.

Most service providers still cannot provide accurate, timely, and, most important, relevant reporting as to their ability to successfully deliver guaranteed services to the customer. In some cases, service providers simply have no idea if they are delivering on QoS entitlements or not. They don't know because there's no one or no system within their organization that can tell them the answers or even where, when, or how to ask the questions.

Over the years, Operations Support Systems (OSSs) and the supporting infrastructure have evolved in ways that make it impossible for service providers to measure and report on SLA compliance consistently. The problems grew each time a new technology was introduced. Organizational politics and the lack of enforceability only added to the inability (or unwillingness) of most service providers to adapt the OSS and infrastructure to deliver a high level of QoS manageability.

When viewed from a Telecommunications Management Network (TMN) standpoint, automating QoS is a difficult undertaking because the two system processes within a service provider happen very far apart.

The billing and financial management systems reside at the very top of the TMN model (within the business management layer), while the services are delivered at the very bottom (in the network element layer). There is a virtual maze of OSSs, work-flow processes, and disparate work groups that make up the day-to-day workings of the service provider.

Although there are numerous SLA management systems currently on the market, they are almost always hardware-centric, and functionality is almost universally limited to setting thresholds on network performance as measured at designated points within the network elements, element management, or network management layers (that is, they collect and manage device-driven statistics).

In light of the evolution of the network and the origins of service level management (SLM) the orientations of the systems originally made quite a bit of sense. Service level management, as the parent of both QoS delivery and SLA management, was initially developed in conjunction with the IT network. It was considered an integral part of network management. Measuring performance is a function of network management, as defined by the Fault, Configuration,

Accounting, Performance, and Security (FCAPS) model. This model is somewhat outdated and has been superceded by the Telecommunications Operations Map, which is discussed in Chapter 4. Because of FCAPS, most current attempts to manage SLAs have been developed by vendors from the network management space (NMS).

Unfortunately, in the context of SLAs as they are used today, managing SLAs from the NMS has not worked (and probably will not work). Current efforts to report on SLAs many times means manually compiling huge volumes of unrelated data from multiple standalone point systems. Once this is done, someone must manually analyze key performance indicators using some common parameters, and searching for violations of undefined origin.

This manual analysis is not very accurate or effective. Hardware-centric network management solutions, by themselves, will not serve the SLA needs of customers. The hardware performance statistics are a major component of a solution, but they are too limited in scope and missing critical capabilities. We will discuss hardware-centric network management solutions in Chapters 4 and 5.

Some Good Examples of Bad Service Level Agreements

Some providers have developed creative work-arounds to their shortcomings. They undoubtedly know that they cannot deliver on the guaranteed service levels. No one can deliver 100 percent availability. Yet competitive pressures to provide SLAs drive some providers to go too far with the available network statistics to prove they are in compliance with regulators and customers. While these statistics are important to some SLA entitlements, they really have little to do with the activity side of SLA delivery.

Creating an SLA then becomes an exercise in wordsmithing entitlements and managing actuarial risk, with none of the facts available to the other side. To these players, the penalties they pay on a few SLA claims are greatly outweighed by the number of violations that go undetected. The result is that a lot of SLA compliance measurement is smoke and mirrors.

This lack of accountability implies, unfortunately, that many SLA offerings are pure marketing ploys, relying on the customer's ignorance of the underlying technology and unrelated to the actual capability of the service provider to deliver, measure, or prove compliance to the entitlements. So without evidence to the contrary, these service providers expect the customers to believe their marketing.

As an example, the following leased-line (including frame relay) SLA excerpts were downloaded in December 2001 from the corporate Web site of one of the Internet's largest service providers. At first glance, the SLA appears to be impressively well thought out. Certain areas have been highlighted through the use of italics in order to point out what we consider deficiencies in the SLA structure. Comments follow that will further explain the deficiencies.

EXAMPLE 1: POINTS OF MEASUREMENT MUST BE RELEVANT

NETWORK LATENCY GUARANTEE SCOPE

Service Company's North American *network latency guarantee* is average round-trip transmissions of 65 milliseconds or less between Service Company–designated interregional transit backbone network routers (*hub routers*) in North America.

NETWORK PACKET DELIVERY SCOPE

Service Company's North American *network packet delivery guarantee* is packet delivery of 99 percent or greater between Service Company–designated hub routers in North America.

COMMENTS

The SLA covers performance between provider-designated network hub routers; this guarantee clearly is not the same thing as the service being delivered to the SAP. But the SLA was probably written this way because the NMS data-gathering capability does not extend out to the SAP. The fact that the service provider selects which hubs to measure performance against is also problematic since it potentially allows the service provider to measure a number of hubs and selectively choose which statistics will be reported.

EXAMPLE 2: THE TIMING OF MEASUREMENT MUST BE RELEVANT

NETWORK LATENCY GUARANTEE PROCESS

Latency shall be measured by averaging sample measurements taken during a calendar month between hub routers. Each month's network performance statistics relating to the network latency guarantees shall be posted at www.ServiceCompany.net/customers/sla/latency.html. No credits will be made if failure to meet a network latency guarantee is attributable to reasons of force majeure (as defined in the applicable service agreement).

PACKET DELIVERY GUARANTEE PROCESS

Packet delivery shall be measured by averaging sample measurements taken during a calendar month between hub routers. Each month's network performance statistics relating to the network packet delivery guarantees shall be posted at www.Service Company.net/customers/sla/latency.html. No credits will be made if failure to meet a network packet delivery guarantee is attributable to reasons of force majeure (as defined in the applicable service agreement).

(continues)

EXAMPLE 2: THE TIMING OF MEASUREMENT MUST BE RELEVANT *(Continued)*

COMMENTS

The performance measurements will be averaged out over a monthly period on the routers designated by the service provider. Not only are these measurements not specific to the SAP, they are not specifically related to the customer's service or any event, such as a network outage. Event correlation is an integral part of network management, yet this SLA appears to dismiss it entirely. The timing and frequency of the sampling is not addressed. How about 2:00 a.m. on Sunday mornings when network traffic is at its lowest? The reports will be posted to a Web site.

EXAMPLE 3: REMEDIES MUST BE APPROPRIATE

NETWORK LATENCY GUARANTEE REMEDY

If Service Company fails to meet any network latency guarantee in any calendar month, customer's account shall be automatically credited for that month for the prorated charges for one day of the Service Company monthly fee for the service with respect to which a network latency guarantee has not been met.

NETWORK PACKET DELIVERY GUARANTEE REMEDY

If Service Company fails to meet any network packet delivery guarantee in a calendar month, customer's account shall be automatically credited for that month for the prorated charges for one day of the Service Company monthly fee for the service with respect to which a network packet delivery guarantee has not been met.

COMMENTS

If the service provider's monthly average performance, on the service provider's selected hubs, at the time that the service provider has designated for sampling misses the entitlement for that month, the customer will automatically be credited with 1 day of free service!

Not only does the remedy fail to address the SAP; it does not even necessarily address the particular customer's hubs. If, by some chance, the sampled average falls below the performance threshold, it is probably because the performance was consistently below the mark during the month. Yet the customer will receive 1/30th of the MRC automatically. Anybody think this is a great deal?

EXAMPLE 4: THE SERVICE LEVEL AGREEMENT MUST BE REALISTIC AND RECONCILABLE

SERVICE AVAILABILITY GUARANTEE SCOPE

Service Company's service availability guarantee is to have the Service Company network (as defined in the applicable service agreement) available 100 percent of the time.

SERVICE AVAILABILITY GUARANTEE PROCESS

At customer's request, Service Company will calculate customer's *network unavailability* in a calendar month. Network unavailability consists of the number of minutes that the Service Company network or a Service Company-ordered telephone company circuit in the contiguous United States was not available to customer, and includes unavailability associated with any maintenance at the Service Company hub to which customer's circuit is connected other than scheduled maintenance. Outages will be counted as network unavailability only if Service Company notifies customer of the outage in accordance with the outage reporting guarantee set forth below, or if customer opens a trouble ticket with Service Company customer support within five days of the outage. Network unavailability will not include scheduled maintenance, or any unavailability resulting from (a) any customer-ordered telephone company circuits, (b) customer's applications, equipment, or facilities, (c) acts or omissions of customer, or any use or user of the service authorized by customer, or (d) reasons of force majeure (as defined in the applicable service agreement).

SERVICE AVAILABILITY GUARANTEE REMEDY

For each cumulative hour of network unavailability or fraction thereof in any calendar month, at customer's request customer's account shall be credited for the prorated charges for one day of the Service Company monthly fee and one day's telephone company line charges for the service with respect to which a service availability guarantee has not been met.

OUTAGE REPORTING GUARANTEE SCOPE

Service Company's outage reporting guarantee is to notify customer within 15 minutes after Service Company's determination that customer's service is unavailable. Service Company's standard procedure is to ping customer's router every five minutes. If customer's router does not respond after two consecutive five-minute ping cycles, Service Company will deem the service unavailable and will contact customer's designated point of contact by a method elected by Service Company (telephone, email, fax or pager).

(continues)

EXAMPLE 4: THE SERVICE LEVEL AGREEMENT MUST BE REALISTIC AND RECONCILABLE *(Continued)*

OUTAGE REPORTING GUARANTEE PROCESS

The outage reporting guarantee is applicable only to service provided in the contiguous United States and is applicable only if customer completes Service Company's customer information form in its entirety or registers for the outage reporting guarantee by submitting the form available at www.ServiceCompany .net/support/sla/sign_up.html. Customer is solely responsible for providing Service Company accurate and current contact information for customer's designated points of contact. Service Company will be relieved of its obligations under this outage reporting guarantee if Service Company's contact information for customer is out of date or inaccurate due to customer's action or omission or if Service Company's failure is due to reasons of force majeure (as defined in the applicable service agreement).

OUTAGE REPORTING GUARANTEE REMEDY

If Service Company fails to meet the outage reporting guarantee, at customer's request customer's account shall be credited the prorated charges for one day of the Service Company monthly fee for the service with respect to which this guarantee has not been met; provided that customer may obtain no more than one credit per day, irrespective of how often in that day Service Company failed to meet the outage reporting guarantee.

COMMENTS

As confusing as it is, this SLA seems to say, "If you ask, we'll check availability for you. In general, the service is available unless we tell you it's not or you open a trouble ticket. But we'll only tell you that service is unavailable if you submit the proper forms or register at our Web site. Then we'll decide how you get notified. Oh, and if we forget to tell you, we'll credit you 1 day of the reporting fee (the reporting fee?), assuming you ask us to.

"The way we know that the service is unavailable to you is by pinging your router, and it could be 25 minutes before we let you know (10 for the pinging, 15 for the notification). So the only outage that counts is if your router is down completely. Latency and packet delivery? Sorry, those are other routers altogether.

"Visibility? No, we don't put availability on a Web site. You have to ask us to look into it, remember? But if we do find that your router has been down, and you filled out the forms, and we did remember to notify you, or you did bother to open a trouble ticket on it, and you ask us to, we'll credit you 1 day for each hour. So if the service is down for 30 hours, we'll refund your MRC. Assuming you ask, of course."

Example Summary

As we've already discussed, ensuring availability is the primary reason that customers use SLAs. The example SLA specifies 100 percent availability. Is

100 percent availability realistic? Perhaps—it depends on your definition of availability.

If we applied the prior examples to the frame relay scenario we discussed in Chapter 2, we would find that there would be no credit due to the e-commerce company. Unless the company requested it, there would be no check on non-availability. Even if there was, availability is calculated on a monthly basis.

The other option would be to open a trouble ticket, which would occur only if the e-commerce company monitored transactions real-time, noticed the drop in revenue over the peak hours, and was able to attribute the degradation in bandwidth. This scenario is somewhat unlikely. But even if it did happen, detecting a bandwidth problem would not matter from a financial reconciliation standpoint.

There is no provision in the SLA for Committed Information Rate (CIR) degradation at the SAP being either monitored or reported. The process calls for pinging the routers at 5-minute intervals. In all likelihood, the ping may have been quite slow, but it probably would have responded.

Availability is defined in the SLA as the network being available to the customer. But in our example of the e-commerce business, the network was available for use; it was just in a temporarily degraded condition owing to congestion on the shared frame relay network. Congestion on the frame relay network is not as bad as it was several years ago, but it can still be problematic unless the network is engineered carefully.

Thirty hours of downtime in a month is about 96 percent availability. Yet in the example SLA definitions, there was no actual downtime. As I stated earlier, the SLAs many service providers use appear to be well thought out. Maybe an SLA with 100 percent availability *is* realistic within the scope of these kinds of examples.

Fortunately, market and government regulations are forcing service providers to seek better solutions. A 2000 study conducted by the TeleManagement Forum (TMF) ranked the management of SLAs as one of the top two priorities across every category of service providers, as shown in Figure 3.1.

Understanding the Complexities in the Network Environment

The challenges that we have discussed in delivering SLAs are merely part of a much larger problem being experienced by the broader industry. Some of the problems go right to the core of the telecommunications industry and are changing the way that the industry has done business, is doing business, and will do business in the future.

A number of external or environmental factors have contributed to the problems being experienced by the industry. Over several years, a confluence of

Drivers for OSS Investment
Service provider respondents to the project survey were asked to rank specified high-level business objectives that might influence OSS implementations and decision making. The results are shown on the following table, with "1" as the highest ranking objective. (The "=" sign indicates equal priority)

	Established Fixed	Established Cellular	New Entrant	ISP/ITSP
Flow-through provisioning	3	3	1	3
Managing SLAs	1	2	2	
Improving staff productivity & reducing operating costs	2	1	3	1=
Integration of new infrastructure	4	4		1=
3rd Party Access / Other		5*	4**	2***

*Quality of services provided by the telco. Speed of deployment and time to market was also cited by one operator.
**Rapid service provisioning, and all factors that aid this are the third business objectives of one new entrant.
***The top level objective of one ISP was the need to centralize the disparate network and operations support systems of acquired companies.

Drivers for OSS Investment

Source: Extract from: Communications Industry Market for OSSs, The Telemanagement Forum (TMF)1999.

Figure 3.1 TeleManagement Forum study documents the drivers for Operations Support System investment.

these factors has outstripped the ability of service providers to respond quickly enough to deliver SLA-based solutions. We will briefly examine the impact of these factors on service providers in general. The environmental factors include the following:

- Explosion of data networking
- New technology
- The premises factor
- New market entrants
- Tight labor markets

Unfortunately, service providers, OSS vendors, system integrators, and other players within the telecom space have also failed to address other, more internal, factors that have increased the difficulty service providers are experiencing in delivering SLA-grade services. The internal factors include organizational stovepipes and workflow complexity.

We will give a brief overview of each of these factors and explore how the combinations of factors have contributed to the problems service providers are experiencing today. Operations Support Systems play such a large role in the overall picture that they are handled separately in Chapter 4.

The Explosion of Data Networking

Over the past two decades, computers have evolved from massive standalone single-purpose machines of the not-so-distant past into vast networks of multipurpose desktop workstations talking to mainframes, application servers, and each other. The invention and evolution of the LANs, wide area networks (WANs), and dial-up modems have paved the way for data to be exchanged between individual computers and networks, changing the way business is conducted, and allowing for wide-scale communications between networks over existing telecom networks.

All this networking enabled the Internet to emerge as a hugely disruptive technology. Corporate, then personal, email forever changed the way people communicate and how business is done. The drastic growth of demand that emerged with the ubiquity of the Internet drove the need for more of everything related to IT. As the speed, storage capacity, and overall capability of workstations increased exponentially each year, so too did the need to network that capability, and in turn manage the network.

The emergence of client-server and peer-to-peer technologies with their increasingly larger networks of faster and more powerful computers passing information over the network has driven the evolution of networking technologies at a dizzying rate. Ethernet (10Mbps), Fast Ethernet (100Mbps), and even Gigabit Ethernet (1Gbps) have all entered the corporate IT environment because of the demand for faster speeds and larger networks pushing more data over the enterprise network.

The demand for more data capacity created a huge demand for large amounts of bandwidth between corporate locations, local networks, remote offices, and other companies via the Internet. The first consequence was that many more special services (*specials*) were ordered and needed provisioning. Data services such as fractional or entire T1s, DS-3s, and even larger pipes were ordered in growing numbers. The *specials* weren't so special anymore.

New Technology

At the same time, the technology development and manufacturing base evolved rapidly to support the growing data requirements. The big established vendors such as Nortel, Lucent, Alcatel, and Fujitsu were quickly joined by hundreds of new data-centric technology companies such as Cisco, Cascade, Juniper, AFC, and a host of others.

A number of different protocols, technologies, and delivery schemes such as ISDN, frame relay, ATM, MMDS, and xDSL were developed to serve different needs, and each had its own advantages, disadvantages, networking requirements, and management idiosyncrasies. The new technologies were offered to the business customer almost as quickly as the hardware vendors could build the boxes.

With a seemingly endless list of options with which to meet the corporate telecommunications need and very little understanding of the technologies, service providers and their business customers tried all the technologies over a relatively short period of time.

The overwhelming number of options contributed to the creation of large numbers of hybrid networks made up of several different technologies, which were delivered on equipment from disparate vendors. The individual networks were connected to, leased from, or otherwise related to (such as through overflow routing agreements) other hybrid networks from other service providers, both established and new. (We discussed coopetition in Chapter 1.)

These hybrid networks were immensely more complicated than the old telephony network and required support personnel to have vastly different skill sets. The newer technologies also required customer premises equipment (CPE) of varying types, complexity, and manufacture, at multiple points in the network. Convergence complicated this issue even further as ISDN PRIs replaced analog lines or T-1s as feeders into switchboards and key systems, frame relay replaced dedicated T-1s, and tech-happy IT departments toyed with *voice-over* technologies (voice-over frame relay, voice-over IP, and so on).

The Premise Factor

The demand for speed has also driven the need for more bandwidth downstream from the large business environment through the small office/home office (SOHO) and even directly into the home for residential use. The end result has been that every customer premise, such as offices, apartment buildings, and even residences, has turned into a potential SAP for the new technologies. Many of the network technologies that deliver these services require that a device of some sort be deployed to the premise.

The variety and amount of hardware that was (and is) being deployed to various premises greatly exceeded everyone's expectations. The volume of service calls requiring that the service provider install premises equipment (such as Channel Service Unit/Data Service Unit (CSU/DSUs)) to deliver the service grew accordingly.

The requirement to deploy equipment in the customer location meant that service delivery became premise-based rather than centralized. From an operations standpoint, the shift from a central-office (CO)-based delivery environment to one that is much more premise-based may be the most significant (and unrecognized) change brought about by the new technology.

The premises factor immensely complicates the entire delivery chain. Until the early 1990s, the only telecommunications providers people had much contact with were employees of the phone company (telephony carriers) and the cable company (cable television providers). The existing phone companies such as Regional Bell Operating Companies (RBOCs) and IntereXchange Carriers (IXCs), (and many of the startups that were to follow) operated in what could be called a traditional telephony environment in that they were primarily voice carriers and extremely switch-centric. While optical, microwave, and satellite transmission technologies dominated the inter-switch networking, the local loops of networks still usually ran on pairs of Category 3 (or below) copper cable from the local CO into the home or office.

Since the customer had long since been able (as a result of a landmark antitrust verdict against AT&T) to own the customer premises equipment (CPE) associated with the voice network (that is, telephones), most phone companies serviced the vast majority of users exclusively from the COs or other even more centralized locations. The number of private lines installed to serve business customers or private LAN/WAN networks was relatively small initially, and rare enough that such orders were called *specials*.

Despite advances in network management systems, the telephony providers have long had problems maintaining current network inventories and configuration control of the network elements. The actual network configurations (in the CO) were often not reflected in or reconcilable with the network inventory databases that supposedly managed the network as part of the OSS.

Over the years, a series of equipment upgrades, undocumented maintenance work, and thousands of adds, moves, and changes made the databases within the OSS inaccurate when compared to the actual network. In some cases, different OSS databases showed very different network configurations, probably none of which were entirely correct. (This disconnect between the logical databases and the physical network elements has been a problem for years. We will discuss it in later chapters.)

Inaccurate record keeping would have made provisioning unmanageable were it not for the fact that each CO had a dedicated pool of technicians that knew every circuit card, cross-connect, and terminal block in the facility. In the CO, the quality of documentation for both equipment and the cable plant depended almost entirely on the initiative of the local technicians. In many cases, the available CO documentation was managed using homegrown (locally developed) systems that were not visible or accessible to anyone outside the CO workforce.

In most cases, the CO technicians simply did whatever was needed to complete the order, many times without properly documenting changes or fixing discrepancies that showed up on the order. Since much of the undocumented work took place in order to provide work-arounds for discrepancies in the orders generated by the OSS in the first place, the problem got worse, not better. In the end knowledge about and visibility of the true inventory and configuration of the physical network were limited to a few people in each CO.

Thus the vast majority of the telephone company's provisioning capability was limited to a relatively small and extremely localized workforce. The years in residence that it took to create expert technicians in every CO also made scaling or redistributing the workforce very difficult. The fact that most of the workforce was also unionized made dynamic adjustments to the labor force almost impossible.

The cable TV companies, on the other hand, evolved from broadcast television, initially a primarily Radio Frequency (RF)-based (UHF/VHF) analog broadcast technology, into a hybrid technology that uses satellite content feeds and many of the same technologies as the phone company's inter-switch network before terminating in the home as coaxial cable.

The cable people fared somewhat better with cable modems. They had three natural advantages: (1) The cable TV technology was better than DSL over copper, (2) they owned the entire route to the premises, and (3) they already had service people used to delivering CPE to the premises.

The cable companies have had the functional equivalent of the CO, called the *head-end.* Unlike at the phone company, however, in order for the cable system to work, a piece of company-owned equipment was normally required at the customer location.This equipment, normally a control box, was usually placed on top of the customer's television set, hence the term *set-top box.* Installing the set-top boxes (a form of customer premises equipment) required the cable companies to employ a larger, more distributed, and mobile workforce—albeit a less technically sophisticated one—which gave cable companies a jump start when it came to dealing with the premises factor.

Even these advantages were not enough to stop cable companies from experiencing most of the same problems the telcos did. But it was enough to get the phone company's attention. Eventually the phone companies bought the cable companies.

New Market Entrants

Customer demand and inefficient service providers allowed alternative providers to the telephone company and the cable people to emerge and create small-scale competition with the incumbent providers. Leveraging the new technologies and free of the regulation and legacy bureaucracies that controlled the incumbent service providers, the new entrants were able to create new markets and capture niches within the existing markets. The opening of

EXAMPLE 5: DELIVERING DSL TO THE CUSTOMER PREMISES

The old problems with keeping the network inventory and configuration current have been magnified by hundreds of times as the CO has been replaced by the customer premises as the focal point of service delivery. The new technology has also made matters much worse by introducing a large number of other complicating factors into the work flow.

As an example, let's review the DSL example used in Chapter 1. The problems attributable to the premises factor started immediately. The service provider had contracted with a third-party installation company to do the installations, and drop-shipped the modem to the customer location. The contract technician usually arrived on-site and found that the modem, Network Information Center (NIC) card, or something else was missing.

In the best-case scenario, the technician had a spare in the truck and got the hardware installed. Unfortunately, the technician qualified to do the hardware installation was not qualified to install the software. So a second technician was sent out, scheduled to arrive a few hours after the first technician had left. Since the installation was performed by a third-party contractor, the loop was qualified by the Incumbent Local Exchange Carrier (ILEC), and the end-to-end test was performed by the service provider, troubleshooting a failed end-to-end test proved almost impossible. Provisioning dragged on, sometimes for months.

Remember the missing modems? Thousands were stranded on the customers' premises since there was no process for canceling service that included retrieving the hardware from the customers. Thousands more were lost as part of the drop-shipping mix-ups. The totals showed that the service provider "lost" over 35 percent of the modems they had ordered.

Especially revealing is how the remaining providers have fixed the problems. In most cases, the service provider now drop-ships everything to the customer for self-installation using better documentation and telephone support. Service providers still lose lots of modems this way, but the labor costs are way down. In the end, the service provider has turned to the customer as a temporary stopgap measure for installing DSL, which everyone expects will be a temporary stopgap broadband technology. What service providers have really done is turn premises installations over to the customer and retreated back to the CO model.

new telecom markets culminated with the passage of the Telecommunications Act of 1996 in the United States and other actions taken by the World Trade Organization (WTO) at about the same time.

The Telecommunications Act of 1996 for all practical purposes deregulated the industry (except for the RBOCs' access to long distance). In the 4 years following passage, an amazing number of new telecommunications carriers emerged. Different types of carriers such as building local exchange carriers (BLECs), competitive local exchange carriers (CLECs), data local exchange carriers (DLECs), integrated telecommunications carriers (ITCs), and any number of other acronyms entered the market.

Cap Gemini Ernst & Young estimates that as of 2000, there were almost 1,500 new competitors created in the United States, nearly 500 in Germany, and 200 in the United Kingdom. Figure 3.2 demonstrates the growth in service providers since 1996.

These new operators, with cash flowing liberally from the capital markets and the largest vendors offering investment packages and favorable financing, went on an unprecedented technology spending spree. Dozens of startup network technology companies, also flush with Venture Capital (VC) cash, swooped in. They offered the latest and greatest innovations in switching, transport, last-mile, digital loop, and almost every other conceivable network area.

The OSS evolution followed the same pattern. Along with the new hardware came a myriad of OSS vendors, systems integrators, and consulting companies, clustered predominantly around the customer care, billing, and network management functions.

Tight Labor Markets

What the vendors found was almost unfair. Although the opening of the telecommunications market had created thousands of opportunities, it had failed to create any additional talent. The data explosion had long before depleted the pool of available IT and telecommunications talent.

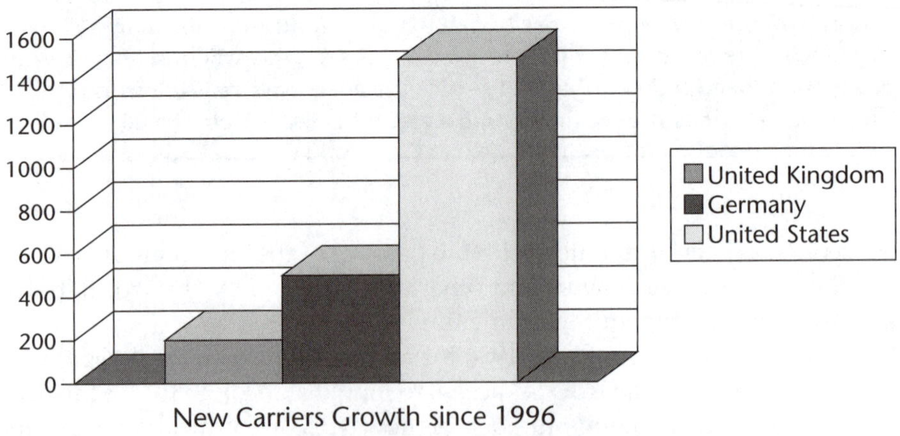

Source: Business Redefine: Connecting Content, Applications, and Customers, EY & CGEY, 2001.

Figure 3.2 Estimates of emerging carrier growth from Cap Gemini Ernst & Young.

According to a January 1998 study, the Department of Commerce estimated that more than 1.3 million additional scientists/engineers, systems analysts, and programmers would be required between 1996 and 2006 (see Figure 3.3). This estimate of new jobs is in addition to the existing (1996) workforce of approximately 1.5 million and an average of almost 138,000 new jobs created per year. Combined computer and telecommunications industry personnel requirements as a whole through 2006 were projected to double in size compared to what was available in 1996. Figure 3.3 depicts the shortages in the marketplace.

With the labor market so tight, the emerging service providers, along with technology companies of all sizes and descriptions, were unable to meet the demand for skilled analysts, engineers, and programmers. Especially problematic was the shortage of experienced telecommunications managers. In late 1997, *X-CHANGE* magazine, a trade periodical focusing on the emerging competitive local exchange carriers, published an article entitled "Could the 1998 Telecom Executive Draft Be Next?"

The article documented the financial bidding war then being waged by emerging carriers for top telecommunications talent, noting that "most top executive performers in the startup market with substantial equity can score between $500,000 and $1 million annually, if the company's stock performs well." *Note*: This article was written long before the bubble burst in late 2000/early 2001.

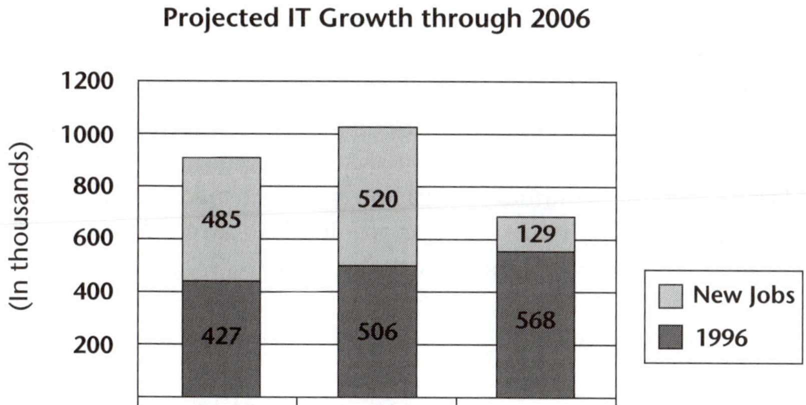

	Analysts	Engineers	Programmers
New Jobs	485	520	129
1996	427	506	568

Source: Bureau of Labor Statistics, U.S. Department of Labor

Figure 3.3 U.S. Department of Commerce projects tight IT/telecom labor markets through 2006.

Needless to say, such inducements motivated tens of thousands of people to make the move from established companies to the emerging carriers. Unfortunately, market dynamics could not overcome simple mathematics. There was no way several thousand startup, spin-off, and associated companies (that is, vendors, system integrators, and consultants) were going to get the talent they needed when the talent pool realistically consisted of the RBOCs, GTE, AT&T, and not much else.

The emerging carriers' demand for experienced personnel and the tightened labor pool led to what amounted to wholesale promotion of entire classes of telecommunications personnel. Technicians became managers, supervisors became directors, engineers became vice presidents, and so on. In reality, many of the CLECs got the exact opposite of what they actually wanted. They thought they were getting experienced talent that could lead them into their version of the next-generation high-tech telecommunications nirvana.

What they actually got was managers, directors, and VPs with no experience managing at the level at which they now found themselves, very narrow skills (owing to specialization in the RBOCs and long-distance carriers), limited exposure to working with other departments or companies, and worst of all, legacy stovepipe organizational and process mind-sets. The problems extended throughout entire companies, most acutely in engineering, operations, and OSS.

Savvy vendors with almost unlimited expense accounts spent extremely large amounts of money on these newly minted executives. Both service provider decision makers and their respective account managers quickly learned how the game was played. Smart startups entertained proposals from several different competitors for each technology procurement.

Aggressive hardware vendors, also flush with cash thanks to the burgeoning stock valuations, did whatever it took to close the deal, including investing in the potential customer and providing liberal long-term credit lines and other incentives. Many times the technology decision was not made on technical merit or business needs, but by which vendor provided the largest investment, best financing, or sweetest deals—whatever that meant.

Organizational Stovepipes

Truly delivering on SLAs to the service access point (SAP) is a process that requires the involvement of much, if not most, of the service provider's organization. Complicating the issue immensely are the challenges associated with the business dynamic known as *stove-piping*. As we originally stated in

Chapter 2, stovepipes are organizations and/or systems that exist in relative isolation from most others within the larger enterprise.

The typical service provider has numerous functionally specific departments and organizations such as the order entry group, provisioning (fulfillment), customer care (service assurance), ops (operations and maintenance), network operations center (NOC) billing (revenue assurance), Carrier Access Billing System (CABS) (actually a form of accounts payable), and the normal corporate finance groups such as accounts receivable and human resources. The different departments can be diagrammed as shown in Figure 3.4

Ideally, service provider systems and departments should work together to create an environment where services can be consistently delivered and the business can be relatively efficient. Instead, these isolated systems and organizations have evolved into bureaucratic bottlenecks that impede productivity and communications.

Because of their isolated nature, stovepipes are inefficient, prone to performing redundant activities, and, in most cases, they lead to departments within the corporate organization becoming highly politicized. The end result of the stovepipe phenomenon is that a large amount of isolated and often hoarded corporate knowledge is unavailable to the company, work flow that is supposedly connected by a series of handoffs becomes bottlenecks and potential disconnects that soon become the most vulnerable points in the entire enterprise. The bottlenecks inherent in stovepipes are shown in Figure 3.5.

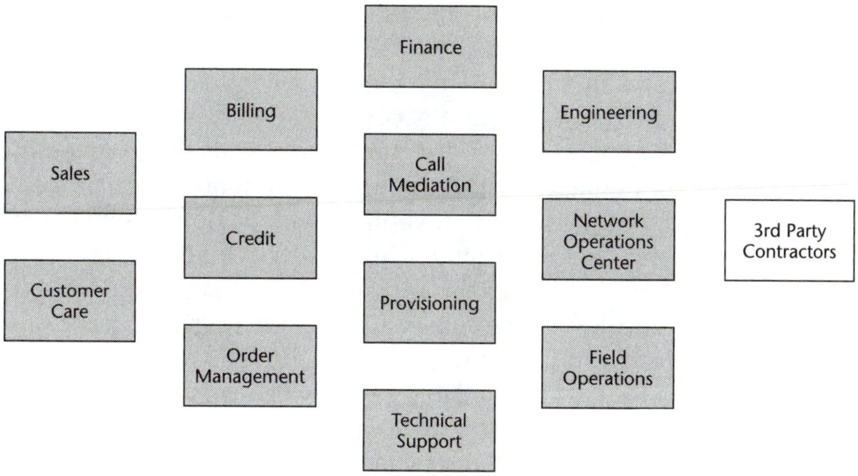

Figure 3.4 Diverse organizations within the service provider.

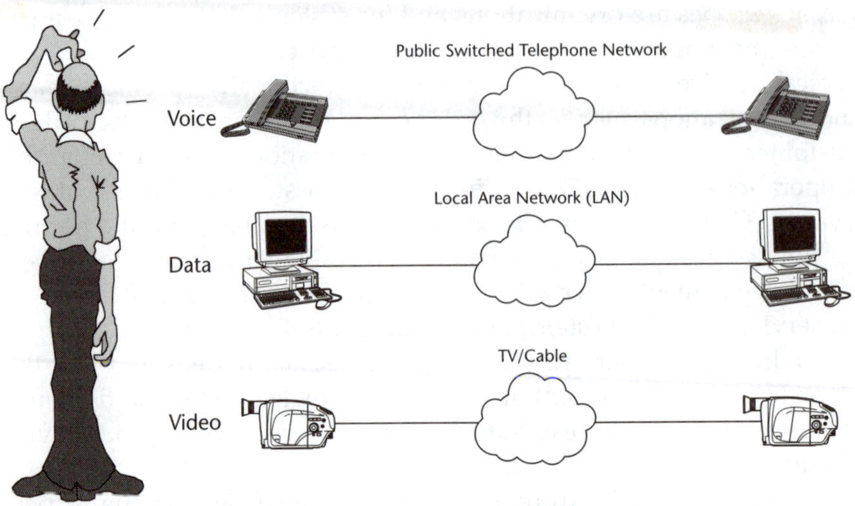

Figure 3.5 Stovepipes cause bottlenecks and disconnects.

Almost all stovepipes were initially created to address a specific functional need. These needs were addressed by creating a group of people with specialized skills. Typically, each group has a core automated system with which it does its job (the system). Almost without exception, the disparate systems are not integrated in any meaningful way. Likewise, the stovepipes have evolved unique work processes, many of which may be work-arounds for perceived deficiencies in their particular system.

Each stovepipe organization is secure in the knowledge that it has the most important business function. Each is equally convinced that its systems, organization, and processes generate the right data to drive the company, and everyone else needs to understand that. To protect the company from the ineptitude of all the other departments, the stovepipe owners adopt a siege mentality that manifests itself as departmental empires or fiefdoms that will protect the department's systems (and accompanying data), organization, and processes at all costs, regardless of the consequences to the larger enterprise.

The defensive attitude adopted by stovepipes is due, in part, to the very limited view of the enterprise that is available to the various stovepipes. Each department within the organization has its own perception of its role within the service provider based on its limited responsibilities, viewpoint, and experience. These perceptions do not necessarily match what everyone else thinks they should be doing. The solution is simple: create another organization that would. In the most extreme examples, legacy service providers have developed entire stovepipe organizations encompassing all the normal functions for individual products!

Protectionism and isolation often foster an over-the-fence mentality. The term *over-the-fence* is used to describe a situation in which one organization (department A) conducts (what it perceives to be) a complete task handoff to a different organization (department B). Department A then totally relieves itself of further responsibility with regard to that particular task. Department A feels that it is (1) no longer accountable for the task, and (2) any remaining actions to be performed prior to the completion of the task are the sole responsibility of department B. In this way, department A distances itself from accountability for the eventual completion of the task. The over-the-fence mentality is depicted in Figure 3.6.

The over-the-fence mentality manifests itself most strongly in large bureaucratic organizations—especially in the telecommunications arena where stovepipe organizations are an epidemic in the legacy ILECs and RBOCs. The most important thing to understand is that when an organization throws a job "over the fence" it has psychologically just passed the buck (accountability) to someone else.

Work-Flow Complexity

A major barrier to successfully implementing, measuring, and delivering on SLAs is the sheer complexity of delivering telecom services. Work flow can be defined as a number of tasks that may be performed in sequence or in parallel by two or more members of a community with the express intent of attaining a common objective. The keys to this definition are that there are two or more parties and the objective is common to all parties.

Figure 3.6 The "over-the-fence" mentality.

In Chapter 1 we introduced the term *coopetition*. Coopetition, along with demand growth, new technology, and large-scale outsourcing, has added more of everything within the definition of work flow. More services, more tasks, more work groups, more members, and much much more work flow.

Of course, work flow (or business processes) such as ordering, provisioning, billing, and many others have been a mandatory part of service delivery in telecommunications since the beginning. But until the early 1980s, these work-flow processes were all taking place within a single company (as shown in Figure 3.7), practically limited to a single product (switched voice)—and, back then, customer service didn't really matter much.

Competition Adds Many More Players

Historically, the monopoly system and local regulation though public utilities commissions as well as the Universal Services Fund ensured that the telephone companies made lots of money with very little oversight. Efficient operations, high levels of line quality, and good customer service were not necessarily mandatory. Although work flow was almost entirely manual, it was relatively limited in scope, volume, and complexity, and it lacked oversight. Customers took whatever the local monopoly phone company (usually AT&T) delivered. There really wasn't any other choice. Most people hated the phone company.

Everything started to change in the mid- to late 1980s as competition and equal access began to offer the consumer choices. The first real taste of the complications that would soon follow happened in the long-distance arena. The emergence of alternative long-distance (LD) carrier networks, such as MCI, LDDS, Williams, and Sprint, forced providers to start interconnecting. Eventually these alternative service providers grew from a few offering LD only into hundreds of emerging carriers offering the entire spectrum of telecommunications services.

Interconnection had a number of implications. First, it introduced new and different players into various parts of the service delivery equation. Interconnecting to other service providers not only meant connecting the two networks but it also meant that some level of cooperation and coordination was required between operations groups, billing departments, and other functional work groups (such as the sharing of information from separate databases, such as those used for 911, 800 numbers, and later local number portability (LNP).

These first steps toward full deregulation added many more process requirements at the same time that much more uncertainty was inserted into the end-to-end work flow. New service offerings proved to be much more process-intensive to implement. For example, Provisioning a POTS (plain old telephone service) line takes an estimated 25 to 40 tasks. Provisioning DSL, on the other hand, requires more than twice the number of tasks to complete.

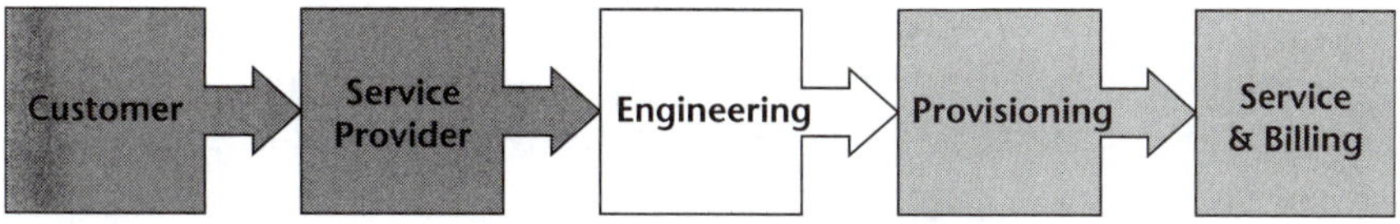

Figure 3.7 A single provider and a single product simplified work flow.

New Technology and Business Models Add More Complexity

The more complicated emerging technologies and disparate provisioning methods greatly affected both the volume and the complexity of internal work flow and also meant that both parties had to develop externally focused rules of engagement and accompanying processes for completing tasks that required cooperation and coordination.

As more external service entities were inserted into the end-to-end process, more and more parts of the work flow were out of the service provider's control and thus practically invisible to management. This external invisibility created black holes in internal work flow and reporting. (The fact that these tasks included processes for stealing customers from each other did not make it any easier.) The interaction between multiple service providers is shown in Figure 3.8.

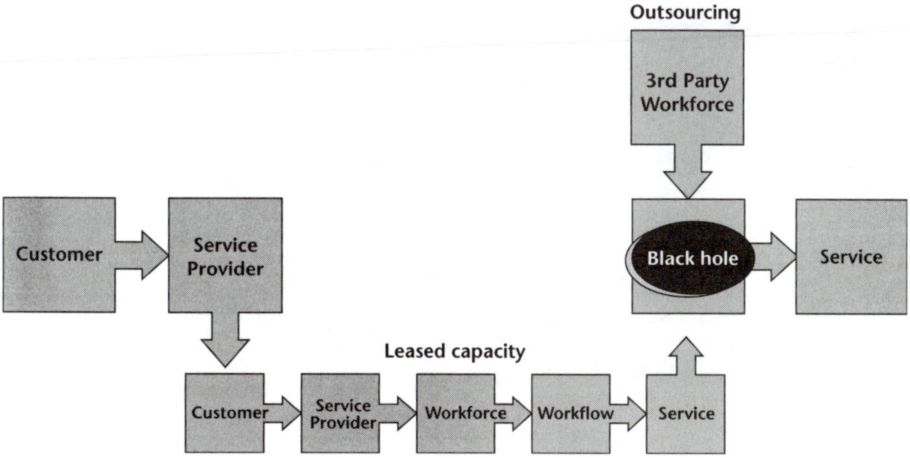

Figure 3.8 Multiple providers add complexity to work flow.

Another evolution that affected work flow was the increasing frequency of leasing of capacity and reselling of services. Equal access had made it feasible to become a telecommunications service provider with little or even no hardware or cable facilities. An emerging provider could own its own switch or facilities, rent facilities from another provider, or any combination of the two. Companies sometimes started out as pure (switchless) resellers, made enough money to buy their own switch, and eventually became full-blown, facilities-based CLECs.

The possible business combinations were endless. So too were the agreements, arrangements, and communications channels that had to be put into place. Everything had a number of options and had to be negotiated, such as who was responsible for operating and maintaining the leased equipment. Sometimes the ILEC did it, sometimes the CLEC did it, sometimes a third party was contracted to do it, and sometimes one party operated the equipment while the other party maintained it, and perhaps neither one actually owned it. Such complex delivery combinations generated many additional interface requirements through all domains within the delivery chain—including the customer, OSS, workforce, and work flow. Figure 3.9 shows the complex delivery chain.

After passage of the Telecommunications Act of 1996, hundreds of new carriers started up, then bought, built, rented, or resold network capacity and began offering every type of telecommunications service available in almost any combination of bundles.

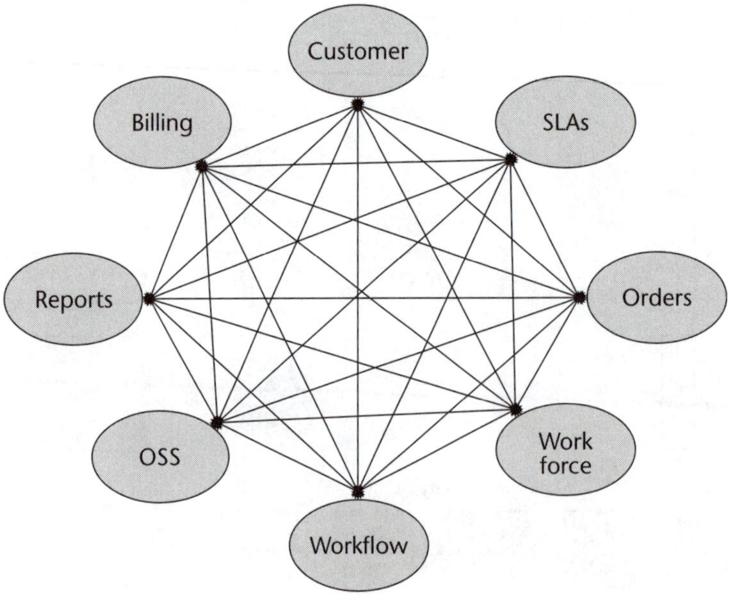

Figure 3.9 Multiple providers and multiple domains complicate the environment.

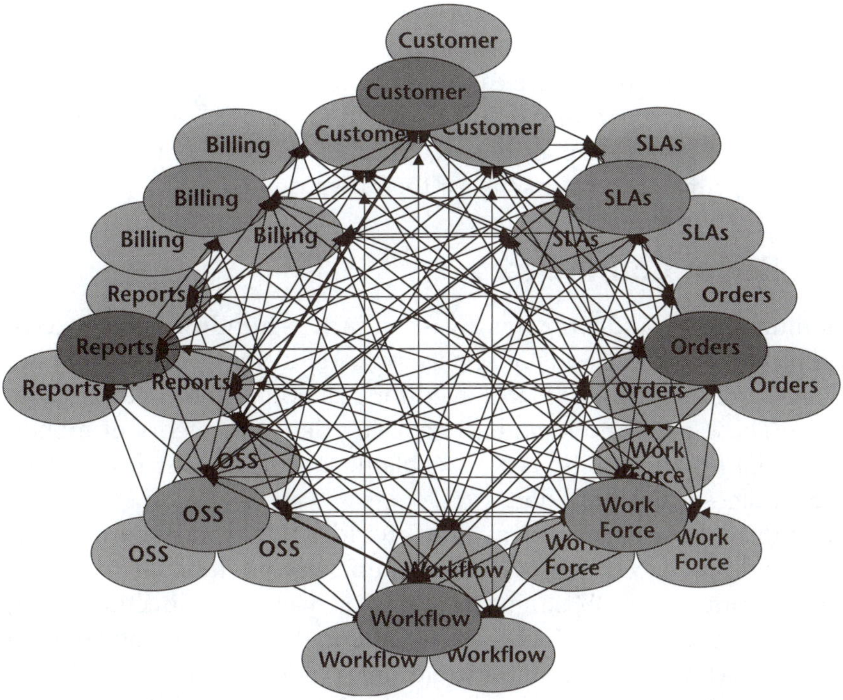

Figure 3.10 Today's work-flow complexity has become unmanageable.

Today, the largest service providers have thousands of different work flows for hundreds of different functions performed throughout the different layers of the organization. These requirements can often be multiplied by the number of interconnection partners, vendors, third-party contractors, and other parties they do business with. Just the sheer volume of work-flow processes—not to mention the complexity, variable options, and players—has overwhelmed the service provider infrastructure. A depiction of the work-flow complexities that can be experienced is shown in Figure 3.10.

Summary: A Confluence of Factors

As we stated in the beginning of this chapter, factors that determined the state of SLAs through 2001 all came together simultaneously. From late 1996 to early 2001, the Internet continued to take off, and the demand for data services exploded. A number of new technologies had been introduced to service the growing needs of the data-centric world. The capital markets at the time funded almost anything high-tech or related to telecommunications. The party lasted about 5 years.

In 2001 the telecommunications bubble burst. Many within the industry and analysts familiar with the landscape have expressed their opinions on what caused the crash. Although credible cases can be made that poor government policy and stalling on the part of the ILECs caused the demise of the CLECs, it must be argued that (with the possible exception of DSL) the new companies themselves were primarily responsible for their own demise.

The Great Boom Commences

The telecommunications industry was awash in cash as hundreds of new technology companies and thousands of service providers emerged. Providers of all sizes, types, and business cases jockeyed for position in the Great Telecom Rush of 1996. These new providers had booming demand, plenty of money, and relatively flat organizations, as well as blank sheets of paper from which to build the perfect service provider.

In addition to all that cash, the many new providers had weak boards, short timelines, green senior executives, even less experienced operational managers, inadequate and unproven OSSs, and no common vision or direction. They, along with everyone else in the CLEC environment, thought they understood the three mandates for the new economy telecom provider: (1) build networks, (2) connect them to everyone else, and (3) take orders and start billing.

At the time, the route to success was perceived to be capturing as much market share as possible, no matter what the cost. Any VC in the high-tech arena could tell you that. The vendors, consultants, and systems integrators brought in to help design and build the network and OSS concentrated on what they knew best: network management systems (NMS) and customer care (Customer Relationship Management [CRM]). That way, service providers could manage the network, take orders, and start billing.

Many millions of dollars went into creating the most impressive network operations centers (NOCs), call centers packed with the latest CRM technologies, and thousand of consultants and systems integrators worked tirelessly to implement all the back-office and OSS technology VC money could buy.

Operational Reality Interrupts the Party

What came next no one on the inside worried about. Just as in their former companies, the managers of all these new providers assumed that they could just throw the orders over the fence and Operations would figure out how to deliver everything. After all, the business was all about building networks and capturing customers. As the old saying goes, Sales is the mother of innovation. It didn't quite work that way.

What a lot of service providers didn't realize, and should have, is that, from the customer's perspective, customer satisfaction is delivered at the SAP.

Period. The customer wants quick, reliable, and reasonably priced service delivered to his or her door. The "Service Level Management: North American Survey 2000," respondents stated that availability is the most important factor in satisfied customers. Availability happens on-site at the SAP. More traditional customer service ranks a distant second. But true customer service also happens on-site. On-site, in the field, on the premises—whatever terms are used is irrelevant. It's the service delivery, stupid!

Operations couldn't deliver the goods. Service providers hadn't gotten widespread delivery to the premises figured out when they started rolling out broadband services. Most had not even identified service delivery as a major concern. Many had already thrown the responsibility over the fence to third-party contractors.

Technology and coopetition had created an entirely different environment. The service fulfillment and assurance processes became exercises in chaos because of the immensely more complex work flow, compounded greatly by the fact that no one knew how to fix the end-to-end work flow. The talent wasn't there to understand and evolve the overall work flow into streamlined repeatable processes.

The lack of talent that could tackle a problem of this magnitude was attributable to a simple process of elimination. Few founders and senior executives came from Operations backgrounds. Many founders were the most entrepreneurial people from Sales and Marketing. They knew very little about actually delivering service.

The talent pool had very few good Operations managers to begin with. The RBOC stovepipes created middle managers who were experienced in single-product or functional areas, with legacy OSS, predictable (unionized) workforces, and stable, relatively well-defined (manual) processes. They were most skilled in day-to-day administration, which did not prepare them for the new environment's challenges.

In the RBOCs and ILECs, those with enough vision, operational experience, and extensible skill sets generally never went into management in the first place. There was simply too much politics. The many bell-heads middle managers that did become new VPs, directors, and department heads spent large amounts of time creating stovepipe fiefdoms in the old RBOC image.

Consultants and system integrators were also a potential source of talent. They understood the latest management theory, had studied up on all the jargon, and could speak the language of the next-generation integrated telecommunications provider. Unfortunately, they didn't know anything about the actual operations of a telecommunications provider.

They didn't know what they didn't know. And it showed. In their first attempt to deliver premises-based broadband services, next-generation service providers have proved one thing: They don't know how to do it efficiently. The inability to reliably deploy and deliver premises-based service has already cost thousands of telecom personnel their jobs, and, in some cases, bankrupted their companies.

These problems were not limited to smaller emerging carriers. After the RBOCs successfully derailed some of the competitive efforts, they found that they couldn't do it either. Remember the high-profile problems experienced by DSL carriers such as Covad and Rythmns? Add SBC, PacBell, and Verizon to the list of companies that experienced huge (read costly) problems with their DSL rollouts.

The real-world example we used in Chapter 2 is just the tip of the iceberg. On the SLA front, many DSL providers and resellers, including the ILECs, had mandatory provisioning SLAs in place, with entitlements as short as 30 days from the date of order. Some of the resellers bet their businesses on it—and lost.

Hundreds of lawsuits have been filed as ILECs, DSL providers, ASPs, ISPs, resellers, and even third-party subcontractors continue to point fingers at each other as to why DSL delivery to the customer takes so long, works so poorly, and loses so much money.

Most troubling to us is the fact that the most widely accepted solution to DSL has been to use self-installation kits drop-shipped to the premises. In effect, the providers are taking their responsibilities back to the CO and throwing the problem over the fence—this time to the customer.

What Issues Lie Ahead for Service Level Agreements?

The premises factor has not gone away. It is still there, waiting for the next attempt at widespread deployment of the next great technology. A word to the carriers on the premises factor: There's no one else to punt to, and soon no one else to blame—think about that.

As we have seen, the largest and most established service providers haven't gotten service delivery in the new environment solved. They are battling the same problems experienced by the emerging carriers: (1) The network is much larger, more complex, and distributed, (2) the workforce is fragmented and not skilled enough, (3) the logistics and OSS support is inadequate, and (4) there are way too many work-flow processes that are undefined, unmanageable, and out of control.

Many service providers would summarize the situation as follows: It ain't pretty, but it works. They are deluding themselves, lying to the customer, or both. Service level agreements don't work. So where does this leave SLAs? More important, where does this leave the customer? Can the service providers transition to a more customer-focused perspective and SLA delivery model?

Only time will tell, but the trend points to continued growth in the use of SLAs. The environmental factors we've discussed continue to march forward unabated and unaffected by the industry's attempts to relieve them. As consolidation continues, the surviving carriers must overcome many roadblocks before much progress can be made, such as migrating from legacy systems, convincing old-school mind-sets, dismantling stovepipe fiefdoms, and dealing with unions. The system, organizational, and work-flow interoperability problems could become even worse as internal politics contribute to the status quo.

Studies have shown that the top people in industry are aware of the problems and are looking to fix them. But in order to effect meaningful change, CEOs, CIOs, and COOs must have a vision that the entire organization can buy in to. That means that the answer lies in the hands of the architects, integrators, and managers of the OSS. Only further systems automation has the potential to establish order from the chaos, to reorganize relationships and transactions, and to make work flow end to end, repeatable, measurable, and reconcilable.

To the OSS managers: Fix work flow—all the way to the premises. Like the old real estate adage, in telecommunications it's Work flow, Work flow, Work flow. Everything else is support. Without work flow under control, SLAs won't be worth the paper they're written on.

Summary

In this chapter, we have examined why delivery is so important in the SLA environment and the problems inherent in current approaches to delivering on them. How some service providers have taken inappropriate (in our opinion) measures to get around the challenges rather than address them. Identified a fairly large number of external factors that came together during a unique five-year period, as well as the primarily negative repercussions on the industry.

We also looked ahead and projected what it will take to address the many problems we discussed. Much of the fix will start with the systems resident within the service provider's OSS. We will spend a considerable amount of time on thorough discussion and examination of the OSS in Chapter 4.

CHAPTER

4

The Operations Support System

In this chapter, we will describe systems within the Operations Support System (OSS), how they function, and how they are used. More important, we will discuss the many problems encountered by service providers in their quest for a top-to-bottom OSS solution that works. We will examine the roles played by the OSS vendors, system integrators, and industry thought leaders. We will undertake a thorough discussion of the evolution of their approaches, the models they espouse, and the relationships that have been developed among them.

We will continue our examination of need hierarchies to understand their place in the OSS equation. As in prior chapters, our discussion of need hierarchies has the potential to show us how we got to where we are, where we went wrong, and where to go next. We will then undertake an in-depth analysis of the OSS environment in the communications boom environment that existed between 1996 and 2001.

We'll explain why the bubble finally burst, why the current situation is as bad as it is, and how it got that way. We'll examine how different business agendas and potential conflicts of interest have influenced and will continue to influence both architecture and implementation. We'll demonstrate our contention that the TeleManagement Forum (TMF), while doing very important technical integration work, also has its own agendas, is too limited in scope, and is too slow in reacting to today's dynamic communications environment.

Finally, we will look at some lessons we have learned through it all. We'll try to understand the implications and provide guidance on where some of the solutions will have to come from. Then we'll finish the chapter with some educated guesses as to where the models that drive the OSS are going to go. So let's get started.

The Operations Support System

In its document *Communications Industry Market for OSSs* the TeleManagement Forum (TMF) has stated, "a key stumbling block is the inability to integrate the many operational support systems (OSSs) used by a company. It isn't possible, for example, to achieve fully-automated order fulfillment, because the systems used for customer contact, order entry, service configuration, network design, installation, dispatch, and account billing were not built to work together" (1999).

Very often, the definition of the term "OSS" depends on who you ask and the role they play within the service provider's organization. To clarify what we mean in this book, we would like to state our own definition: The OSS is made up of all the computer software applications, systems, and accompanying processes that allow a service provider and its separate organizations to conduct their defined business and operational roles within the communications industry environment. The TMF makes a further distinction between those systems and functions related to service management and network operations and those more closely or directly related to customer care and billing by using the term *business support system* (BSS) to describe the latter. By separating a service provider company into OSS and BSS, the TMF has created an artificial partition that reflects the evolution and current scope of the TMF as an organization but is not based on industry needs, as we will discuss. We will use the broader definition of the term *OSS*, encompassing BSS functions as well.

On the SLA front, vendor claims to the contrary, there is no single answer to SLAs. An automated OSS system that is capable of fully measuring and reporting compliance to SLAs across the enterprise has yet to be developed. This lack of appropriate tools is not singularly related to SLAs but merely indicative of the problems that have been experienced by service providers when they have tried to build modern OSSs.

Today's OSS landscape is really made up of a number of point solutions that address very specific needs of individual departments. Even the broadest of suite-based solutions from the leading enterprise resource planning (ERP) or customer relationship management (CRM) vendors can provide only a fraction of the total system functionality needed by the communications service provider.

Customer care and billing systems are not readily integrated into the network management systems, and both areas are separate from the network inventory, design, and planning systems used by the company's planning and engineering groups. Provisioning is normally accomplished by using an order management system, as well as a workforce management system that automates the activities of the field engineers, while trouble management systems may be related to the order management system, network management system, or many times it is an entirely separate system altogether (such as the extensive use of the trouble ticketing system "Remedy"). The breadth of the disconnect among systems has been shown in Figure 4.1.

This convoluted systems architecture has evolved because internal software development groups and independent software vendors have long built functionally specific systems for stovepipe organizations. While the use of disparate systems was initially somewhat manageable when there was a single telephone company offering a limited number of services through an internal organization operating on its own network, a single provider environment is far from the reality that we are faced with today.

As we discussed in earlier chapters, the global communications environment has become a hodgepodge of service providers, offering myriad services to millions of new data-hungry customers. Hundreds of types of network hardware, software, services, and OSS vendors, in addition to systems integrators and consultants, ply their products and services to carriers hoping to establish their product as the next *must-have* technology.

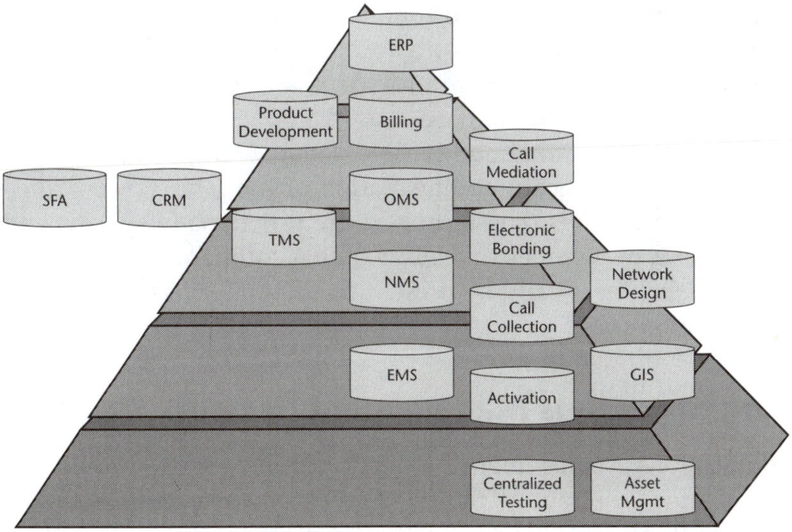

Figure 4.1 Disconnected systems within the Operations Support System.

Thought Leadership and Industry Models

The situation is convoluted, confusing, and dynamic, especially in the OSS arena. In order to discuss, and, we hope, understand, the current situation, it is first necessary to have a working knowledge of the role of the TeleManagement Forum, the Telecommunications Management Network (TMN) model, the Telecommunications Operations Map (TOM), and the Systems Integration Map (SIM). We will be exploring these in addition to more need hierarchies to understand the evolution of OSS; to look into the current relationships between OSS and service providers, customers, and SLAs; and to attempt to project future trends.

The TeleManagement Forum

The TeleManagement Forum (TMF) has arguably become the most influential single entity within the communications OSS arena. The TMF is an industry-driven organization that provides thought leadership, strategic vision, and standards guidance, as well as solution development projects specific to the communications OSS environment. TeleManagement Forum membership is made up of incumbent and new-entrant service providers, network equipment vendors, independent software vendors (ISVs), systems integrators, and large communications or networking customers.

The stated mission of the TMF is "to be universally recognized as the leader and enabler for automating operational management and business processes within the global communications industry and related supply chains by advancing the available technologies and solutions."

The TMF accomplishes its mission by organizing a number of committees and forums where OSS vendors, service providers, and other members can compare and exchange information, as well as define standards and make recommendations for OSS interoperability. TeleManagement Forum catalyst projects demonstrate the practical implementation of the latest TMF principles, concepts, and architectures. These projects are functionally specific and supported by a number of member (usually vendor) companies. These vendors obviously realize business value by presenting their offerings as solutions to the defined problem areas.

The Telecommunications Management Network Model

The Telecommunications Management Network (TMN) model provides a common framework for OSS interoperability. The TMN was originally developed by the International Telecommunications Union-Telecommunications

(ITU-T) Services sector (formerly the Comité Consultatif Internationale de Télégraphique et Téléphonique [CCITT]) in order to support deployment and network management of multi-vendor (hybrid) communications networks and the accompanying services.

The TMN standards have been widely adopted throughout the industry and have been used as a reference point by other organizations such as the TMF, European Telecommunications Standards Institute (ETSI), and Telecordia (formerly Bellcore), the Synchronous Optical Network (SONET) Interoperability Forum (SIF), and the Asynchronous Transfer Mode Forum (ATMF).

Modeled in part after the Open Systems Interconnection (OSI) management framework, the TMN is intended to be multi-vendor, interoperable, extensible, scalable, and object-oriented, and it approaches communications management from several viewpoints. It defines frameworks for both the logical and the functional aspects, as well as standardized interface points.

The TMN logical model divides the day-to-day aspects of the service provider into five functionally specific management layers, as shown in Figure 4.2. The model is such that each management layer starting with the physical network builds a foundation of systems, activities, and processes that enables execution and operations at the next higher level. Starting from the bottom, these management layers include the following:

- Network element layer
- Element management layer
- Network management layer
- Service management layer
- Business management layer

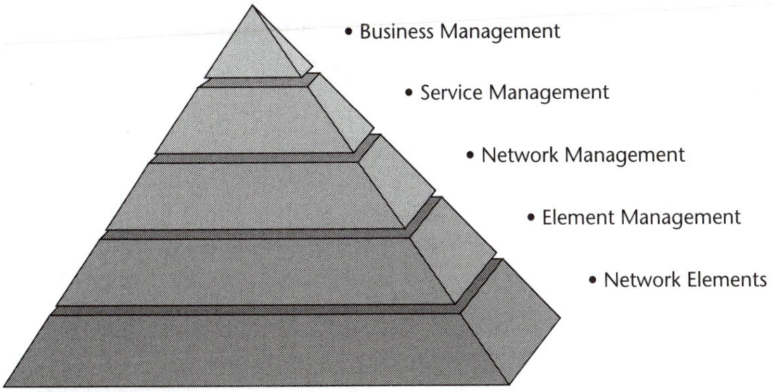

Figure 4.2 Overview of the Telecommunications Management Network logical model.

The Network Element Layer

The network element layer (NEL) is made up of the network hardware and software that enable communications. For example, a router or a class 5 switch would be considered a network element, as would a channel bank or Digital Subscriber Line (DSL) access multiplexer (DSLAM).

From a functional standpoint, the network management layer is often called the *physical* layer of the network. It is through the network elements that the communications products and services are actually delivered.

It is important to remember that the end-users/customers and their service access points (SAPs) physically exist on the network element layer. In the many discussions on OSS, the customer becomes a euphonious logical entity made up of database objects that are passed back and forth through the various OSS subsystems that reside on the service management layer.

It is equally important to understand that the majority of service delivery activities, from the customer's viewpoint, occur on the customer's premises. Almost all service delivery (as opposed to service management) happens at the network element layer.

The Element Management Layer

The element management layer (EML) is generally made up of the software management tools that allow for direct oversight and management of a specific group or subset of network elements. Normally this grouping is managed on a vendor-specific basis. (Nortel INMS is used to manage Nortel DMS-series circuit switches, the Fujitsu is used to manage Fujitsu FLM-600s, and so on.)

Functionally, element management systems (EMS) actually make up most of the functionality that is aggregated as the network management system, but they are limited in breadth because of the technology differences among vendors. In many cases, different network elements manufactured by the same vendor have different element managers. Therefore a relatively large number of element managers exist that enable the service provider to manage a variety of network elements.

The Network Management Layer

The network management layer is made up of tools that allow the service provider to see the various elements and EMS within the network as one large (probably hybrid) entity. There are many responsibilities within the network management layer. These have sometimes been represented by the acronym FCAPs, a collection of the following tools:

- Fault
- Configuration

- Accounting
- Performance
- Security

These tools provide a centralized fault detection, alarm indication, correction and testing capability via data collected from various EMS and network elements. The network management system provides real-time data and analysis of network systems, detecting possible problems and degradation of service quality throughout the network so that they can be corrected before they become problems.

The network management system can modify alarm thresholds for alarm activation for particular users and elements if need be. All alarms and statistics gathered either in real time or in batch mode are archived for later analysis and historical record. The network management system, in conjunction with other systems within the network management layer, provides configuration and optimization of the system, manages traffic surge capabilities, and controls network growth.

The functions of network security management are especially important. Security elements include user identification and authentication, access controls, passwords, audit trails, real-time alerting, and a number of other network security measures.

The Service Management Layer

The service management layer (SML) is made up of the systems and functions that enable ordering, delivery, ongoing support, and billing of customers. There are a number of different types of systems that reside on this layer, including:

- Sales force automation
- Customer care
- Order management
- Provisioning
- Call collection and mediation
- Billing
- Product development
- Trouble management

These tools support a number of functional departments within the service provider, such as the call center, the provisioning group, the credit department, the billing group, and so on. In some cases, integrated software suites falling under the general term of customer relationship management (CRM) packages are used to provide support for a number of functional requirements, taking the place of multiple applications.

The Business Management Layer

The business management layer (BML) is made up of systems that support the high-level business needs of the communications service provider. The business management layer is more inwardly focused than the service management layer is, because the financial viability of the service provider is its priority. The business management layer includes systems that enable the service provider to perform functions such as planning, goal-setting, negotiating contracts, reconciling financials, and other forms of decision support.

These functions can be supported by several systems or by application suites specific to the BML, known as enterprise resource planning (ERP) systems.

The Telecommunications Operational Map

Together, the different levels of the Telecommunications Management Network allow the OSS and, by extension, the service provider to support functional activities at a number of levels. These activities or operational processes must be managed in an automated manner in order for them to be efficient. The stated mission of the TMF is to enable end-to-end automation of the operational processes. The Telecommmunications Operations Map (TOM) is the framework for accomplishing this.

Based on the TMN, the TOM has mapped required business functions into the TMN layers for network management and service management. The required business functions have been identified as follows:

- Customer care processes
- Sales
- Order handling
- Problem handling
- Customer Quality of Service (QoS) management
- Invoicing and collections
- Service development and operations processes
- Service planning and development
- Service configuration
- Service problem management
- Service quality management
- Rating and discounting

- Network and systems management processes
- Network planning and development
- Network provisioning
- Network inventory management
- Network maintenance and restoration
- Network data management

The TOM is intended to be a framework for service providers that will assist the industry in developing common definitions, a common process model, and eventually common processes. In addition to the functions identified within the TOM, the TMF has identified a number of process interface or touch points into the core framework. These include processes for customer interface management, network element management, and management of the physical network elements.

The TOM also identifies three end-to-end processes that together form the critical process flow for delivering services to the customer: service fulfillment, assurance, and billing (FAB). Fulfillment, assurance, and billing makes sense because the customer calls to (1) order or end service, (2) report a service outage, or (3) reconcile billing issues. The end-to-end process areas are then overlaid on the TOM to produce a blueprint for defining and implementing the work-flow processes that are actually used in the service provider environment, as shown in Figure 4.3.

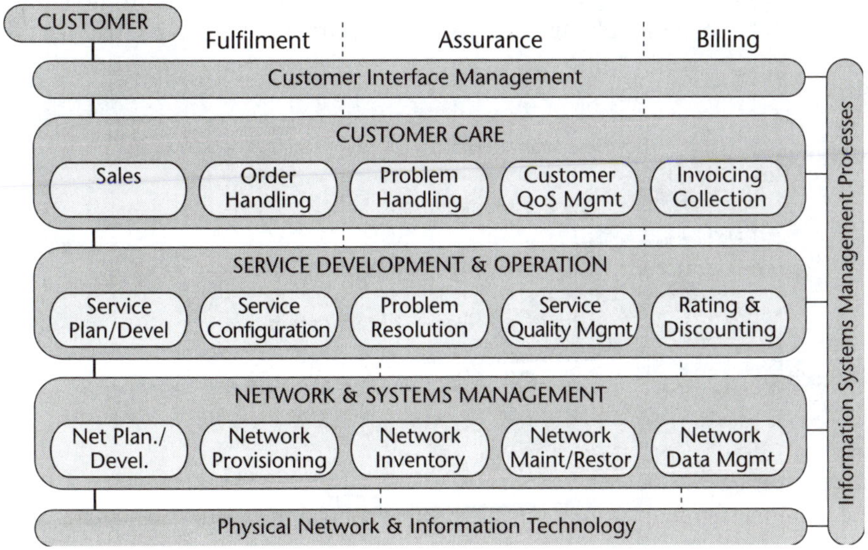

Figure 4.3 The Telecommunications Operations Map.

The adoption and use of the TOM framework will enable the industry to begin the long journey toward integrating processes, but it is a very long road. Current integration efforts still center on the technical integration of the data structures. To realize process integration, several other issues must be addressed first, such as semantic integration (see Chapter 7).

Understanding the Models

In some ways, the TMN and TOM models are very similar to Maslow's hierarchy of needs, which, as we discussed in Chapter 2 , theorizes that lower-order needs such as physiological and security requirements must be satisfied before higher-order needs such as belonging and realizing potential can be addressed. This comparison is shown in Figure 4.4.

As you can see, we have mapped the different layers of the TMN to Maslow's hierarchy. Although this may seem somewhat unconventional, examining the TMN and, by extension, the TOM in this manner is a valuable exercise in understanding why things work, why they don't, and where they should go if the models hold true. The TOM really starts at the network management layer, so we will begin our examination there.

The Evolution of Network Management

The systems and functions (FCAPs) that come readily to mind when the term *network management* is used reside on the lower three layers (the network element layer, element management layer, and network management layer) of the TMN model. These levels are, for the most part, hardware-centric. Even

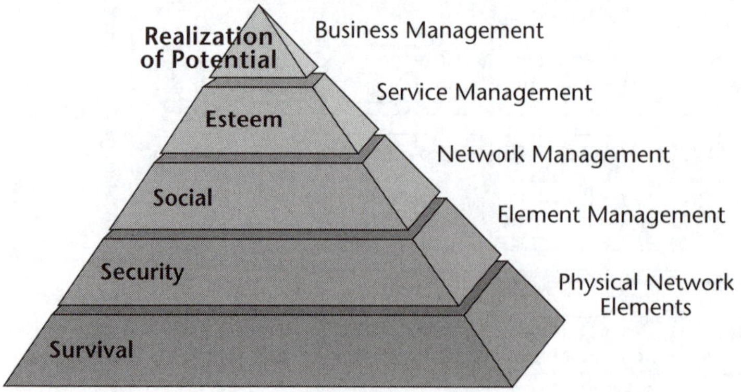

Figure 4.4 The Telecommunications Management Network and Maslow's hierarchy.

with a manager-of-manager (mom) application overseeing individual element management systems (EMS), the systems are all designed to monitor, control, indicate, and report on hardware.

As we've shown, the physical network, as well as element management, equates with Maslow's physiological needs. The *organism,* to use Maslow's term, must first have its physiological needs met in order to allow the higher-order needs of security to become important. Accordingly, network management is futile without first establishing consistent order and control of the network elements.

In the beginning of modern telecommunications, legacy plain old telephone service aside, network managers and OSS vendors were initially overwhelmed by trying to solve the hardware and software problems involved in wide-scale networking. Maximum efforts were made to bring the network under control and to understand all the physical infrastructure, connectivity, and interoperability issues that came with the territory.

Initial element management systems were (and to some extent still are) vendor-proprietary and unable to be readily integrated. Since then, good element management systems have been developed that can monitor, control, and report on network elements (EMS). With the adoption of standardized interface protocols (thanks in large part to the TMN recommendations) such as Simple Network Management Protocol (SNMP), Common Management Integration Protocol (CMIP), and TL-1, the capability to integrate a large number of elements from various vendors came to fruition as the *manager-of-managers* concept. This integration seemed to fulfill the TMN requirements for network management quite nicely.

The TMF evolved in parallel with network management. In fact, until a few years ago, it was known as the Network Management Forum (NMF) and originally concentrated its efforts on standardizing interfaces from the network elements into the network management systems.

As the interoperability issues within the network management layer started to become less of a concern, the NMF broadened its scope to include the service layer and changed its name accordingly. Today its members are involved in defining the standards and developing the models for almost every aspect of automating communications OSS operations, including hardware, software, processes, and vendor interoperability.

An obvious indication of the broader scope of the TMF is the TOM. The TOM has been developed as the common framework by which communications service providers can understand the relationships among individual process flows. The TOM, approved by the TMF membership in early 2000, takes the TMN model and overlays processes and functions to add a second dimension to the model. One important point to note: The TOM does not yet cross the boundary between the service layer and the business layers within the service provider and pays only cursory attention to the element management and network element layers.

Looking at our need hierarchy, we have reached a point technically where the lower-order (network element layer, element management layer, and network management layer) needs have been addressed and the higher-order (service level management [SLM] and business management [BML] layers) needs are now the priority. The remaining network management layer questions are mainly a by-product of convergence as additional network technologies (including voice and video) are integrated onto the hybrid network over Sonet, IP, frame relay, DSL, Asynchronous Transfer Mode (ATM), and so on.

Element and network management systems will continue to evolve as vendors and integrators jockey for their share of the market and standards continue to be implemented. It is fair to assume that in the future, both hardware vendors and network management application developers will continue to build their offerings in compliance with the latest TMN and open-architecture standards. We have moved up the hierarchy from physiological needs to security. What really matters today is the service management layer.

The Transition to Service Management

As we discussed, the service management layer of the TMN is much more customer-oriented. The transition from network-centric requirements driving systems requirements to the customer-centric service management environment has been an ongoing process.

The TMF has understood for quite some time that the needs of the customer would become increasingly important. The TMF recognized these changes within the need hierarchy fairly early and transformed itself by expanding its focus from network management to include the service management layer as well. The new focus was obviously a necessary transition if the organization was to remain relevant to its membership.

Other people and organizations also recognized the need for change. Industry analysts have forecast for a number of years that with the maturation of the network management system, expected growth and spending would be more pronounced in the customer care and billing areas of the TMN compared to network management. Figure 4.5 shows OSS spending projections from 1997, as shown in *Tele.com* magazine.

The Telecommunications Act of 1996 was propelled, in part, by customer dissatisfaction with the limited options that were available before competitive communications became a reality. The wider introduction of alternative carriers made customer service a bigger priority.

Within the TOM, the service management layer of the TMN has been divided into two domains: (1) service development and operations and (2) customer care. This distinction in the model is particularly interesting because it creates two separate functional domains. This division clearly represents the fulfillment of security needs for both the service provider and the customer, further validating our use of need hierarchies as a tool for understanding the OSS.

This book is devoted to exploring the particular needs of both the service provider and the customer within the context of supporting SLAs. The real value lies in applying these principles. The principles should be deployed in a way that is both useful in the present and provides future guidance for increasing effectiveness.

In the following section, we will continue to discuss the evolution of the service management layer. We will look at the OSS as it is used today, recount recent industry experiences, and further analyze some of the recent difficulties, as well as the reasons behind them. We will also look at some of the lessons learned and recommend approaches service providers can take to correct current deficiencies and avoid making the same mistakes in the future.

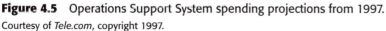

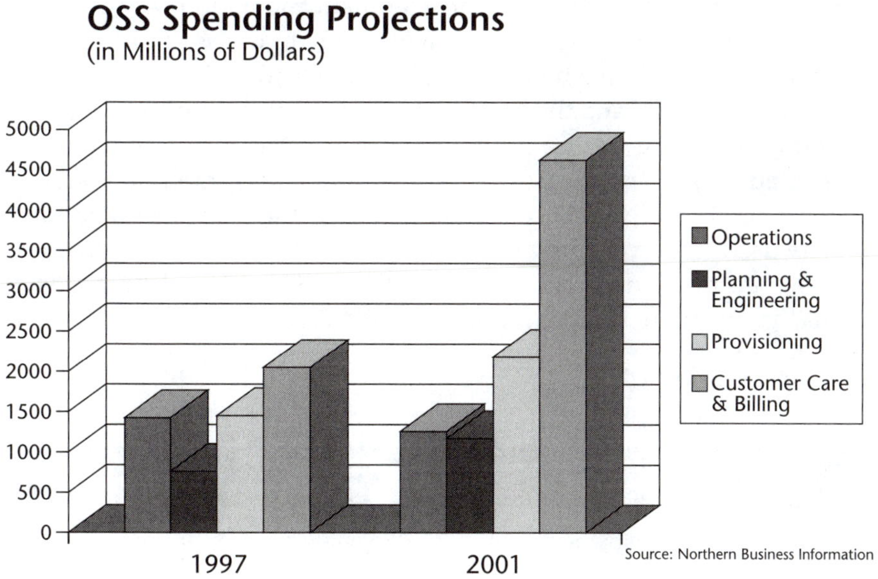

Figure 4.5 Operations Support System spending projections from 1997.
Courtesy of *Tele.com*, copyright 1997.

The Emergence of Best-of-Breed

The biggest constraint to effective SLA-grade service delivery has been the fractured service provider infrastructure. The requirements of an innovative OSS—effective organizational infrastructure and well-thought-out work-flow processes—are of equal importance for service provider success. The three components of systems, people, and process (plus logistical parts support) must converge in a way that is complementary and that allows the strengths of one to compensate for the weaknesses of the other.

The great majority of service providers have done an extremely poor job of orchestrating this collaboration. Instead all three areas have succumbed to the stovepipe phenomenon that originated in the people (or organizational) component. The organizational dynamics of a stovepipe are adddressed in Chapter 9, and we talk about the advantages of collaborative work flow in Chapter 11.

Prior to 1984, the communications industry was much simpler, although much less efficient. There was basically one service provider per country. Providers developed their own systems internally, and the stovepipes weren't as important because efficiency and customer service were not a major concern. Processes changed little immediately after the divestiture of AT&T, but slowly the evolution picked up momentum. The deregulation in 1996 was the impetus for a real change in service provider practices.

The ITU-T developed and published the document sets for the TMN beginning in the early to mid-1990s. Since the development and widespread adoption of the TMN principles, service providers, with the help of system integrators, have used the TMN to help them understand, design, and build their OSSs.

In some ways, the TMN and the TOM are actually counterproductive to creating smoothly operating service providers. Because the TMF's active membership is made up primarily of OSS vendors and established service providers, the TOM had, in essence, documented the then current operational methodology used by service providers. By doing so the TOM had segmented the processes into many different functions. The many different functions of network management are shown in Tables 4.1 to 4.3.

Table 4.1 Network Management

FUNCTION	OPERATIONS SUPPORT SYSTEM SUBSYSTEM TYPE
Network planning and development	Engineering
Network provisioning	Element managers
Network inventory management	Asset tracking
Network maintenance and restoration	Dispatch/scheduling system
Network data management	Data warehouses/reporting

Table 4.2 Service Development and Operations

FUNCTION	OSS SUBSYSTEM TYPE
Service planning and development	Product development
Service configuration	Network provisioning and/or activation
Service problem management	Trouble management
Service quality management	Network management
Rating and discounting	Billing

Table 4.3 Customer Care

FUNCTION	OSS SUBSYSTEM TYPE
Sales	Sales force automation
Order handling	Order management
Problem handling	Trouble ticket—Customer Relationship Management
Customer Quality of Service management	Service level agreement managers
Invoicing and collections	Billing

Startup OSS vendors then used the TMN and TOM to build different software for each function without understanding how it would affect the service provider's organization or work-flow processes. As a result, the market was overcrowded with OSS vendors. Some of these vendors created products to serve needs that did not exist. Those vendors didn't last very long.

System integrators and OSS vendors were responsible for much of the adoption of the TMN in the service provider environment. The TMN provided an easily understandable way for OSS vendors to explain to OSS managers why they needed to buy their particular products. The model also provided an easy way for those managers to explain the complexities of the communications OSS to their executives.

Having an easily understandable industry-accepted model greatly benefited the system integrators who provided both solution recommendations and implementation services. The TMN gave them a way to convince service providers that their services were absolutely necessary to make the whole TMN work. Needless to say, the OSS vendors, system integrators, and OSS managers were generally members of the TMF. So the same people who developed the models also made the recommendations, sold the software, did the implementation, and integrated the data. Needless to say some very complementary relationships were developed and it wasn't long before *best-of-breed* (BoB) was born.

Best-of-breed (BoB) is an OSS systems architecture wherein the service provider divides the overall systems requirements into a number of classes or *breeds*, such as ERP, CRM, provisioning, and network management systems. The service provider selects from the competitors in each class and integrates the best solution for that class into the overall OSS architecture. Best-of-breed can be mapped against the TOM and TMN as shown in Figure 4.6.

Best-of-breed evolved because there were too many new OSS vendors with too many products that did too few things. The complexities in the work flow, changing requirements from the service providers, and the rate of change in the industry made it impossible for a single vendor to provide very broad applications that would serve a large portion of the service providers' needs. There were many competitors of each system type, and it seemed that more OSS companies were starting every month. These systems were not interoperable even horizontally across the models, let alone vertically.

The need for OSS interoperability was so acute that it spawned a new industry. The *enterprise application integration* (EAI) or *middleware* vendors emerged in the late 1990s promising to be the medium that would allow the disparate systems to communicate with each other effectively.

Initially, middleware technologies were immature and functioned as little more than meeting points for the different applications. Successfully integrating the myriad possible product combinations into a single system proved to be impossible. Failure of generalized middleware caused dominant OSS vendors, with the assistance of the major system integrators, to narrow the field by creating strategic partnerships among their companies and building prepackaged interfaces among their applications. Many of these alliances were conceived as part of a TMF catalyst project or systems integrator's *model* architecture.

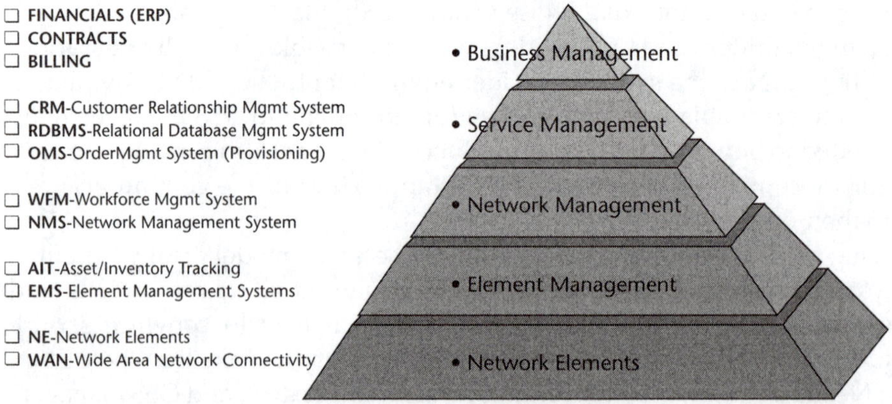

Figure 4.6 The relationship between telecommunications management network and best-of-breed.

Best-of-Breed Problems and the OSS Spiral of Death

There were a number of problems inherent in best-of-breed OSS architectures. First, they were extremely expensive to implement fully. In many cases, service providers spent in excess of $50 million to provide top-to-bottom TMN functionality to their personnel. Much of the cost was not the software itself, but the high price of implementing and integrating services from system integrators.

The success of middleware depended on the Application Programming Interfaces (APIs) made available by the OSS vendors, and in the late 1990s these were somewhat rudimentary and lacking in functionality. While some of this still holds true, middleware has gotten much better in recent years. Chapter 7 is dedicated to interoperability and integration techniques.

Furthermore, the disparate systems and the limited distribution capabilities (most of these were client-server applications) encouraged stovepipe organizational structures built around OSS product functionality. The operational disconnects actually created more handoffs, both human and electronic, adding to the workflow complexity. We discuss workflow techniques in Chapter 9.

In addition to the problems inherent in BoB architecture, the competitive local exchange carriers (CLECs) and other emerging carriers compounded the problems by the way they implemented their systems. Many emerging carriers bought and implemented parts of the model architectures piecemeal, without giving much consideration to the TMN or organizational, process, or data integrity issues.

Poorly integrated systems were not entirely within the carriers' control. Pressures to capture built networks, market share, and offer broadband services to the captive customer as quickly as possible drove the majority of deployment decisions. Furthermore, the systems integrators that service providers depended on to guide them through the process had their own agendas for which systems needed to go in and when. Many times system integration was based more on the system integrators's vendor relationships than on the needs of the service provider.

Financial pressures and the sales backgrounds of many founders drove CLECs and the like to concentrate on capturing customers and generating revenue as quickly as possible. The rush to revenue meant that the first things to go into the OSS architecture were the order management system (OMS) and billing systems, which suited the integrators just fine.

In many cases, the carriers put the network management system in place as soon as the internal OSS resources were available. Systems integrators liked building network operations centers (NOCs), and carriers enjoyed showing them off to customers. A lot of money was spent on superior audio-video capabilities in NOCs. The rush to get the new carrier up and running as quickly as possible created a situation where the network was built, and the provisioning, billing, and network management systems were brought on-line practically simultaneously. With the simultaneous activities being conducted by disparate groups within the service provider, many times using separate integrators, huge functional gaps occurred between applications. It was as if the new carriers were asking for trouble.

Eventually, many emerging carriers experienced an almost predictable startup cycle that included a pattern of recurring setbacks related to the implementation, integration, and operation of their OSSs. These setbacks often resulted in the failure of the OSS, the service provider, or both. These failures happened often enough that industry observers developed a timeline of 18 to 36 months for what they nicknamed the CLEC spiral of death, illustrated in Figure 4.7.

As shown in Figure 4.7, the following steps led the service provider inevitably into the spiral of death:

1. Company funded.
2. Network build started.
3. Marketing blitz launched.
4. Provisioning and billing on temporary systems up and running.
5. Demand outstrips delivery capacity.
6. Network operations center built.
7. Inventory control lost.
8. Customers lost.
9. Professional telco management hired.
10. Best-of-breed so called world class systems bought.
11. Data integrity, migration, and interoperability problems encountered.
12. Delivery capacity continues to degrade.
13. Revenue targets missed.
14. Company fails.

Once the disparate systems (billing, order management system, and network management system) started being used to provision services, the problems we discussed in Chapter 3 started taking their toll on the CLECs. Customer orders entered the order management system and came out the other side as a service order that needed to be provisioned. The order was then thrown over the fence to another organization, such as the NOC or field services group, normally in the form of (paper) work order forms and circuit layout records (CLRs) or design layout records (DLRs). The CLR or DLR was most often generated as a function of the order management system, or sometimes using a separate drawing package or Geographic Information System (GIS), such as AutoCad or Mapinfo.

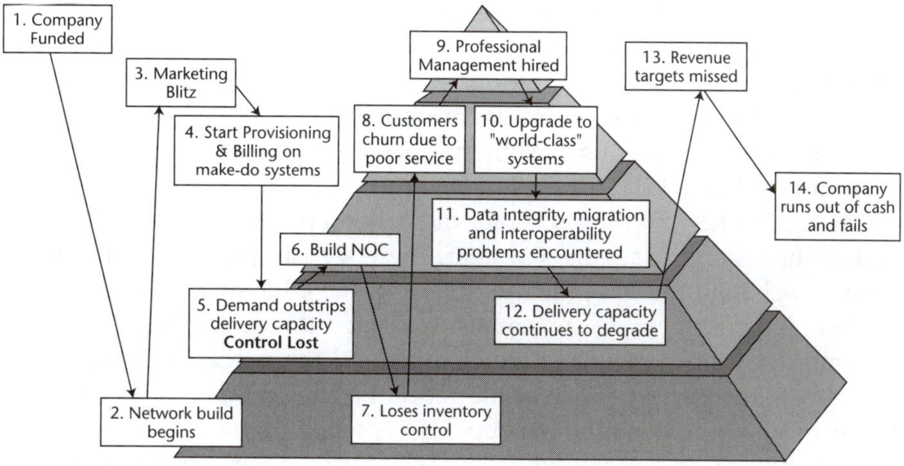

Figure 4.7 The competitive local exchange carriers' spiral of death.

On the receiving end, the work orders were entered into a different system, often manually, because the field technicians did not have access to the order management system. They then did the work as engineered in the CLR or DLR, did the appropriate notifications, and tested the circuit in conjunction with the NOC. Once the NOC was able to verify that the circuit was completed and tested *good,* then the technician was released and the work order was closed. The NOC then assumed control of the circuit and monitored it. The disparate systems and the roles they played in the end-to-end work flow are depicted in Figure 4.8.

At first, this manual method got the job done—before reality interceded. The work flow worked only if everyone did precisely as the CLR or DLR directed. The port assignments, cable pairs, and jumpers had to be completed exactly as engineered in the drawing over the entire route. Assuming workers followed directions, everything was fine.

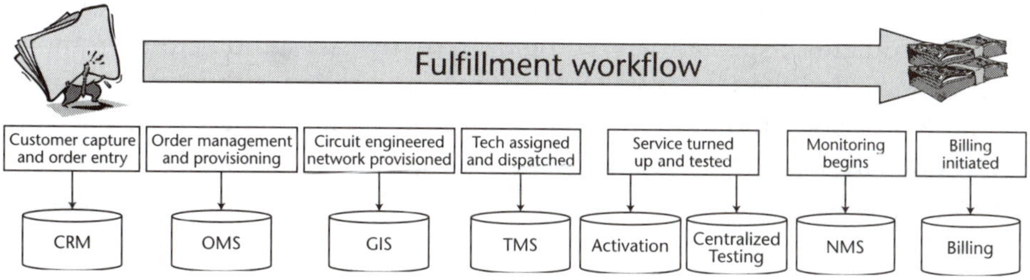

Figure 4.8 The Operations Support System relationship to end-to-end work flow.

But in reality not all systems worked as expected. So when the technician tried to use the cable pair that was designated in the CLR, sometimes the pair was bad. Similarly, sometimes the exact ports specified couldn't be used. To the technician, the answer was simple; he or she simply used another pair of cables or another physical port. Sometimes the technician documented the new pair or port in the local cable plant records.

Unfortunately, the new pair of cables or physical port record rarely, if ever, got back to the order management system. There was simply no practical feedback loop to change the assignments made in the CLR or DLR—especially when the order management system also included the design functions. The systems had no way to reconcile the change, and the processes were not in place to throw the order back over the fence. Besides that, over many years technicians had adopted a mind-set of pride in getting the job done, regardless of the instructions that came down from the order management group. So the technicians simply made each system work and moved on to the next job. There were always plenty of jobs.

Yet the order management system is not the only source of change on the physical network. Cables get cut, cards fail, preventive maintenance (PM) gets done, and many other things affect the configuration of the network. Trouble tickets make up a large percentage of work and are documented in the trouble management system (TMS). Preventive maintenance schedules also dictated that work be done, and many adds, moves, and changes (A/M/C) made to the network were totally undocumented.

The end result of the work flow in best-of-breed systems was that a lot of adds, moves, and changes to the network were not reflected in the order management system. Each instance created at least two data integrity problems. The first was that the order management system understood that a circuit was to be running over certain network elements and cable pairs when it was not. The second was that the order management system understood that certain elements or cable pairs were available—but they were not. The data integrity problem was further compounded when the order management system assigned what it thought was available resources, which were actually in use, to another work order. Then the whole cycle started over again, resulting in several more data integrity problems. The data integrity problem is illustrated in Figure 4.9.

It did not take too long for service providers to feel the effects of data integrity problems, especially in the field. In many cases, the field operations group disregarded the CLR and DLR entirely and relied instead on the local stovepipe processes and systems. The work-flow situation had gotten so bad that, by one estimation, one of the country's largest service providers never got its orders right the first time.

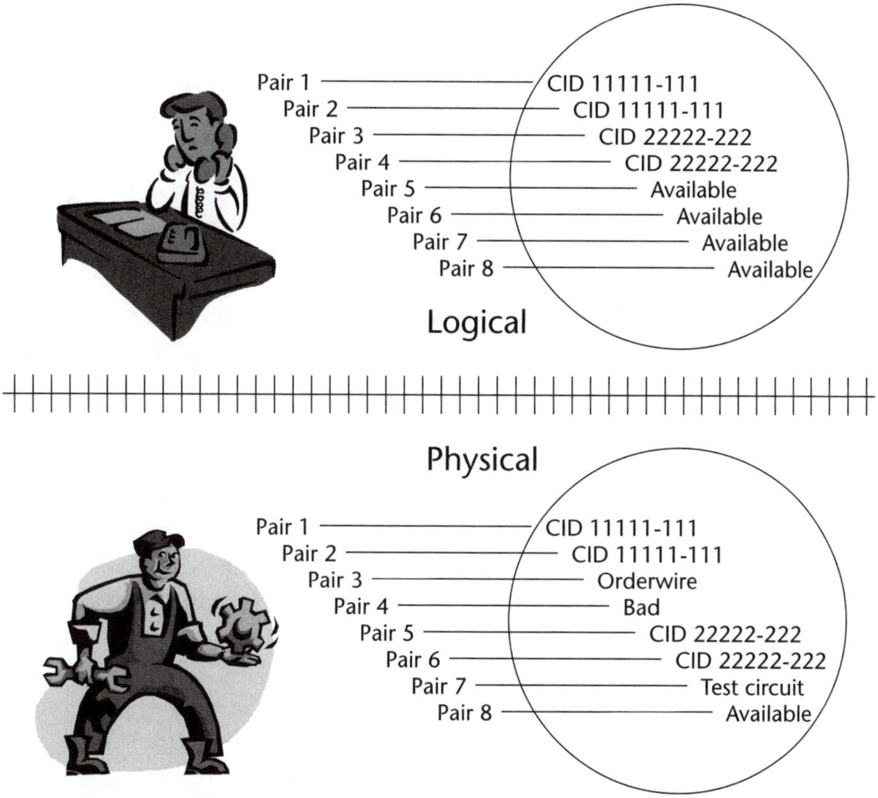

Figure 4.9 Disparate systems cause physical-logical data integrity problems.

In reality, that *never* estimate is probably exaggerated, but much of the work done was wrong, and corrective action usually resulted in the service provider expending two or three times the required effort. The financial implications of the errors were staggering. One service provider estimated just over $100 per DSL installation, but the actual cost was over $400.

The combination of the application disconnects, the fragmented (and often invisible) work flow, and physical asset management that was marginal at best, resulted in huge data and process integrity issues. Integrity issues meant that the OSS became practically unusable after some length of time. The length of time depended on the volume of orders since more orders corrupted the database more quickly. In the beginning, the effect was not very noticeable, but as order volume increased, so did the integrity corruption issues.

It was extremely difficult to escape from the death spiral. Some carriers threw out their integrators' first attempts and started over with new integrators and new BoB models. Besides being extremely expensive, replacement solutions didn't usually work because the underlying problems were still there. The only way to ensure that work-flow problems would not continue on a permanent basis was to establish data integrity between the logical and physical layers of the OSS. Uniting the physical and logical layers took a concerted effort and required a number of intermediate steps that many service providers simply couldn't afford to take.

One of the first steps was to establish and maintain good asset and inventory tracking of the network elements. Accurate inventory required that detailed physical audits of the network be performed in order to get accurate data. In many cases the audit process required *lockdowns* (periods where no changes may be made) of audited sites for some time. The audits also required that a sustainable repository of this data be implemented and maintained.

Once the audited physical data was available, it was used to revise the data that would reside in the order management system. Updating the order management system usually meant that someone was doing manual data entry and overwriting the discrepancies. Manual fixes created huge amounts of work for the provisioning group, but they also had the desired effect of restoring data integrity between the logical and physical layers of the network, which allowed for better service delivery and increased revenues. Figure 4.10 shows the steps to recover from the spiral of death.

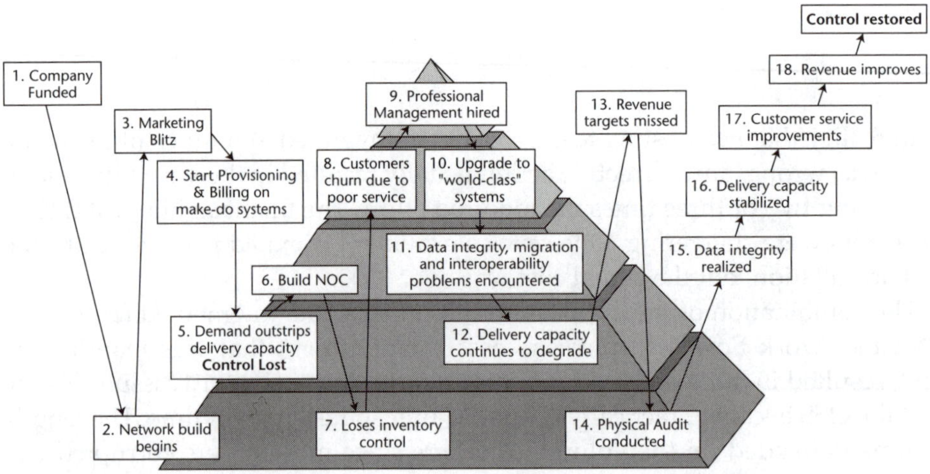

Figure 4.10 Death spiral recovery depends on establishing data integrity.

Obviously, service providers had to develop a process that would prevent the recurrence of data integrity and work-flow problems. The most effective solution would have been to build an interface between the different systems within the OSS. Unfortunately, an interface was not always possible; the systems that managed the logical and physical layers of the network were so far apart that many times the update process consisted of regularly scheduled physical audits. With scheduled updates, the data integrity problems existed only for a limited time. The manual updates managed but did not correct the data integrity situation, but many carriers had no other choice.

Lessons Learned

The telecom bubble that existed between 1997 and 2001 was a good opportunity to observe service providers, systems integrators, and OSS vendors at their best (and worst). The sheer number of emerging carriers building OSSs from scratch as well as existing carriers trying to keep up with new entrants meant that there were many more examples to examine. As active participants on telecom projects, we have a number of lessons to share:

- Build your OSS from the bottom up.
- Asset management is important.
- Understand the functional and semantic gaps.
- Work flow is the glue that binds the organization together, not middleware.

In hindsight, the data integrity issues that became the death spiral were avoidable. What the carriers and their system integrators failed to understand was the hierarchical need relationship between the TMN layers. As we've discussed, the lower-order needs must come first to make possible the higher-order ones. In this case, the requirements of the physical network elements must be satisfied first. The CLECs didn't follow the hierarchy. Instead they first implemented systems that managed prices, products, and a virtual view of the network.

Service providers are built from the ground up. As we have seen with our examination of need hierarchies, for each move up the pyramid—whether it is the data generated within the OSS, the functioning of the network, or the processes that drive the service provider's organization—the foundation must be solidly in place before the rest of the house can be built. Going back to the delivery elements of parts, people, process, and time, systems must be able to support all the elements all through each layer of the TMN.

The foundation of the OSS is its ability to manage and control the physical layer (the actual network elements), which is the cornerstone of all delivery capability. This foundation takes the form of good physical asset tracking first, followed later by the network inventory available on those elements, and followed after that by the logical inventory enabled by those elements, the revenue generated by the logical inventory, and finally by the profits realized at the top of the pyramid. Figure 4.11 shows the OSS element pyramid relationship.

As we move up the value chain, managing the virtual representations of the network becomes equally important, once the physical layer has been taken care of.

NOTE Let us state that again for emphasis: *once the physical layer has been taken care of.* As our detailed examination of need hierarchies has shown, the ability to satisfy higher-order requirements is very dependent on lower-order competency.

The virtual representations include, but are not limited to, OSSs that document the network capacity to deliver services such as element management systems, the network management system, GIS, and engineering and design systems, that is, anything that manages network inventory such as OC-48S, DS-3S, T-1S, and the accompanying electronics from a configuration standpoint. Inventory management systems must also have the data from the physical layer presented to them in a usable information format that can then be further processed and sent up the pyramid.

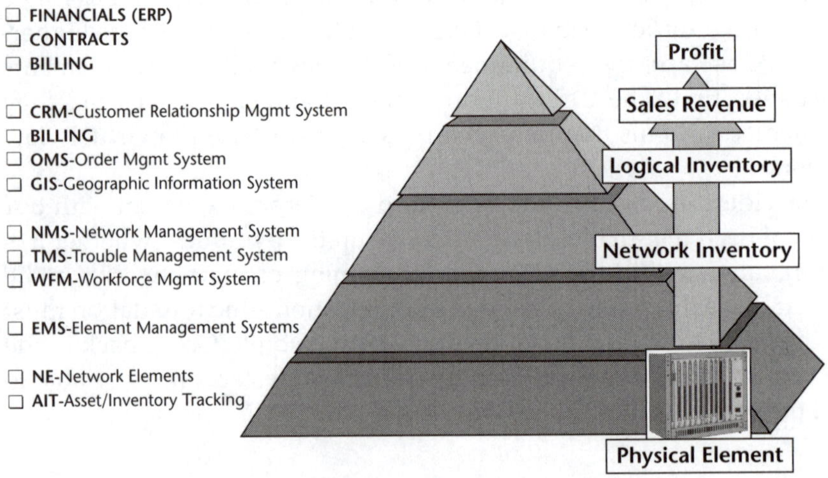

Figure 4.11 Understanding the network element value chain.

The benefits of maintaining data integrity as you move up the model will also be realized at the logical layer, once the virtual representations are taken care of, and so on. The point is that the service provider's need hierarchy dictates that OSS integration strategies should concentrate on engineering the OSS in almost the reverse order of current thinking. In effect, the TMN model should be inverted to determine subsystem importance and sequence when the OSS is being designed. The first systems you add to the OSS should not be order management and billing at the logical layer. You should add asset management and related work flow first in order to establish control of the physical layer. Doing otherwise will almost certainly result in data integrity disconnects that will eventually compromise the service provider's provisioning capabilities.

Asset Management Is Important

As we've discussed, many millions of dollars were spent on implementing and integrating certain OSSs (by system integrators, naturally), primarily the customer care system, billing, the order management system, network management system, and trouble management system. One of the problems with both the TMN and the TOM is that they do not place much emphasis on the physical aspects of the network element layer. By ignoring the physical aspects, many emerging service providers (and their system integrators) neglected asset and inventory tracking of the physical network.

Asset management has long been a recognized problem among service providers. It is conservatively estimated that many major carriers lose between 5 and 7 percent of network assets every year owing to poor asset management. They will continue to take multimillion-dollar write-offs every year because they simply can't find what they have. Considering that many carriers own $1 billion or more in physical network assets—that's real money. The premise factor adds even more importance to good asset tracking. In the DSL case we examined in Chapter 1, the carrier couldn't account for over a third of the modems that it had bought.

Asset tracking is often perceived as a financial function within the service provider. The very large amounts of money that have been invested in the network and the importance of realizing a return on those sizable investments probably contribute to this mind-set. Consequently, the task of asset management is many times relegated to accounting personnel in the headquarters or regional office. Typically, the ERP system is used to do the tracking.

Sorry, folks. Adds/moves/changes don't happen in the carrier office headquarters. Changes happen in the warehouses, central offices, and customer premises; that is, changes happen in the field. These field changes must find their way back into the ERP, and once-a-year inventories from a computer printout won't cut it. When was the last time you saw a technician who had access to the ERP system?

Asset management problems continue because the tasks related to asset tracking are not being handled at the appropriate layer, by the appropriate people, with appropriate systems for carrying out the task. Unless asset tracking systems and processes that are appropriate to the field are implemented to capture and document changes to the network (the entire network, not just the manageable devices or items over some artificial cost basis) as they happen, service providers will continue to have problems tracking assets. Again, the premises factor makes near real-time asset tracking crucial.

The management systems at the physical level are often vendor specific. The fact that they are out of scope (and outside the skills competency of most integrators) is another reason that asset management was often overlooked. Below the network management system, system implementation and integration were primarily done by network equipment vendors, as part of the network build-out. Some executives in the emerging carriers assumed asset and inventory management was done by the NOC. Unfortunately, the NOC is primarily responsible for managing fault notification and is two levels removed from the physical layer.

You can more closely depict the entire physical network by using robust network inventory and asset systems. Good network inventory and asset control systems will capture the parts of the network that the network management system does not, as well as depict aspects that are vitally important to service assurance, such as physical locations of elements, cable runs, access points, and so on.

Since robust systems were not usually available, physical layer information (such as cable plant records) was usually documented in a separate (stovepipe) system by the technicians on-site. The technicians had very little choice. The networks were being built so quickly and by so many subcontractors that there was really very little visibility of what was going on in the physical layer. The carriers brought the electronics on-line and offered services over them almost as soon as the last subcontractor had packed up his or her tools. Many CLECs never completely established control over the assets and inventories residing on the physical layer. In hindsight this lack of attention to assets on the physical layer was a mistake and was a major contributor to the physical-logical disconnects.

Understanding the Functional and Semantic Gaps

From a functional standpoint, the largest gap that exists in the OSS is between the order management system (and the systems above it) and the network management system (and the systems below it) as depicted in the TMN model.

As we have discussed, this gap had its origins in the institutionalization of the "sales versus operations" organizational stovepipes and was systematically documented by the TMN model. Subsequent TMN- and TOM-compliant systems development did little to address the problem.

Because of the functional differences between the roles of the systems and the needs of their respective users, integrating the order management system with the network management system is not a natural fit. The order management system is really an administrative system. Its users manage logical entities that exist only in databases. Furthermore, its function is to push information up the TMN model that eventually results in revenue generation.

The network management system, on the other hand, is immensely more technology and systems oriented. Its function is to gather information that will eventually result in information and direction being pushed down the TMN model to manage activities that affect the network elements at the physical layer.

The order management system to billing (OMS/billing) and trouble management system to network management system (TMS/NMS) integrations are much easier to understand because of the natural functional flow. We believe that the functional gap between the order management system and network management system is simply too wide to bridge effectively through technical data integration.

Figure 4.12 illustrates the importance of understanding the functional gap between the order management system and the trouble management system.

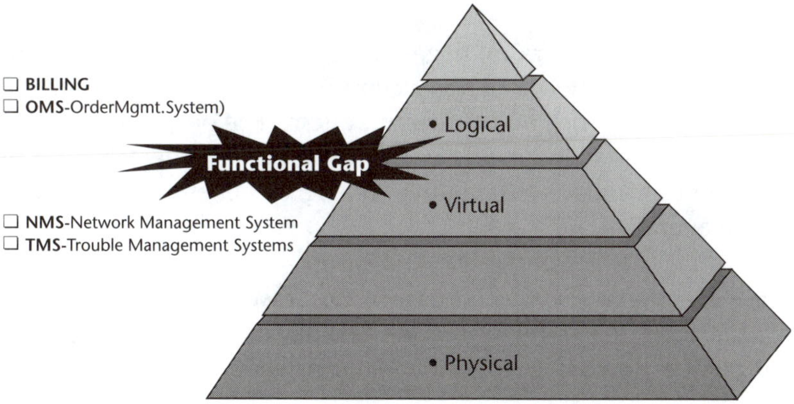

Figure 4.12 The impact of the order management system/network management system functional gap.

The functional gaps also translate into semantic gaps. Semantic gaps severely affect interoperability. For example, in a network inventory system, a circuit card may represent 16 ports of capacity, in an asset tracking system it may represent a $2,500 subassembly of a switch, and in the network management system it may represent an originator of SNMP messages.

NOTE Semantic as used here refers to the interpretation of the meaning behind a term or object. A semantic agreement would mean that all parties would have the exact same understanding and interpretation of an object.

Under all the bells and whistles, the order management system is a database that relates the customer with the service provider through the provision of a service. Like all databases, the order management system database is *normalized* through the use of a unique identifier. In the case of the order management system, the unique identifier that is used to relate the customer to the service normally takes the form of a telephone number, circuit ID, or CLLI code. These identifiers are *logical* entities that exist only in databases.

The network management system, on the other hand, is often misunderstood and perceived as being the physical layer. It must be understood that the network management system is not the physical network. It is not even an accurate *virtual* representation of the entire network. The physical network is made up of much more than the devices that are managed by the network management system. The physical network also includes cable plants, non-managed devices, such as Channel Service Unit/Data Service Unit (CSU/DSUs), many modems and other customer premises equipment (CPE), as well as things such as relay racks, central offices, punch-down blocks, and so on, that are not monitored.

So, more accurately, the network management system is a *virtual* representation of the portion of the network that is electronic, monitored, and actively reporting to the EMS or network management system. The network management system is a snapshot of the configuration data being generated at any given moment, although most systems are capable of generating historical data and statistical averages, and so on.

NOTE We have used the term *virtual* because in most cases the network management system and, to a larger degree, the EMS rely on database interpretations of configuration data being received from the network elements.

The logical (OMS) and virtual (NMS) entities are enabled by the *physical* network elements such as switches, routers, and the like that are cross-connected to one another through jumpers, patch panels, and extensive cable plants. They are not the physical layer. Hence, the physical/logical disconnect actually included a virtual layer sandwiched in between the logical and the physical layers. The addition of the virtual layer created a second gap. The second gap is also both functional and semantic in nature. Figure 4.13 shows the functional and semantic gaps between the physical, virtual, and logical layers.

Work Flow Is the Glue That Binds the Organization, Not Middleware

The functional and semantic gaps are both very much related to the division of work and organization of departments within the service provider. Yet closing the functional or semantic gaps is not the integration issue that system integrators and middleware vendors thought they needed to solve for the emerging providers. Vendors and integrators have instead concentrated on integrating technical data among the different OSSs, often assuming that the ability to exchange data between the systems was the most important aspect of building an end-to-end OSS solution. The integrators and vendors were only half right.

In Chapter 3 we defined *work flow.* We can paraphrase the definition as a number of tasks performed by members of a community in order to attain a common objective. We know that both the tasks and the objectives are often perceived differently at the various organizational layers.

For example, a technician at the physical layer may perceive a work order as just another cross-connect to be made, while someone in the NOC may see the service order as just another configuration change to a fiber mux; meanwhile, the customer service representative tracking the order may see the order as one of a hundred orders closed that day. Moreover, those hundred closed orders also mean that the billing system can start sending invoices and generating revenue, which eventually gets analyzed as financials in the executive boardroom.

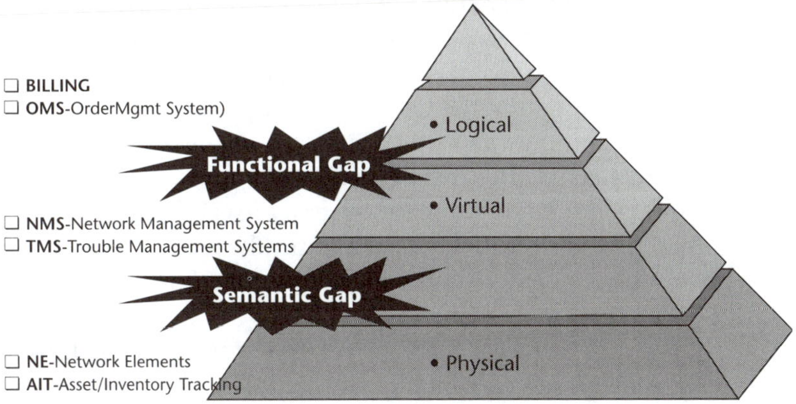

Figure 4.13 The functional and semantic gaps within the Operations Support System.

Therefore it is the ability to exchange information, not data, that is one of the most important aspects of building an end-to-end OSS solution.

Information is distinguishable from data in that it has usually been processed into a format that can be displayed to a receiver and perceived in such a way as to enable the receiver to gain additional knowledge, make a decision, perform a task, or otherwise effect a change based on the contents of the information. For example, an SNMP stream may have been processed by the element management system and displayed as a color-coded visual fault alarm. A receiver can perceive the color to mean that a certain response is needed. The perception can be classified as semantics.

Data can generally be defined as unprocessed machine or network output. An example might be an SNMP text stream generated by a network element to its element management system. Until it is processed further, it is not usable by a receiver in a practical sense. Data is the basis of all information, yet because it has not yet been perceived by a receiver, semantics is not mandatory.

The difference between information and data is the inclusion of the semantic relationships. In other words, there must be some level of agreement as to what the data means. The need for semantic agreement exists at two levels; between the OSSs and also between human users of the information. In an ideal world, every application and every person would have a common semantic understanding of every object. A universal understanding of all objects is obviously not possible.

For reasons we will discuss in Chapter 7, we do not believe that even the semantic integration of the systems is achievable end to end within the foreseeable future. Nor do we feel that end-to-end semantic integration is absolutely necessary. That is not to imply that the technical integration work being done by the TMF is futile. Far from it—we feel that technical integration is absolutely mandatory.

But we do believe that the best way to overcome integration gaps is by automating work flow. As we've stated, the common denominator between all of the carriers' systems is that they are used by a number of different departments to support fulfillment, assurance, and billing work flows. The commonality means that the order management system, network management system, and almost every other system within the OSS are already related.

A fulfillment, assurance, or billing work flow uses a process or set of processes to unite the components related to service delivery: people, parts, systems, data, information, and time. Service providers place orders, provision services, run reports, and so on. Each task is performed as semantically understood by the application and person performing it. Whether or not it is documented or automated, every task is completed based on a semantically complete work-flow process. Within a large service provider there are a large number of work-flow processes. Individually, each of these is semantically complete.

If there were a way to integrate and automate many of these task-level processes into a work flow that delivered service end to end, including semantics, then the different OSSs would not need to be semantically related to each other. They would instead need to be semantically related to the work flow. Don't worry, we'll get to the hows and whys of creating semantic work-flow relationships starting in Chapter 6.

The Outlook for Operations Support Systems

Having examined OSS models, the evolution of the TMF, the TOM, and the correlation to the industry service provider needs hierarchy, we can make some educated guesses about the future of OSSs.

In the future, the TMF will continue to expand its reach, perhaps eventually beyond communications. The TMF's strategic plan includes initiatives to expand into customer care and billing, B2B, and e-commerce, as well as trying to attract more membership from emerging companies built around the latest technologies such as wireless ISPs, Application Service Providers(ASP), Content Delivery Networks (CDNs), hosted ERP, data mining, and data warehousing.

Likewise, we expect TOM to continue its process-mapping approach in roughly the same directions. The TMF will eventually add the business management layer to the TOM.

As the customer demands more real-time visibility into multiple layers of the service provider's operations, customer interface management will move from its horizontal orientation above service level management into a more vertical arrangement that interfaces with several layers. The transparency will also be driven by the needs of suppliers, trading partners, clearinghouses, and other entities within the service provider's sphere of influence who need to access certain information that resides at each layer.

Although the process map in the form of the TOM has not yet been defined, it is clear that some of the problems we've spoken about have been recognized by the TMF. This awareness is very evident in the most recent OSS model to be circulated to the membership—the next-generation OSS, or NG-OSS, model.

The NG-OSS is a specification framework for the technical integration of disparate OSS systems into the service provider environment. The current work outlines the use of a work-flow engine to distribute shared information services to other applications through a common middleware interface bus. Much of the current specifications detail the use of well-defined contract interfaces that will be developed for each transaction type.

Next-generation efforts are undoubtedly based in part on the TMF's decision to support CORBA and XML as the common protocols for the middleware bus. Multiple data sources can provide or contribute data that is then aggregated with other data to produce information. This information can then be provided in the form of shared services to users through a common presentation platform.

Summary

The disparate needs of the service provider will not be met anytime soon with the current approach, whereby (1) system integrators and vendors experiment with technical interoperability through TMF-sponsored catalyst projects, (2) the TMF documents those efforts in multiple revisions of the TOM or NG-OSS models, and (3) systems integrators provide services to the carriers based on the member-approved methodology.

Quite simply, the technology and business environment has moved too quickly for service providers to wait for the TMF process to be completed. In addition, the focus on interoperability by the TMF has concentrated primarily on technical integration, although the NG-OSS is starting to define the need for common semantic domains.

The NG-OSS approach to the middleware bus circulating information services through the use of defined contract interfaces is sound and should result in large gains that will resolve some of the functional and semantic gaps that exist within service providers over the long term.

While there are very good asset tracking systems that properly implemented and integrated should relieve many of the service providers' problems with the physical network, it will take good high-level architecture and integration methodologies to relieve the logical-physical data integrity problems.

Integrating the OSS is only a part of the solution. Even if the technical *and* semantic data interoperability problems were solved, the impossible task of manually managing all tasks contained within the end-to-end work flow would still force service providers into stovepipe organizational hierarchies.

The real missing link in the OSS is the remarkable absence of a true workflow automation tool that will allow for managing many work flows, revising them, and be open and distributable enough for a number of the disparate OSS entities to be able to input or extract work-flow information at the appropriate points in time. Without the availability of a robust work-flow (human, not data) manager combined with a secure distributable presentation capability for those shared services outlined in NG-OSS, the service provider will continue to fall further and further behind the curve.

It already appears that we may be falling behind when it comes to supporting SLAs. While many strides have been made in managing SLAs from a network standpoint, there has been relatively little success in truly implementing systems that support the service aspect of SLAs, that is, the human activities required for service fulfillment and assurance.

But there is a glimmer of hope. Several vendors have emerged recently (Comanage, Sirius, Trendium, and so on) with fresh approaches to SLA management, and they have the potential to succeed should they manage to develop their offerings in the right ways and be successful enough to create critical mass. The jury is still out on the approaches the vendors have taken.

We can, however, explore some of the other SLA approaches that are out there. In Chapter 5 we will undertake an examination of the business models, the motivations, and the pros and cons of recent SLA developments. We'll describe how the various elements and systems within the OSS should be related in order to base delivery on an SLA model. All of which should bring us closer to possible solutions to the difficult problems we have explored thus far. After all, that's why you're reading this book.

CHAPTER 5

Service Level Agreement Models

The basis for almost all SLA implementations existing today is the *SLA Handbook* published by the TeleManagement Forum (TMF). And yet different implementations of SLA models have different focuses, different strengths and weaknesses. In this chapter we build on the TMF SLA model and describe two examples of how companies in the telecommunications arena have chosen to implement an SLA model within their product suites. In Chapter 6, we will continue to use the TMF's SLA model and build the concept of the integrated SLA model.

The two SLA models we have chosen to explore in depth are based on the product suites of important vendors in the telecommunication industry—Amdocs and the combination of the Micromuse suite along with the Orchestream (or Crosskeys) suite. These vendors are fundamentally different in terms of their product suite, their company history, the markets they dominate, and more. Yet both companies view themselves as having an SLA solution. The competing views of Amdocs and Micromuse/Orchestream illustrate the importance of coming up with an integrated SLA model—which, in many ways, unifies the concepts implemented in the two product suites to create a single end-to-end SLA model. Focusing on the two vendor models is therefore important for when we discuss the integrated and collaborative model described in Chapter 7.

The Amdocs Service Level Agreement Blueprint

Amdocs is one of the dominant players in the telecommunication market providing information solutions to the leaders of the communications and IP industry. Amdocs offers customer relationship management (CRM), billing systems for communications providers, and business support systems for directory publishing companies. The Amdocs installed database includes over 150 leading telecommunication providers throughout the world.

Amdocs delivers end-to-end software solutions, supporting multiservice operations, emerging markets, and next-generation services across all lines of business—wireline, wireless, broadband, electronic, and mobile commerce and IP services. Amdocs offers voice and IP capabilities with a comprehensive single-customer view and convergent product catalog.

Customer-Facing Processes

Amdocs as a company grew around the customer-facing processes. Its Ensemble customer care and billing product is known throughout the world as one of the most comprehensive packages for large telecommunication providers. Amdocs is not a company that specializes in certain verticals. Instead it covers all areas of telecommunications including wireline, IP, broadband, wireless, 3G, and so on. Within all these spaces Amdocs provides solutions to the customer and Business Support System (BSS) layers of the Telecommunications Operations Map (TOM) (shown in Figure 5.1). Amdocs aims to dominate the customer interface management (CIM) processes, provide a full set of CRM solutions to the telecommunication markets, and provide a set of products that will cover all customer care processes. From the Amdocs perspective, the *customer* entity managed within a telecommunication provider is the most valuable asset, and the entire handling, management, and maintenance of the customer entity should reside within the Amdocs product sets. Amdocs's focus is complete in that the company does not try to reach into the lower-level processes in service development and operations, and certainly not into the network processes.

This focus on the customer care processes and the CIM layer explains best of all the reasoning behind Amdocs's SLA blueprint. Rather than *growing from* the service quality management box, which seems to be where most of the traditional SLA vendors grew from, Amdocs views SLAs as first and foremost a tool for enhancing customer care, ensuring customer satisfaction, reducing costs, and driving new revenue opportunities. The focus on the customer layer is an important distinguishing feature of the Amdocs SLA blueprint. An SLA is viewed as a term or service that is part of a contract with a customer. Just like any other product or service that is added to the contract and may be charged-for by the provider, an SLA may also be charged for, very easily creating a situation in which SLAs generate revenue even before they start costing the provider money (in terms of the assurance processes and the compliance verifications). In fact, the SLA is part of the standard product catalog as opposed to being a separate and different entity. The commitments defined on the contract as part of the SLA definitions may include commitments made by the customer to the provider; this arrangement can create revenue for the service provider. For example, the customer can commit to a minimum number of service access points or a minimum length of service. If the customer later falls beneath the required number of SAPs or wishes to terminate a certain service, the same assurance mechanisms that usually work to ensure that the customer's quality of service remains on par now work toward ensuring that there is no lost revenue for the provider.

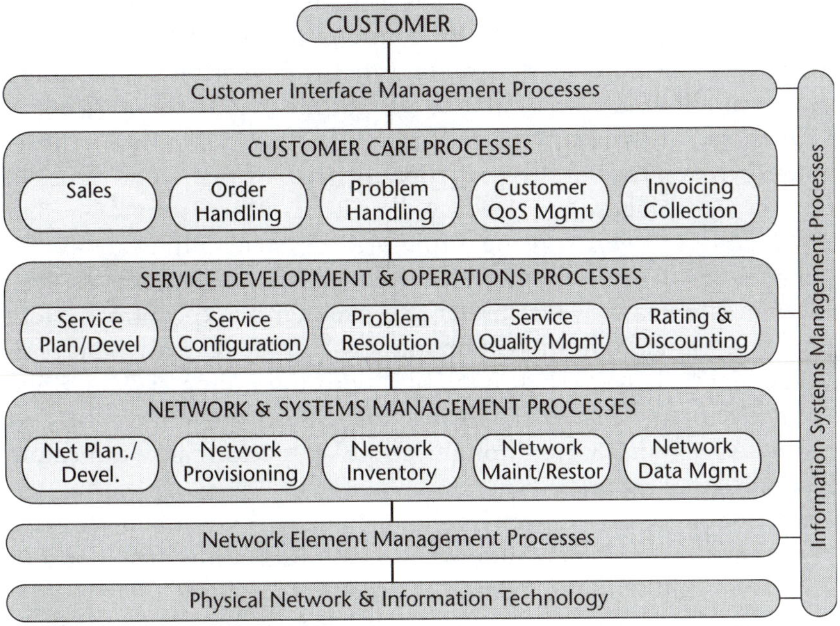

Figure 5.1 The TeleManagement Forum Telecommunications Operations Map: The business process framework.

Service Level Agreements in a Customer-Centric Approach

According to the Amdocs philosophy, Quality of Service (QoS) and SLAs must be negotiated with the customer, agreed upon before activating the service, and embedded in the contract or agreement formed between the customer and the provider. Once they become part of the contract, SLAs must drive all aspects of order handling and problem handling as well as (through interfaces) drive the processes at the operations level.

Once the contract is in place and the service has been activated a rule-based system is used to ensure that the commitments defined in the contract are addressed correctly. The rule-based system allows the parameters defined by the SLAs in the contracts to drive not only penalties and reimbursements as part of the billing cycles, but also the various processes such as proactive alerts and notifications that can be used to prevent such penalties from being incurred. This rule-based monitoring and control system is a generic platform that is used in several Amdocs product suites.

Figure 5.2 shows the TOM with an overlay of the main Amdocs products that form the Amdocs SLA blueprint. All of these product families have facilities to generate and manage SLAs as well as elements that are guided by the SLA definitions and rules. For example, the contracts module defines the SLAs within the context of the contract generation process. The order management system can also modify SLA definitions as part of the negotiation process as well as be influenced in terms of how the order is managed and how instructions are sent down into the various provisioning systems (using interfaces to the operations layer)—all based on the SLA definitions. The assurance system continuously monitors the SLAs using a rule-based system and, using events that flow from the lower layers in the system, through a set of interfaces. This assurance system is in many ways similar to a command-and-control system in that it proactively and continuously monitors compliance with SLAs, creates violation events when needed, interfaces with the billing system when either the provider or the customer violates any part of the agreement, and allows for continuous monitoring through sets of key performance indicators (KPIs) and performance reports.

The key from the Amdocs perspective is to manage the end-to-end life cycle of the SLA within the Customer Support Systems (CSS)/Business Support Systems (BSS) layer—all within the Amdocs product families. The main flow is shown in Figure 5.3. Much of the focus of the Amdocs SLA blueprint is on the template and contract creation, the SLA life cycle management within the contract life cycle flows, and the compliance verification processes. Therefore much effort has been put into creating the best user experience for OSS personnel (as well as the best experience for customers through the use of the CRM navigator) in terms of flexible and intuitive user interfaces and work flows.

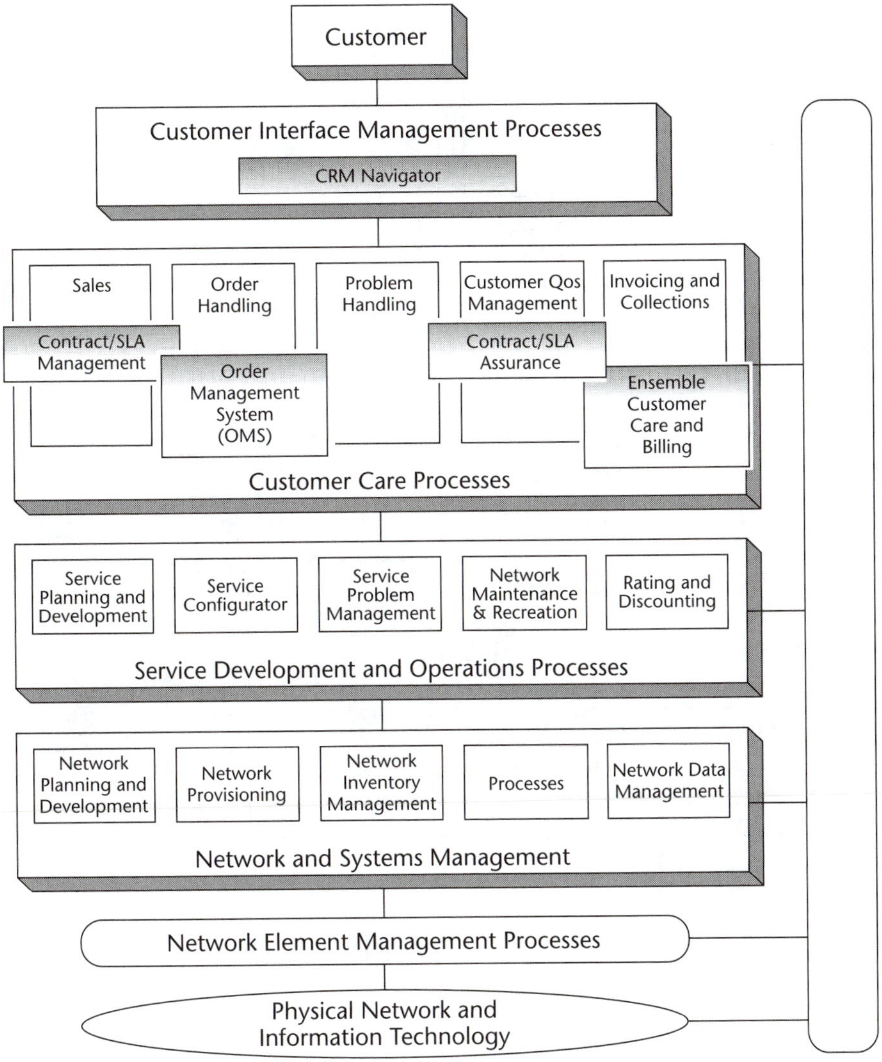

Figure 5.2 Overlay of Amdocs products forming the Service Level Agreement blueprint.

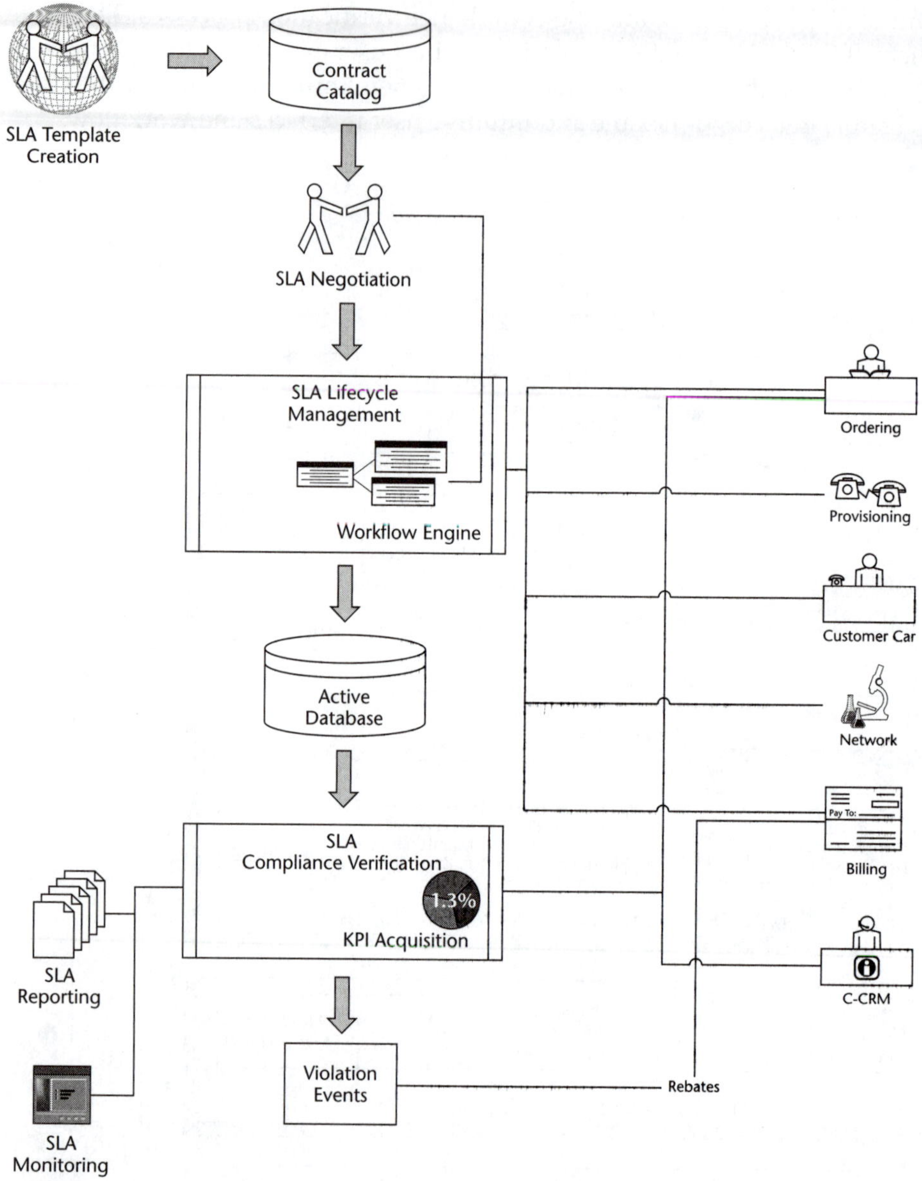

Figure 5.3 End-to-end Service Level Agreement life cycle management.

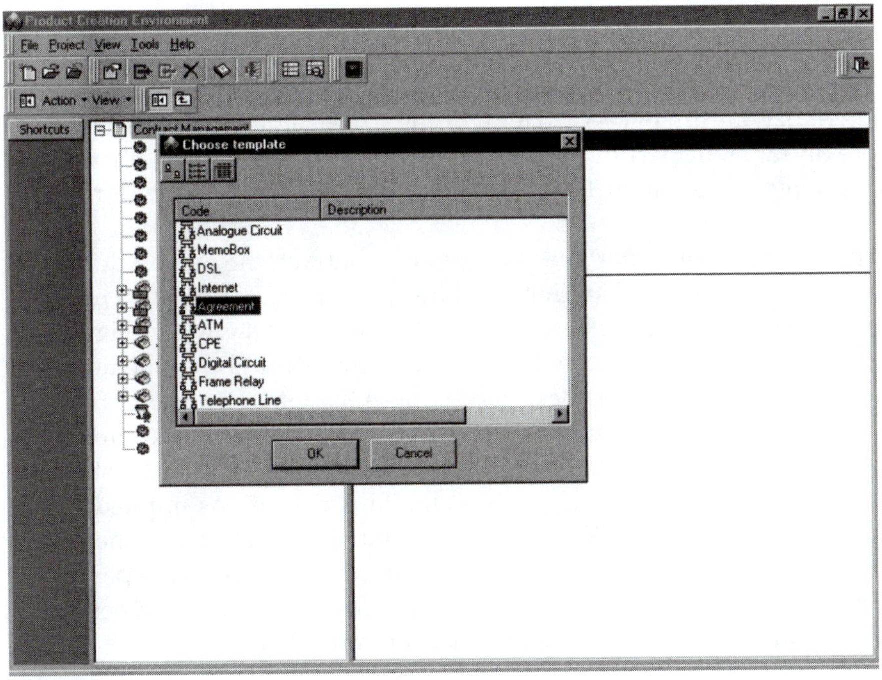

Figure 5.4 Selecting a template within the product creation environment.

Creating a Contract Offering

As an example, Figure 5.4 shows the start of the process for creating a contract offering (or a template) within the Amdocs product creation environment. In this example, the role responsible for defining the available products (for example, the Marketing department) defines a template of a contract for a frame relay product. The agreement properties are shown in a categorized tab-based view that provides easy access to all informational categories (Figure 5.5). The template is given a name and a date range in which it can be used and during which it can be sold. Now comes the really interesting part—the selection of various QoS parameters. Figure 5.6 shows the product configuration definition tab for the frame relay product. The lower left-hand panel is an explorer-type widget that is very common for displaying and selecting items within a product catalog. The SLA specs are shown here as products—they are first-class citizens in the product catalog! The SLAs are therefore an inherent part of the product that can be structured for the customer—therein lies some of the inherent strength in the Amdocs concept of SLAs.

When the service provider needs to create a contract, the person drafting it selects a contract template (offering) as shown in Figure 5.7, thereby creating a new instance of the contract based on the template. As shown in Figure 5.8, this contract has prepopulated values based on the definition of the template. The contract type is shown as Basic since this is the template that defines the contract's structure. By clicking on the Offering tab, the contract administrator can review the composition of the products and services supported by the contract. In this case, Figure 5.9 shows how the SLA definitions implied by the offering convert into a set of KPIs that are defined by the contract. These KPIs are the drivers that ensure that the SLAs are enforced. The KPIs are part of the contract and are used later in the assurance processes to monitor whether the service provider is adhering to the contract commitment.

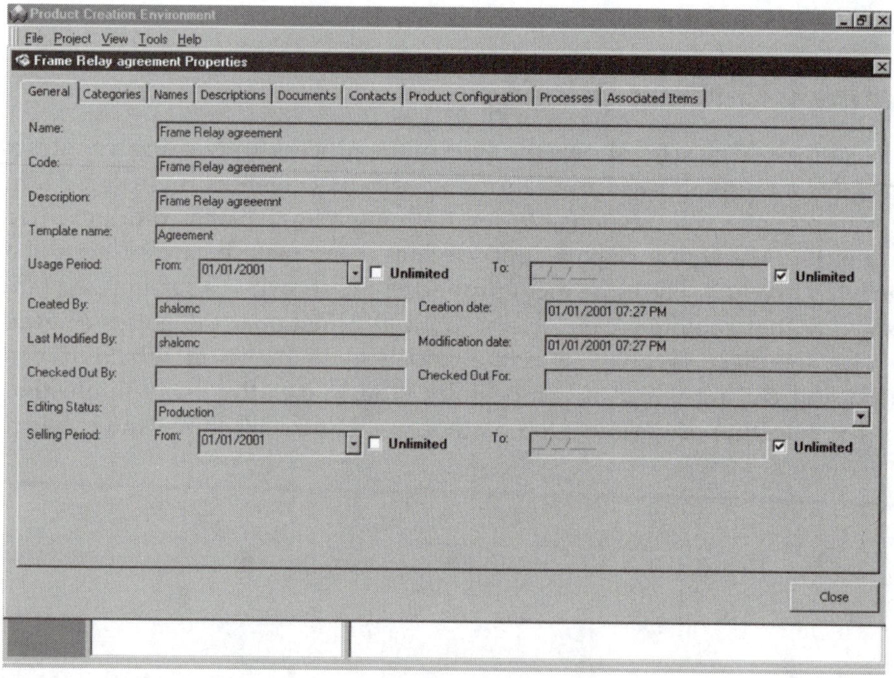

Figure 5.5 Agreement categories.

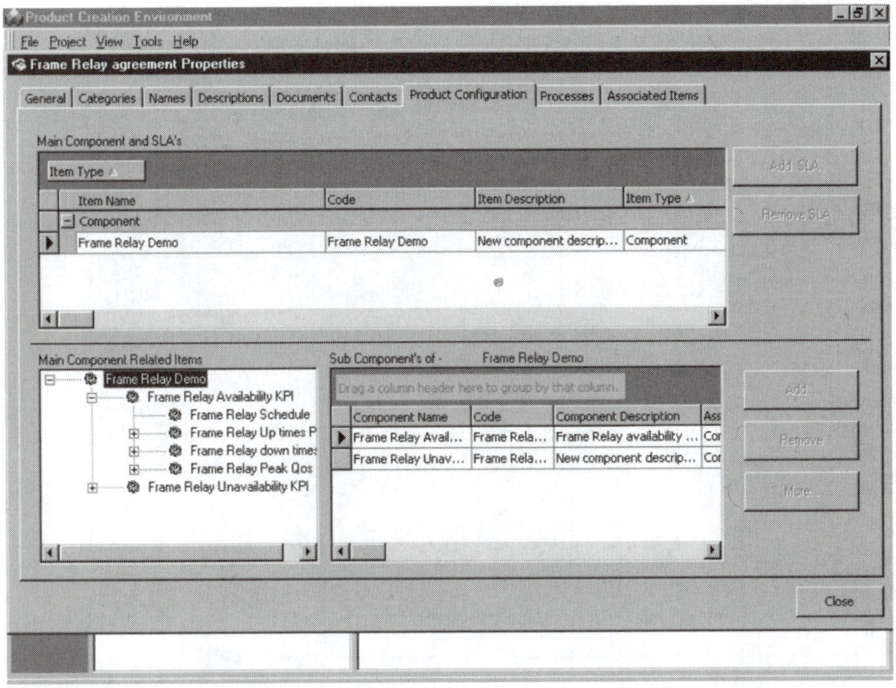

Figure 5.6 Service Level Agreement elements added to the agreement.

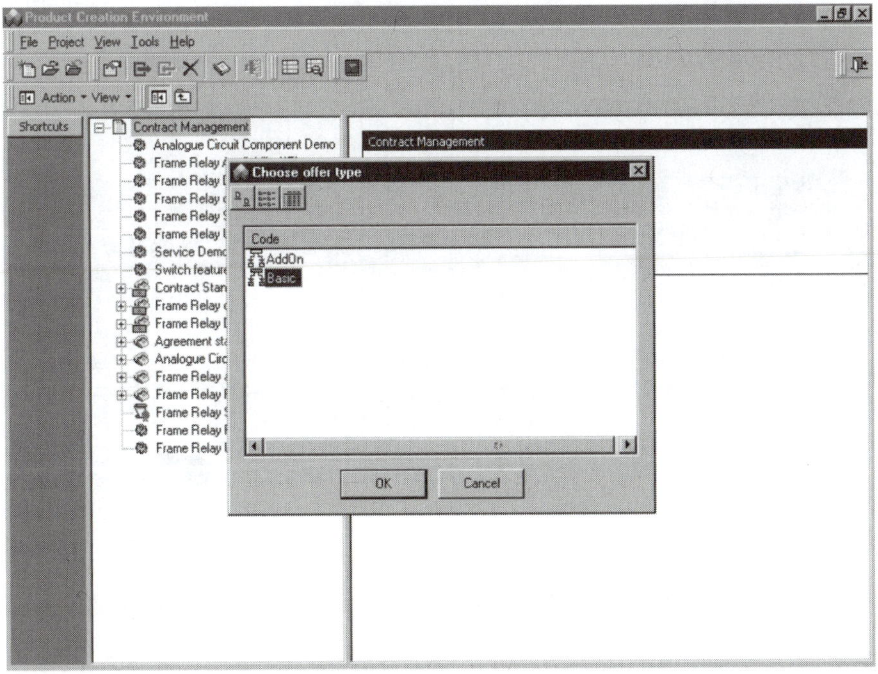

Figure 5.7 Selecting the template for the contract.

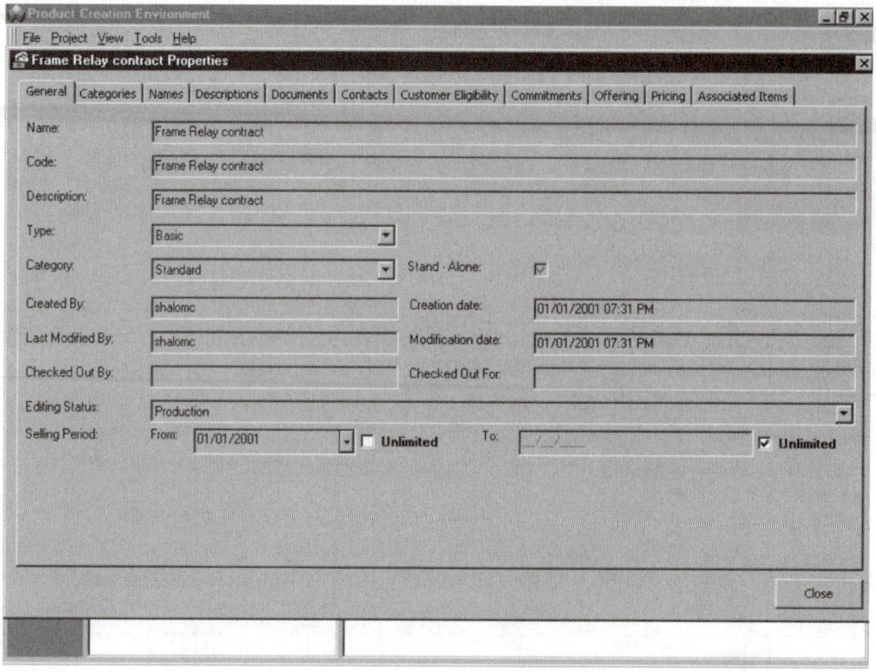

Figure 5.8 Creating the contract.

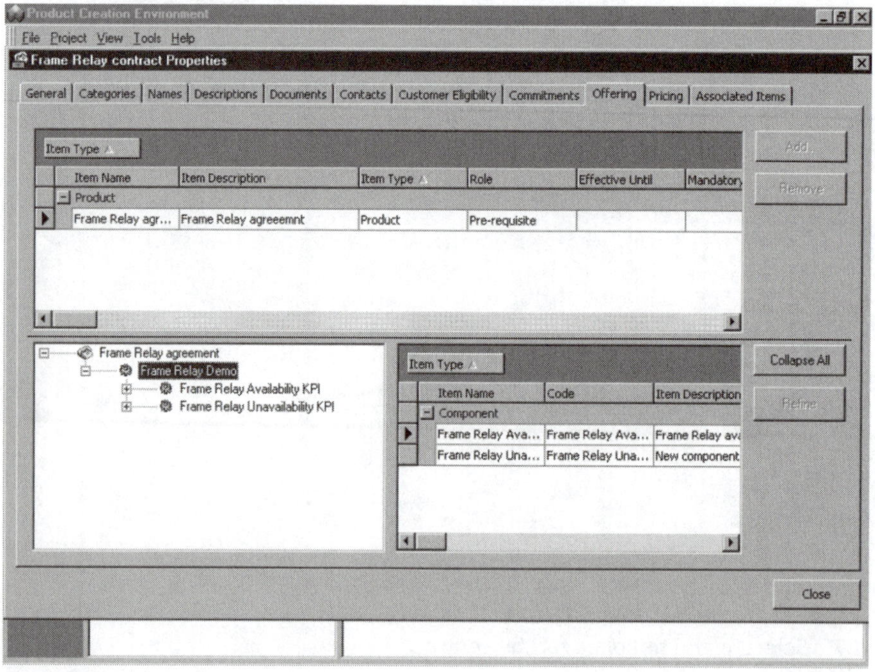

Figure 5.9 Key performance indicators in the contract.

Contract Life Cycle

Let's look at another process within the contract life cycle—one in which we will set not only a QoS commitment that the provider needs to adhere to, but also a termination term, under which a customer commits to a certain period of service. In this example, a salesperson is adjusting the products sold to the General Motors corporation at RB Telco and defines the QoS attributes for an Integrated Services Digital Network (ISDN) connection as well as a frame relay Permanent Virtual Circuit (PVC). Using the contract management screen shown in Figure 5.10, the account manager or salesperson adds a contract with a period of 12 months renewed automatically every 2 months as shown in Figure 5.11. As can be seen from this contract management flow, the system is based on a set of wizards that guide the user along based on the work-flow policies of the provider. As part of the definition of the contract, the service class and QoS values are determined. After defining the customer contact for the contract (remember, one of the emphases in the Amdocs suite is the complete modeling of the customer entity), the salesperson reviews the price plans available to the customer for the selected products and performs the negotiation process, as shown in Figure 5.12. As part of this plan, the provider must commit to certain performance levels, and the customer must commit to a service period of 12 months with possible exit points every 2 months The end result of this negotiation process is the actual agreement as shown in Figure 5.13, as well as the kickoff of the processes required to initiate the service.

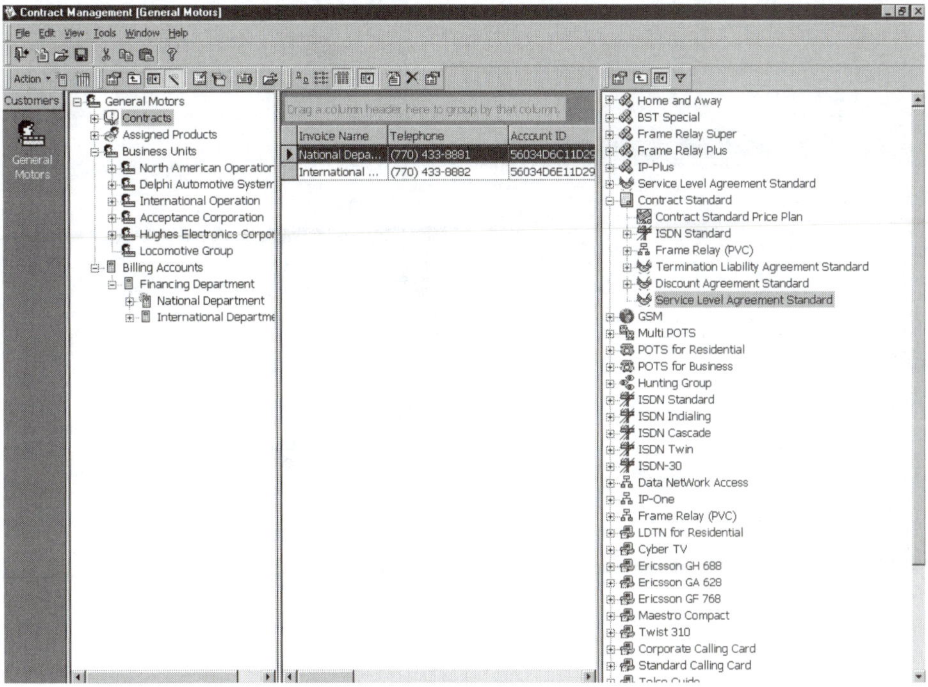

Figure 5.10 Contract management view for General Motors example contract.

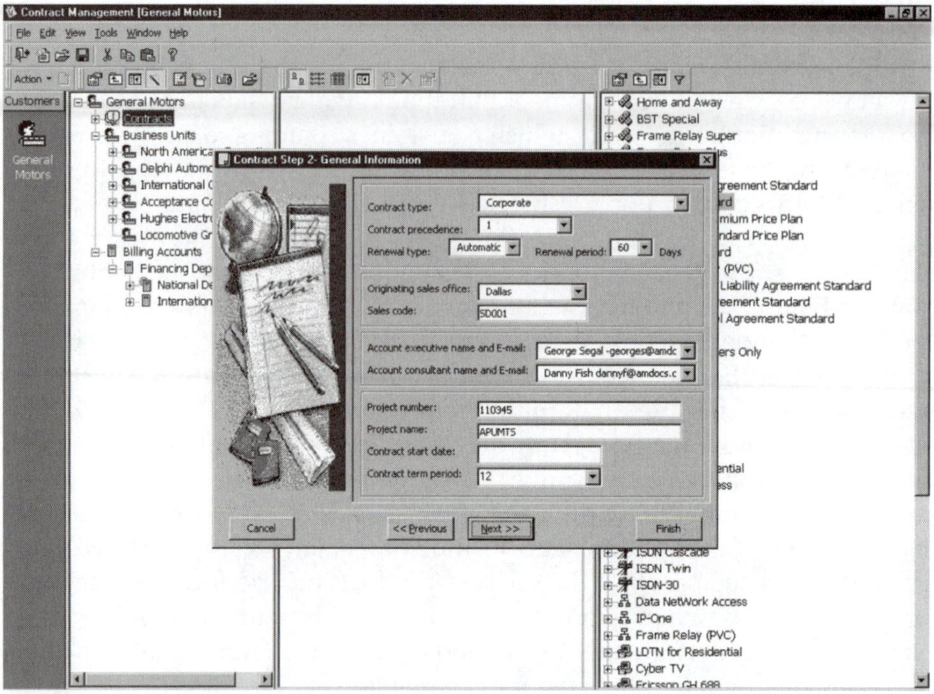

Figure 5.11 Setting the contract renewal policies and general details.

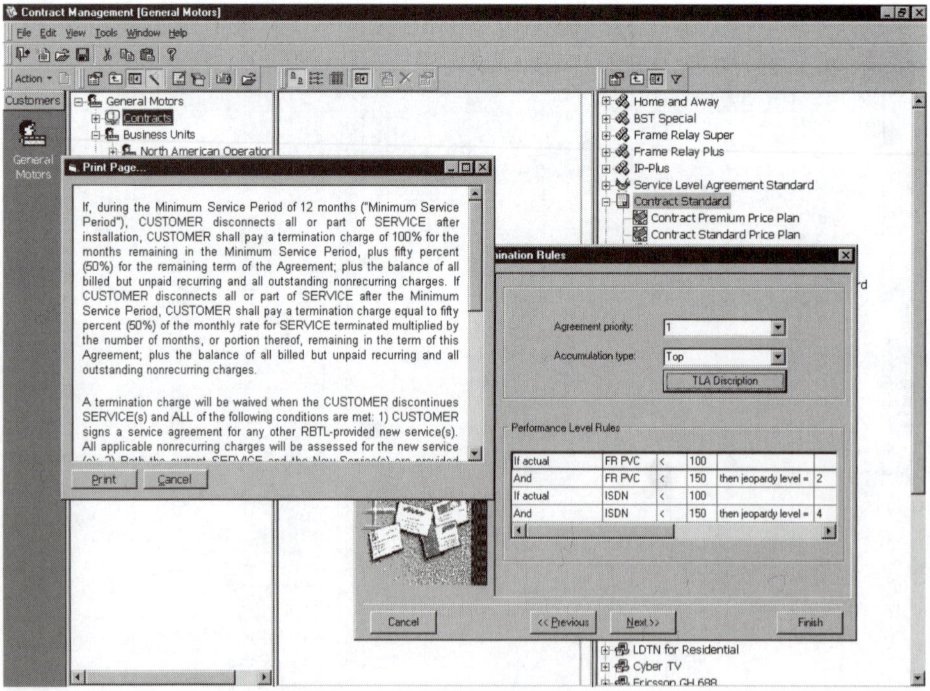

Figure 5.12 Selecting a price plan.

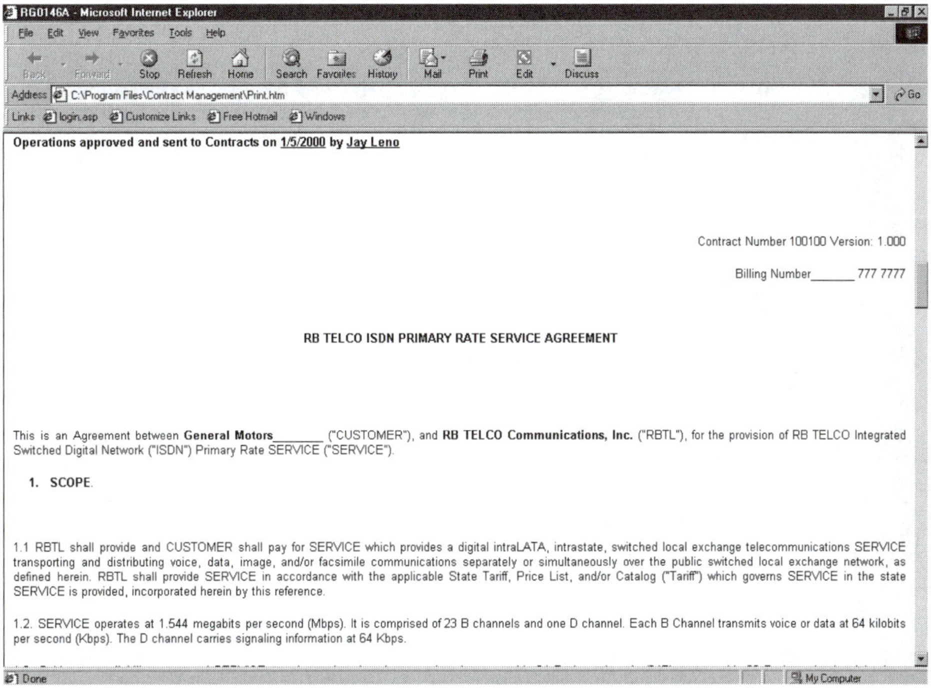

Figure 5.13 Generated agreement.

Once the service has been activated the compliance system can be used to ensure that all SLAs are being met. Since the central focus of the SLA blueprint is the customer and the contract in which the SLAs are defined, the system supports monitoring views for ensuring contract compliance. Using the hierarchical view shown in Figure 5.14, we can see that any contract for any business unit may be inspected. The user can click on one of the organizations within the customer's organizational hierarchy and view all information pertaining to that organization, as shown in Figure 5.15. The system provides a hierarchical view showing products within the set of contracts created for this organization. All SLA levels are shown in addition to relevant alerts based on the contractual SLAs. Since the KPIs were defined as part of the contract, the system enables the user to drill down and view the KPI information including historical service compliance, QoS values, and more (Figure 5.16). Further drilling down is also supported because behind it all is the actual contract with the definitions of the terms and liabilities. The user can always review the implications that might result if the SLA is not met.

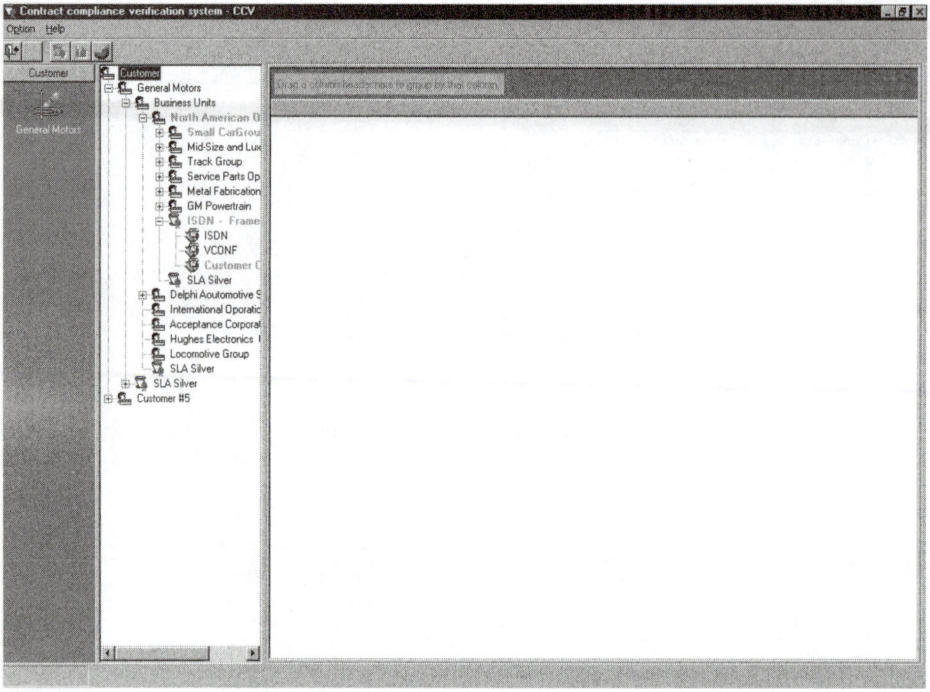

Figure 5.14 Inspecting contracts and Service Level Agreements within the customer hierarchy.

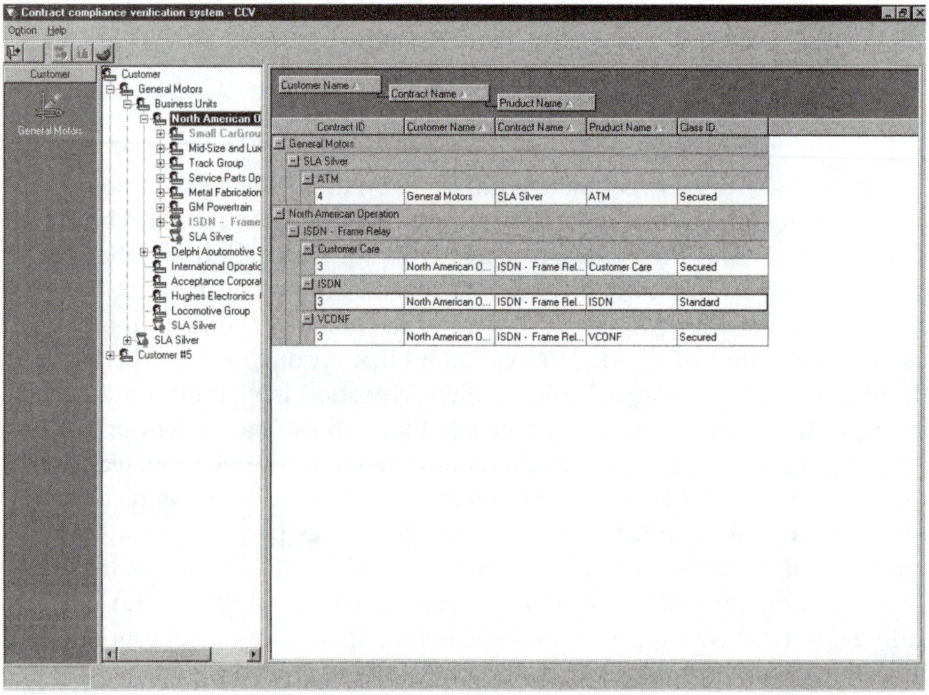

Figure 5.15 Service Level Agreements and alerts for products on customer contract.

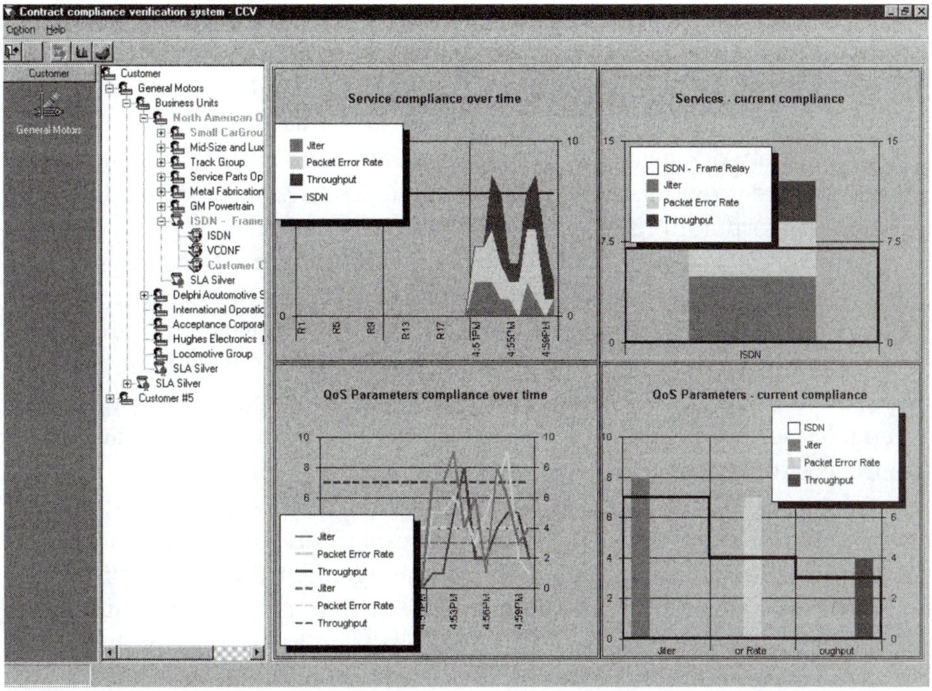

Figure 5.16 The key performance indicators view for the customer unit contracts.

Service Assurance Model

In this section we describe an example of an SLA model that focuses on the service assurance aspects and addresses SLAs at the service development and operations layer of the TOM. This traditional emphasis of SLA assurance differs from the blueprint described in the previous section. Here the focus is less on the customer-facing aspects of the SLA and more on the network monitoring and assurance processes that need to occur in order to guarantee that the service provider adheres to SLAs.

In this section we describe a solution that integrates two offerings. The first component is Micromuse's Netcool suite for real-time fault management and service assurance. Integrated with this suite is Orchestream's Resolve product for QoS and SLA management. This component provides a more complete view of network and service information by consolidating business-level information such as customers and services.

Micromuse Netcool

Micromuse develops software that monitors and manages the elements of information technology infrastructures. The company's Netcool suite collects and consolidates network data and events. Netcool features a desktop tool that customizes network information and enables operators to automatically resolve service problems. Orchestream (based in the United Kingdom) develops software that helps telecom companies and Internet service providers expand their network service offerings. Its software prioritizes Internet traffic, enabling service providers to offer faster service for higher prices and making it possible for corporations to send time-sensitive material at a faster pace than lower-priority information. Orchestream Canada (formerly Crosskeys) develops software that helps telecommunications service providers track network traffic and performance (Resolve), control network infrastructure and traffic (NetworkWare), and manage equipment (CrossControl). Orchestream Resolve is a portfolio of service and network performance management applications that enables service providers to maximize their revenue potential and minimize the cost of running their network. The Netcool Suite provides real-time fault management and service assurance solutions. It supports almost any network environment, providing over 300 probes and monitors that collect event information from Simple Network Management Protocol (SNMP) and non-SNMP management applications, voice or data networking equipment, Internet and wide area networks (WANs), and IT infrastructure within enterprises. The suite monitors networks for events such as alarms, alerts, faults, and informational messages and reports on them in a customizable manner. The suite has a rules engine within the event engine that allows intelligent response based on the alarms arriving at the server.

Figure 5.17 shows the Netcool/OMNIbus system architecture. The elements that comprise this suite include the following:

The Netcool Object Server. A memory-resident instance of the Sybase database optimized for collecting event information and applying filters and rules to derive intelligent information from a massive flow of data from the probes.

Probes. Passive software elements that collect event information from more than 300 types of sources.

Monitors. Polling elements that monitor the function of applications and services on the network.

Event lists and event list consoles. Display and management applications showing summaries of events that require handling or generating an alert. Figure 5.18 shows how the event list is displayed to someone working in the network operations center (NOC) and how the application allows assignment of tasks directly from the event list.

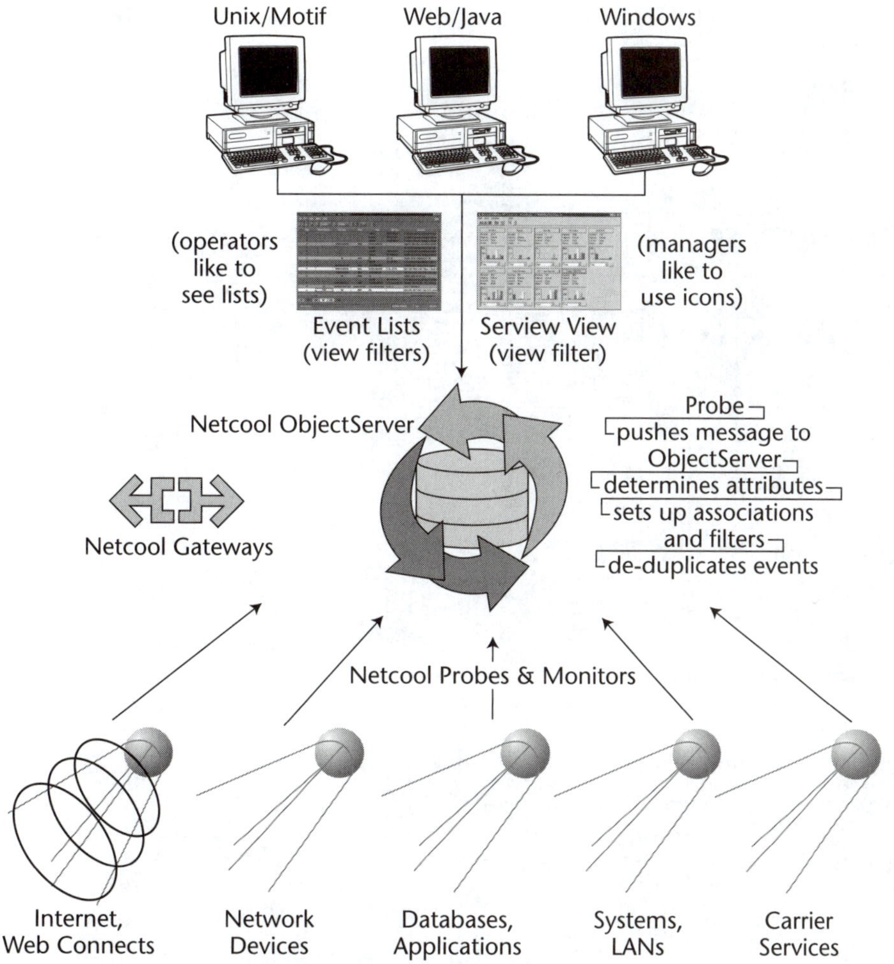

Figure 5.17 Netcool system architecture.

Displays. A set of user interfaces used by Operations Support Service (OSS) personnel. An example status screen is shown in Figure 5.19.

Gateways. Bidirectional interfaces that are used to integrate other products with the Netcool suite.

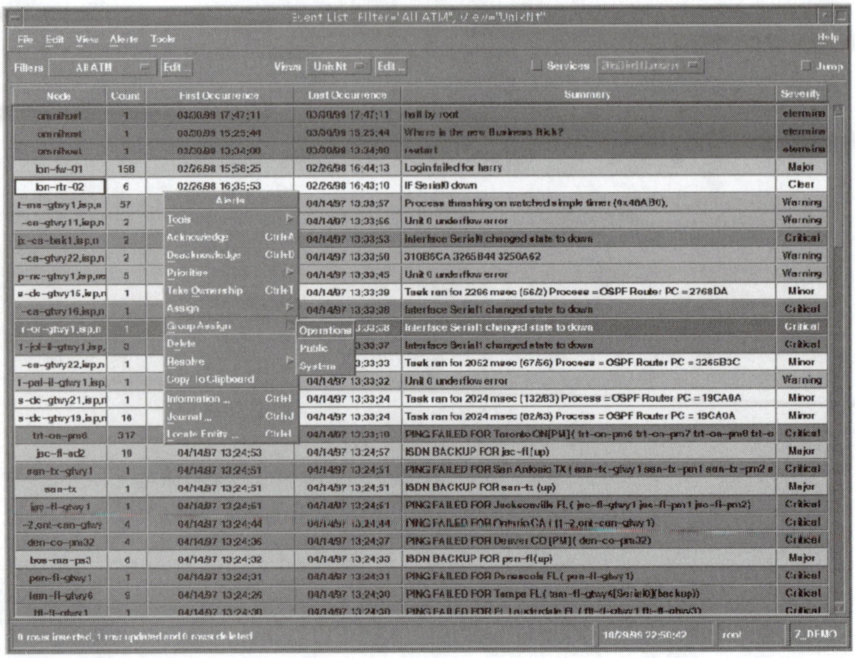

Figure 5.18 Netcool event list.

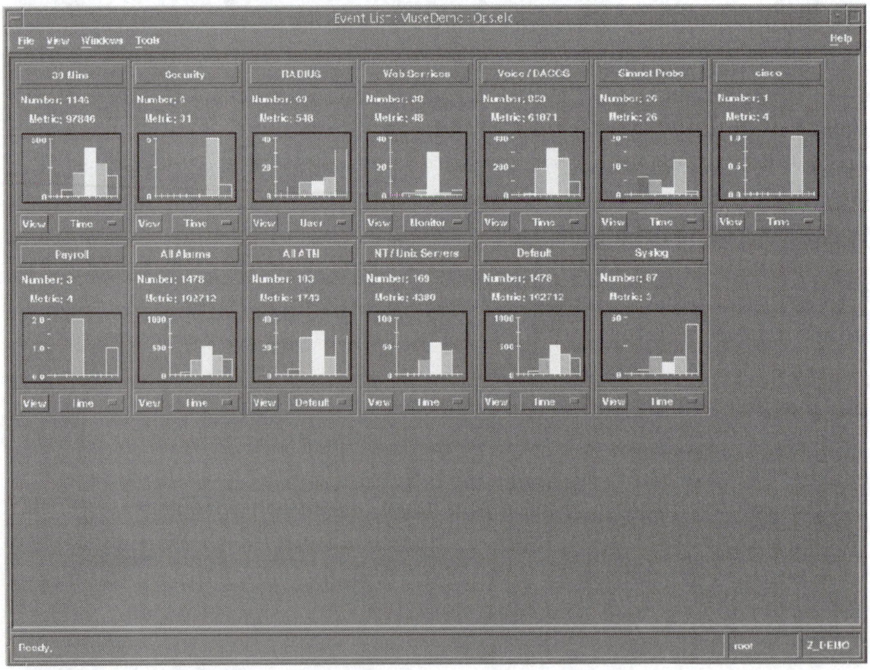

Figure 5.19 Netcool status display.

Orchestream Resolve

Orchestream's Resolve product suite (Orchestream acquired Crosskeys) provides network and service performance management applications. The suite enables providers to adhere to SLAs and manage the changes required to eliminate SLA violations. Resolve models the relationships between entities at the business and customer levels with the network-level objects. This matching allows Resolve to build automated and proactive threshold monitors based on business-level SLAs and notify Netcool when threshold crossings have occurred or are about to occur. It also has a good reporting engine and provides a complete set of standard reports for QoS and SLA monitoring.

The combined solution is enabled through the Micromuse Netcool OSS Gateway Module for Resolve. This component runs on the Resolve server and allows Resolve to send information regarding thresholds that are at risk. Resolve provides a more complete view than Netcool since it can consolidate business-level information such as customer and service information with network information whether the information is related to assurance or to provisioning. The gateway allows Resolve to send notifications to Netcool based on QoS and SLA degradations detected at the network level. The events are sent to Netcool as alerts and can be viewed and handled using the event list monitors.

Summary

In this chapter we have presented two somewhat different approaches to implementing an SLA model. These differences stem from differences in company focus and from the history of the product suites. We believe that the true implementation of SLAs must merge these two somewhat distinct approaches into one integrated SLA model. Merging these approaches means that both the customer-facing life cycle as well as the service and operations processes must all be merged to provide full SLA management. The model and architectural blueprint for how an integrated SLA solution can be implemented within the context of an OSS is the focus of Part 2 of this book and makes up the detailed discussion in the remaining chapters of the book.

One of the major problems in defining an integrated SLA solution is that it must deal with almost every aspect of the OSS/BSS. Many of the systems defined at the different levels of the TMN have some claims on supporting SLAs. Obviously, every one of these systems and vendors believes that it is the true keeper of the essence of SLAs and that all other information flows need to be integrated based on its model. Given this state of affairs, the integration and middleware vendors too have claims on being the true owner.

There are two major viewpoints regarding SLAs that need to be merged into a consistent architecture. One is *customer-centric* in the sense that it deals with customers, contracts, and billing cycles. The second is *network-focused* and deals with quality of service metrics, network fault tolerance, failover capabilities in which a backup takes over for a failed master system, and NOCs. These views are related. On the one hand the QoS is the basis for the definitions existing in the customer-facing contract. On the other hand the NOC is responsible at an operational level for ensuring that the provider does not lose an arm and a leg through rebates. The rebates themselves need to be paid to the customer based on the contract terms if the service does not meet the QoS defined in the contract. The third important viewpoint is that of *service delivery*—both from a customer-facing perspective (for example, sales, call center and NOC personnel, and so on) as well as from the network-facing workforce (for example, the field technicians in the service assurance groups, the network build-out groups, and so on). The main concept of integrated SLAs involves a merging of all these viewpoints, a topic we explore in Chapter 6.

PART

Two

The Solution

CHAPTER 6

The Integrated Service Level Agreement Model

In this chapter we describe how the various elements and systems within the OSS should be interconnected in order to base service delivery on an SLA model.

The *integrated SLA* (ISLA) model is based on the authors' belief that the only way to drive efficiency and ensure Quality of Service (QoS) commitments are consistently met is to drive the business processes directly from the SLA definitions. Using ISLA is very different from relying on business processes that periodically check to see if business results are in compliance with the SLA, which is the basis for the vast majority of current SLA initiatives. While these initiatives may improve reporting (almost anything would), these initiatives also add more stovepipe systems and complexity to the service environment and do nothing to correct the underlying problems.

Our approach is to create a distributed computing environment that is capable of supporting a large, diverse user community. We automate the wide-scale business process and enable collaboration of the different constituencies at a number of levels. Then we use well-defined SLA entitlement templates to bring order to the complex work-flow environment and manage the millions of relationships that are being created daily. We have termed this collaborative environment the *integrated SLA (ISLA) framework.*

The objective of establishing this environment is to bring together all the different community members, OSS applications, relationships, processes, and domains of the service provider into a single big-picture representation of the service provider's activities.

As discussed in preceding chapters, we believe that the key to successful SLA delivery lies in optimizing the work flow. Once the environment has been established, advanced work-flow automation and workforce management systems enable SLA entitlements to automatically drive the business processes and the participants within the work flow. This new model allows both work flow and the support community related to it to be optimized for SLA delivery in real time and end to end. We have termed these major innovations *dynamic work flow* and *dynamic work-flow communities*, respectively.

The framework is integrated with the existing Operations Support System (OSS) architecture through machine-machine interfaces and Application Program Interfaces (APIs). Integration occurs at four levels: (1) organizational, (2) process, (3) data interchange, and (4) the collaborative level, which combines the integration of the other levels into a single work-flow presentation. The four integration levels serve a number of defined domains, including data interchange, which consists of both technical and semantic aspects.

Once the framework is in place, communications technology developed for the Internet makes it possible to then securely break down the big picture into executable work flow and accompanying tasks. We can then distribute permissions, activities, and information related to the collaborative work flow in real time to those work-flow participants that are best situated to act effectively

Optimized work flow is possible because the man-machine (presentation) environment can be easily tailored to meet the needs of the individual community members. Every community member is part of the bigger picture and is able to access huge amounts of information (assuming he or she has permission to do so) from throughout the service provider, break down the information into understandable chunks (that is, so that the participant will see only those portions of work flow that relate directly to him or her or tasks that are to be done within a certain timeframe), and view the information in a manner that he or she is most comfortable with. This concept is known as *unified presentation*.

The combination of the collaborative big-picture representation, the dynamic work-flow capabilities, the dynamic work-flow community concept, and unified presentation then allows the service provider to fully automate and integrate people, products, processes, systems, and the related activities, transactions, and relationships in a way that was impossible until very recently. Integration serves the purpose of eliminating the data, processes, organizational isolation, and tunnel vision that are endemic in stovepipe organizations.

The Origin of the Integrated Service Level Agreement Concept

We believe that the ISLA approach presents an innovative solution to many current OSS problems, not the least of which is managing SLA-compliant delivery. We developed the concept behind the ISLA model based on two very important observations.

First, the performance of specific tasks (human, electronic, or man-machine)—related to larger business processes or work flows—is the central activity of the telecommunications service provider. The business work flows are, in turn, usually driven by a generating event, such as the submission of a service order or the opening of a trouble ticket. The chain of related events (Figure 6.1) starts with a generating event, which in turn generates a supporting work flow, which generates a number of tasks within the work flow, which results in the performance of the tasks, the last of which finally closes the event.

Identifying the work flow led to the observation that, for the most part, each event generates one or more lower-level and associated work flows. These lower-level work flows are made up of different tasks, with different participants performing the tasks and making different contributions to the work flow. Most times the work flow changes from job instance to job instance, even for the same product.

The confluence of many tasks creates a multiplier effect in which millions of work-flow relationships (varying in depth, length, and complexity) and transactions are being executed every day, yet there is no real way to understand them. The different domains created to develop and manage the OSS, business process, and organization infrastructure are interdependent on each other within the work flow, but each functions as a stovepipe, with no meaningful linkages existing between them. We felt that the disconnect contributes to poor SLA reporting capabilities.

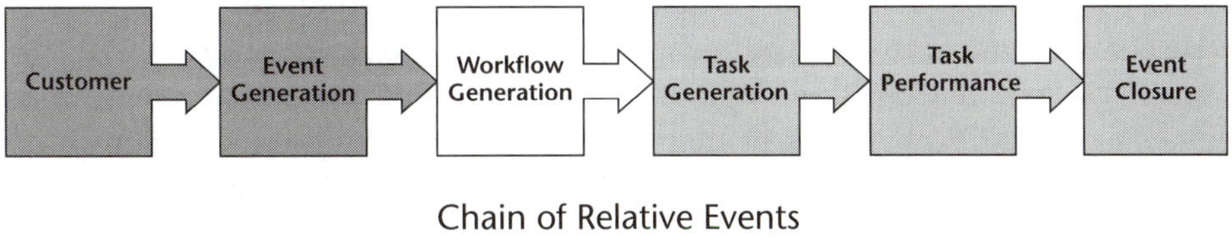

Figure 6.1 The chain of relative events.

The second observation is the more important. As we stated in Chapter 2 (end-to-end definable), the SLA measures the service providers' operational capability to deliver, not the product per se—an important distinction. Although the SLA and the product definition are related, they are not directly linked initially. A single product may have a number of SLA options defined for it. A selection is not normally made until the product is ordered, so the SLA is linked with the delivery criteria for the product on an *event-driven basis.*

The final piece of the puzzle fell into place with the realization that almost all the parties and support infrastructures in place to support SLAs within the service provider are also event-driven, including the OSS, most internal organizations, and even the customer. The implication is that it is possible to create a synergy between SLAs and the business process.

We concluded that to create the synergy one has to control the work flow, the workforce, and the customer in such a way that very large volumes of complex work flows become manageable. Harmonizing the SLAs and business processes would also require an environment that could relate the different parties, software applications, processes, and domains of the service provider so that everyone is on the same sheet of music. The music obviously has to be the SLA.

We needed a conductor capable of directing the work flow. Because everything is event-driven, the emphasis has to be placed on organizing the processes. The conductor eventually evolved into the ISLA framework.

Technological Reality Check

Is the technology available to build the solution? Is it proven Commercial Off The Shelf (COTS) technology? Is it relatively affordable? Surprisingly, the answer is *yes*. We have developed the ISLA framework as a roadmap for service companies and integrators to make it possible to understand and manage the myriad relationships in the day-to-day operations of telecommunications companies. The ISLA framework gives the service provider a realistic vision of what the environment should look like, the technical architecture that is needed to support it, and a realistic transition path to getting to an SLA-based delivery model that is flexible, robust, accurate, and manageable.

Yet it is important to note that achieving this level of integration is a departure from current OSS thinking. The ISLA framework is not intended to replace existing OSS systems or methodology, especially the important interoperability work being done by the TMF. Instead the ISLA framework is an extension of that work and is built on the foundation laid by groups such as the TMF and the Work-flow Management Coalition (WfMC).

Even the TMF's New Generation Operations Systems and Software (abbreviated as either NGOSS or NG-OSS) initiative does not yet contemplate the entire ISLA environment; instead it concentrates primarily on the technical data interchange specifications and related technology needed to enable interoperability of their more narrowly defined OSS. This approach is valid considering the scope and agenda of the TMF membership. But in our view it is only a part of the solution.

Telecommunications service delivery requires hardware, software, people, and process. As we have discussed, the current telecommunications industry is in chaos on all four fronts. People and processes are by far the most dynamic (and expensive) variables in the equation, so they must become manageable in order for service providers to optimize efficiency. The danger lies in the potential for even an open-standards NGOSS environment to become a large stovepipe if there is no capability to manage organizational dynamics and work-flow evolutions across the entire business.

Because we espouse the integration of people, processes, logistics, and time, in addition to systems, many aspects of work-flow automation, workforce management, and distributed collaboration techniques described in the following chapters diverge from and go beyond even the most recent TMF catalyst projects. Yet, this is far from a theoretical exercise.

The Integrated Service Level Agreement Framework

The ISLA framework is enabling because it introduces advanced work-flow automation and community management technology into the OSS environment, thereby creating a number of core capabilities that can be divided over seven functionally oriented logical domains, which will be discussed later in the chapter.

The three framework components are as follows:

1. Enabling technology and concepts
   - Dynamic work-flow automation
   - Dynamic work-flow communities

2. Capabilities
   - Universal access
   - Intelligence
   - Collaboration
   - Automation
   - Integration
3. Logical domains
   - The presentation domain
   - The information domain
   - The product or contract domain
   - The process or work-flow domain
   - The data domain
   - The workforce domain
   - The supply chain domain

The ISLA framework is shown in Figure 6.2.

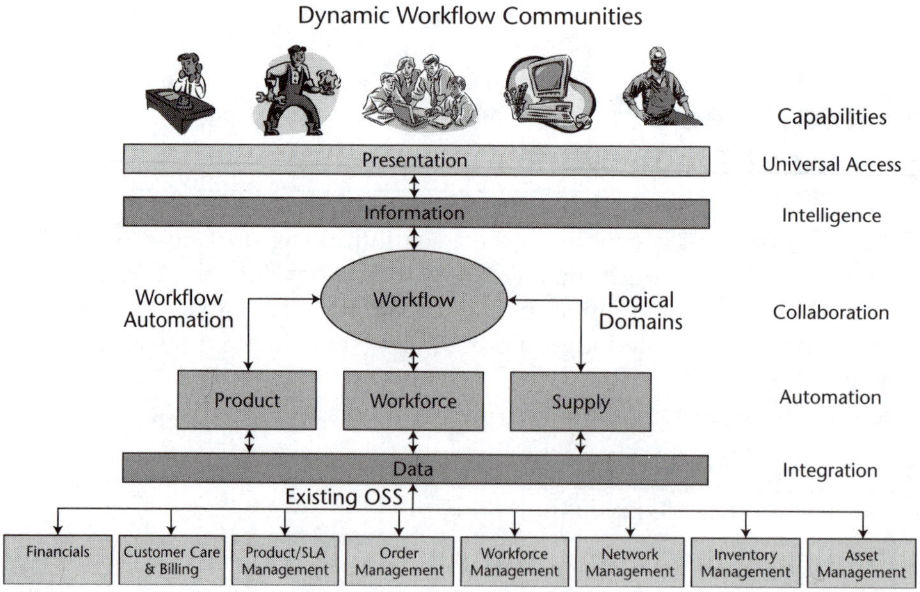

Figure 6.2 The Integrated Service Level Agreement framework.

Enabling Technologies

The ISLA framework can only be implemented due to recent advances in distributed computing technology, specifically true work-flow automation. These advances include the ability to create dynamic work flow and dynamic work-flow communities.

Dynamic Work-Flow Automation

Dynamic work flow, just like it sounds, is the ability to manage changing work flows dynamically, that is, in real time and on the fly. Through the implementation of robust work-flow automation, the tasks to be performed (and therefore the entire work flow) can be defined, driven, managed, measured, and presented based on defined SLA service entitlements.

Service Level Agreement definitions would determine the initial work flow to be implemented, then dynamically drive performance requirements at the task level down to the work-flow participant based on the selected SLA entitlements. For example, the system would use the entitlement definition to determine how long a technician may work on a trouble ticket before it is escalated.

The task would then be sent to a participant. A work-flow participant may be human, electronic, or even logistical in nature. Each work-flow participant has a specific objective, role, and tasks that he/she/it is required to support. The system then monitors the progress of the task to determine the next appropriate action. Intelligent work-flow automation enables the system to determine what the next appropriate action will be, based on the results of the current task.

For example, a platinum-level QoS work flow may require that trouble ticket escalation happen at the 1-hour mark, as opposed to the silver-level standard of 4 hours. The work-flow management system, performing as a work-flow participant, would automatically trigger the escalation process at the appropriate time, if the technician had not yet finished the task, or alternately the system would capture the task completion time entered by the technician then trigger a handoff to the next task. The two work flows are very different, yet the one selected is entirely dependent on whether or not the technician completes the job on time. As in this example, the work flow can be dynamically adjusted based on actual task performance.

The next task to be initiated may again consist of human intervention, an electronic interface (via XML, CORBA, email, an Internet query, or access to a data repository), or millions of other possibilities as determined by the policies defined in the SLA and all the possible work-flow options defined within the system. The work-flow automation would intelligently route and track the work flow to completion, again based on the SLA entitlements. The work flow may have been dynamically modified dozens of times en route to completion.

Dynamic Work-Flow Communities

Telecommunications is an event-driven business. Certain initiating events occur that set off a chain reaction for other events, tasks, transactions, timeframes, and oversight that require that work efforts be put forth by a number of people, applications, or systems. Examples of initiating events include a customer placing an order, a preventive maintenance action coming due, or a backhoe cutting a fiber optic cable.

Any single event can necessitate that many different tasks and activities will happen serially or in parallel to each other. Some of these events are recurring, some of them are periodic, and many are one-time occurrences. In most cases, the parties gathered to support the end-to-end work flow related to this chain of events are dynamic in that the parties, tasks, applications, and transactions are not exactly the same each time.

Following are the community participants:

- Customers
- Service provider(s)
- Internal organizations
- Third-party suppliers
- Applications
- Systems
- Interfaces
- Transactions

The participants within a community can be defined up front, dynamically over time, or through a combination of the two. For example, the customer ordering a service will probably not change throughout the life cycle of the order. He or she will always perform the role of customer in the work flow, regardless of when or how many times human intervention from the customer is required to complete the work flow.

On the service provider's side, work-flow tasks are usually assigned to a department or functional area. The same person is not likely to be involved in any one work flow end to end, and it is unlikely that any one person will carry out all instances of a single task performed in that work center. Likewise, dynamic work-flow adjustments, necessitated by unplanned events, such as accelerated provisioning timeframes, customer scheduling conflicts, and even a technician calling in sick, prohibit the service provider from hard-coding the participants in the work flow.

As with work flow, the community dynamics will also be influenced in real time by the progress made on the tasks within the work flow. As in the earlier example, once a task assignment is received, the community member must complete the tasks within the prescribed timeframes or the work-flow engine will involve other community members in an attempt to resolve or preempt SLA violations through notification and progressive escalation. Managers or other personnel may be inserted into the work flow who would not otherwise have been involved.

The ISLA framework uses work-flow automation in conjunction with workforce management to establish dynamic work-flow communities to collaborate on the tasks associated with the work flow. The framework supports up-front work flow and task assignment, dynamic assignment, or any combination thereof.

Core Capabilities

To support the ISLA framework and the needs of the work-flow communities, a number of capabilities must be present and available to all community members and domains within the dynamic work flow on a near real-time basis. As with the need hierarchies we have already discussed, each higher layer is enabled by the foundation built on the layer below, without which it is unable to function. The capabilities (shown in Figure 6.3) include the following:

- Universal access
- Intelligence
- Collaboration
- Automation
- Integration

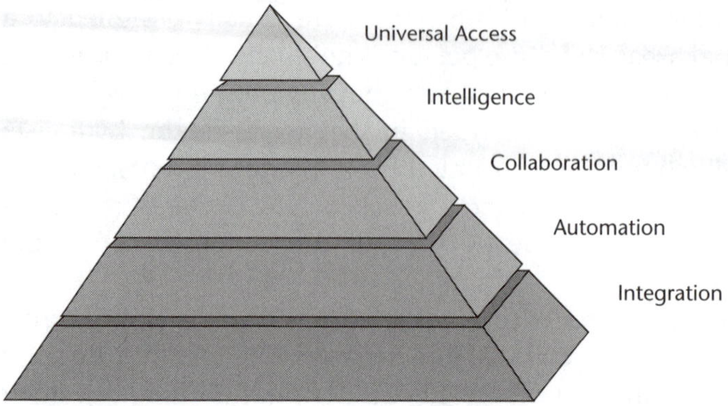

Figure 6.3 Integrated Service Level Agreement capabilities.

Universal access. The concept that all participants involved in any work flow, both human and electronic, must be able to securely access the environment in a convenient user-friendly manner. For humans, this may mean via the Web, wirelessly, or over the telephone. For electronic access, this may mean an Electronic Data Interchange (EDI) transaction, a database call, CORBA, XML, or other standards-based transaction.

Intelligence. The environment must provide very high levels of appropriate SLA compliance and other business intelligence to community members. Intelligence may take the form of real-time or periodic work-flow monitoring, key performance indicators, monitors, or reports. The systems within the environment must also function within the work flow and be able to recognize threshold violations and subsequently initiate task generation or trigger automation of predefined actions, such as notifications, escalations, queries, and so on.

Collaboration. The environment must support many different entities and parties working together in series, parallel, or in a combined manner. Collaboration too requires the ability to seamlessly support both human and electronic participation in collaborative efforts.

Automation. Certain types of tasks and, more important, task handoffs between work-flow participants must be set up so they can be initiated, managed, transferred, and completed by the system without unnecessary human intervention. Automation must span the work flow end to end and capture activities in the most efficient manner possible that were formerly performed by both human and electronic participants.

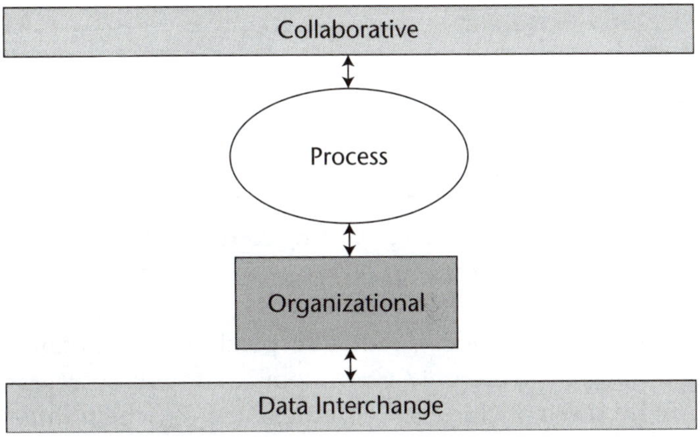

Figure 6.4 Integrated Service Level Agreement integration levels.

Integration. The environment must bring together participants, applications, processes, and interfaces seamlessly into a common management environment. Integration occurs at four levels: (1) organizational, (2) process, (3) data interchange, and (4) the collaborative level, which combines the integration of the other levels into a single work flow (see Figure 6.4). Furthermore, the data integration is made up of both technical and semantic aspects.

Domains

The activities related to providing access, intelligence, collaboration, automation, and integration must occur on and, hence, be manageable on all functional layers and available to every domain. The ISLA framework recognizes a number of domains as being critical to SLAs. The ISLA domains (Figure 6.5) include the following:

- Core domains
  - The presentation domain
  - The information domain
  - The product domain
  - The process or work-flow domain
  - The data domain

- External domains
  - The workforce domain
  - The supply domain

The domains can be functional, logical, semantic, or technical in nature depending on the application need. For example, they can provide a logical partition for managing the four primary work-flow components: people, parts, process, and time. These components are addressed in the *workforce, supply,* and *work-flow* domains, respectively.

In addition, the ISLA domains provide a semantic partition for creating common understanding among the different OSS systems that must interface with each other. An example could include the product catalog, which must unite the semantic interpretations of the product that are represented in the provisioning system, billing application, workforce management system, and supply chain application. Semantics play a big part in the supply, workforce, and customer domains because they provide information and resources to the work-flow domain.

Finally, several domains are primarily functional, such as the data and presentation domains, which are responsible for data integration, and man-machine interface, respectively.

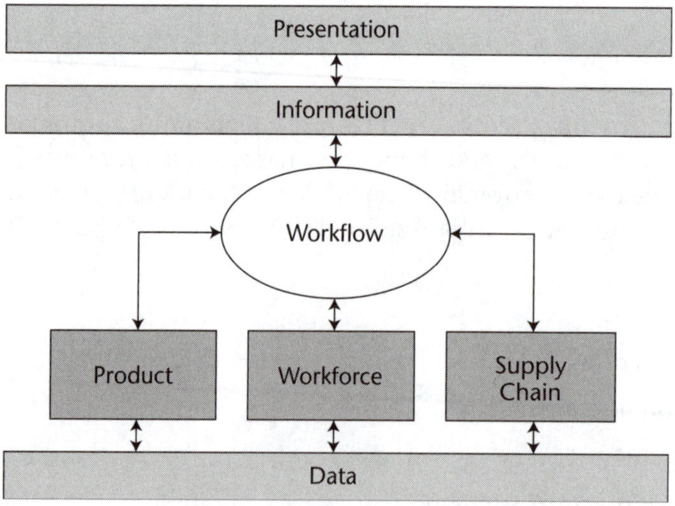

Figure 6.5 The seven Integrated Service Level Agreement domains.

NOTE **The customer domain, which is arguably the most important facet of the SLA equation, is not included in the core domains for two important reasons: (1) in general, there are very few semantic issues related to the customer between OSSs; that is, almost all systems have the same data field that means the same thing (such as name, location, billing address, and so on). (2) In most case, the customer is responsible for causing event generation, and although he or she is a party to reporting and notification throughout the work flow, he or she is normally a passive observer of work flow, rather than an active participant. The overriding consideration is the semantic issue, which in our opinion does not warrant a separate domain definition for *customer* within the framework. The issues are capably handled by the individual systems.**

The Presentation Domain

The *presentation domain* is enabled by the ISLA portals and is responsible for providing universal access, community management, security, communications, and presentation of the man-machine interfaces (graphical user interfaces, or GUIs) needed to perform work-flow tasks. This domain provides a central access point through which service can be obtained or delivered, supports the formation of work-flow communities, provides access to all external systems, and provides advanced capabilities such as publish and/or subscribe, proactive alerts, and search facilities.

The portal also enables the management functions of the dynamic work-flow community and serves as the entry point to the community, whether access is provided for employees, customers, or business partners. A sophisticated profile is maintained for each community member. User ID management; security; and the granting of permissions for access to information, activities, and other systems is enabled by a sophisticated combination of process and algorithms that allow service providers to define, create, and manage the communities over the Internet.

The Information Domain

The *information domain* is enabled by the business intelligence module and is responsible for storing, providing, and managing the information that will be made available to the presentation domain. Information can be processed and displayed in an almost infinite number of ways, including on Web pages; through application GUIs; in text documents, spreadsheets, audio or video files, through multimedia presentations, and so on. Each format must be supportable within the domain and be accessible by the presentation domain.

Although the information domain deals with large amounts of data, you should understand the difference between its role and that of the data domain. There are three categories of data within the ISLA environment:

Raw data that can generally be classified as unprocessed machine or network output. An example might be a Simple Network Management Protocol (SNMP) text stream generated by a network element to its element management system. Until it is processed further, it is not usable by humans in a practical sense. Raw data is the basis of all information.

Information that is distinguishable from raw data. This data has usually been processed into a format that can be displayed to a human to help him or her to gain additional knowledge, make a decision, perform a task, or otherwise effect a change based on the contents of the information. For example, the SNMP stream may have been processed by the element management system and displayed as a color-coded fault alarm.

Business intelligence that is the highest level of information and potentially the most valuable to the service provider. Business intelligence is certain types of information that have been processed in such a way that they can provide the user with knowledge that can impact the business operations of the service provider; examples of such information include key performance indicators (KPIs), reports, financial projections, or information on historical performance or upcoming trends.

The Product or Contract Domain

The *product domain* and, more specifically, the *product catalog*, are the brains of the ISLA framework. Product, QoS, and SLA and work-flow definitions converge in the provider domain. The ISLA framework calls for end-to-end work flow to be developed dynamically and managed based primarily on the SLA entitlements. Service Level Agreement entitlements, as we have stated before, are the contractual component of QoS related to a product or service. The contractual entitlement is one of two key elements in the SLA value proposition (the other is performance that is in compliance with that entitlement).

The product domain is probably the most problematic one to execute successfully. Complications can arise in the semantic issues related to the notion of the product catalog within the various OSS systems. Enterprise resource planning (ERP), order management, billing, workforce management, and even some inventory systems each have some representation of product entities.

The semantic descriptions within the disparate systems must be brought together to form a common understanding of products and services, including SLAs.

The product catalog should be semantically managed from within the framework, as should workforce management and the supply chain. But the master repository for product entitlements should also reside within the framework. The reason is that in addition to the semantic aggregation, certain capabilities (such as the ability to set thresholds that can be electronically monitored) must be present in the contract management system in order for the system to support real-time SLA management.

The product catalog is linked both semantically and technically to the other OSSs via integration performed in the data domain. Because of the different semantic interpretations of the product entity within the different OSSs, we recommend that you consider establishing a master-slave relationship, perhaps using publish-subscribe as the preferred technical integration scheme.

The Process or Work-Flow Domain

The *process domain,* also called the *work-flow domain,* is the core aspect of the ISLA model. The work-flow domain is responsible for work-flow instance management, modeling, editing, and reporting as well as all task-level management responsibilities, such as rule enforcement, role-relationship definition, and tracking-auditing.

The work-flow domain is enabled by the capabilities of the advanced work-flow automation systems that have recently come onto the market. We cover the objectives, capabilities, architectures, implementation, use, and benefits of such systems in detail in a number of the remaining chapters of this book, including much of Chapters 8, 9, and 11.

The Data Domain

The *data domain* is enabled by the integration server and is responsible for managing the electronic data interchange between the ISLA framework, disparate OSSs, and other electronic interfaces, such as email (simple mail transfer protocol, or SMTP) systems. This domain handles the transfer of raw data, information, and intelligence from many different automated systems and repositories, including the Internet.

The data domain can support technical and semantic integration through the use of a common integration server, a message-oriented middleware (MOM) bus, publish-subscribe technology, or some other technical integration scheme. The disparate OSSs reside beneath the data domain and are transparent to community members until these systems are called upon by the work-flow engine to provide support to a process through an electronic transaction or GUI presentation.

We will discuss the integration server and the functions of data integration in Chapter 7.

The Provider or Workforce Domain

The *workforce domain* is responsible for managing the contributions made by the human components of the work flow. The workforce domain is considered to be a semantic one because the primary management systems (workforce management) related to these activities are external to the ISLA framework, and therefore functionality depends on successfully integrating data at both semantic and technical levels with the work-flow domain.

The workforce management system is an external OSS that is responsible for role management and for providing a repository for information related to the availability of human work-flow participants. The different personnel, departments, organizations, and service companies are profiled and catalogued in the workforce domain using a variety of dynamically definable criteria. Business rules are then employed to ensure a more efficient response that prioritizes service calls.

The system matches the customer entitlements stored in the provider domain against the location, capabilities, and status of each member of the community. It then searches for, identifies, and dispatches field engineers based on the work-flow requirements and the skill sets of community members. Having accepted a call, the community member can report work against it, such as travel, labor, and wait times. The system automatically tracks work-flow arrival and departure times and downtime.

We talk about organizational use of the workforce management system in Chapters 9 and 11, and we address technical and semantic integration in Chapter 7.

The Supply Domain

The *supply domain* is responsible for managing assets and inventory, and, like the provider domain, the supply domain is dependent on an external OSS for much of its functionality. The supply domain is enabled by the supply chain or logistics system. It is also touched by the financial and billing systems.

The supply domain is a semantic domain that manages the contributions made to the work flow that are not human or electronic. In the telecommunications industry, the terms *nonhuman* and *non-electronic* generally refer to physical network elements or parts, such as terminals, switch ports, circuit cards, or modems—but these terms can also refer to logical inventory such as cable pairs or Permanent Virtual Circuits (PVCs).

We discuss the integration of the supply chain and the logistical aspects of bringing ISLA into the organization and its processes in Chapters 9 and 11.

Sample Technical Architecture

In general, the ISLA architecture is based a multitiered, multiserver environment that uses logical domain definition to deliver functional partitioning of the core capabilities. The ISLA architecture is server-centric. Its *n*-tier architecture consists of application servers, in which most business logic is performed, as well as several database servers.

One sample of the ISLA architecture uses IBM's WebSphere as its application server. These application servers can be deployed as a single virtual server, providing improved performance, fault-tolerance, and fail-over capabilities. Application servers are available to clients through a corporate intranet, or over the Internet.

The IBM WebSphere Application Server (WAS) is used with the IBM HTTP Server and can be deployed to allow for maximum performance in various topologies depending on the client's volume and activity. The database server is typically installed on a separate machine. The HTTP server and the WAS can be installed on a wide range of topologies.

The ISLA architecture has three primary databases:

1. The *operational database* is used for managing presentation, work flow, workforce, and integration applications.
2. The *data mart* incorporates service-related information that is extracted from the operational database and other repositories and used by the reporting framework for creating business intelligence.
3. The *document repository* maintains reports, documents, pointers to operational data, and many other elements that together form the bulk of the service providers' knowledge.

The ISLA architecture is standards-based and platform-independent. We designed the ISLA framework around COTS software written in Java and using object-oriented methodologies. Modules deployed on the Web are also written in Java and are deployed as servlets or Java server pages. Most of the application frameworks are based on XML, as is the integration framework. All external interfaces conform to the API standards, where such standards have been published.

There are several core application modules that drive the specific functionality within the respective domains, including the work-flow management system, which is used to relate all functions across the domains. We will discuss the core modules, their fit within the ISLA framework, and the architecture behind them. The core modules are as follows (see Figure 6.6):

- Portal architecture
- Business intelligence architecture
- Work-flow automation architecture
- Integration architecture

Portal Architecture

The presentation layer is built around the capabilities of the ViryaNet Service Hub Web portal built on IBM WebSphere. The Web portal—combining user, content, and product information—serves as the hub of all service-related operations. Using a Java- or Dynamic Hyper Text Markup Language (DHTML)-based interface, the portal offers a unified view of service that serves as both the end-user and the administrative view into all the functions provided through the ISLA's other modules and the extended OSS environment.

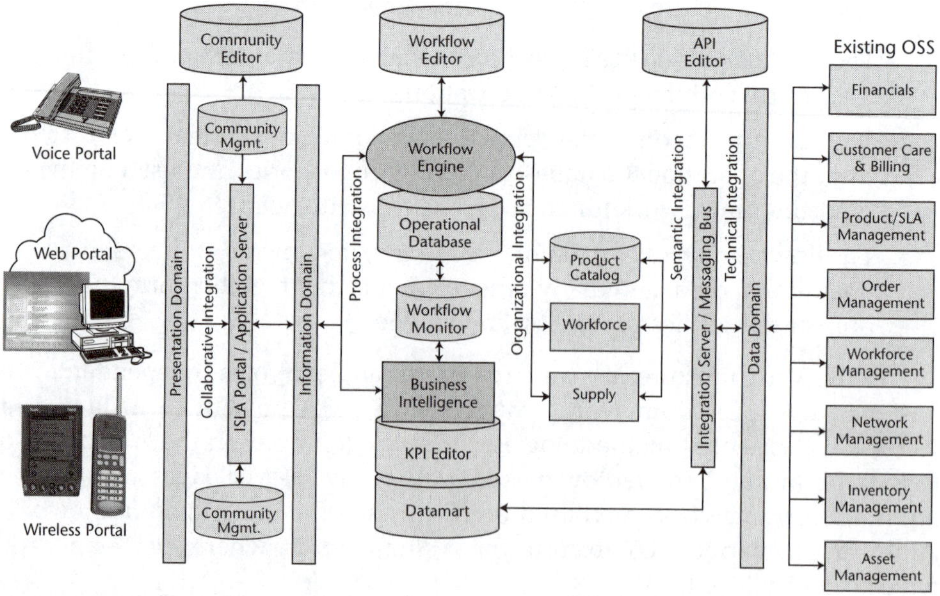

Figure 6.6 Integrated Service Level Agreement architecture.

The Web portal is based on an information repository that unifies all content under one meta-model and indexes documents, data, queries, reports, and Web pages. Users can therefore immediately obtain access to both the correct information and the appropriate applications. The architecture uses a combination of pull and push elements that support alerts, notifications, and queries—all within the single Web front end, as shown in Figure 6.7.

The User Interface

The ISLA user interface is based on various technologies:

Dynamic Hyper Text Markup Language (DHTML) pages. Most of ISLA functionality uses dynamic HTML pages generated by Java Server Pages (JSP).

Java Swing. Configuration tools such as the Work-flow Editor and the APIS Service Definition Tool use Java Swing components.

Client/Server. The *ISLA Windows Client* is a client-server application.

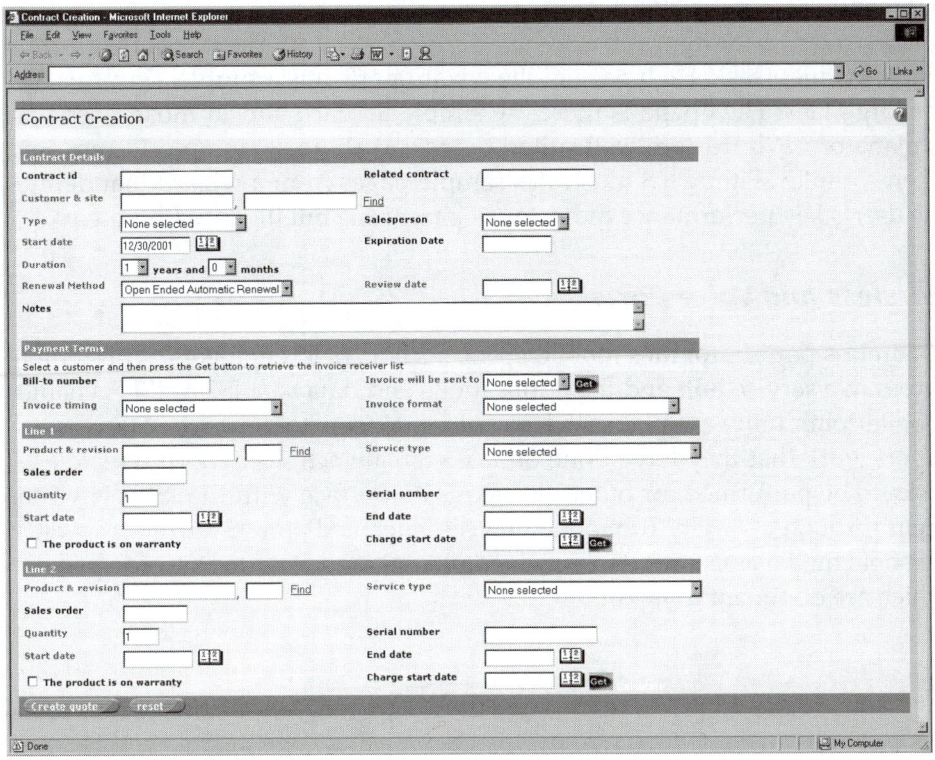

Figure 6.7 An example contract creation front end.

We have made every effort to ensure that all of the interfaces are consistent. Therefore the Web interfaces include not only forms but also dynamic tables, trees, and so on. The code is based on HTML, JavaScript, OM, and style sheets. The Web pages are very lightweight and function in both Netscape Navigator and Microsoft Internet Explorer. Where the browsers differ, the code is differentiated, so that instead of writing to the lowest common denominator, the ISLA Web pages offer the best user interface possible in each browser.

All elements of the DHTML user interface can be customized without code changes. Possible changes include both visual attributes (such as component visibility, color, and font), and validation properties (such as mandatory fields and the ordering of columns in a table). Work-flow customization can affect the ordering of pages in a work-flow process to support the presentation needs of the dynamic work-flow concept.

Many processes involve intricate user interfaces, which place a heavy burden on users, who must learn a complex series of pages and operations in order to complete a task. In addition, some of these processes are used infrequently, making the cost/benefit ratio too low. To resolve this issue, ISLA makes extensive use of wizards, and we have also adopted a *finder* based on the Macintosh finder concept and Microsoft's Windows Explorer finder. Finders help users find objects, including products, sites, calls, contracts, processes, or any other business object.

The wizard paradigm is based on a series of very simple pages that form a single business task. Each page in the wizard performs a simple, single part of the large task. Each page is therefore simple to learn and in most cases self-explanatory. Wizards are well suited to tasks that are seldom performed and often complex. Figure 6.8 illustrates sample pages from a wizard that defines the user's key performance indicator as part of the intelligence framework.

Wireless and Voice Portals

A wireless portal provides mobile users, such as field engineers, with remote access to a service hub and the applications and data w/i ISLA. ISLA enables mobile community members such as field engineers to view work-flow tasks, report work that they have done on tasks, create activity reports, create new tasks to be performed, or otherwise request interface with the ISLA environment through a variety of mobile devices, such as PalmOS and WindowsCE personal digital assistants, Web-enabled phones, and I-mode DoCoMo phones, which are dominant in Japan.

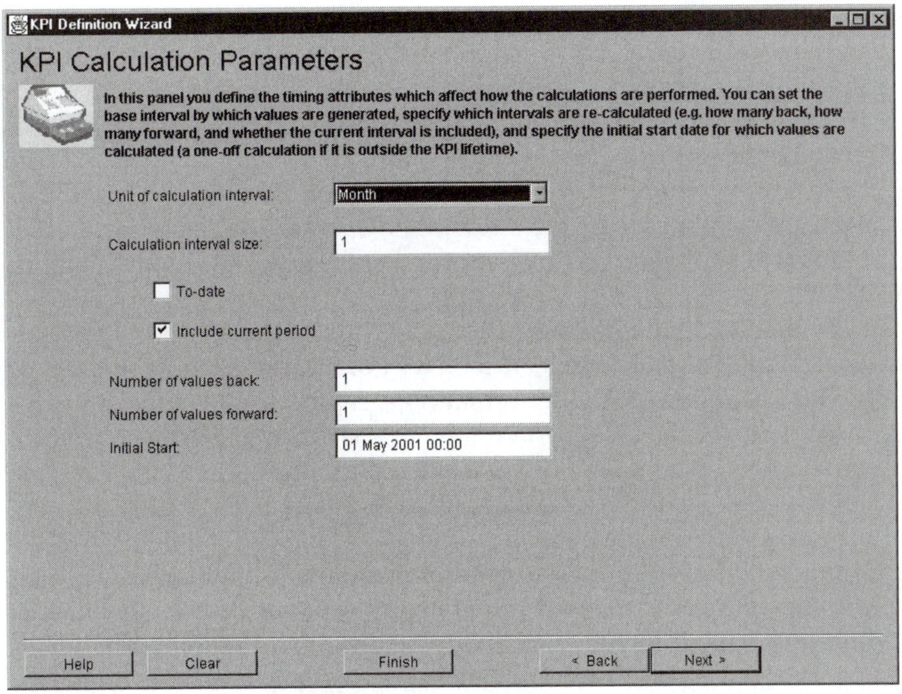

Figure 6.8 A key performance indicator wizard sample.

The voice portal allows community members to access new calls, obtain detailed information about assignments, and report time-critical information, such as labor, travel time, and expenses using natural voice commands from any land-line or cellular phone. The voice portal uses VoiceXML, an emerging standard, to communicate with the voice server and generate voice sessions with the end user.

Business Intelligence Architecture

The information domain is supported by two databases—the data mart and the document repository—that together form the capabilities behind the business intelligence module. The data mart incorporates service-related information that is extracted from the operational database and other repositories and is used by the reporting framework for creating business intelligence. The document repository maintains reports, documents, pointers to operational data, and many other unstructured elements that together form the bulk of the service provider's knowledge. This repository is the basis of much of the content that is managed by and displayed in the portal.

Business intelligence architecture allows users to monitor the performance of the work-flow community and take action based on informed decision making. It analyzes information extracted from the operational database, stores it in an appropriate format in the data mart, and creates graphic representations of the results.

Business intelligence architecture is based on the collection of key performance indicators that track data on the basis of criteria such as work-flow tracking, financial trends, SLA performance, service rates, revenue, and cost per product type. It also allows you to define your own performance indicators, monitors, and reports, as well as to create graphs and charts. The data mart captures over 80 different data points among its KPIs, and carries out monitoring and reporting functions.

Reporting technology allows service administrators to capture service metrics and compare them to defined goals. Reporting tools operate in conjunction with the data mart to generate a wide-ranging set of reports. Analysis is facilitated via a wizard-based interface that allows administrators to define the information that is important from a roster of the KPIs that are captured.

Active monitoring and reporting enable the service provider to understand where performance may not measure up to SLA entitlements, and then take steps to make both dynamic adjustments, that is, immediate reallocation of resources, and strategic changes involving the alteration of the work-flow process template. These adjustments form the basis and enable the execution of both the dynamic work flow and the dynamic work-flow community concepts.

Work-Flow Automation Architecture

A robust work-flow engine that allows service providers to graphically define work-flow processes manages the work-flow domain. The work-flow engine links work-flow activities with system events, such as generating API calls according to business rules that are defined by a wizard-driven graphical tool. With the portal's capabilities to reach all members of the service process, the work-flow engine coordinates activities among users inside and outside the enterprise, as well as connects to other OSS applications, such as CRM, ERP, and so on, which augment the service process.

The work-flow engine allows the service provider to define and apply rules to automate the movement of documents, work orders, and information between community members. The work-flow engine includes the work-flow editor and a work-flow monitor, which is a tool for monitoring active processes and auditing completed processes.

The work-flow engine provides a working environment that guarantees maximum flexibility. It treats each process as a module, consisting of a series of steps, and assigns each step to a user or user group. Once a step has been completed, the engine determines the next step to be performed, by whom, and when. Work-flow processes and application functionality are packaged in a very flexible way. This packaging is based on a number of key elements that ensure that implementation cycles are performed quickly and efficiently, while still allowing all aspects of the applications to be customized to the service provider's requirements. These key elements are:

- The work-flow engine
- The business transaction framework for managing business events
- The business rules framework

The Work-Flow Engine

The Integrated Service Level Agreement is based on a *work-flow engine* that manages the process flows within the system. The engine conforms to the work-flow model defined by the Work-flow Management Coalition (WfMC) and by the Object Management Group's (OMG's) Work-Flow Facility and supports processes, nested processes, time-outs, and so on.

It is possible to customize each work-flow process, and it is easy to define new processes. All such modifications are made using the work-flow editor, as shown in Figure 6.9, and these alterations require no code changes.

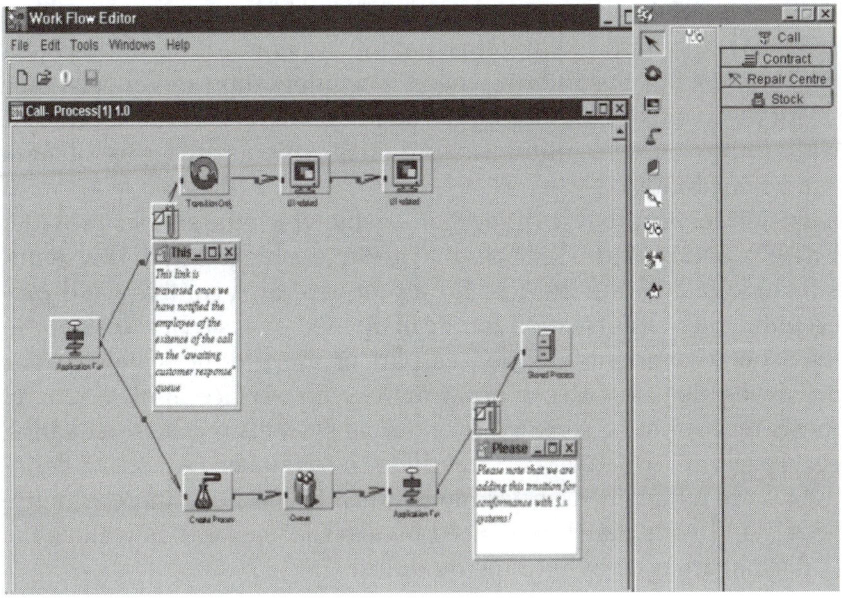

Figure 6.9 The Work-Flow editor.

The work-flow engine, in combination with the integration server, is a powerful tool for gluing external application to the ISLA and synchronizing activities in various systems. Using scripting languages, the work-flow processes can implement complex customer-specific business logic.

Business Transaction Framework

The *business transaction framework* allows any occurrence in the system that is of interest in a business context to be defined as an event, and makes it possible for custom behavior to be attached to such events. You can tailor effects based on events. The business transaction framework links to the work-flow engine and the integration framework, and it allows tailored business processes to be triggered by business transactions, as well as allowing business processes to initiate business transactions.

Business Rules Framework

Much of the functionality in the ISLA applications is based on a data-driven paradigm. This data forms the core of the business rules framework through which the behavior of the system can be customized to reflect the requirements of each organization without requiring code changes.

Integration Architecture

The ISLA must interface with a multitude of other OSSs including financial systems, billing, provisioning, call center and help desk systems, as well as interactive voice response (IVR) systems, paging systems, and ERP products. The *integration server* fills this interface need. The integration server runs on a Java application server. The packaging of the integration server as a separate server yields improved scalability and provides benefits in terms of fault tolerance and availability.

The integration server provides a mechanism by which the service provider can publish APIs, and provides services that are accessible to external systems. Examples include calculating the cost for a proposed SLA contract, and providing SLA entitlement information for a call opened by a service desk application (based on the variants defined as part of the product catalog). The integration server also provides a uniform way for service applications to make requests that are to be serviced by external systems (such as activating an engineer's pager to dispatch a service call to the engineer). All object definitions and APIs are maintained uniformly in an API repository, thereby defining the models and APIs that can be used by external systems as well as the outgoing calls that are used by internal modules.

The following can be viewed as the chronical usage of the integration server:

1. *Application 2 provider* implements a service that will be called by *application 1 requester*. *Application 2* publishes the object definitions and the service definition. It defines a set of *components* and a *service* and publishes it to the *API repository*. The *components* are objects used by the API (that is, the signature of the *service*) and the definition of possible outputs.

   For example, if the service to be provided is a quote calculation service, then the following items must be defined within the API repository:

   - The structure of the quote object (object definitions include version numbers)
   - The output structure (in this case simply a set of numeric values)
   - The specifier of the service (the provider name, in this case the *contract*, the service name, in this case *calculate quote,* and the version).

2. Once an API has been published, the *application 2 provider* registers with the *service registry*. The *service registry* is implemented using a Java Naming and Directory Interface (JNDI) namespace, allowing multiple physical integration servers to function as a single logical server. This approach allows users to develop scalable systems by balancing the transaction load over multiple servers.

3. When *application 1 requester* wishes to invoke the service published in the API repository, it creates a *service request object* (part of the adapter). This object encapsulates the request parameters, including the URL of the integration server, the input to the service request, and attributes defining whether the request should be invoked as a synchronous call or as an asynchronous one. It also defines how results should be returned and to whom.

4. The service request communicates with the packager, which translates the request parameters to XML, by using the definitions maintained by the API repository. The adapter then makes an HTTP connection to a Java program running on the server called a *servlet broker*. This broker sends the XML, forming the service request.

5. The servlet broker functions as a separate thread, passing the XML to the performer. The performer parses the XML into a Document Object Model (DOM) structure based on the service definitions. The performer validates security attributes and validates the correctness of the service request. It then looks for service providers registered with the service registry that can perform the requested service, and passes the request to the *application 2 provider*.

XML and the Integration Server

The integration server is based on XML in two respects: (1) messages are XML, and (2) configuration and other internally structured using files use XML. Application program interfaces (APIs) are defined using XML and are stored in the API repository that can be queried and investigated. This repository allows applications to publish their APIs in a way that can be used by other applications to determine how to form the call. Once an API has been published to the repository, a message may be sent.

The message structure itself is also an application of XML. Adapters allow the integration server to be used from multiple implementation platforms. They are used by applications built using various tools, programming languages, and development paradigms. For example, a Java/RMI adapter allows any Java application to use the integration server. Adapters that are part of the integration server include the following:

- The *email adapter* uses a URL to allow messages to be sent and received using email.
- The *database adapter* provides a facility in which a database application can interact with ISLA. The facility is implemented as a set of tables and stored procedures, through which calls can be made by inserting data. Once the messages have been inserted into the tables, a daemon process on the integration server picks up the messages and forms XML service requests, which are handled by the integration server.
- The Web adapter allows service requests to be issued using any protocol that can be based on HTTP.
- The file adapter provides the capability to access the API's services using ASCII files placed in a dedicated input directory. This adapter is very useful for massive multiple activation of services, typically during data upload.

Integration Server Tools

The integration server offers three customization and management tools:

- A *development tool* for defining components, bindings, and services
- A *monitoring tool* for displaying information pertaining to the processing of managed services
- An *administration tool* used to control the various components of the integration server

The development tool is used for defining components, component bindings, argument bindings, and services (that is, APIs). The tool is a visual editor for the API repository objects and is used by implementation teams and system integrators that require access to external applications.

Figure 6.10 shows the definition screen of an output structure, which includes the condition under which this output structure will be generated and what the output structure will contain.

The monitoring tool, also shown in Figure 6.10, is used by implementation teams when they set up and optimize the system and by system administrators in daily operations.

The monitoring tool allows the viewing of runtime information that is useful both for debugging and for daily maintenance. The tool includes five subtools:

1. The *service registry viewer* displays the contents of the service registry.
2. The *event log viewer* shows all events logged by the integration server within a specified time period.
3. The *message queue viewer* displays the contents of the message queue, including priorities, scheduled times, and so on. It supports a drill-down capability that allows users to view the message's entire XML structure.

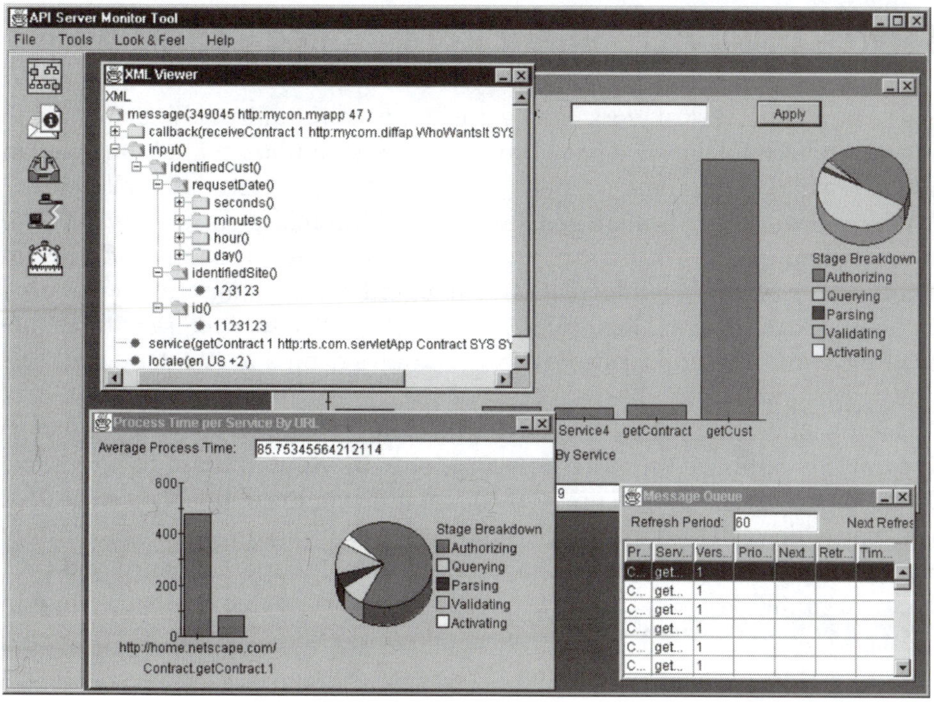

Figure 6.10 API development and monitoring tools.

4. The *throughput monitor* displays statistical information regarding the integration server throughput within a given time period, and supports a drill-down capability that shows throughput per service.
5. The *process time monitor* displays statistical information regarding the process time of the services managed by the integration server, including drill-down capabilities for viewing process time breakdown per service.

The integration server includes other components. These components provide additional capabilities, such as synchronization, queuing, and auditing.

NGOSS Architecture

The TeleManagement Forum's recommendations, publications, and continued work with OSS vendors and service providers, especially the Catalyst projects, have greatly contributed to the creation of the ISLA framework. We recommend that any party undertaking integration of the ISLA framework consult the TMF's *NGOSS Architecture Technology Neutral Specification [TMF 053], Performance Reporting Concepts and Definitions Document [TMF 701], Service Provider to Customer Performance Reporting Business Agreement [NMF 503], SLA Handbook [GB 917],* and *Telecom Operations Map (TOM) [GB 910].*

Service Level Agreement Compliance Reporting

The same architecture of work-flow automation, community management, and integration technologies we have brought together and discussed thus far can also be used to realize previously unattainable levels of business intelligence.

When all work flow is managed through the ISLA framework, every instance of an assignment, work performance, status tracking, updates, and closure becomes important QoS information that is continually compared in real time to the SLA entitlements. Real-time tracking is, of course, necessary to enable dynamic work flow and work-flow communities related to events such as service provisioning or trouble ticket response.

On the operations side, detected threshold violations are then used to dynamically optimize the work flow and/or work-flow community to resolve the problem. All activity becomes historical information and is then stored for analysis, which can lead to changes in the work flow or work-flow community templates, providing a feedback loop based on actual performance and producing a continual optimization cycle. The new ISLA value chain is shown in Figure 6.11.

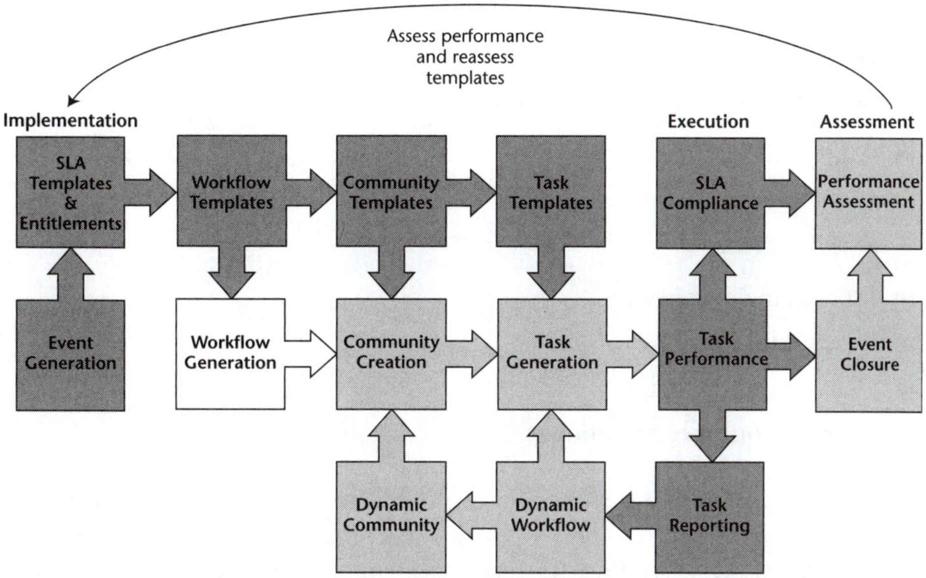

Figure 6.11 The Integrated Service Level Agreement chain of events.

We discuss the ISLA value chain and its impact on the service provider's operation in detail in Chapter 11. In this chapter we will discuss the methodology behind realizing real-time SLA compliance through the ISLA framework.

The concept behind ISLA compliance reporting is to combine the ISLA framework's automated work-flow capabilities (work-flow domain), the SLA entitlements within the product catalog (product domain), and the OSS integration realized through the integration server (data domain). This integration is accomplished by defining and implementing a work flow that is specifically designed to measure real-time compliance to SLAs. We term this methodology *ISLA compliance (ISLAC) work flows.*

An ISLAC work flow would consist of a number of steps that would resemble the ISLA value chain yet serve an independent purpose. An ISLAC work flow should contain the following tasks (see also Figure 6.12):

- Defining entitlements
- Generating events
- Identifying provisioning and /or troubleshooting work flows

- Extracting performance data
  - Work-flow activity
  - Network statistics
- Analyzing performance
  - Real-time
  - Historical
- Identifying exceptions
- Responding
- Calculating financial impact
- Carrying out reconciliations

The ISLAC work flow is then overlaid onto the delivery work flow, which results in every product having a work flow for service delivery that is the parent to a child ISLAC work flow for reporting. For example, a DSL service order event would result in the DSL work-flow template creating the appropriate tasks within the work-flow engine. One of the initial tasks within the DSL work-flow template would be to generate the DSL-ISLAC work flow.

Work-flow generation creates a mirror effect in which all activities reported against a parent delivery work flow, compliant or not, are automatically recorded and compared to the SLA entitlements in real time at a number of points within the ISLAC work flow, as shown in Figure 6.12.

The work-flow community defined for the ISLAC would consist primarily of OSS systems, applications, and the work-flow engine. A number of OSS

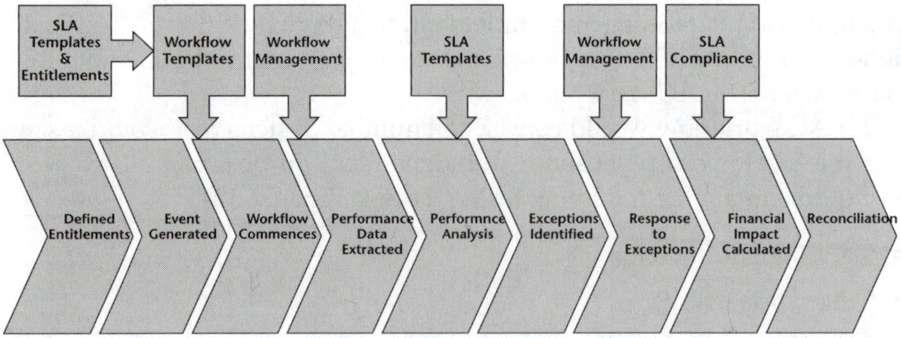

Figure 6.12 The Integrated Service Level Agreement Compliance-Operations Support System work flow.

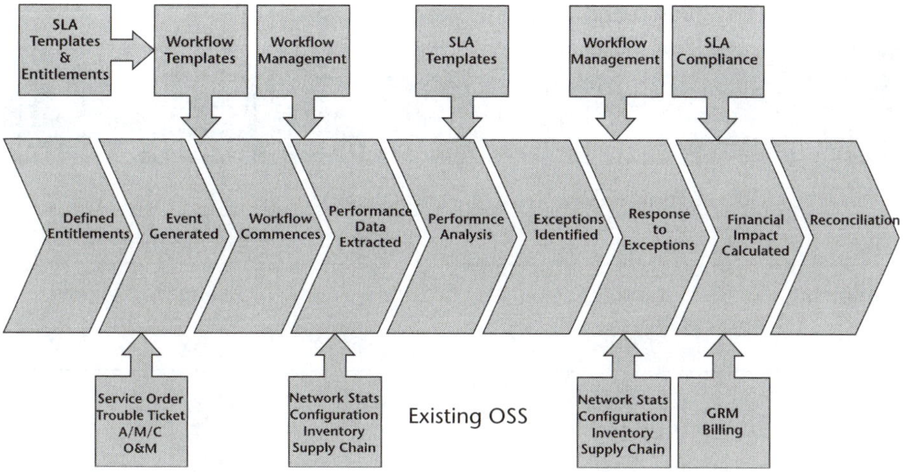

Figure 6.13 The Integrated Service Level Agreement-Operations Support System Service Level Agreement contributions.

contributions are needed to truly manage SLAs. In managing the ISLAC work flow, the work-flow engine automatically integrates with the underlying OSS system gathering, storing, and archiving information received as part of the delivery work flow, as shown in Figure 6.13.

Because some of the master repositories of information do not reside directly within the ISLA framework, the different OSSs must contribute the required information. This OSS contribution provides the most critical SLA information to the data mart. The types and sources of this information are shown in Table 6.1.

The information is then related through the use of KPIs into a unified view of the environment. This business intelligence can then be broken down using different criteria, into a number of reports that are made available to community members.

More accurate reporting allows service providers to develop entirely new classes of KPIs that will better serve the specific needs of the disparate community members. The KPIs, as proof of compliance, can then be made available in real time, on demand, to all levels of management within the service provider, and extend out to a widely distributed vendor, employee, and customer base. Metrics and performance reporting, including the use and development of KPIs, are covered extensively in Chapter 12.

Table 6.1 Work-Flow Information Types and Sources

DATA TYPE	OPERATIONS SUPPORT SYSTEM MASTER	METHOD	OPERATIONS SUPPORT SYSTEM SLAVES
Penalties	Financials	Calculated	
Rating	Billing	Extracted	Financials
Entitlement	Product Catalog	Core	Billing, Work Force Management (WFM)
Customer	Customer relationship management	Extracted	All
Activity	Work flow	Core	All
Network	Network management system	Extracted	Element management system
Network Configuration	Network Inventory	Extracted	Geographic Information System (GIS)
Asset & Inventory Stock	Supply Chain	Extracted	Geographic Information System (GIS), ERP, WFM, Financials

Core: Stored internally
Extracted: Data provided to datamart via integration
Calculated: Formulated by usiness ntelligence from two or more source inputs

Service Level Agreement Risk Mitigation

The biggest benefit provided by the ISLA framework is the reporting and visibility it makes possible for the service provider. Good KPI definition will make the financial liabilities associated with the SLA commitments visible for the first time.

Finally, faced with the financial liability outlined by the SLA provisions, carriers would invariably want to mitigate the risks associated with those commitments. Strong ISLA reporting capabilities can assist service providers in setting concrete limits on offerings to avoid signing on to unrealistic agreements that would be technically impossible or too expensive to deliver.

In order to avoid expensive financial remedies, service providers will also need to take advanced action to fix deteriorating service before it violates the entitlement threshold, thereby implementing a strategy of penalty avoidance. Service Level Agreement penalty avoidance strategies should encompass several tiers, such as network planning, field service management, and financial risk management.

The most obvious form of risk mitigation is to build additional network redundancy and survivability into the carrier's backbone so that hardware failures in the network do not result in downtime at the SAPs. Carriers would take proactive measures to assure compliance; that is, network designers and service managers would consider SLA commitments when making operational deployment decisions. A carrier may be more inclined to install redundant backup circuits at its own cost if it understands the financial liability. Redundancy, when it is available, is probably the most cost-efficient method of mitigating risk. But most network redundancy does not extend all the way out to the SAP.

Another mitigation strategy would be to properly staff and train field service organizations to respond to SLA-prioritized work. We will discuss implementing ISLA capabilities into the operational environment in Chapter 11.

One of the ways to limit the actual financial liabilities is to monitor the flow-down of penalty clauses. Monitoring ensures that off-net facilities carrying traffic are in turn covered by SLAs from the off-net provider. Relating the services in the data mart and developing the appropriate KPIs and reports make monitoring flow-down manageable.

Once the financial liabilities associated with delivering SLAs become visible to service providers, auditors, and stockholders, we should expect that more conventional financial risk management strategies will be utilized to reduce or spread out the largest liabilities. Risk management techniques could potentially take the form of SLA insurance or even the formation of a central exchange that trades SLA liabilities along with the bandwidth on which they ride—possibilities we explore in Chapter 15.

Summary

In this chapter, we have introduced the ISLA framework. We have explained the observations that lead to our belief that event correlation may hold the key to solving many of the problems that now exist within the OSS. While our approach is clearly a breed apart from the current emphasis on technical integration, it is based on what we feel is sound logic and takes full advantage of the most current technologies.

We discussed the concepts of dynamic work-flow automation and explained how the technology can also be used to drive dynamic work-flow communities. We also explored the impact that the ISLA could have on SLA compliance reporting, and touched on the kinds of risk mitigation that service providers might use once the liabilities become measurable.

But we didn't stop there. We demonstrated our belief that the technology for implementing ISLA is commercially available by providing a detailed architecture model based on COTS software that we are familiar with. The software packages we used are not the only ones that can deliver ISLA capabilities, just the ones we are most familiar with. There are a number of possible combinations that can deliver the solution.

But any of these solution sets must be able to deliver the core capabilities we've outlined as: universal access, business intelligence, collaboration, automation, and integration. They must also be able to reconcile the technical and semantic issues related to the domains on which we have based so much of our solution, such as:

- The presentation domain
- The information domain
- The product or contract domain
- The process or work-flow domain
- The data domain
- The workforce domain
- The supply chain or logistics domain

Reconciling these domains means solving the problems remaining in technical integration and at least starting to resolve some of the more challenging semantic issues. As we have shown in other areas of discussion and in other chapters, almost everything has a need hierarchy behind it. The ISLA framework is no exception. The foundation upon which the ISLA framework is built is the integration of the disparate OSSs into a single collaborative domain. In Chapter 7 we begin to lay that foundation.

CHAPTER

7

Integration Techniques

In this chapter we will discuss integration techniques and then describe how to build an integrated and collaborative SLA model. The convergence of topics is no coincidence, since integration is at the heart of the integrated SLA model and at the heart of the Operations Support System(OSS)/Business Support System (BSS).

Integration has always been, and continues to be, of core interest to the IT industry. The high-tech community as a whole is fascinated with integration, and the telecom industry is no exception. The trade press is always full of discussions on integration, and although the terms and names change with the fashions, the essence remains the same. Although we use various terms such as *integration*, *interoperability*, *middleware*, and *enterprise application integration* (*EAI*), the business drive is still always the same. We have many different systems that we would like to see behaving as one single, integrated, and well-running system that can be used to conduct business in the most smooth and efficient manner.

Technical Integration

The convergence of the data communication world with the classic telecommunication world, coupled with the number of technologies and the sheer size and complexity of the networks, creates a reality in which the operational, management, and customer-care systems that are needed to run the service provider's business form one of the most complex information systems on earth. In addition, these systems need to run very efficiently, with very high uptime and under extreme conditions, so it is no surprise that each software vendor within the OSS specializes in a certain area. The disparate systems need to operate efficiently and manage end-to-end processes well. To work together smoothly, the systems must be well integrated from both a technical as well as a semantic perspective.

Distinguishing between technical and semantic integration is important. *Technical integration* requires resolving issues that result from different systems being built on different platforms, running on different operating systems, being written in different programming languages, using different data management systems, and so on. The technical integration effort requires a common information and communication bus. We will not attempt to define an information bus at this point, and we certainly do not mean to imply that a certain middleware approach is advisable. Whether we use a bus platform, messaging middleware, publish-subscribe backbone, or any other solution, all technical integration is accomplished by agreeing on a common way to describe data and pass it from one system to another. The data transfer makes use of adapters that translate data, events, and function calls from the systems' native forms to a common form.

A great deal of work has been done in terms of technical integration over the past decade. This work has been difficult, but it has achieved quite a lot of success. The work of the Object Management Group (OMG) in creating CORBA has influenced the OSS—specifically the integration aspects within the provider environments. Technical integration work also includes the relative newcomer—eXtensible Markup Language (XML)—and the even newer kids on the block—Simple Object Access Protocol (SOAP), Web Services Definition Language (WSDL), and Universal Description Discovery and Integration (UDDI), which form the *Web services* platform.

Semantic Integration

Technical integration is relatively easy to tackle, and for IT people it is usually a fun thing to do (hence the plethora of middleware solutions that exist). The semantic integration problem is much more challenging, requires different skill sets, and is not as much of a science as is technical integration. *Semantic integration* is about agreeing on the relationship of symbols and their meanings—and this is much harder than agreeing on data formats and invocation protocols. Semantic integration is about making sure that when one system talks about an SLA or a contract and communicates this information to another system, they both can agree on what an SLA is and what a contract is. Actually, we cannot hope to go that far—we will be happy if there is a clear and good enough semantic mapping between what one system means and what the other system means. This is true for almost any entity managed by the relevant systems—including an SLA, contract, location, customer, product, and more. Nothing regarding semantics should be taken for granted—even agreeing on the semantics that are today encapsulated within Common Language Location Identification (CLLI) codes took a long time and was driven by a very dominant central authority (Telcordia/Bellcore).

Semantic integration requires agreement at the modeling level—which is difficult to carry off because the model is the least exposed part in any system. The internal nature of the model is also the reason that semantic integration holds much more promise of benefiting the provider than does technical integration. The only real way to make all systems work together as a single system is for them to agree on a common model that drives all events from the inside out. Unfortunately, we (the authors) do not believe such a model is fully attainable. The people promoting the model would have to be as much politicians and psychologists as technologists, and they would have to have far-reaching influence within their respective companies. In fact, a lot of work toward this end has been done by the Common Information Model (CIM) group—so although we do not think this model will be adopted by the vendors, we are keeping our fingers crossed. In the meantime, we can amuse ourselves with technical integration and with data mapping and transformation techniques, which are technical solutions provided to help solve semantic integration problems. These integration techniques will be the central focus in this chapter, since they are also required to implement the integrated SLA model using existing OSS solutions. We will, however, mention some of the groups working on true semantic integration and their influence on the SLA model—and especially the work that is being done within the TeleManagement Forum (TMF).

Concepts of Distributed Computing

Distributed computing is a paradigm used to build complex application structures that are based on the notion of multiple components and processes working toward combined goals. It has become the dominant (if not only) paradigm within computing for solving complex problems and building robust information systems. All of the integration technologies that we will discuss in this chapter and that dominate the OSS fall within the paradigm of distributed computing. All of the middleware and enterprise application integration (EAI) vendors that are common in telcos are based on the distributed computing paradigm and provide different flavors of solutions to the problems inherent in the interaction of distributed systems.

Batch Processes

Integration between systems in the OSS/BSS takes two forms: data uploads/conversions and interfaces. Data uploads and various other batch processes are often used to move information from one system to another. While the names may imply that this kind of interfacing is done only once when the system is put in place, the reality is that batch runs that extract data from one system, transform it, and put it into another system are probably still a very common type of interface in the OSS.

The advantage of such interfaces is that they are relatively easy to build, easy to run and manage (since, for example, they may run only nightly), and avoid a lot of the difficult questions related to timing, transaction bracketing, and so on. These interfaces usually use either flat files with some kind of ASCII format as the data format and protocol, or staging tables in some database. When files are used, the system from which the information is coming exports a file according to some format.

Often the file is a Comma Separated Value (CSV) file, where each row corresponds to a record or a message to be sent and the data is separated by commas (as shown in Figure 7.1). The receiving system will take this file and create transactions, usually one per row in the file. If a database table is used for the interface, then the two systems agree on the table structure and a table (usually called the staging table) is created in one of the two systems' databases. The system from which the information comes then inserts records into the staging table, and the receiving system either removes a record once processing of the record is complete or changes a status column.

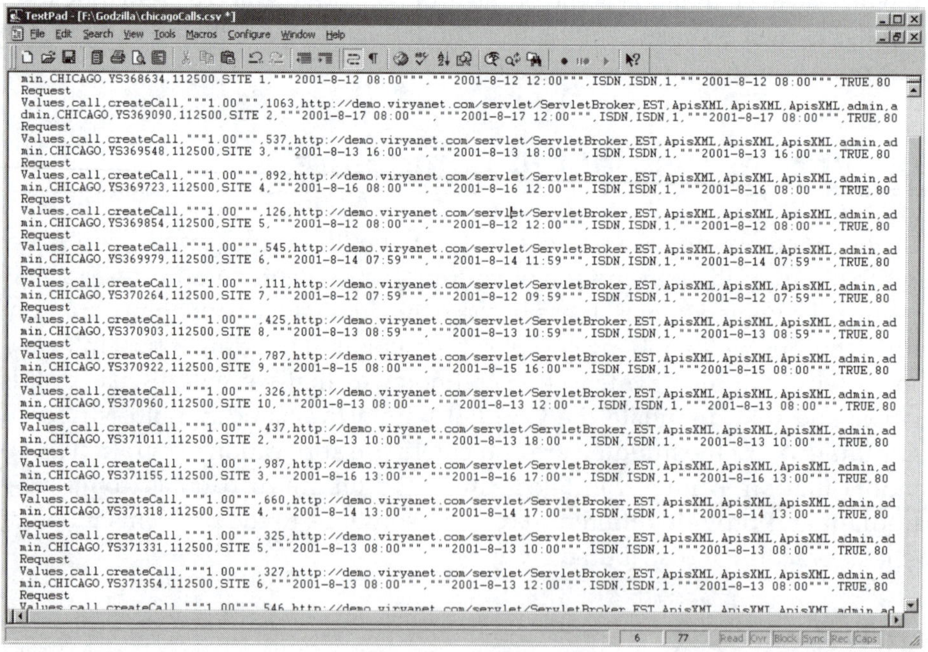

Figure 7.1 A Comma Separated Value file used for system integration.

Real-Time Integration

The category of static batch interfaces is well proven, but it is fast losing ground to a second form of interfacing that has been used for over 10 years, and is becoming the dominant and preferred interfacing method. This form of interfacing supports more integration scenarios, real-time information flows, the use of multiple systems within a single integration bus, and more.

We already mentioned that the challenge facing the parties responsible for building the OSS is to take many disparate systems and make them hum together like a well-tuned machine. From the perspective of those building the OSS, they are trying to build a *single system*. The fact that it is made up of multiple systems, each one with its own different attributes, is unfortunate but a fact of life. From this perspective the OSS is a complex instance of a distributed computing environment.

Integration Paradigms

In a distributed environment, each component or system functions in an autonomous manner. These systems need to interact with each other in order to satisfy the end-to-end processes handled by the OSS. Interaction between these systems normally follows one of three primary paradigms: an invocation paradigm, a messaging paradigm, or a publish-subscribe paradigm.

The Invocation or Remote Procedure Call

In an invocation paradigm (sometimes called a remote procedure call [RPC] paradigm) one system needs a service that is implemented within another system. The system that implements the service defines how calls are made to activate this service. Examples (which we will detail later) include CORBA invocations and XML-based invocations such as SOAP. For the system making the invocation, the call is similar to what a local function call might look like, apart from various different calling attributes such as timing, the fact that the call must be based on a published application program interface (API), the fact that the call may more easily fail, and so on. The call itself may be synchronous or asynchronous. In a *synchronous* call, the calling thread blocks until the result is returned by the implementer. In an *asynchronous* call, the caller usually supplies a callback routine, which is called once the action has been performed and the reply is ready. Every invocation has a client (the caller) and a server (the implementer), but roles may change among different invocations.

Message-Oriented Middleware

The asynchronous mode leads us into the second common paradigm—*Message-Oriented Middleware* (MOM). Products supporting this paradigm manage the transfer of messages from one system to another using a messaging bus. This mode is often called *store-and-forward*. An asynchronous invocation can sometimes be categorized as a case of MOM, but in general MOM-type solutions tend to better support decoupled distributed systems, while Remote Procedure Call (RPC) solutions tend to be suited to highly coupled systems.

Publish and Subscribe

The third common paradigm is *publish-subscribe*. This paradigm is based on the concept of a business event. Publishers make information available in the form of a business event. They place this information on a common bus that all systems can access, both to read events from as well as to publish events to. Subscribers subscribe to the bus and register to receive certain business events. Channels and Topics may be used to categorize and organize the business events and provide more focused data delivery mechanisms.

Integration Paradigms and OSS

Many middleware and EAI systems today support all three paradigms of distributed computing. Vendors who specialize in this technology have recognized that they need to offer all forms of integration architecture. Incidentally, there is a natural progression between the paradigms. Once an RPC-based system allows asynchronous invocations with callbacks, the road to MOM is fairly short. Similarly, once a messaging bus is implemented, it is quite natural to progress to the advanced feature allowing subscribers to register to receive messages that are published on the bus.

Since many of the systems that need to be integrated in order to support the integrated SLA model are built using advanced technology, they almost always can be used as participants within a distributed system using either invocation-based, messaging, or publish-subscribe integration. The choice of which paradigm is used is primarily a question of the overall design of the OSS. Regardless of which primary mode is used, the integration of the systems will be based on published APIs provided by each of the systems and by a middleware backbone provided either through one of the EAI vendors or as a component in one of the systems comprising the OSS.

Although there are examples of all three integration paradigms within the OSS, there is a clear effort within the OSS to build integration as a *decoupled distributed system*. This is especially true for the integrated SLA model. One of the distinguishing features of the integrated SLA model is that it requires integration and collaboration between systems at all levels of the Telecommunications Operations Map (TOM). These systems do not live in exactly the same environment, they do not operate in the same timeframes, and they represent domain entities differently. A tightly coupled model cannot work.

One point that makes this obvious is the issue of transaction management. A service implemented by one system and used by another system is providing functionality as well as transaction management. Any integration solution that requires the caller to manage a transaction that is really occurring within the system implementing the service makes integration very difficult and makes for point-to-point stovepipe interfacing. An integration paradigm that is based on each system being responsible for its own transaction bracketing makes loose integration much easier.

CORBA

The Object Management Group (OMG) is the world's largest and most notable software consortium. The OMG was founded to work within the software industry to provide an open architecture to support multivendor, global, heterogeneous networks of object-based software components. The Object Management Architecture (OMA) Guide was published as an architecture to serve as the foundation for the development of detailed specifications and infrastructure and to form the future of object-based systems. The OMA defines many components that together enable the implementation of the OMG's vision. The most important architectural piece defined in the OMA, and essentially the basis for CORBA, is the *object request broker* (ORB).

Object Request Brokers

The OMA revolves around the object request broker (ORB). The ORB is the facilitator for sending and receiving messages between different components and objects. Other important ingredients of the OMA are *object services*, *common facilities*, and *application objects*. Object services provide low-level *system*-type services that are necessary for developing applications, such as object persistence, transaction capabilities, and security. Common facilities provide higher-level services that are semantically closer to the application objects, such as document management, mailing facilities, and printing facilities.

Object Services

As mentioned, the ORB is the most central component in the CORBA architecture. It provides the common ground for all object interaction, and it does that in a location-independent and platform-neutral manner. Yet the ORB does not provide enough substance for application programmers to use it for developing applications. This substance is provided by *object services*, also known as CORBAServices (COS). Here are some of the services defined in the CORBA architecture:

Naming service. Allows lookup of CORBA objects by name.

Event service. Facilitates asynchronous communication between CORBA objects.

Object transaction service (OTS). Enables CORBA objects to perform transactions. This service has a lower layer that implements the mechanics of transactions and a high-level interface for defining the scope and boundaries of transactions.

Concurrency control service. Allows multiple clients to interact with a single resource concurrently, via locks.

Interface Definition Language

The ORB needs to act as a bridge between different components, implemented in different programming languages and running on different environments. In order to allow such diverse components to communicate, the ORB needs to translate the various object models used by the different components into a uniform representation. A uniform representation is required (as opposed to sets of translation mechanisms between pairs of languages) since CORBA was intended to be ubiquitously available and support interoperability among a large set of programming languages.

The uniform object model for CORBA is implemented through the OMG's Interface Definition Language (IDL). This language defines in a uniform manner the services offered by objects. Client programs can use the IDL as the basis for their object invocations. Object implementations need to comply with the definitions of the IDL, implementing the methods defined in the interfaces. Separating the definition from the object implementation provides clear separation between object definition and implementation, and makes the object definition portable and language neutral.

It is important to note that the IDL is not used for writing code; rather it is used only for specifications. In other words, neither client code nor object implementation is written in IDL. The object specification is provided in IDL, and the client code can use the IDL specification to perform calls in its native programming language. The client can make such calls because the IDL interfaces are mapped to the programming language.

Mapping from IDL to a concrete programming language involves the creation of stubs on the client side and skeletons on the server side. *Stubs* are methods implemented in a specific programming language that act as a proxy for the CORBA object. The client code may call these stubs to initiate invocations transparently, even when the real object is remote and implemented in a different programming language. When an invocation takes place, the object implementation skeleton for the invoked object is activated. This is the *skeleton* that was created as a result of mapping the IDL to the object implementation's programming language. The mapping defines an empty skeletal implementation of the object, and it is the job of the object developer to provide a full implementation in the native programming language.

Mapping of the IDL to concrete programming languages such as C++ or Java includes mapping of all the following elements:

- Data types
- Constants
- Object references
- Object attributes
- Object method signatures
- Exceptions

Storing and Retrieving Information

In CORBA there are two repositories used for storing and retrieving information. The *interface repository* holds representations of the IDL definitions. This information is used extensively by the ORB, for example, for performing type checking and method signature checking, or for parameter marshalling. The *implementation repository* maintains object implementations (for example, Java class files for objects implemented in Java). The implementation repository does not have a standardized definition in CORBA—it is specific to an operating environment.

Invoking an Object

In order for a CORBA client to make an invocation of an object, the client must hold an object reference, allowing it to activate operations for this object. Such object references in CORBA are opaque, allowing CORBA to achieve the objective of location transparency: The client code has no information regarding the location of the object implementation, the language used to implement it, or any other details about the implementation. It has only a specification for an operation request that is part of the interface. The ORB delivers invocations made by the client to the serving object.

The actual handling of invocations can be done in one of two ways. *Static invocations* are used in case the service interface was defined in advance and this interface was available as IDL at the time the client code was developed.

In this case, client code invokes stub code locally, and this invocation translates into a remote invocation mediated by the ORB. On the receiving side, the skeleton code is invoked to serve the request.

If no IDL interface was available at compile time, it is possible to use *dynamic invocation*, via CORBA's Dynamic Invocation Interface (DII). With dynamic invocations, a request is constructed at run time without the use of IDL stubs. This runtime construction allows a client to directly specify an object, an operation, and a set of parameters and invoke this request. The DII is common to all objects and all operations, and does not make use of the stub routines generated for each operation in each interface. Information regarding the parameters and the operation itself is usually acquired from the interface repository. Figure 7.2 shows the schematic outline of a CORBA invocation.

Object Request Broker Interoperability and TCP/IP

Since different systems in the OSS embed different ORBs, interoperability between ORBs is critical. The *General Inter-ORB Protocol* (GIOP) is an ORB interoperability protocol that can be mapped onto any connection-oriented transport layer. In GIOP, each request is associated with a connection. The General Inter-ORB Protocol assumes that the connection is reliable, that it maintains message ordering, and that it provides some form of delivery acknowledgment and connection-loss notification. Although GIOP is defined in a general manner, you might have noticed that TCP/IP meets all the required conditions. Thus the mapping of GIOP to TCP/IP, called the Internet Inter-ORB Protocol (IIOP), is quite natural.

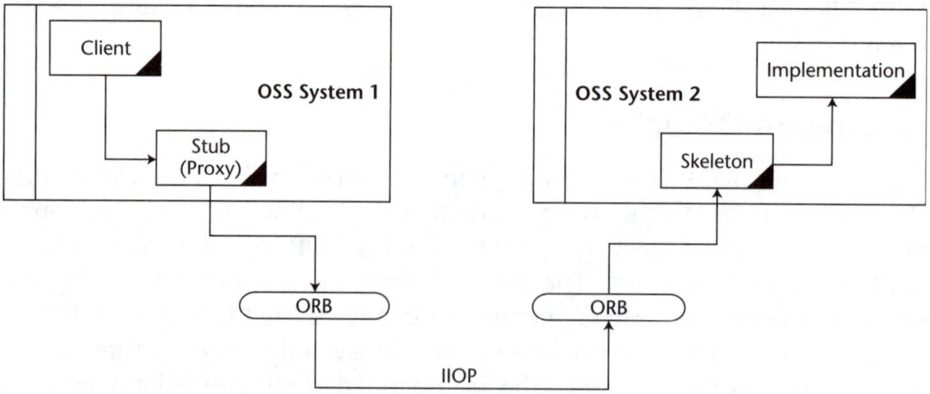

Figure 7.2 An outline of a CORBA invocation.

The GIOP specification consists of the Common Data Representation (CDR) and the GIOP message specifications. The CDR maps Interface Definition Language (IDL) types into a byte stream representation forming the GIOP transfer syntax. The message specification defines which set of messages may be exchanged between the participators in a session and how these messages are formatted. Common Data Representation defines encoding for IDL, data types, exceptions, object references (as Interoperable Object References, or IORs), and information relating to a request such as its context and principal (caller identification for security purposes).

The Internet Inter-ORB Protocol (IIOP) is a specific version of the GIOP mapped to the TCP/IP transfer protocol. Since TCP/IP is so ubiquitous with the proliferation of the Internet, IIOP is the prevailing flavor of GIOP. In fact, IIOP became the standard ORB protocol.

The telecommunication industry has been the most active as a market segment in adopting CORBA and implementing it both within products and as an architectural backbone for integration. We cannot think of a solution used within the OSS that does not support a CORBA interface. Some solutions have gone to the extreme of making CORBA *the* interface layer, so that APIs are defined in IDL and all of the functionality of the system is exposed using CORBA.

Although the use of CORBA has definitely served the telecommunications industry well and helped providers integrate systems within their OSS, CORBA is limited in its capabilities. CORBA requires that systems communicating over an ORB be fairly tightly coupled. The OSS architecture, on the other hand, and the systems required to manage integrated SLAs must be built up as a decoupled distributed system. For example, one cannot assume that object references need to be maintained from one system to the other. From this perspective, providers and Independent Software Vendors (ISVs) alike have recognized that CORBA cannot be relied upon as the integration backbone for the OSS. A new set of technologies—in the form of XML and Web services on the one hand and messaging middleware on the other—have been identified to better serve the OSS (and the New Generation OSS—NGOSS). This does mean, unfortunately, that the ISVs that have solely (or primarily) invested in CORBA as their interfacing layer have a lot of work to do.

Incidentally, CORBA is far from dead. In fact, it has been given a new lease on life for the next decade in the form of the J2EE's Enterprise Java Beans (EJBs). CORBA is the native invocation technology for Enterprise Java Beans. Regardless of the use of EJBs within the OSS, CORBA is still less appropriate for use in integrating loosely coupled systems.

Message-Oriented Middleware

The Aberdeen Group defines *middleware* as "a collection of enabling software, based on widely accepted industry standards, that creates bridges or conduits between and among a rich set of computing services found on disparate computing platforms and the applications that need easy access to those services. In addition to providing access to computing services, some middleware offerings enable disparate applications to communicate with one another." (Aberdeen research report on EAI - Feb 2001)

This broad definition covers quite a lot of ground, including application servers, Web servers, and database access methods. Another definition that we like because of its simplicity is that middleware is *software glue* that enables communication across heterogeneous platforms by providing services that let systems running on different machines and platforms interact across the network. In the broad categories of middleware, the category we are most interested in within the OSS is *messaging systems*, and *publish-subscribe systems* as a subcategory. We believe that a messaging and publish-subscribe paradigm is the right one to use when one is implementing an integrated SLA architecture.

Message-Oriented Middleware systems provide APIs for moving messages among disparate systems. They also manage the message queues, ensure that the messages are persistent, provide guaranteed delivery features, ensure that messages arrive at their destination, and carry out various additional tasks without which integrating applications through message flows would be a nightmare. The actual message structure is always flexible, and any data structure can be encapsulated within a message. These messages (or events as they are also often called) are most often defined using a metadata layer that ensures that the message structure can be queried and inspected so that the message can be inspected and extracted. Figure 7.3 shows a simple scheme in which two OSSs use a MOM infrastructure to communicate. In this example, alerts are discovered and analyzed by a network management layer and then are packaged up as a business event that is used by the SLA assurance system.

The two systems used in the example of Figure 7.3 are very dissimilar. They belong to different levels in the Telecommunications Management Network's structure, run by different groups in the organization, and they almost certainly come from different vendors. There is really no reason to make any form of assumption regarding the similarity of these systems. More likely, we should assume the following:

- The systems are written in different programming languages.
- The systems run on different operating systems.
- The communication path between the two systems cannot be guaranteed to be up all the time.

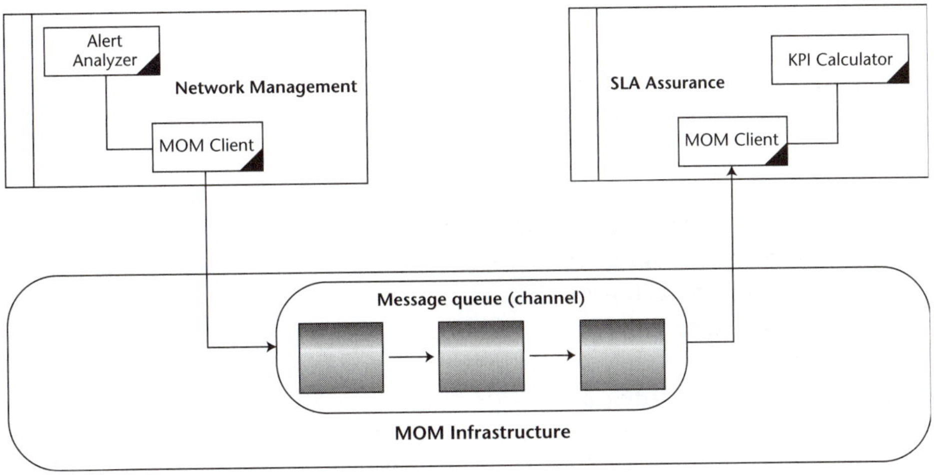

Figure 7.3 Message-Oriented Middleware-based integration.

- The downtime of these systems will not necessarily be coordinated.
- The data models will differ, and, more important, the operations exposed by one of these systems may not match the functional model that the other system encapsulates.
- Each of the systems might undergo software (and therefore possibly functional) upgrades at different schedules.

Given these assumptions, RPC-based integration has drawbacks owing to the tight coupling required. For example, RPC-based integration would require both systems to be up when information needs to flow from one system to another. Since we cannot make this assumption (see points 3 and 4), the applications will have to implement the added complexity of caching the information and retrying the invocation until the other system is accessible.

Business Events

Message-Oriented Middleware is more suited to loosely coupled distributed system interaction, and therein lies its success within the OSS. All major players in the middleware market support this paradigm, including Vitria, TIBCO, MQSeries, WebMethods, and so forth. On the semantic side, MOM also has an advantage in that it promotes loosely coupled integration. Whereas RPC-based integration requires the parties to agree on the operation and signature that will be invoked, MOM defines an event that is fundamentally a data structure that is passed from one system to another. The difference seems slight, and, in fact, one can implement a business event paradigm using invocations (and as a friend keeps telling us—everything is just a bag of zeros and a bag of ones anyway). The fact remains that message-based integration architectures promote the notion of agreeing on events as opposed to operations. Events by nature are more stable than are operations, and the agreement on a business event is easier and more stable in the long run.

Figure 7.4 shows an example of how such a business event may be defined in a tool. The metadata for the events can be defined using tools as in the figure, using IDL as in Vitria, using UML as in Kabira, using XML, and so on. Note that, fundamentally, a business event is a recursive data structure—simple and straightforward (which is why it works so well).

Even at the semantic level, business-event-based integration provides better results than RPC-based integration. It is quite easy to create an event structure that is either a lowest common denominator that is useful for all systems participating in the information flow or a superset of all of these structures. Each system can then provide the data transformers using a set of tools that are usually also provided by the MOM vendor. An example is shown in Figure 7.5. The fact that the event structure can be dynamically changed so long as mandatory fields are maintained is of extreme importance.

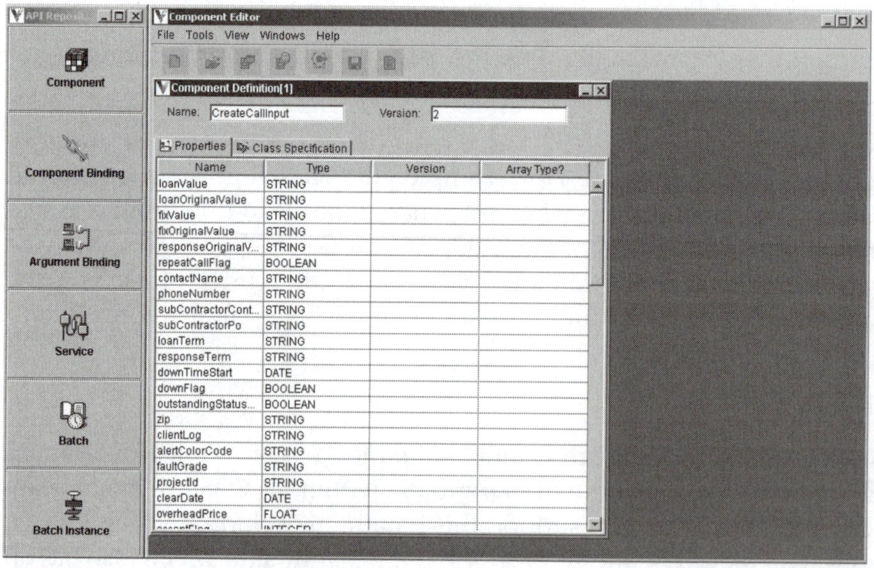

Figure 7.4 The business event editor.

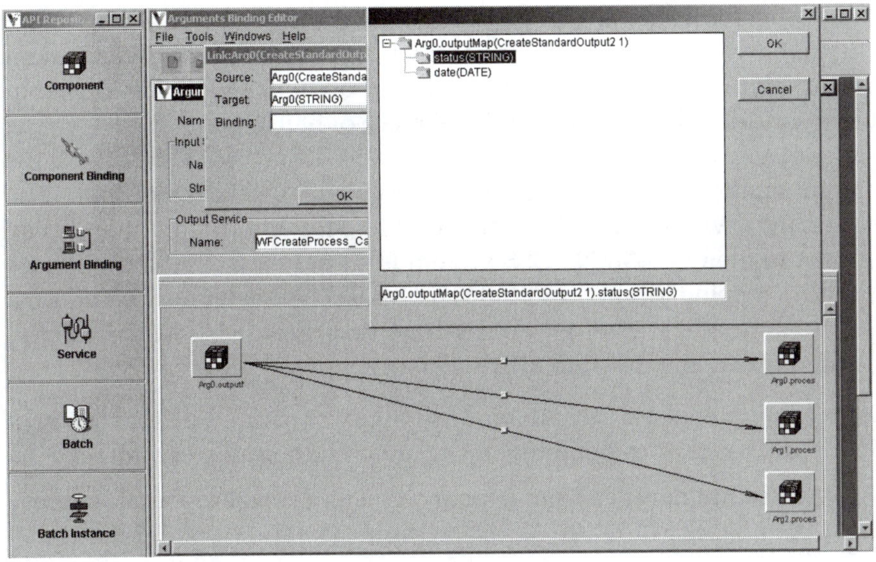

Figure 7.5 The data mapping (transformation) editor.

Publish-Subscribe

Finally, MOM-based systems naturally extend to a *publish-subscribe* metaphor. The main difference is that in a direct-messaging architecture a business event is sent from one system to another (through a queue or channel), whereas in a publish-subscribe architecture the producers and consumers of events do not have to be predefined. The added flexibility is provided through the concept that a system can be a producer (publisher) of events. Occurrences in the system that the architect deems important enough to publish to the outside world are published as an event on a common bus (or channel or queue). Subscribers register with the bus and declare what their interest is (that is, they subscribe to a channel or a type of event depending on the actual solution). When an event is published, all subscribers that have registered interest are notified and provided with the event information. This solution is even more robust than simple MOM since no up-front communication paths are required. If, for example, at a later point in time in the life of the OSS more features need to be added, there is a good chance that the incremental work required will be exactly that—incremental, as opposed to a complete reworking. Figure 7.6 shows the publish-subscribe scenario in which a new workforce management system is added to the OSS where a field technician needs to be dispatched in case of high-priority alerts on some critical piece of hardware.

The advantages of MOM have not been ignored by the TMF. In fact, the technical foundation of the NGOSS is a publish-subscribe concept. The NGOSS initiative within the TMF is intended to deliver a true plug-and-play environment to the OSS. An NGOSS system is characterized by the software entities within it being loosely coupled. The NGOSS framework is based on a business event paradigm over a MOM infrastructure, which satisfies the following criteria (as defined by the TMF):

- Software components can run independently of each other, and the operation of one does not interrupt or affect the running of another.
- Software components can run over any cluster configuration as long as they are networked.
- Software components may be added or removed without affecting the other components.
- Information communicated over the network is typically owned by the OSS as a whole as opposed to one software component or another.

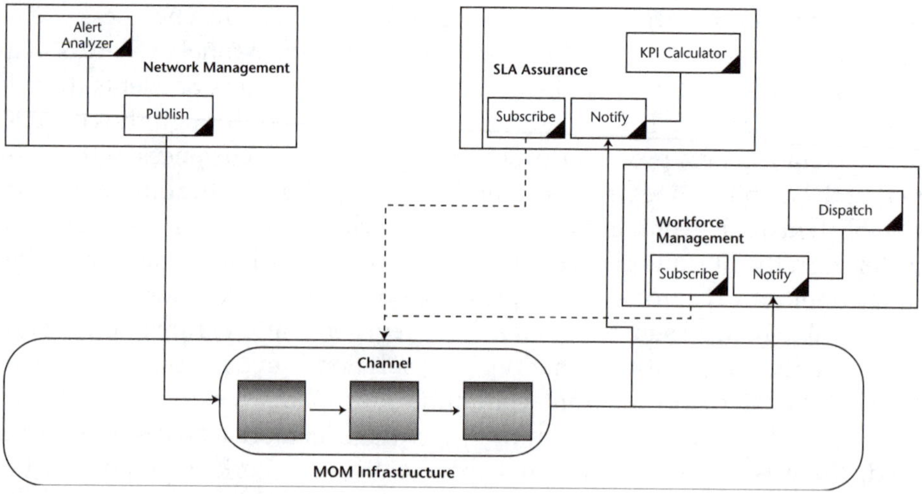

Figure 7.6 Publish-subscribe integration.

Extensible Markup Language

Extensible Markup Language (XML) is the new silver bullet—that is, the solution to all of IT's problems. It is a language that is being used today as the basis for integration and automation—the two keys to efficient deployment of complex information systems. In addition, it is perhaps the one, singular, most important infrastructure component for ebusiness since it is the key to allowing systems created by different vendors to talk to one another and share data. It is also the basis for *enterprise application integration* (EAI) systems such as Vitria, WebMethods, TIBCO, MQSeries, CrossWorlds, and more.

Everywhere you look you see vendors and developers scurrying to XML—and for good reason. Extensible Markup Language is a standard developed by the World Wide Web Consortium (W3C) to forward the notion of data sharing and formatting over the Web, and in general it supports the notion of tagged data in a way that preserves the semantics of the domain. Extensible Markup Language is an application (or subset) of the Standard Generalized Markup Language (SGML), but it is much simpler to deal with. It is more powerful than HTML, and, in fact, HTML can be seen as an application (or subset) of XML. Therefore XML is just the right combination of SGML's powerful expression options and HTML's simplicity. It is already slated to become the lingua franca of the Web. Obviously, this will take time, but we are quite certain that it will be a dominant player in the future of the Web. In addition, XML promises much in other areas, such as business-to-business applications, Electronic Data Interchange (EDI), document management, and so on.

Extensible Markup Language is the center of intensive research and development both within the W3C and throughout the industry. As a standard, it is the basis for many other standards that are being developed by the W3C—standards such as the eXtensible Linking Language (XLL), the Document Object Model (DOM), the Simple API for XML (SAX), and the eXtensible Style Language Transformation (XSLT). All of these specifications may be found in the W3C site at www.w3.org, as well as at other sites, such as OASIS and at the sites of pretty much every major vendor, such as IBM, Microsoft, Sun, Oracle, and so on.

Extensible Markup Language Document

Extensible Markup Language is a format in which documents are structured. Therefore the primary entity described by the XML standard is the XML document. Each XML document has a physical structure and is composed of entities. Each XML document has exactly one entity called the *root entity*; all other entities must belong to the root entity. Entities are defined with a start tag and an end tag, much like many elements in HTML and any language that is a derivative of SGML. When one entity is embedded in another, the start and end tags of the embedded entity must both reside within the start and end tags of the embedding entity. For example, if we want to describe a customer who has a name, an ID, and a phone number, we can describe the customer as follows:

```
<customer>
   <id>IWUDHFIREH</id>
   <name>Jane Doe</name>
   <phone>973-861-7533</phone>
</customer>
```

XML *embedded structures* are very common since real-world structures are recursive in nature. If, for example, the customer we are describing includes an address (which itself may be a structure that has an important semantic notion), then the describing XML may be as follows:

```
<customer>
   <id>IWUDHFIREH</id>
   <name>Jane Doe</name>
   <phone>973-861-7533</phone>
   <email></email>
   <fax/>
   <address>
      <street>9060 Palisades Ave.</street>
      <city>North Bergen</city>
      <zip>07047</zip>
      <state>NJ</state>
      <country>USA</country>
   </address>
</customer>
```

The most fundamental concept of XML (and where its name comes from) is that the tag set in XML is not fixed but rather extensible. What this means is that different applications of XML define their own tag set and in effect create a new language for describing elements in a certain domain. This is a very powerful notion, since it means that instead of trying to box every type of information using the same set of descriptive rules, we are now free to build languages that are well fitted for that particular domain. Still, if we invent a new language every time, we must make sure that the rules of the language are well known to anyone trying to use this XML document (in the same way that we need to learn grammar and vocabulary before we can start using a language). Extensible Markup Language introduced the notion of a *document type definition* (DTD). The DTD describes the rules of the tag set used by an XML document. It specifies the available tags and how they may or may not be put together. A typical XML document will then include DTD in the document so that readers of the document (especially tools and programs) know how to interpret and validate the document. Note that DTDs are not mandatory and many XML documents do not include DTDs. In fact, there is a movement away from DTDs, in which the description of the new language is itself phrased in XML.

Why Extensible Markup Language?

Integration and interoperability are certainly not new to the software industry—so why all the fuss about XML? The answer is not in the *how* but in the *what* (that is, not in how systems work together but rather in *what* is passed among the different systems).

Until recently, interoperability was viewed primarily as being related to communication and invocation paradigms. As already mentioned, interoperability does not usually address integration and interoperability at the semantic data level. Therefore, while interoperability solutions did provide a mechanism by which systems could talk to one another, these solutions did not define what these systems would talk about—and so they didn't.

Extensible Markup Language, on the other hand, goes one step in that direction. Extensible Markup Language is a language for describing data. Data takes the form of sets of values. For example, an address record in a database or some other data store could consist of the following data elements:

- 9060 Palisades Ave.
- North Bergen
- NJ
- 07047

Pretty simple, right? Well, this seemingly innocent example is a simple example of the primary reason for most of today's integration and interoperability problems. True, if you know it is an address you can probably figure out what the different pieces of information are. But what happens if you come from a very different culture? A culture with no street names—possibly only a village name. Or what if the actual data is in a language that is foreign to you—would you be able to decipher this or would you not know anything except that the record has four fields of data? Most important, what if you were a computer and didn't have the benefit of growing up with loving parents who taught you all about addresses—would you be able to understand and use this data? The answer is invariably *no*.

Enter XML. Extensible Markup Language simply states that a description should be placed around each piece of data. This descriptor (called a tag or a markup element) is not part of the data—it is a structural definition that can help us know what this piece of data represents. So in our simple example we can use the following tags:

```
<ADDRESS>
   <STREET>9060 Palisades Ave.</STREET>
   <CITY>North Bergen</CITY>
   <STATE>NJ</STATE>
   <ZIP>07047</ZIP>
</ADDRESS>
```

Now things are much clearer. First, if you were to come across this chunk of data (assuming you knew the XML rules), you would be able to understand what the whole record is—it is an *address*. You would also be able to make out what the individual segments are—after all, it's written right there. And most important, software that is XML-aware would also be able to understand this data. Moreover, even if that software represented addresses differently, conversions would be easy, and different systems could finally be made to work together.

At this point it should be clear to all that XML is simple—almost trivial. Much of today's integration platforms are based on the premise that XML is all that is required to solve the complex issues of application integration in the convoluted world of software. Two questions immediately come to mind in this context. First, how can such simple technology solve such a complex problem? Second, why only now?

The answer to the first question is that *only* a simple technology can solve such a complex problem! The inherent complexity of integration between OSSs is a result of the so-called real world:

- Operations Support Systems are large and provide a lot of functionality. They often have a monolithic self-contained design.
- Operations Support Systems live for a very long time (since the cost of replacing them is so high). Therefore different systems are often based on completely different technologies.
- Operations Support System integration involves organizational and responsibility-related issues—which are much more complex than purely technical issues.
- In order to run an OSS, many systems need to work together and share data.

Given this *base complexity*, any complexity introduced by technology (and specifically the technology aiming to provide the integration backbone) is immediately amplified proportionally to the organization's size. Therefore the technology *must* be simple—as is XML.

The answer to the second question is (as it seems always to be the case these days)—the Web. The Web provides a ubiquitous infrastructure for communicating between different systems and organizations as well as a backbone for delivering on the promise of distributed systems. The Web and the Internet are everyone's answer to the *how*. Although it is clear today that the real question has always been the *what*, computing professionals were always so preoccupied with the technical details and the mechanics of making things work and were not able to see past the *how* until that part was completely clear.

Document Type Definitions

Document Type Definitions are files that describe the structure of an XML document. One of the important features of XML is that it is self-describing. This trait is important because XML documents need to be shared among different people—the DTD allows a reader of an XML file to interpret what he or she is viewing, and it helps the creator of an XML file create something that can be well understood by others. Document Type Definitions define sets of constraints with which an XML file can be validated—it defines elements, attributes, and rules such as whether or not they are mandatory, whether or not there are defaults, and so on. The disadvantage of DTDs is that they do not provide nearly enough information about the XML structure to make XML truly self-explanatory.

The new trend in the industry is XML schemas. A schema is itself an XML file but one that describes the XML. An XML schema is a meta-data element that uses the flexibility of XML to provide a complete description of the XML it is being referenced from.

Document Object Model

The Document Object Model (DOM) is an API for HTML and XML documents. It provides a programmatic paradigm to provide access to the objects represented by the document. Interfaces are provided for building documents and navigating documents and entities within documents, view and edit attributes, and practically anything that might have to do with a document. The Document Object Model is also a standard defined and supported by the W3C. By promoting it as a standard, the W3C wants to assure a standard API for managing XML and HTML documents that will allow developers to build portable code and further promote XML.

Each XML (and HTML) document can be parsed and broken down into a hierarchical structure of objects. This is fundamentally what DOM does; it defines how forests (sets of trees) are created from XML documents (and vice versa). Since the tree structures are objects defined by DOM, an API is provided for manipulating these trees, and through it, the document. Since DOM is primarily an API for manipulating these objects, it is phrased in CORBA IDL. Since IDL is a specification language that can then be mapped to multiple programming languages, the DOM APIs can be processed to create sets of libraries in many programming languages, all the while maintaining a single consistent API.

Simple Application Program Interface for Extensible Markup Language

The Document Object Model provides the capabilities for processing any XML document. You, as the programmer, can use the DOM APIs to build the tree structures for the XML document and then traverse the trees to manipulate the elements, extract information, or do any other kinds of processing. Still, the process can sometimes be highly inefficient. For example, if the XML document represents all of the contacts that the company has, the XML will certainly be a very large document. If we need to parse this document, build the trees and then traverse them, we might be in for a long wait. If we really need to go through all of the elements in the XML document, we have no choice, and the solution provided by DOM is probably as efficient as any other. But if all we need to do is some processing on a subset of the elements (and potentially a much smaller set), then there is another, better alternative.

The Simple API for XML (SAX) is an event-based API for processing XML documents. Being event-based means that SAX provides a way for an application developer to express interest in certain elements without requiring all elements to be pre-built before application-level processing begins. The benefit of this feature is that structures that are not necessary will not be built; instead a callback into the application code will be called whenever any interesting event occurs. Simple API for XML is not only much more efficient when we need to process a subset of the elements, it can also be a useful tool if we need to process very large XML documents. In this case, even if we do need to process all elements, we may run into memory problems because building so many objects can be very memory-intensive. Simple API for XML, on the other hand, does not need to build anything; processing is done in *real time* as opposed to in a number of passes.

Using SAX is very simple. It involves two stages. First we need to use the SAX APIs to define what we are interested in. For example, we may say that we are interested in the contact names only or (in a larger context) in the contacts for the contracts that should be renewed this month. Once we've defined our interest, we can go ahead and fire up the parser that will parse the XML document. As the parser goes through the XML document, it comes across the element tags and generates events (for example, START ELEMENT CONTRACT, END ELEMENT CONTRACT, START ELEMENT CONTACT, and so on). Some of these events will be of no interest to us, so nothing will happen (the parser will continue with its job). When an event occurs that we have expressed interest in, the event will cause the application callback to be called, and processing of that particular element can begin.

Extensible Style Language Transformation

Extensible Style Language Transformation (XSLT) is a subset of XSL (actually half of it is—the second half is the formatting language) that defines a language for transforming XML documents into other XML documents. Extensible Style Language Transformation is very important in the grand scheme of XML. Extensible Markup Language documents are based on a certain tag set defined by the creator of the XML document. It will often be the case that two parties who want to exchange data in the form of XML documents do not completely agree on the tag set. In such an instance it is often feasible to perform a mapping between the two XML tag sets using XSLT.

In the context of OSS integration, XSLT is immensely important. All of the middleware vendors have an XML interface by now. This is also true of many of the product vendors in the OSS. Unfortunately, most vendors have their own XML structures, and there is no standardization. So, while all of these endpoints can accept XML, transformations at the XML level must be performed.

Extensible Markup Language transformations are precisely what XSLT is best used for. By applying XSLT sheets to XML created by one such endpoint, we can easily flow the information into the next endpoint. Hence, the data transformation solution in an XML-based integration scheme is based on XSLT.

Extensible Style Language Transformation is itself an application of XML that defines a tag set that allows for the definition of transformation rules. These rules define how a source tree constructed from an XML document is processed into a result tree that can then be used to generate the resulting XML document. Each transformation rule has a pattern and a template. The pattern is matched up with the source tree to identify the constructs that are identified by this rule—the base for the transformation. Once the pattern has been matched, the template is applied to the source tree to create an element of the result tree. Obviously all of this activity is performed recursively, so while the template is being applied, other transformation rules may also be involved. Templates can be quite involved, and XSLT has a lot of expressive power when it comes to the templates—almost anything is possible, but unfortunately not simple.

Extensible Style Language Transformation Rules

Each rule has a pattern. This pattern defines when the rule is valid and can be applied to the source tree to create the result tree. Patterns have expressions that are based on the XPath specification. These expressions select the node that is appropriate for processing. For example, an expression can include conditions on nodes (for example, the type of node), on attributes of the node, on ancestors of nodes, on descendants of nodes, and any combination of the above.

Once an expression has been evaluated, causing the template to be matched, processing of the template begins. When the expression is matched, a current node is always identified. This node is the one matched by the pattern. All processing of the template is based on this node. For example, if we include a directive to traverse all subnodes, then this directive will apply to the node matched by the expression.

The following code segment shows a (very) simple XSLT sheet. Here we define some simple processing instructions— in terms of both the patterns we try to match as well as what we do when a pattern is found. The example processes an XML file and creates an HTML output that is convenient to view using a Web browser. Therefore, right after we match the root node (match="/") we output an <HTML> tag. Then we start processing each message element.

```
<?xml version="1.0"?>
<xsl:stylesheet xmlns:xsl="http://www.w3.org/1999/XSL/Transform"
version="1.0">
<!-- Root template - start processing here -->
<xsl:template match="/">
 <html>
   <xsl:for-each select="message">
<!-- *********************** exceptionOutput
**************************-->
   <xsl:for-each select="exceptionOutput">
     <head>
     <title>Service failure</title>
       </head>
       <body BGCOLOR="silver">
            <xsl:value-of select="exMessage"/>
       </body>
   </xsl:for-each>
<!-- *********************** end exceptionOutput
**************************-->
<!-- *********************** output **************************-->
   <xsl:for-each select="output">
    <xsl:choose>
    <!--********** output = 0 ***************-->
      <xsl:when test="outputMap=0">
     <head>
     <title>Returned successfully</title>
```

```
        </head>
        <body BGCOLOR="silver">
              Returned successfully; serial created
        </body>
       </xsl:when>
     <!--********** end output = 0 ***************-->
     <!--********** output != 0 ***************-->
       <xsl:when test="outputMap!=0">
      <head>
      <title>Servise failure</title>
        </head>
        <body BGCOLOR="silver">
              Service failure
        </body>
       </xsl:when>
    <!--********** end output != 0 ***************-->
    </xsl:choose>
    </xsl:for-each>
 <!-- *********************** end output **************************-->
    </xsl:for-each>
  </html>
 </xsl:template>
 </xsl:stylesheet>
```

Extensible Style Language Transformation is a complex language and one that takes a long time to fully understand and learn. The interested reader is referred to www.w3.org/TR/WD-xslt, where more details can be found.

Web Services

The notion of a new model for running business applications in a cooperative manner is not a new one. It has been discussed in theory for many years within academic circles. But today's technological world has brought us to a point where a new model is doable—and doable within the mainstream. These are very exciting times for anyone involved in building the new world. We are actually in the midst of a technological change in the way in which decoupled systems are integrated and in the way new business features are delivered to users. This new model is called *Web services*.

The Web services model revolves around functional elements that are accessible using standard Internet protocols. This model is, in a way, the marriage of the experience attained by the industry in component-based development and usage along with Web-based access and invocation and middleware integration systems. The basic ideas are not new; they are similar to various technologies we have grown accustomed to over the past 10 years. But the Web services model is unique in two respects.

The Web services model is natively based on Internet protocols and therefore is optimally suited to make use of the ubiquitous connectivity of the Internet—including any networking paradigm within the OSS. It can deliver on the promise of all that is involved with tapping into a practically endless availability of information, functionality, and computing power. Since all OSSs pride themselves on having Web-enabled offerings, the use of the Web services model presents a new opportunity for systems integration within the OSS.

Miraculously, Web services are being supported by both the Microsoft camp and the non-Microsoft camp. This is the first time we can remember such a miracle happening.

The promise of the new Web services model is huge. For providers, Web services hold the promise of low cost and quick deployment, highly functional systems, continuously improving systems, flexibility, and extensibility. For solution and OSS providers this new model promises more revenue opportunities and lower development costs. And, most important, for the infrastructure vendors Web services hold the ultimate promise of new license revenue. So everyone is on board.

The Three Elements of Web Services

The elements required to support a Web services model are actually fairly simple. Web services are functional elements deployed somewhere and accessed over the Internet. For Web services, there is no limit to the programming language, the functional element it can be written in, or the operating platform it can be deployed on. Therefore the following three elements are required for delivering the promise of the Web services model:

1. A standard way to represent data and messages or invocations that activate such functional elements
2. A standard way to describe what a Web service does in a way that is usable by the user of a service (typically another functional element that makes use of the Web service)
3. A standard way to discover providers of Web services

Fortunately, all three elements are already here. The three technologies that together deliver on the promise of Web services are the Simple Object Access Protocol (SOAP), the Web Services Description Language (WSDL), and the Universal Description, Discovery, and Integration (UDDI) mechanism. Interestingly enough, all three are applications of XML, proving without a doubt that XML is the lingua franca of the Web.

The real benefits of Web services are best realized in a loosely coupled model—precisely the environment of all OSSs (and the NGOSS). For Web services to work, HTTP must be the underlying protocol, and XML must be the language of choice. This fact has been acknowledged by all—including IBM and Microsoft. (Yes—both are *cooperating* and are the main drivers for the standards being formulated for Web services.) As atypical as it is—the cooperation between IBM and Microsoft on a technological basis gives anything that is produced a tremendous amount of clout, and the result is widespread industry acceptance. For example, many other vendors are already buying into the IBM/Microsoft lead initiative, including Ariba, BEA, HP, Iona, SAP, and Software AG. A recent breakthrough in the acceptance of these standards and in the fight against fragmentation is Sun's announced support for SOAP and UDDI as part of the Sun Open Network Environment (ONE) initiative. Analysts, too, are in agreement. In a research report issued by the Gartner Group in April 2001, analysts estimate that "IBM and Microsoft will exert leadership in defining Web services standards" with 0.8 probability.

The Simple Object Access Protocol

The Simple Object Access Protocol (SOAP) uses HTTP to carry messages that are formatted using XML. It provides a standard object invocation protocol built on Internet standards using HTTP as the transport layer and XML as the encoding layer. It is extensible in nature—both because it uses XML for the body as well as because of the approach it takes to the addition of headers—so that messages can evolve over time. The Simple Object Access Protocol therefore functions at the level of HTTP clients and servers. It does not care about operating systems, programming languages, and other such issues. Hence it can truly serve as the foundation for interoperability. Since SOAP is built on HTTP and XML—both simple technologies—it is quite simple, much more so than the previous generation of interoperability invocations such as CORBA and DCOM. The Simple Object Access Protocol also allows for messaging-type interaction where the *message payload* packaged as an XML document (the business event if you will) is wrapped by a header that defines routing attributes.

The Web Services Description Language

Once basic communication between disparate systems is available, we can start talking about Web services. Obviously SOAP provides the ability to make the invocation—but this is not enough for creating the fabric and essence of Web services. The next step in the standards process was the creation of the Web Services Description Language (WSDL) by IBM, Microsoft, and Ariba. Web Services Description Language defines an XML grammar for describing network services as collections of communication endpoints capable of exchanging messages. This includes both document-oriented and procedure-oriented s ervices (that is, it supports both MOM and RPC-type interaction). Web Services Description Language allows for defining both the abstract notion of the messages as well as protocol-specifics that are required in order to make communication possible. All of this is done without limiting message types, protocols, services, or anything else. With WSDL, one can define the endpoints of a system that are used for communicating, and these endpoints can be aggregated into collections that can be exported out to the world as Web services.

Universal Description, Discovery, and Integration

The last piece of the puzzle is Universal Description, Discovery, and Integration (UDDI), which was also developed by IBM, Microsoft, and Ariba. Successful ebusiness requires that businesses be able to discover each other, make their needs and capabilities known, and integrate services using different processes. The model that UDDI is meant to support is one in which a business can connect to discover and learn about other businesses, learn about capabilities, and continuously discover additional services and capabilities. Universal Description, Discovery, and Integration as an initiative defines what is required for supporting such business scenarios. Universal Description, Discovery, and Integration enables businesses to quickly, easily, and dynamically find and transact business with one another. It is all about having a means by which a business can describe its services and processes through the Internet and by which a business can dynamically discover and interact with other businesses via the Internet. Universal Description, Discovery, and Integration is, of course, also based on SOAP, XML, and HTTP. The actual functions supported by UDDI are described in the UDDI Programmer's API Specification—a document that defines a set of more than 30 SOAP messages that are used by both publishers of Web services information as well as those inquiring about the availability of various Web services. The SOAP messages defined by UDDI allow Web service providers to register themselves within UDDI registries, and allow Web service consumers to find providers of Web services and match them with specific requirements.

The TeleManagement Forum's System Integration Map

Having dealt quite a bit with technical integration, data representation, and transformations, let's go back to semantic integration. As we already mentioned at the beginning of this chapter, semantic integration holds within it the prospect of bringing the most benefit to the OSS. In line with this, semantic integration is also very difficult to achieve and requires an agreement on the essence of what the entities are, and not only on how the communication is to be performed.

The only organization that has such a focus, enough clout, and a good community process is the TMF. As part of the TMF process, the Systems Integration Map (SIM) specifies a high-level model of *coarse-grain* components organized as a set of domains in areas of interest to the provider—and among them many of the components necessary to build an integrated SLA model within the OSS. This map does not go into a deep description of the components. It defines only the high-level functional responsibilities of the respective components and domains. Therefore it cannot be used to form data structures for the events used in an event-based integration architecture (which is what we would have wished for). Still, it can and should serve as a guideline and as a tool for validating that the integration solution put in place makes sense. It is therefore an important part of the integrated SLA model, and in the following paragraphs we provide a brief overview of the semantic definitions. This is not a complete account of the SIM; please refer to the System Integration Map documents published by the TMF.

The domains described by the SIM are as follows:

- The customer domain
- The invoicing domain
- The sales/marketing domain
- The portfolio domain
- The product domain
- The network service domain
- The equipment domain
- The technology domain
- The work domain
- The business management domain

Of these domains the ones that are most important in the context of the integrated SLA model are

- The *customer domain,* including the handling of the customer contracts and customer data. This domain includes all functions for managing agreements and SLAs and measuring QoS performance against those agreements.
- The *invoicing domain,* which encompasses all actions related to the invoicing of customers, collection of payments, credit management, and, among other things, credits, collections, and adjustments owing to SLAs.
- The *product domain,* managing the instances of products and services supplied to customers throughout the products' full life cycle. This

is a crucial domain because it includes service provisioning, trouble management, order management, service performance testing, and service configuration.

- The *network service domain,* which includes the network-level data and monitoring for service performance, maintenance, and restoration.
- The *work domain,* which is crucial in ensuring that the way the provider schedules and dispatches work will ensure adherence to SLAs.

Summary

Any operation that is based on many systems is heavily dependent on integration. The OSS is no exception, and providers require sophisticated integration methods to ensure that SLAs can be used to drive the business. In essence, what providers need is a *glue layer* on which the systems can reside. Contrary to popular belief, integration is not enough. The other important element is work-flow automation, which is the subject of the next chapter.

CHAPTER

8

Work-Flow Automation

Automation is one of the most important foundation points of an integrated Service Level Agreement (SLA) architecture. Automation is about building an information system that manages and performs handoffs automatically that in traditional systems would be manually processed. Work-flow automation reduces costs; ensures better quality, reliability, and predictability; and allows for tracking and auditing.

Managing Business Processes

Telecommunications providers are among the largest companies in the world, providing a very wide range of services to huge communities. Their offerings are diverse, change very quickly, and are technologically intensive. The customer base is massive and the organizational structures are complex. Given all of this, it is no surprise that a telco's organization and operations include a large set of complex business processes. These processes cover the end-to-end operations of the telco and primarily the Operations Support System (OSS). In many ways, the business processes that model the telco's operations are the backbone of the provider's business. Without such business processes to use as a map, the provider would be in a total state of chaos.

Manual Work Flow

Business processes map out what needs to be done, by whom, when, and with whose collaborative assistance. There are many ways to implement a business process. First, you need to analyze possible processes and define the best-practice process. Then you can model the business process and create a set of documents, guidelines, and instructions. There are two possible next steps after you have created the models for the business processes that are to drive operations. The first possibility is to leave the processes as a set of documents and implement the processes by educating the organization—creating manual handoffs between various people and systems that are part of the business process. The advantage of this manual method is that it is relatively simple to carry out and involves no IT work.

The disadvantages of the manual method are obvious. It relies on manual work and therefore on people adhering to instructions. It requires more work from the individuals who need to perform the handoffs, and it is very sensitive to *process leaks*—usually owing to manual errors. For a number of reasons, the manual method does not scale—it cannot handle the process management for very large numbers of people. This is perhaps the most important reason that manual process management is not an option for the telecommunications provider. Another disadvantage is that there is no way to monitor and easily track individual flows and/or all processes, there is no easy way to handle escalations and alarms when a process is in jeopardy, and more.

Since a service provider must offer efficient service, the operations of the provider must be based on automated business processes. In our view of the OSS, business process automation is a fundamental axiom. It is also a must-have for implementing the integrated SLA model. We believe the only way to drive efficiency and ensure that SLA commitments are met is to base the business processes on the SLA definitions. We cannot stress enough how important this point is. We believe that the right way to implement an SLA-based business is not to have business processes that periodically check whether SLAs are maintained. The right way is to have SLAs drive the business process. Business processes should be modeled and built with SLAs as part of the model itself. Thus the business processes must be automated. Business processes need to be modeled, automated, and managed centrally based on SLA definitions—meaning that the entire operation of the provider is inherently based on the SLAs and that all of the OSS is aligned toward SLA adherence. From an implementation standpoint, this means that the business rules defining the transitions within the process flows are also based on SLA assurance metrics.

NOTE The only way to drive efficiency and ensure that SLA commitments are met is to base the business processes on the SLA definitions.

Work-Flow Management Systems

Business process automation is achieved through the use of a work-flow management system. Simply put, *work-flow management* is a technology that makes possible the automation of processes involving combinations of human- and machine-based activities.

The more complex a business process is, the more an organization can benefit from its automation through a work-flow management system. Complexity is not always a good thing, and overly complex business processes can sometimes mean that a better way can be found to do things. But having a complex process does not mean that the model is incorrect; life truly is complex. The complexity of a business process can be mapped onto two dimensions—the number of activities and conditionals that exist in the process and the number of organizational boundaries the process needs to cross. The more organizations a process touches, the more complex it is. Work-flow management deals with both of these dimensions and is suited to handle business processes that span several areas in a company as well as parties that the company interacts with—parties including customers, suppliers, subcontractors, and so on.

Work flow has become a dominant theme in information systems and in the OSS. It has become so dominant that every vendor in the OSS claims to have work-flow technology. Unfortunately, *work flow* is a term that is often misused and sometimes not fully understood. While introducing the concept of SLA-based work-flow automation we will also strive to define work-flow automation and provide a detailed blueprint of what a work-flow management system really looks like. Work-flow automation is so important that in our opinion a deep understanding is mandatory for building a good OSS and for building SLA management.

Work-Flow Definitions

Work flow is not a new concept. It has been around for over 20 years and has even been well formalized by the Work-flow Management Coalition (WfMC). The WfMC was founded in 1993 and is a nonprofit consortium that includes more than 200 vendors, customers, and users whose mission is to promote the use of work flow through the establishment of standards for software terminology, interoperability, and connectivity between work-flow products. The following definitions appear in the WfMC glossary:

Business process. A set of one or more linked procedures or activities that collectively realize a business objective or policy goal, normally within the context of an organizational structure defining functional roles and relationships.

Work flow. The automation of a business process, in whole or in part, during which documents, information, or tasks are passed from one participant to another for action, according to a set of procedural rules.

Work-flow management system. A system that defines, creates, and manages the execution of work flows through the use of software, running on one or more work-flow engines, which is able to interpret the process definition, interact with work-flow participants, and, where required, invoke appropriate IT tools and applications.

Three Elements of Work Flow

Work flow automates processes in instances where information and tasks are passed between participants according to a defined set of business rules. *Automates* is the key word here—the essence of work flow is the replacement of manual business process management with an automated system. Such a system is called a work-flow management system. In order to support such automation, a work-flow management system needs to support three categories of features:

Build. A work-flow management system needs to provide tools with which a business analyst can design and assemble a process definition made up of the activities that need to be performed, the roles that participate in the work flow, and the flow between the activities based on a set of business rules.

Process engine. A work-flow management system must include a runtime engine that manages the processes and walks each process through the set of activities as specified by the process definition. The engine needs to perform the actions and needs to evaluate the business rules to determine how the flow proceeds.

Runtime user interface. A work-flow management system must include user interfaces through which people can interact with the system. The work flows modeling the business processes almost always include a large set of activities that require human intervention; the system must therefore manage a set of screens to allow this. In addition, the process engine should have a user interface component to allow users to monitor and control the engine and the processes running within the engine.

Since work flow has become such an important concept and every vendor seems to have a work-flow system, there is a lot of confusion as to what it really means to be able to implement work-flow automation. The danger is that the hype and misnomers used by various vendors will cause work-flow automation to be overlooked entirely. To avoid this pitfall one should distinguish between work flow and work-flow automation—these terms are not synonymous. Many products have work-flow features but are not work-flow automation systems. Examples include the various document routing, document management, and document collaboration systems. Applications that route documents using email, shared repositories, and data stores can claim to support work flow simply because they can be used to flow work from one person to another.

The same caution is true for Enterprise Application Integration (EAI) systems. Since EAI and middleware systems are often used to route data from one system to another and perform invocations, message passing, and data transformation, they claim to route work from one system to another. But business related concepts—such as work—is not like routing data. The last example includes provisioning systems that manage work queues and allow tasks to be moved from one work queue to another. None of these systems falls into the category of work-flow automation. The distinction is akin to that between the simple Paint application and desktop publishing systems or between Notepad and a word processor. One last word of caution: Lotus Notes is not a work-flow management system. Neither is Microsoft Exchange, Vitria BusinessWare, or Metasolv TBS. All these applications may have work-flow features, but they cannot be used to manage and automate business processes.

CAUTION **Work-flow features and work-flow automation are not the same. Beware of products that tout work-flow features.**

The Process Editor

Process automation (work-flow automation) starts out during the design phase of a system. The business processes that are to be used in order to run the OSS or the integrated SLA model need to be translated from a human language into computer language. We don't mean that we need to write machine code here; what we mean is that we need to have a way to paraphrase business concepts in a way that can be used by the work-flow engine.

All work-flow products come with a process editor—a tool that allows you to build the process flows. In fact, the process editor is one of the identifiers of a true work-flow system—every work-flow system must have one. The concept behind automating the business process is to build the business process within an information system and support the ability to continue tweaking the automated process to match exactly how we want the business to be implemented by the various systems. In order to build automation into the information system, the process must be defined and maintained within the work-flow system and cannot be hard-coded into any of the systems being glued together in the course of automating the business processes.

Process Templates and Tokens

Process editors are used to build process templates. A *process template* is the structural definition of the process that needs to be activated at run time. This template defines the *type* of work flow and is used at run time as the basis upon which process instances are created. The template is the definition of the state machine—the steps and the transitions between the steps—that form the process. The process editor allows us to build the templates that are used by the process engine at run time. Although the full terms are *process template* and *process instance,* we will often just refer to *process* and assume that it is clear from the context whether we are discussing the template or the instance.

Process editors take many forms. Primitive work-flow systems will have a text-based editor through which processes can be designed. More advanced systems have a visual tool for allowing processes to be built and modified. An example of a visual tool is shown in Figure 8.1. The tool has two primary areas—the canvas and the palette. The canvas area allows us to edit a process. More than one canvas may be open within the process editor, as shown in Figure 8.2; each canvas represents a single process template.

Process templates consist of a definition of a state machine. The state machine has activities that must be performed by the engine at run time and transition rules that define the business rules according to which the process progresses. In addition to the steps and transition rules, every process has a *token.* The token is a data structure that can be accessed by all steps in the process. From an implementation perspective the token is usually implemented

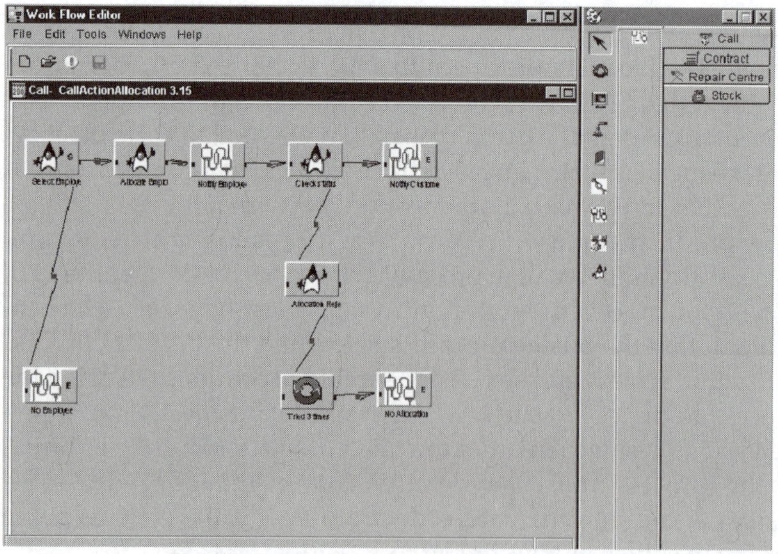

Figure 8.1 An example process editor tool.

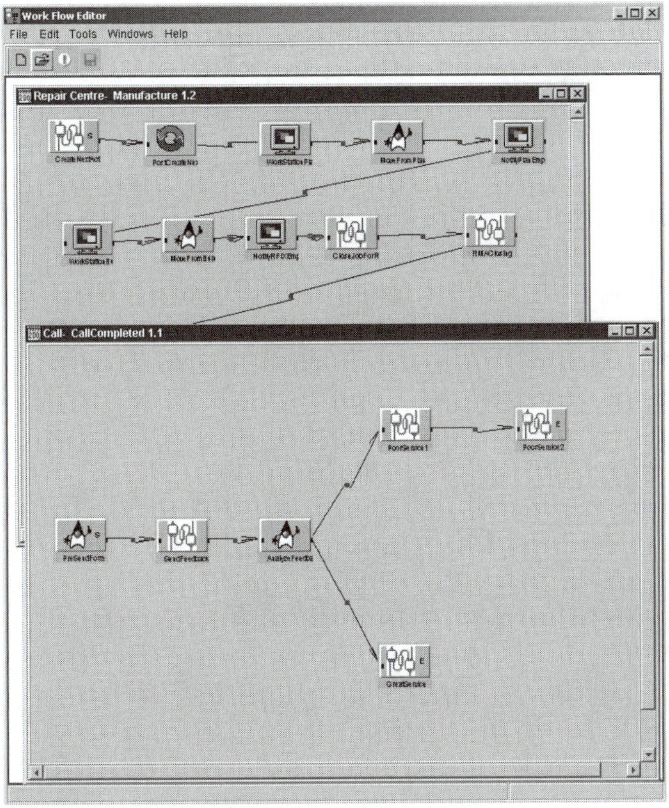

Figure 8.2 Editing multiple process templates.

as a dictionary that includes name-value pairs. In advanced work-flow systems, the values can be objects (or at least complex data structures) as opposed to only primitive elements. Conceptually the token is the context that is the common thread throughout the process instance at run time. The token allows data to be passed from one step to another, and most transition rules are based on data in the token or data that can be derived from objects in the token. Figure 8.3 shows an example of a token in a process template. The token editor allows us to edit the token definition. Each entry in the token dictionary has a name (this name is later used to query and update information in the token), the type of the object in the token, whether this entry is mandatory, and whether it is the main object in the token.

As an example, in the context of the integrated SLA model we may want to have an escalation process in the case where a ticket is open on a case for which a fix-time SLA exists. In such a case the ticket will most probably be within the token as well as the SLA or the customer (the customer can be referenced from the ticket and the SLA from the customer).

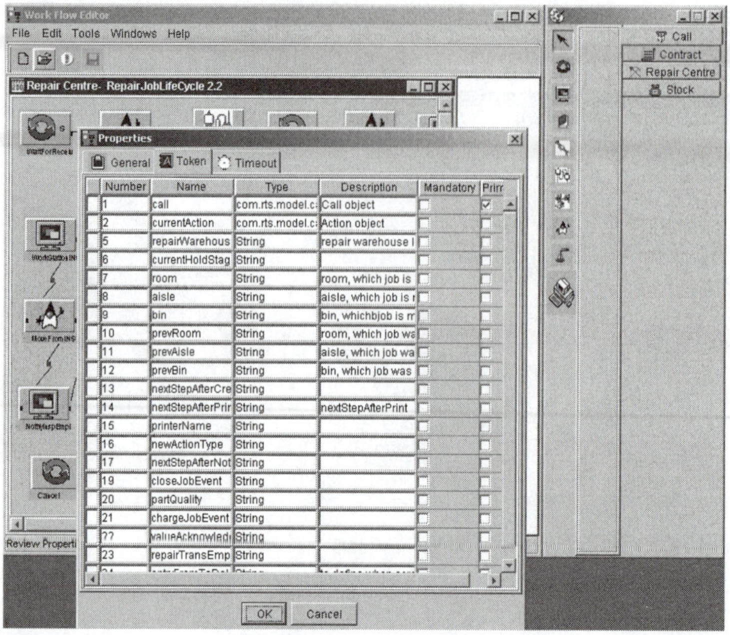

Figure 8.3 The process token.

Process Steps

Steps are added to a process template by dragging them off the template. The template includes a set of step types. Each step type represents a type of activity that may be required. An example is a functional activity with which we invoke an application function. Another example is a notification function through which we either send email, send a page, or use some other kind of notification method to send a message to someone. Unfortunately, while each work-flow system includes a set of step types on the palette that represent a common set of capabilities, there is little standardization in the step types, and each work-flow system has a slightly different set of step types.

Properties

Once a step has been dragged from the palette onto the canvas, the attributes of the step need to be defined. The step type plays the first part in determining what will happen in a step—but this is far from enough. The attributes are mandated by the simple fact that if we have 10 application function steps, we would usually want each step to perform a different function. In such a case

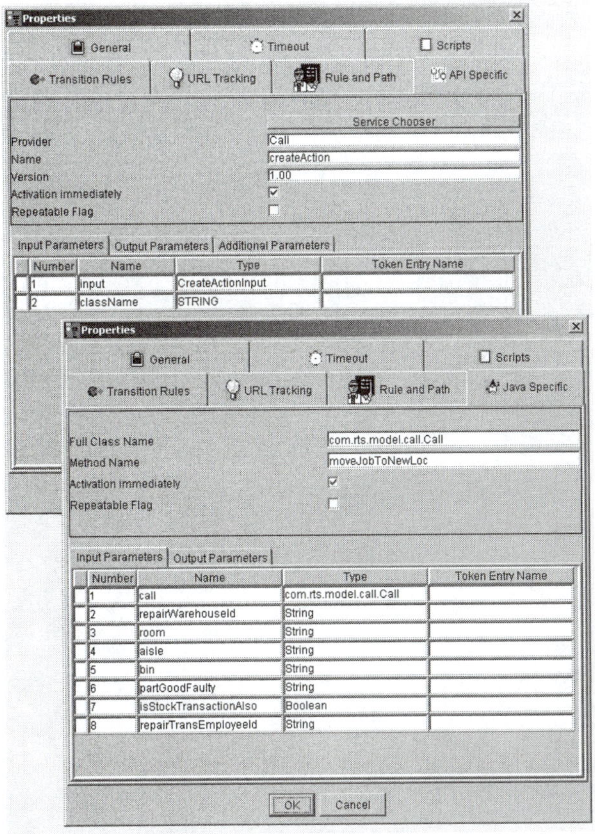

Figure 8.4 Step property sheets.

the attributes define the actual functional element that will be invoked within this step. Figure 8.4 shows an example of two property sheets through which we may define the attributes of steps.

As can be seen in Figure 8.4, there are two types of properties—those that are common to all steps and those that are specific to the step type. The common property sheets include general properties such as whether the step is a start step or an end step (Figure 8.5). Another set of common attributes includes time-out properties through which we can define the time-out periods. Time-outs allow us to implement business rules that control the limits to which the engine should force a transition out of the step owing to a time-out condition. Time-out alerts are important to ensure that processes do not get stuck just because someone is not doing his or her work in a timely manner or for any variety of other reasons. A time-out property sheet is shown in Figure 8.6.

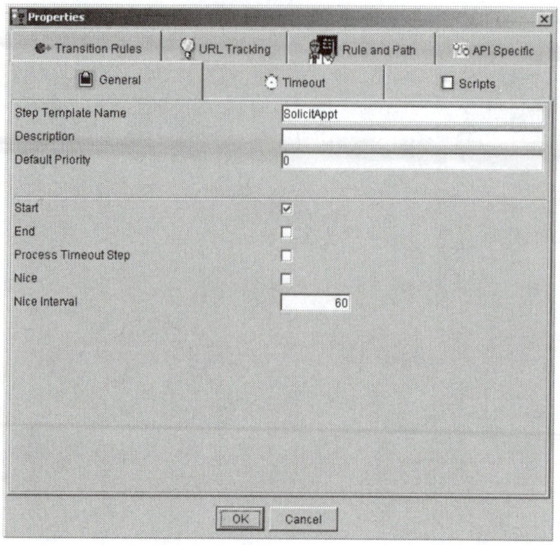

Figure 8.5 A general property sheet.

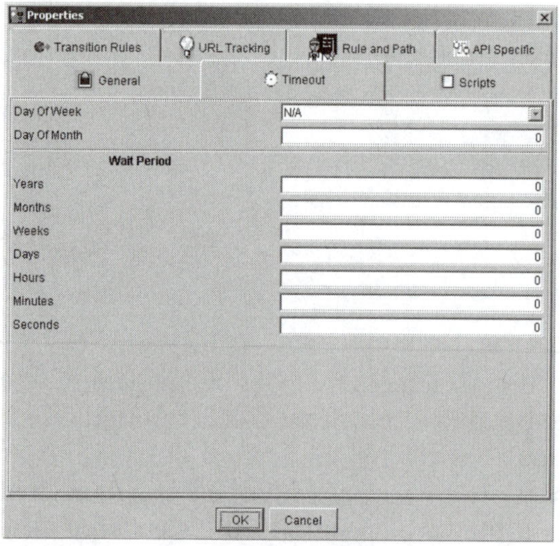

Figure 8.6 A time-out property sheet.

In addition to the properties that are common to all steps (that is, those properties that can be controlled by the very essence of the engine managing the steps), each step type has some attributes that are specific to the step type itself. For example, for an application step we would need to define which functional element to call. If, for example, the work-flow system is implemented in Java, the functional element would translate to specifying which method in which class to call when the step is activated. A functional element property sheet is shown in Figure 8.7.

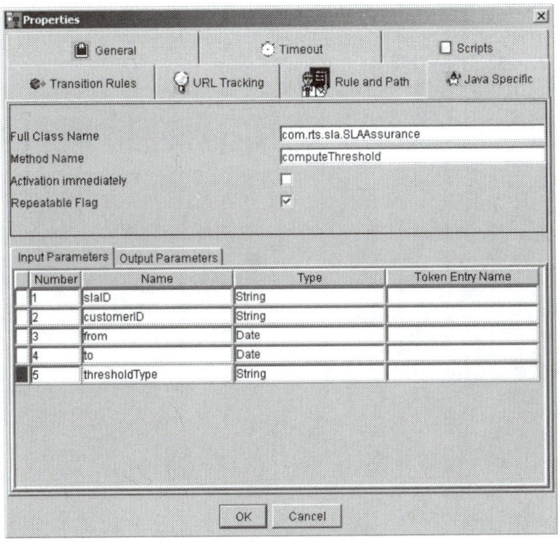

Figure 8.7 A functional element property sheet.

Obviously it is not enough to define only the class and the method to be called (note that at run time this class will need to be in the classpath of the Java Virtual Machine [JVM] running the work-flow engine). Since methods almost always require arguments to be passed as the method's parameters, we need to define the data elements to serve as these values. Normally these data elements will be extracted from the token. If the token names match the parameter names to be passed into the method, then we do not need to explicitly specify the token names or the path by which we can access this data (as in the case of Figure 8.7). Otherwise we would need to specify the path with which we can get at the data (for example, a path like troubleTicket.customer. sla.fixResponse).

Figure 8.8 shows a property sheet for another step type. This sheet is for a User Interface (UI) step type—one in which we intend a user to interact with the system. In this case, we need to specify the screen (or a uniform resource locator [URL] if the system is a Web application) with which the user will work in interacting with the system when the step is active. Note that different people (different roles) may have access to the same step, and it is very likely that we want to provide different views and application screens to different people. This view customization is shown in Figure 8.8 with multiple line items—with a screen (URL) for every role that should have access to the step. Note that since a certain user may belong to more than one of these roles, the step definition includes a priority value, which is used by the system to select which screen to use in such a case.

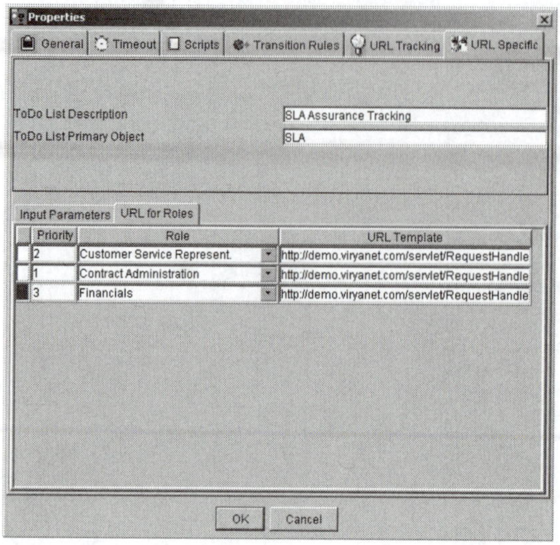

Figure 8.8 A User Interface property sheet.

Figure 8.9 shows yet another property sheet—this time for a notification method—or an email send in our case. Once more, arguments required for this email send are extracted from the token.

Subprocesses

The last property sheet we will show (Figure 8.10) addresses a very important step type—the step that allows us to spawn a subprocess. Processes can become

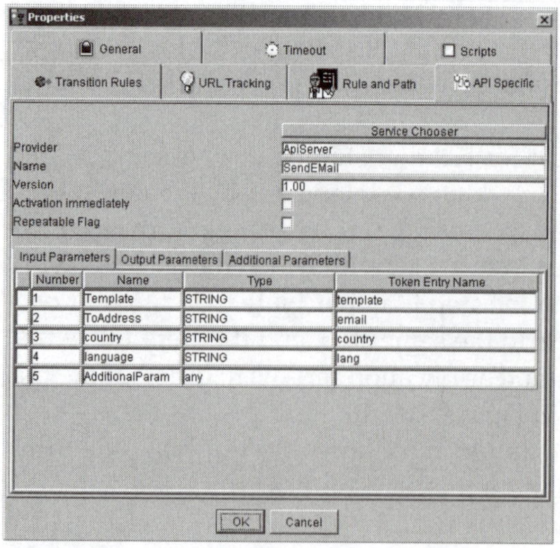

Figure 8.9 A notification property sheet.

fairly complex. Trying to maintain a full end-to-end process as one monolithic definition is not a good idea. In addition, such an approach would not promote reusability very well. It is far better to define each process as carrying out one segment of the complete automation.

Using these process definitions we can then go on to assemble *higher-level automations*. We do this by using subprocess steps as shown in Figure 8.10. A subprocess step causes a subprocess to be spawned when the main process enters the subprocess step. The main process continues with its process normally, and a new step is created. The token of the subprocess is derived from the token of the main process that existed when the subprocess was spawned. After the creation of the subprocess, both process instances continue their progress somewhat independently. The interaction between the subprocess and the main process occurs when the main step enters a synchronization step in which the main process waits for the completion of the subprocess. Normally the main process will also receive values from the subprocess (after all—it was probably sent out to do some work on behalf of the main process).

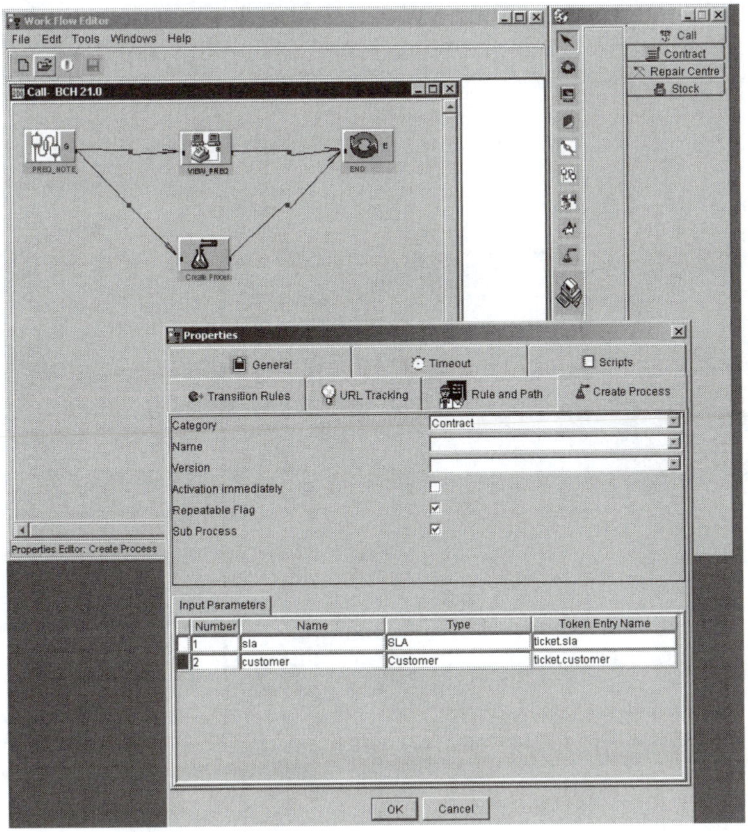

Figure 8.10 Spawning a subprocess.

When we are designing a process template, the step composition is obviously very important since these are the activities that will be performed as the process makes progress. The other set of definitions that are very important are the *transition rules*. The transition rules implement the business rules that define the conditions under which the process moves from one step to another. Also it is very common for a step to be able to transition to a second step or a third step—depending on the business rules formulated in the transition rules. Figure 8.11 shows an example transition rule. In this case the transition rule is formulated in JavaScript; it is common to formulate transition rules using a simple scripting language as opposed to a complex programming language because the intent of the process editor is to allow nonprogrammers to modify the business process definition.

Exporting Work-Flow Definitions

Process templates are the core of automation within the integrated SLA architecture. It is therefore no surprise that a lot of work goes into defining the process templates. While the process editor is a convenient tool to use, it also needs to have import-export capabilities that can help us when we want to adapt someone's existing process for our own use. Examples include a vendor who can help us by providing a template developed within the core development group—the so called *best-practice* process—or even a process developed for another customer.

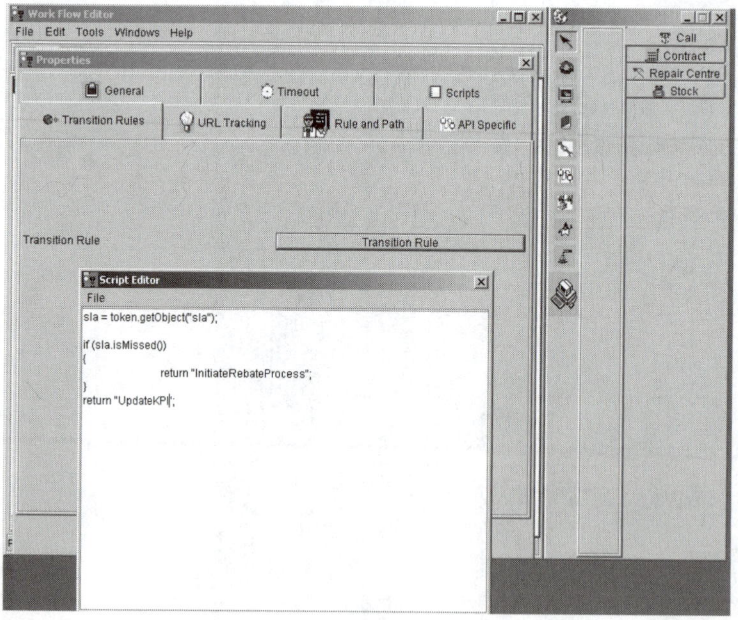

Figure 8.11 A transition rule.

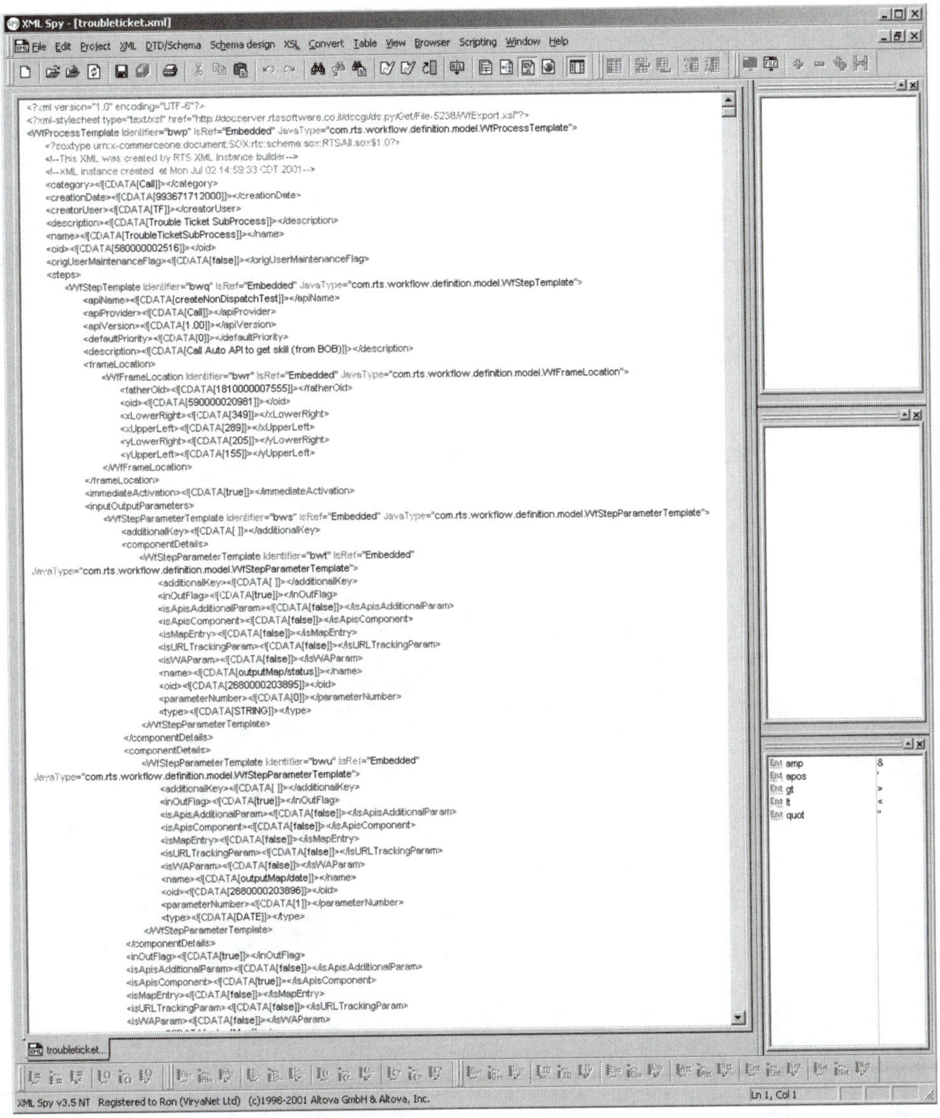

Figure 8.12 An Extensible Markup Language export.

Figure 8.12 shows an example XML file that represents the steps, transition rules, and attributes of a process. The actual format is not important—the part that is important is the ability to export a process template definition and later import it back into the same or another work-flow engine. The example in Figure 8.11 shows the export to be an XML file in the Commerce One SOX format. Using XML is simply a convenience since both people and machines need to be able to read the process. Machines—clearly—since this is the goal of the export-import capability. People—because the process template embodies within it the business process and it would be nice to be able to validate the process definition and maintain some form of documentation of the process.

Although XML is readable by humans, the file shown in Figure 8.12 is not that easy to read. By adding an XSL style sheet we can go a step further; we can provide an intuitive report format for the business analyst who needs to view and comment on the process definition. The result of applying such an XSL sheet to the XML document is shown in Figure 8.13. Note that we can even display a *process map* that uses a matrix to display which steps can transition into which other steps.

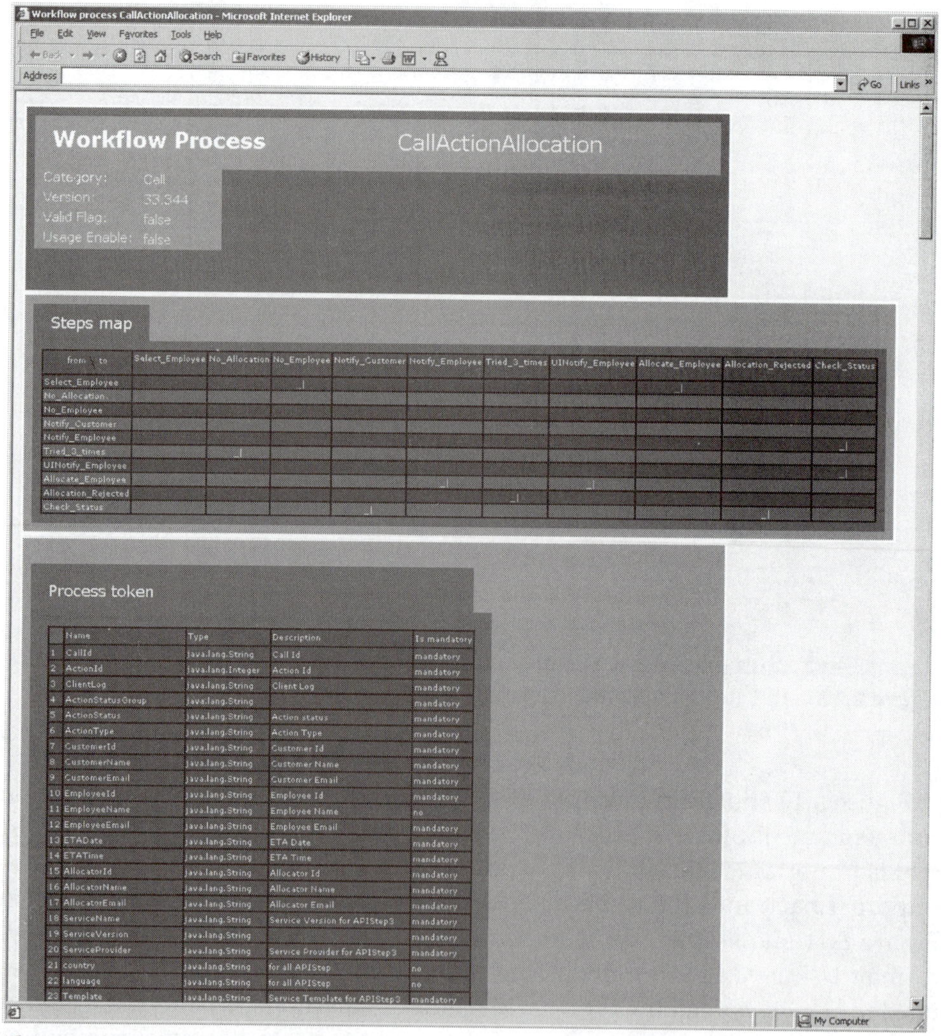

Figure 8.13 An HTML report.

The Process Engine

The process engine is a runtime component that is at the heart of the integrated SLA architecture. It is the main process that manages the creation and management of the process instances. A process engine is the main component that manages the automation aspects of the integrated SLA architecture. It is therefore not surprising that the process engine needs to be very robust, be implemented using a threaded architecture, and have at least one (and usually many) redundant copies for fault tolerance and fail-over.

During run time, there are many process instances. *Many* is often an understatement because it is very normal for a process engine to be managing tens of thousands and even hundreds of thousands of process instances. Each process instance has only a single active step at any point in time. The process engine loops through all the active processes, and for each one it looks at the active step. It then inspects the transition rules to see whether the process should transition out of the step that is currently marked as active. If the process engine determines that a transition needs to be performed, it calculates where the process should transition to and performs the transition. It marks the new step as being the active step in the process and activates the step itself. For example, if this is a functional step, the application function will be invoked.

Working and Monitoring

The process engine is responsible for making the transitions between steps in the active process. This happens at run time and is the heart of a fully automated system. The engine is, however, a back-end component and not usually visible to users.

There are two forms of interactions between people and the process instances at run time. One interaction point involves system administrators (or work-flow administrators, as we prefer to call them). These people are responsible for managing the process engine, monitoring the process instances, and modifying runtime statuses. For example, a work-flow administrator can determine that a process needs to be suspended or aborted, or conversely, resumed. In addition, the work-flow administrator can decide to reassign the active step of a process to some individual.

The Work-Flow Monitor

Figure 8.14 illustrates the work-flow monitor query screen (or *finder,* as we prefer to call it). This screen allows the work-flow administrator to look at the process instances that are currently running within the engine based on any set of query parameters. Once the query is invoked, the work-flow administrator gets a list of all the active processes that match the search criteria that are being managed by the process engine as shown in Figure 8.15.

Using the action buttons, the work-flow administrator may select any set of processes and perform the actions upon these process instances. If need be, the work-flow administrator can view a full audit trail of any of these processes as shown in Figure 8.16. This view shows all the steps that the process went through, when the transition was made, and even the business rule that caused the transition (as shown in the pop-up window in the figure). Since the token is the context of the business process, the work-flow monitor allows the work-flow administrator to peek into the token and see all the objects that are being maintained within the process context (as shown in Figure 8.17).

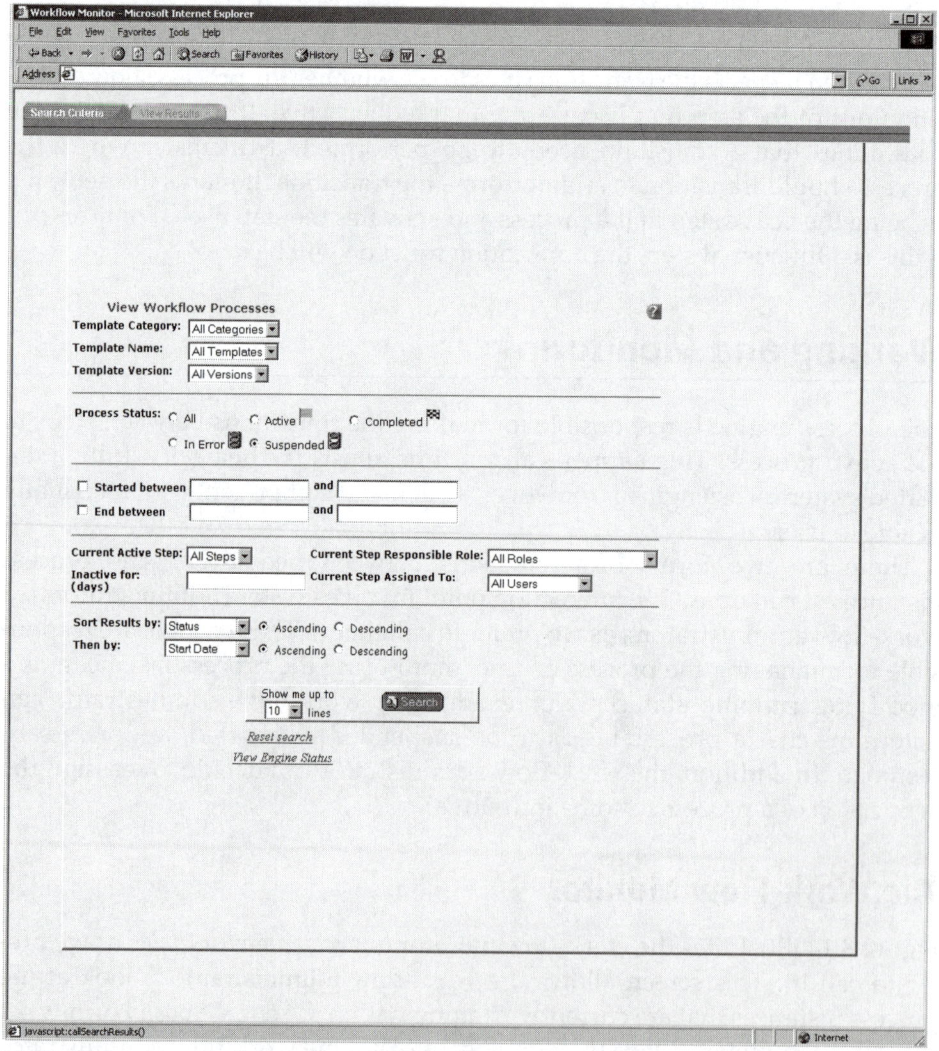

Figure 8.14 A work-flow monitor finder screen.

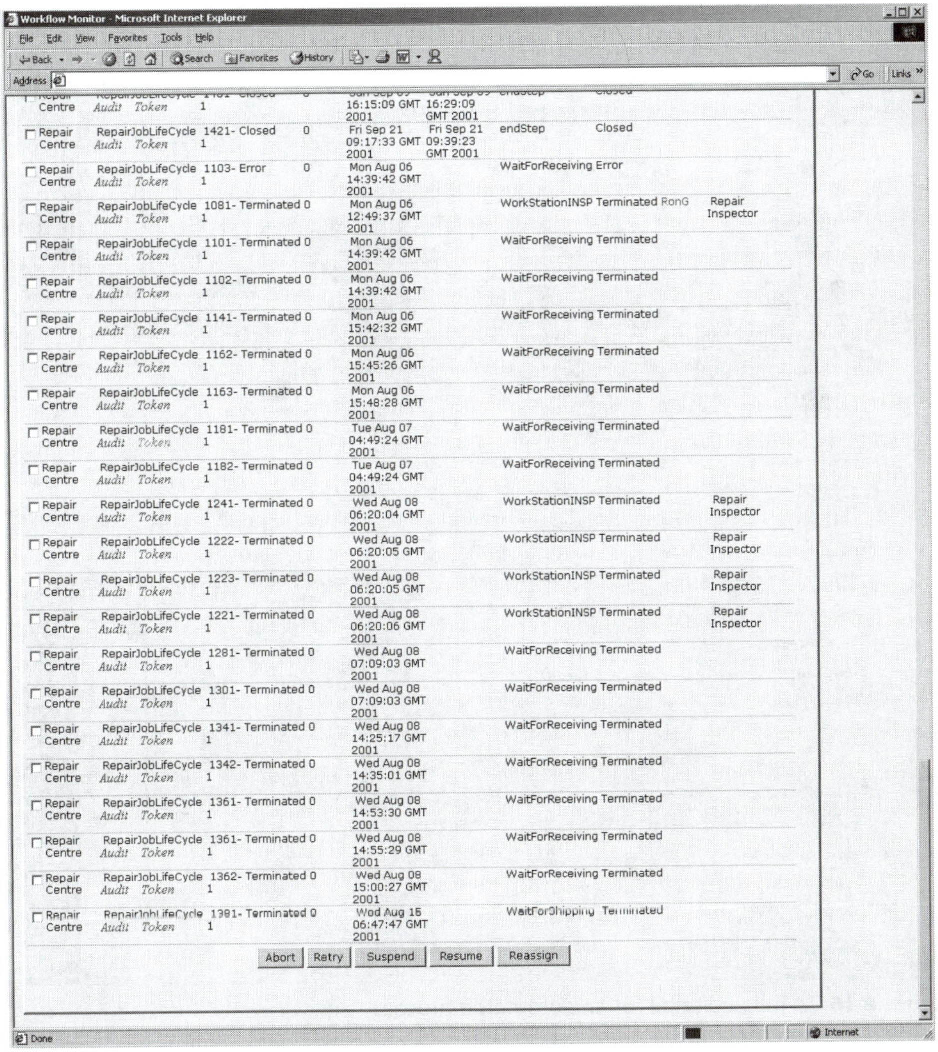

Workflow Monitor - Microsoft Internet Explorer
File Edit View Favorites Tools Help
Back Search Favorites History
Address
Go Links
Centre Audit Token 1 16:15:09 GMT 2001 16:29:09 GMT 2001
Repair Centre RepairJobLifeCycle Audit Token 1421- 1 Closed 0 Fri Sep 21 09:17:33 GMT 2001 Fri Sep 21 09:39:23 GMT 2001 endStep Closed
Repair Centre RepairJobLifeCycle Audit Token 1103- 1 Error 0 Mon Aug 06 14:39:42 GMT 2001 WaitForReceiving Error
Repair Centre RepairJobLifeCycle Audit Token 1081- 1 Terminated 0 Mon Aug 06 12:49:37 GMT 2001 WorkStationINSP Terminated RonG Repair Inspector
Repair Centre RepairJobLifeCycle Audit Token 1101- 1 Terminated 0 Mon Aug 06 14:39:42 GMT 2001 WaitForReceiving Terminated
Repair Centre RepairJobLifeCycle Audit Token 1102- 1 Terminated 0 Mon Aug 06 14:39:42 GMT 2001 WaitForReceiving Terminated
Repair Centre RepairJobLifeCycle Audit Token 1141- 1 Terminated 0 Mon Aug 06 15:42:32 GMT 2001 WaitForReceiving Terminated
Repair Centre RepairJobLifeCycle Audit Token 1162- 1 Terminated 0 Mon Aug 06 15:45:26 GMT 2001 WaitForReceiving Terminated
Repair Centre RepairJobLifeCycle Audit Token 1163- 1 Terminated 0 Mon Aug 06 15:48:28 GMT 2001 WaitForReceiving Terminated
Repair Centre RepairJobLifeCycle Audit Token 1181- 1 Terminated 0 Tue Aug 07 04:49:24 GMT 2001 WaitForReceiving Terminated
Repair Centre RepairJobLifeCycle Audit Token 1182- 1 Terminated 0 Tue Aug 07 04:49:24 GMT 2001 WaitForReceiving Terminated
Repair Centre RepairJobLifeCycle Audit Token 1241- 1 Terminated 0 Wed Aug 08 06:20:04 GMT 2001 WorkStationINSP Terminated Repair Inspector
Repair Centre RepairJobLifeCycle Audit Token 1222- 1 Terminated 0 Wed Aug 08 06:20:05 GMT 2001 WorkStationINSP Terminated Repair Inspector
Repair Centre RepairJobLifeCycle Audit Token 1223- 1 Terminated 0 Wed Aug 08 06:20:05 GMT 2001 WorkStationINSP Terminated Repair Inspector
Repair Centre RepairJobLifeCycle Audit Token 1221- 1 Terminated 0 Wed Aug 08 06:20:06 GMT 2001 WorkStationINSP Terminated Repair Inspector
Repair Centre RepairJobLifeCycle Audit Token 1281- 1 Terminated 0 Wed Aug 08 07:09:03 GMT 2001 WaitForReceiving Terminated
Repair Centre RepairJobLifeCycle Audit Token 1301- 1 Terminated 0 Wed Aug 08 07:09:03 GMT 2001 WaitForReceiving Terminated
Repair Centre RepairJobLifeCycle Audit Token 1341- 1 Terminated 0 Wed Aug 08 14:25:17 GMT 2001 WaitForReceiving Terminated
Repair Centre RepairJobLifeCycle Audit Token 1342- 1 Terminated 0 Wed Aug 08 14:35:01 GMT 2001 WaitForReceiving Terminated
Repair Centre RepairJobLifeCycle Audit Token 1361- 1 Terminated 0 Wed Aug 08 14:53:30 GMT 2001 WaitForReceiving Terminated
Repair Centre RepairJobLifeCycle Audit Token 1361- 1 Terminated 0 Wed Aug 08 14:55:29 GMT 2001 WaitForReceiving Terminated
Repair Centre RepairJobLifeCycle Audit Token 1362- 1 Terminated 0 Wed Aug 08 15:00:27 GMT 2001 WaitForReceiving Terminated
Repair Centre RepairJobLifeCycle Audit Token 1381- 1 Terminated 0 Wed Aug 15 06:47:47 GMT 2001 WaitForShipping Terminated
Abort Retry Suspend Resume Reassign
Done
Internet

Figure 8.15 A work-flow monitor process manager.

To Do List

The second interface point between the process engine run time and the user is the *to do list*. This represents all the tasks a user should be working on based on the process automation that exists within the organization (and is managed by the process engine). This concept is probably the most important one, and we need to elaborate not only on the implementation and the presentation to the user but also on the concept behind it.

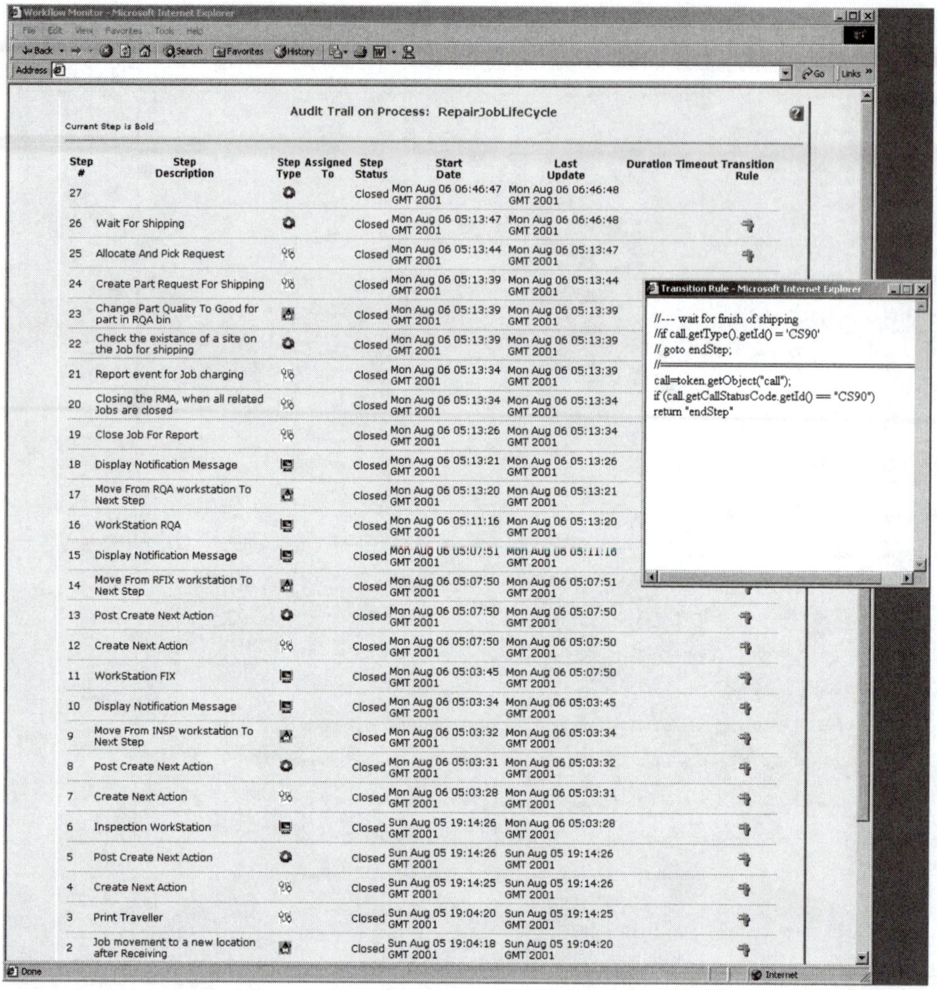

Figure 8.16 A full audit trail for an automated process.

The main concept behind automation based on work flow is that the business process is embedded in an engine that drives the process flow and automates the handoffs between different systems and different roles based on the business requirements. The handoff between systems is fairly clear and involves calls made to APIs defined by the systems. The handoff to roles (people) is a little trickier since it involves a user interface. The concept of work

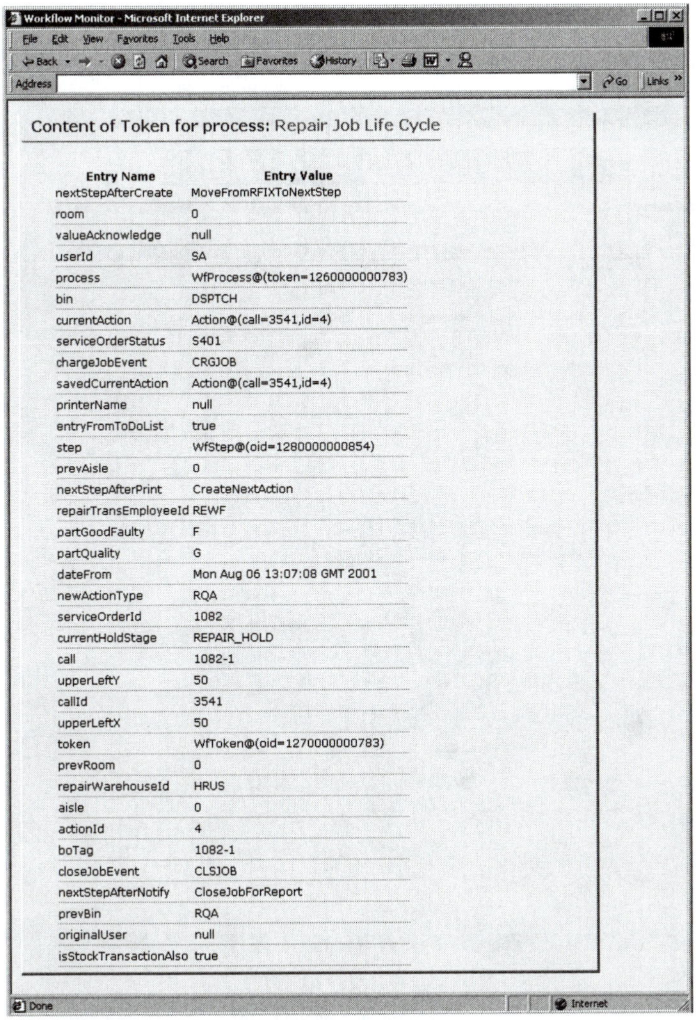

Content of Token for process: Repair Job Life Cycle

Entry Name	Entry Value
nextStepAfterCreate	MoveFromRFIXToNextStep
room	0
valueAcknowledge	null
userId	SA
process	WfProcess@(token=1260000000783)
bin	DSPTCH
currentAction	Action@(call=3541,id=4)
serviceOrderStatus	S401
chargeJobEvent	CRGJOB
savedCurrentAction	Action@(call=3541,id=4)
printerName	null
entryFromToDoList	true
step	WfStep@(oid=1280000000854)
prevAisle	0
nextStepAfterPrint	CreateNextAction
repairTransEmployeeId	REWF
partGoodFaulty	F
partQuality	G
dateFrom	Mon Aug 06 13:07:08 GMT 2001
newActionType	RQA
serviceOrderId	1082
currentHoldStage	REPAIR_HOLD
call	1082-1
upperLeftY	50
callId	3541
upperLeftX	50
token	WfToken@(oid=1270000000783)
prevRoom	0
repairWarehouseId	HRUS
aisle	0
actionId	4
boTag	1082-1
closeJobEvent	CLSJOB
nextStepAfterNotify	CloseJobForReport
prevBin	RQA
originalUser	null
isStockTransactionAlso	true

Figure 8.17 A sample work-flow token.

automation is that a person should be able to view all the work that he or she should do based on the active processes managed by the process engine. Since all these flows are automated, at any point in time the engine has the correct active steps that need to be worked on. The to do list (an example is shown in Figure 8.18) is the user interface that presents the list of things to do to the user.

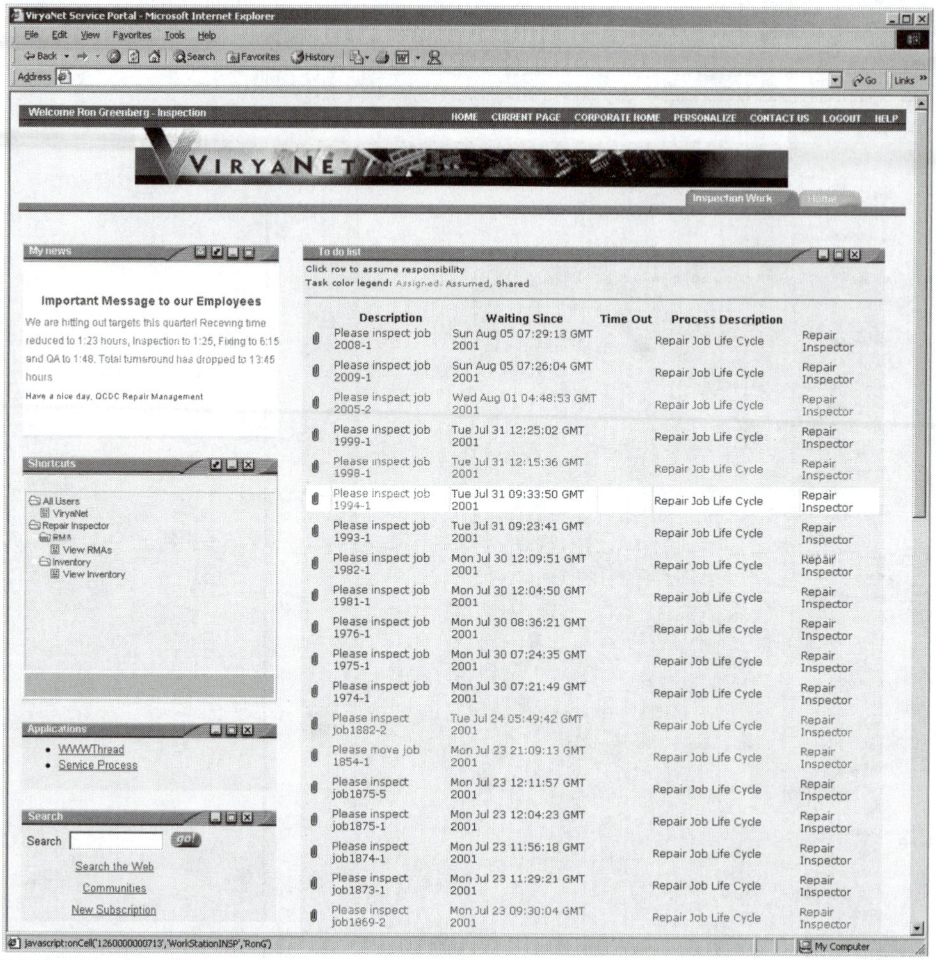

Figure 8.18 The to do list.

Personal Assignment and Role Assignment

In terms of defining what work needs to be done by a user, every work-flow system has two important assignment concepts—*personal assignment* and *role assignment*. Personal assignment means that as part of the flow, an active step is assigned to a named individual. This means that only that individual can work on this process at the time. From a user interface perspective it means that the task will appear on only one person's to do list.

Every work-flow system is based on a role metaphor. A user may belong to more than one role. Processes that are managed within the process engine have definitions in which each step can have a role assignment. This step-specific assignment means that when a step is the active step in the process and is assigned to a certain role (for example, contract administrator, network planner, and so on), each user belonging to that role will see this work task on his or her to do list. In effect the to do list behaves like a shared queue. When a user selects a task off the to do list, that step is automatically assigned to the individual. This assignment is done in order to avoid situations in which more than one person works on the same task (without the sharing of the task being explicitly defined as allowed). If a person does not want to work on a particular task, he or she needs to release it back to the shared pool (or the work-flow administrator can do so using the reassignment function as shown in Figure 8.15).

Dynamic Queues

The notion of work-flow-based work delivery and automation is very powerful—much more powerful than is immediately apparent. The to do list and the role assignment are a perfect example. From reading the preceding description you may understand that the process engine and the role-based assignment manages a set of queues.

In fact, the work-flow concept is about *dynamic queues* and is much more powerful than are static queues. The notion of dynamic queues is implemented by queries on active steps. At any point in time, every process instance at run time has one and only one active step. Therefore, if we were to take a snapshot of the process engine at any single point in time, what we would really see is a set of active steps. Each one of these steps, if related to interaction with a person (as opposed to interaction with a system), has a definition of the roles for which it is relevant along with possibly other parameters that affect on whose to do list this work should appear. The to do list is created at run time through a dynamic query. Based on the user's profile and the work-flow definitions, a query is created and applied to the set of all active steps to determine which of these steps are relevant to the user.

For example, the role handling a certain SLA definition process can be a contract administrator. But if the provider is organized into geographical areas, then we will not want this work item to appear on all contract administrators to do lists—rather we will want it to appear on the to do list for any contract administrator working in the region for which this contract and/or customer is relevant. Since any process will have its own categories and since business policies tend to be very dynamic, it is much better to base such categorizations on flexible and dynamic queries than on static queues.

This dynamic work-flow assignment is precisely the main theme in work-flow-based automation. Instead of defining a set of queues and continuously changing them, we define business rules by which we can decide at run time whether the work item should appear in someone's to do list. The business rules are built by defining the required attributes (per work-flow step) for inclusion in a to do list. For example, Figure 8.19 shows a step definition in which not only do we define that the work should appear on a contract administrator's to do list but we also define an additional condition that explicitly restricts access to those contract administrators who belong to a service center in the region that matches the region defined within the process context (that is, token).

Summary

Along with integration, automation techniques form the technical foundations for an integrated SLA model even when many disparate systems compose the OSS. Unfortunately, even when the technology is fully aligned, change management and organizational issues cause providers to fail with the integrated OSS model. It is therefore very important to also manage the organizational issues, which is the topic of the next chapter.

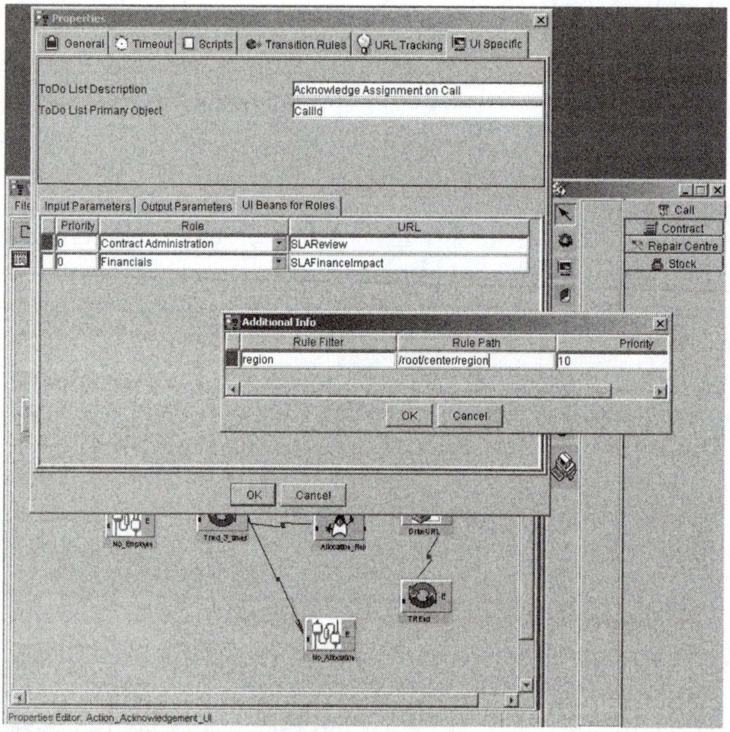

Figure 8.19 Query definitions.

CHAPTER

9

Organizational Issues

In this chapter, we will discuss how you, as a service provider, can optimize your business by organizing your workforce and relationships with your business partners.

The Stovepipe Service Provider

The most difficult part of implementing an environment based on the Integrated Service Level Agreement (ISLA) framework will undoubtedly be the organizational change management the service provider will need to undergo. The challenge will be greatest in the largest, most established carriers.

For many years, large service providers have been plagued with bureaucratic stovepipe organizations. We have repeatedly looked at the impact stovepipes have on different aspects of the service provider. In this chapter we will again explore the stovepipe with a view toward understanding why it exists and the characteristics that make it so damaging to a service provider.

One of the most obvious effects of stovepipe organizations is poor communications between departments within the service provider. Since no one knows what anyone else is doing and communications between departments are regimented owing to turf concerns, working together to solve even simple problems becomes a grueling exercise. For example, it is not at all unusual for the customer to make an inquiry to the call center on the status of an order or the expected arrival time of a technician. The customer service representative then makes a phone call that starts a flurry of phone calls down the center chain in order to get an answer.

NOTE **The center chain is an organizational oddity where only key people in centralized work centers talk to anyone external to the work center. There can be many centers in a service provider, and there is generally a pecking order.**

This example starts when the customer talks to the call center, and the call center then calls the provisioning center. The provisioning center calls the operations center, the operations center calls the dispatch center, and the dispatch center finally calls the technician.

If the technician can be reached, a series of verbal updates proceeds back up the chain until it eventually gets back to the call center. The call center then updates the customer. Figure 9.1 shows the call center chain that a trouble ticket often follows.

The end-to-end work flow, in many cases, is just as convoluted and invisible as is status tracking. Most work centers can do a fairly good job while a trouble ticket is within their control; the problems come with the handoffs.

Because a number of disparate systems exist within the stovepipe environment, each subsequent handoff sends the job to the end of the new work

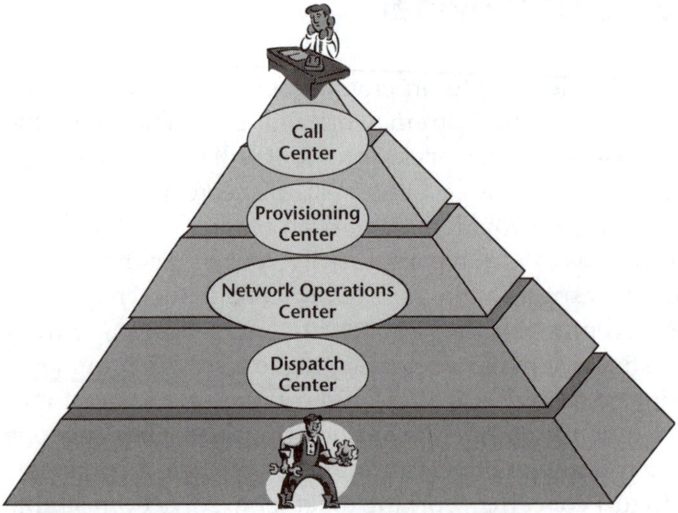

Figure 9.1 A service provider's center chain.

center queue when it arrives. The overall process and delivery timing receive little oversight. The result of center-centric communications and work flow is inefficiency.

Based on our experiences, we estimate that work center personnel perform fewer than 16 hours (2 days) of actual work in provisioning the most common types of services. Yet delivery times for these services routinely range anywhere from 30 to 60 days, sometimes longer. During the other 28 to 58 days, the order sits in one queue or another somewhere in the process.

Many work centers get their orders out almost as quickly as they come in. But it takes only one backlogged work center to gum up the works. Because there is little visibility of workloads between the work centers, the work centers at the end of the delivery chain are subject to the ebbs and tides of all the work centers that come before them in the process.

Delays are exacerbated by the tendency for the preceding work centers to use up most if not all of the available time. Some days are extremely slow, while on other days huge amounts of backlogged work show up that force certain work center employees to work through the night. From a productivity standpoint, there is no consistent way to measure or forecast the efficiency of the operations.

It is important to note that service fulfillment and assurance work flows progress through the service provider vertically, when mapped against the Telecommunications Management Network (TMN), much more often than horizontally. As an example, Figure 9.2 depicts the vertical nature of the fulfillment work flow.

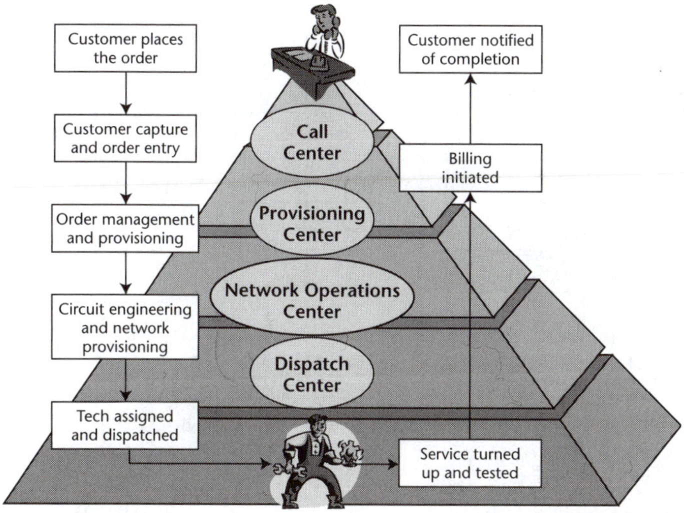

Figure 9.2 The vertical nature of fulfillment, assurance, and billing (FAB) work flows.

Because each work center, in essence, fends for itself, there is much duplication of effort. In fact, much of the impetus driving the technical integration of the Operations Support System (OSS) is the requirement to enter the same data into multiple systems as the job progresses through the service provider. While an observer might think that systems integration is undertaken to ensure data integrity, this is a naïve assumption. Integration is most often undertaken to reduce the need to reenter the data in various stovepipe systems.

There is also a tendency for organizational duplication as a result of stovepipe mentalities. In many cases, separate organizations have mandated the use of totally different systems, personnel, and work flows even for virtually identical tasks.

For example, technicians who reside in the provisioning group often have the exact same skill set as those in the operations group. They may even work in the same facility. Yet the provisioning technician performs work only in response to service orders, while the operations tech only performs routine maintenance or responds to trouble tickets. In both cases, the task the worker performs may be exactly the same, such as running a bit error rate test (BERT) using common test equipment.

The fact that there is little if any measurement of the productivity of these organizations almost guarantees that massive amounts of money are being wasted through inefficient organizational planning. In the most extreme cases, it is not all that uncommon to see entire organizations built to service a single product offering, even though the resources already in place are being used at less than full capacity. Figure 9.3 shows product-specific stovepipes.

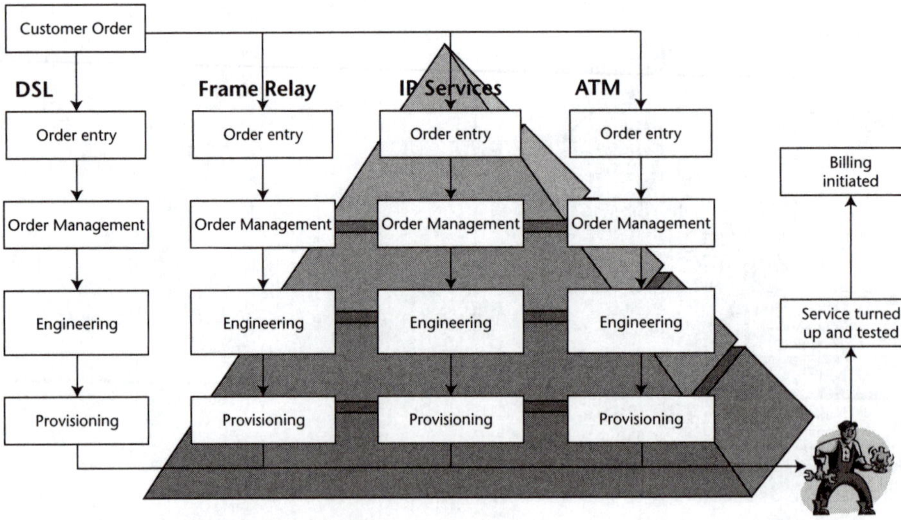

Figure 9.3 Product-specific fulfillment stovepipes.

These organizational deficiencies have led to some very bloated organizations with ineffective processes for delivering services. Obviously, these kinds of organizations are not conducive to delivering SLA-based services. So a number of changes must be made. Specifically, the isolation and proprietary data-hogging that are so common in the environment must be reduced. We can start by improving communications, encouraging resource and information sharing, and figuratively tearing down the walls by replacing the work center chain with a new delivery model: the collaborative community.

Integrated Service Level Agreement Change Enablers

The ISLA framework is designed to enable service providers to develop collaborative communities; manage organizational changes; and continually develop, operate, and optimize the organization based on the true needs of the business. There are several inherent ISLA framework capabilities that work together to allow service providers to transition from the bloated stovepipe environment into a more tightly integrated and efficient community. These capabilities include the following:

- Unified presentation
- Dynamic work-flow communities
- Dynamic work-flow automation
- Workforce management
- Business intelligence

Unified Presentation

Unified presentation of the same information puts everyone in the community on the same sheet of music. Being able to present the big picture of activities in smaller, more manageable views while maintaining the integrity of the background information sources is absolutely crucial to the service provider's ability to transition out of the need for stovepipes.

Also important is the ability to distribute the information in a view and through an access method (such as a PC, pager, Personal Digital Assistant [PDA], and so on) that is appropriate to the individual community member within the operational environment. Unified presentation and universal access to work-flow information create one large support community with many disparate roles.

Dynamic Work-Flow Communities

Communities are related by a commonality. In the case of neighborhoods, this commonality is the physical proximity of neighbors to each other's homes. In the case of telecommunications, the commonality is a service order, trouble ticket, or other type of related task.

Service providers have had work centers that were essentially isolated unto themselves for many years. Although the work centers knew the neighborhood was there, they really didn't know or care about their neighbors. Everyone just threw the work over the fence as quickly as possible. Dynamic work-flow communities allow service providers to build event-driven teams specifically for delivering on individual service orders, addressing trouble tickets, and so on. The roles individual community members play are determined by their ability to contribute to the many tasks contained within the end-to-end work flow.

Dynamic Work-Flow Automation

The ability to reliably automate the hundreds of different fulfillment and assurance work flows can be used to change the ways that organizational departments relate to each other. Rather than being dealt with by an isolated stovepipe that provides little visibility into the activities of other work centers, the service order becomes a series of smaller work flows with the individual work centers contributing to the end result.

The former stovepipe departments become part of the larger enterprise. While the relationship has always existed, the stovepipe departments had no way to understand who else was involved, what the status of work was, or the roles they themselves played in success or failure of the end goal. Because the entire end-to-end work-flow tasks and performance can be made visible to the entire work-flow community, every community member becomes accountable to every other for delivering the product.

A comparison can be made to an assembly line with the product being moved along on an automated conveyor system that doesn't stop moving as the community members make their contribution to the rolling product. As with the assembly line, parts, personnel, and other resources of the service provider must be available at each station in time to meet the window in which the contribution must be made; otherwise the entire line gets backed up. If the line backs up or stops, everyone knows. The fact that there are many resources that have been idled is very apparent, and it is clear to everyone that action needs to be taken to correct it.

Workforce Management

Advanced workforce management can close the loop by providing visibility of the capabilities of the entire collection of human resources that are available within the community to support the work flow. This capability includes managing the roles, skills, locations, schedules, availability, and costs associated with each resource relative to the task requirements indicated in the work flow.

Workforce management allows the service providers to use the work-flow management system to make intelligent decisions as to which resources to allocate and assign to support the work flow based on defined criteria or requirement limitations, such as geographic locations, specialized skill sets, or equipment needs.

By distributing (or integrating with) the workforce management capabilities to subcontractors, suppliers, trading partners, and so on, the service provider can get full visibility of the entire delivery environment. In addition, this style of management allows for full accountability of the human resource utilization in relation to the actual task loads generated by the work flows.

Business Intelligence

Business intelligence, in the form of key performance indicators (KPIs), can be used to provide statistical validation to the service provider that the workforce is performing efficiently. It can be used to measure individual, departmental, and organizational contributions to the business case of the service provider.

Relating the service requirements to the contributors allows decisions to be made about productivity targets, departmental utilization goals, and any number of metrics related to human resources. These measurements enable the service provider to better adapt the workforce to the organization's true business needs.

Integrated Service Level Agreement-Based Organizational Optimization

True business needs are established through measurement, analysis, and presentation of KPIs that indicate the actual operational performance provided by the community organizations and individual contributors. By auditing each work flow, as well as aggregating them into larger enterprise views, the service provider can optimize the mix of organizations, people within them, and skills within the workforce that will deliver the best performance for the service provider's needs.

For example, a service provider may set a target of 100 DSL orders per day. This is based on market estimates put together by product development. An order may have to pass through order management, engineering, logistics, installation, and test groups. Order management may be passing 100 orders a day just fine, while engineering is capable of completing only 50, even though the department is working everyone overtime.

Further down the work flow, the installation group has staffed up in anticipation of a growth in demand and has actually padded the staffing to accommodate up to 150 orders a day. The test group has staffed incorrectly and is able to pass through only 75 of the 100 orders per day. This example is depicted in Figure 9.4.

In the stovepipe environment, order management would have passed the orders to engineering, and that would be the end of the order department's involvement. Engineering would probably handle the orders as best it could, but obviously things would begin to backlog once 50 orders per day were exceeded. Logistics and installation would think that product development had overestimated demand by quite a lot, while the test group would perceive the overestimation to be smaller, while assuming that its department had gotten its staffing correct.

Sooner or later, a big enough backlog would develop that staff would start working weekends to catch up. Meanwhile, impatient customers would cancel their backlogged orders (but if the cancellations were not caught soon enough, the orders would be provisioned anyway). In the end, nothing would change.

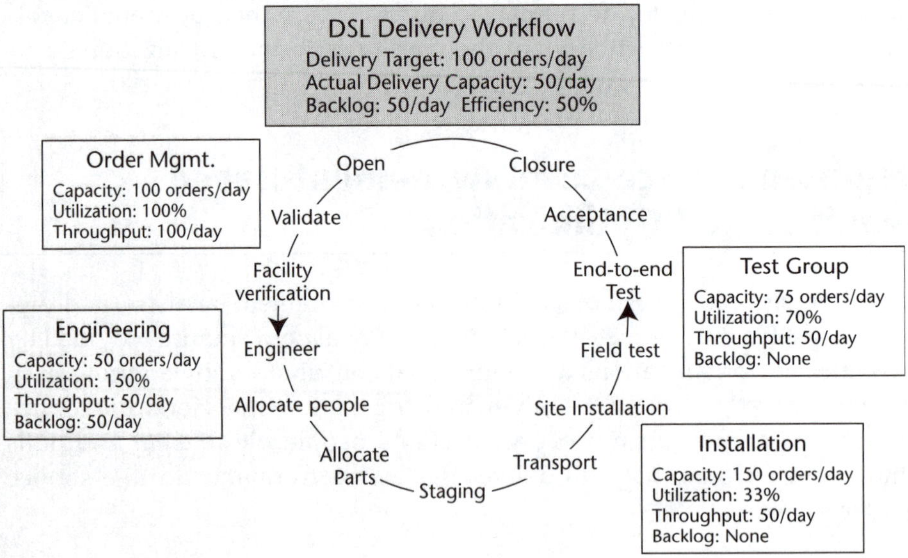

Figure 9.4 A DSL work-flow optimization example.

An examination of the KPIs developed for resource utilization would tell a somewhat disturbing story. Order management would show full utilization, while engineering would show 150 percent utilization at the same time that engineering would start to build a backlog. Because logistics wasn't turning over inventory as planned, it would have slowed ordering by half. Installation, on the other hand, had utilization numbers under 40 percent, and the test group had utilization numbers closer to 80 percent.

Armed with accurate utilization statistics, the service provider can make corrections on several fronts. The carrier can choose from a large number of options, such as decreasing the order volume target (although this is highly unlikely); increasing the engineering staff by 100 percent; decreasing the installation staff by 33 percent; or augmenting the testing staff by another 25 percent.

By doing the last three things simultaneously, the service provider should be able to correct the staffing levels to better support the required order volume. After a short amount of time, the service provider would be able to analyze the KPIs to determine if the organizational changes that had been made had the desired effects on work-flow performance. If not, another optimization cycle could be undertaken.

The Work-Flow Community

The kind of organizational engineering and optimization we are talking about is possible only through good end-to-end work-flow tracking, reporting, and analysis. The success of organizational optimization is directly related to how far the service provider is willing to go in effecting change through the workforce. As we stated earlier in this chapter, organizational change management will be the most difficult part of implementing the ISLA framework.

But the capability to perform organizational optimization is the end result of a long process of relating the components and factors of service delivery into the big picture represented by the ISLA framework. The starting point, from an execution standpoint, is to relate the various entities in the service provider environment to each other in a way that is also conducive to creating the relationships that will be needed later, that is, relating them to work flow. This concept is known as a community.

In their broadest sense, communities can be centered on any common interest or theme, such as the company picnic committee. The purpose of the communities brought together by the ISLA framework is very specific: to collaborate in delivering telecommunications products and services within Quality of Service (QoS) parameters defined in the SLAs.

The ISLA concept of dynamic work-flow communities is based on organizing the disparate community members in certain ways that can be understood by the work-flow engine and other OSSs that support the environment. Once the work flow is established, we then map these community members to the work-flow contributions needed to deliver the aforementioned products and services. By leveraging the systems capabilities, we can match work-flow need with work-flow contributors.

NOTE Because this chapter deals specifically with the service provider's organization, we will discuss only the human community members (as opposed to systems, application program interface [API] calls, automated transitions and intelligence, and so on).

Definition Hierarchy

Relating the members of the work-flow communities is done by establishing a definition hierarchy, which will be used by a number of different systems within the ISLA framework to understand the relationships between the participants and such things as communities, work flow, permissions, information, and allowable activities. An overview of the definition hierarchy would include the following:

- Users
  - User parameters
  - User roles (if applicable)
  - User authentication
- Groups
  - Group category
  - Groups
- Communities
- User types
- Roles
- Companies
- Customer type

Users

All human community members are understood by the system to be users. A user has many attributes and parameters that the system needs to understand in order to relate one user to other users, groups, communities, work flows, and so on. The primary relational attributes that will determine user permissions to access information, perform activities, and so on re group category and user role(s). These are covered under the Group section.

NOTE **The role within the user's attributes corresponds to one or more of the groups, which means that the attributes and permission sets related to those groups must be in place before a user is assigned a role.**

There are also many types of information that are nonrelational but are important to the system, such as the preferred notification method, that are stored in the user profile. The user profile contains both secure (system) and nonsecure (user) data fields. Secure data fields are structures that are mandatory for system functions, such as maintaining authorizations and security, and are normally hidden from users.

Non-secure data fields are normally provided by and made available to the user. Some nonsecure data is mandatory for system functionality (such as user ID, passwords, last name, and so on). While other data is optional to the system (such as title, employment data, and so on).

Much of the secure data in the user profile is dedicated to providing system and user security. There are a number of security measures that are designed to protect all users from each other, including robust authentication procedures. For example, an employee of one company must not be able to access information from another company by creating a bogus profile or entering a different company name.

Data protection is addressed through a secure authorization profile developed by system administrators that is masked from the user by an authorization number. The authorization profile is developed prior to user registration as part of the system implementation.

Users are then able to register with the portal, enter nonsecure data, and begin participating as a community member. An example of the user registration screen can be seen in Figure 9.5.

Groups

Many users have common attributes, responsibilities, or interests. These users can be grouped into a formal entity that the Workflow Management System (WMS) can understand as being specific in purpose. Groups are often developed to simplify community management for the service provider. Groups allow the service provider to create template permission sets that give users within a group specific permission to perform certain activities or access certain information.

For example, a user in the repair technician group may be able to access his or her own calendar, order parts, and update trouble tickets, but may not be able to access the KPIs detailing trouble ticket performance for the entire department. A second user in the dispatcher group may be able to access the calendars of all field engineers in his or her region and see the KPIs for the department, but may not have permission to order parts.

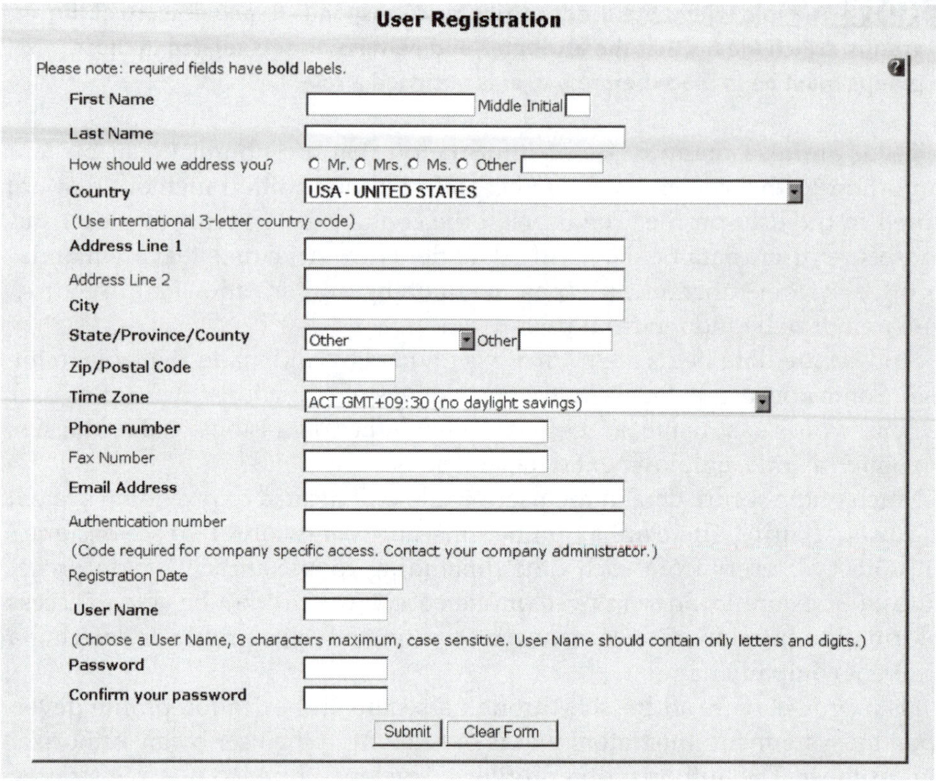

Figure 9.5 A user registration screen.

The regional repair supervisor may be able to perform all those functions for the entire region, while the repair manager may be able to perform all those functions as well as access KPI information for every repair department within all the regions.

Like users, groups are also assigned to one or more categories that help to further define the uniqueness of the group in relation to the service provider and other groups. Any number of different group categories can be developed to reflect different relationships that exist within the service provider's environment. Within the model architecture, described in Chapter 6, the following categories have been predefined as default groups:

- Service company
- Employee (internal)
- Customer (external)
- Supplier (external)
- Registered user (not a service company employee but not linked to a customer or supplier)

The model architecture has also predefined a number of groups. Of course, the service provider is not limited to using the default groups. Any number of additional groups may be defined and assigned attributes and permission sets. These groups are then mapped to group categories, which are also assigned attributes and permission sets. The default groups include the following:

- Registered user (ureg)
- Customer (cust)
- Supplier (SUPP)
- Field engineer (FE)
- Dispatcher (DISP)
- Warehouse employee (ICRK)
- Customer service representative (CSR)
- Repair supervisor (RSUP)
- Repair receiving clerk (RRCV)
- Repair QA (RQA)
- Repair technician (RTCH)
- Repair inspector (RINS)
- Repair shipping clerk (RSHP)
- Repair account manager (RAMN)

Groups and group categories (along with the accompanying permission sets) can be developed that will serve the needs of almost any type of relationship that exists within the service provider's environment. By assigning a user to more than one group, along with individual user attributes, the service provider can accurately manage the roles played by each community member and securely provide user access to activities, information, and reporting. Examples are shown in Figure 9.6.

Role management can also help the service provider understand the makeup of its support organization. For example, if the service provider knows that it needs a certain number of Cisco Certified Internetworking Expert (CCIE) engineers, it may use the group's function to maintain visibility of who has been assigned to the engineering group and what permissions those workers have. By designating certain user attributes (such as specialized certification) as mandatory for entry into the CCIE engineer group and tracking those attributes within the work-flow management (WFM) system, the service provider can understand what actions must be taken, with which users, within which departments in the organization in order to have more certified CCIE engineers.

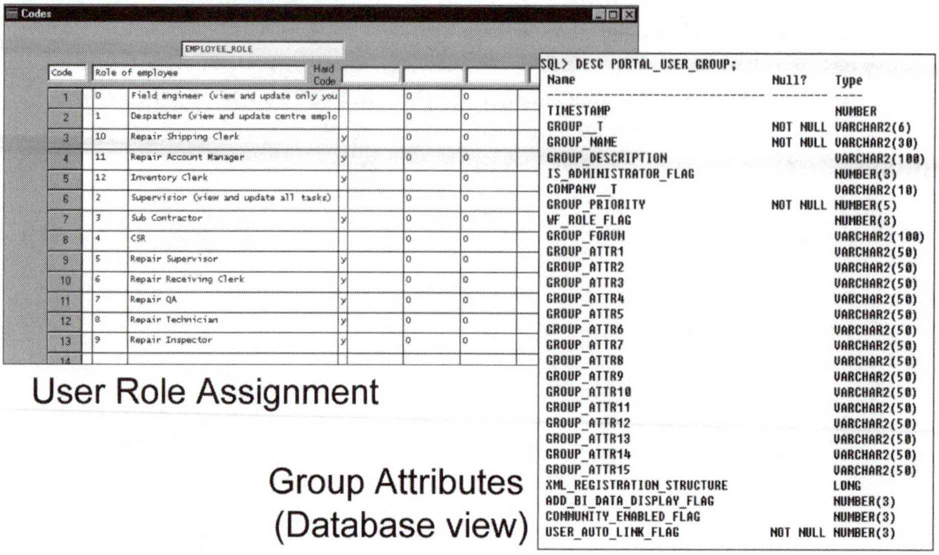

Codes
EMPLOYEE_ROLE
Code
Role of employee
Hard Code
1 0 Field engineer (view and update only you y 0 0
2 1 Despatcher (view and update centre emplo 0 0
3 10 Repair Shipping Clerk y 0 0
4 11 Repair Account Manager y 0 0
5 12 Inventory Clerk y 0 0
6 2 Supervisior (view and update all tasks) 0 0
7 3 Sub Contractor y 0 0
8 4 CSR 0 0
9 5 Repair Supervisor y 0 0
10 6 Repair Receiving Clerk y 0 0
11 7 Repair QA y 0 0
12 8 Repair Technician y 0 0
13 9 Repair Inspector y 0 0
14
User Role Assignment
SQL> DESC PORTAL_USER_GROUP;
Name Null? Type
TIMESTAMP NUMBER
GROUP__T NOT NULL VARCHAR2(6)
GROUP_NAME NOT NULL VARCHAR2(30)
GROUP_DESCRIPTION VARCHAR2(100)
IS_ADMINISTRATOR_FLAG NUMBER(3)
COMPANY__T VARCHAR2(10)
GROUP_PRIORITY NOT NULL NUMBER(5)
WF_ROLE_FLAG NUMBER(3)
GROUP_FORUM VARCHAR2(100)
GROUP_ATTR1 VARCHAR2(50)
GROUP_ATTR2 VARCHAR2(50)
GROUP_ATTR3 VARCHAR2(50)
GROUP_ATTR4 VARCHAR2(50)
GROUP_ATTR5 VARCHAR2(50)
GROUP_ATTR6 VARCHAR2(50)
GROUP_ATTR7 VARCHAR2(50)
GROUP_ATTR8 VARCHAR2(50)
GROUP_ATTR9 VARCHAR2(50)
GROUP_ATTR10 VARCHAR2(50)
GROUP_ATTR11 VARCHAR2(50)
GROUP_ATTR12 VARCHAR2(50)
GROUP_ATTR13 VARCHAR2(50)
GROUP_ATTR14 VARCHAR2(50)
GROUP_ATTR15 VARCHAR2(50)
XML_REGISTRATION_STRUCTURE LONG
ADD_BI_DATA_DISPLAY_FLAG NUMBER(3)
COMMUNITY_ENABLED_FLAG NUMBER(3)
USER_AUTO_LINK_FLAG NOT NULL NUMBER(3)
Group Attributes
(Database view)

Figure 9.6 Group and user roles.

Communities

Communities are created when a number of users and/or groups are brought together to satisfy a specific need, work-flow requirement, or simply because they share a common interest. Through their personal attributes and group membership, community members are provided with access to activities and information (including things such as documentation, chats, and forums) that will allow them to perform their defined roles within the community. Community maps can be built to identify every community need within the service provider's environment. A very simple example of community mapping is shown in Figure 9.7.

Communities can be permanent, ongoing, or temporary. In our quest to deliver SLA-grade service, we are creating communities to satisfy the needs of specific fulfillment and assurance work-flow instances. Once the work-flow instance is completed and the last task is closed, the needs that created the community no longer exist. This means that almost all fulfillment and assurance work-flow communities are temporary in nature.

The billing associated with a specific customer, on the other hand, may generate the need for an ongoing community (which exists as long as the customer continues to be billed). The service provider's employee community is an example of a permanent community (unless the service provider goes out of business).

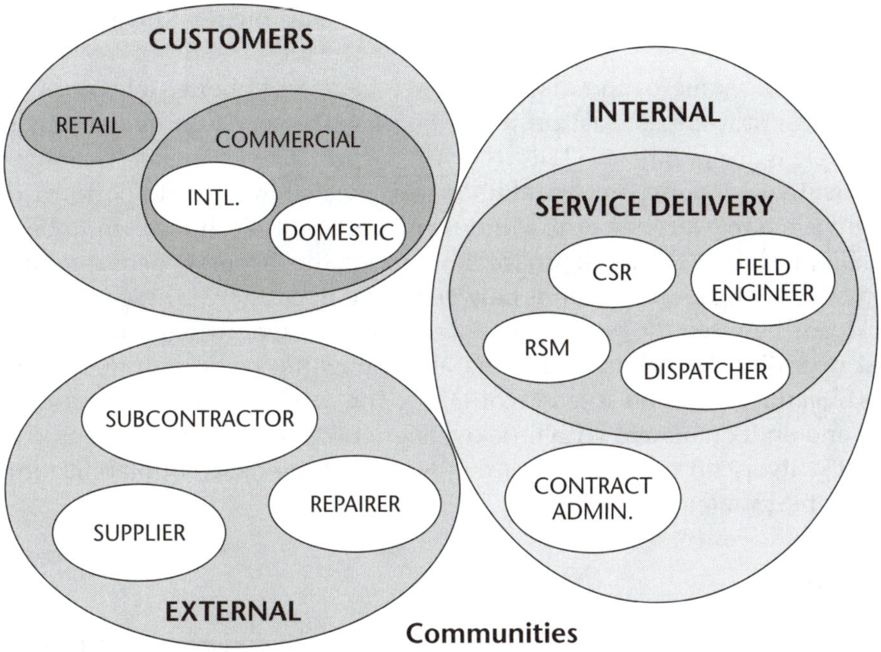

Figure 9.7 A simple community map.

Based on our discussions of users and groups, it is obvious that not all community members are created equal. Nor are all work-flow community members necessarily allowed the same level of access to activities or information related to the work-flow instance(s) that they are working on in common.

The Integrated Service Level Agreement-Aware Service Provider

Over several of the previous chapters, we have discussed the reasons that stovepipe organizations have evolved and continue to exist within large service providers. The ISLA framework corrects many of the system deficiencies that have contributed to the evolution of stovepipes. In this section we will discuss how the ISLA framework can reduce or eliminate many of the problems inherent to the stovepipe organization.

We will also create an example of an ISLA-aware organizational structure and try to understand the roles of the several mandatory support entities that the ISLA framework requires in order to function most effectively. While we are not naïve enough to believe that removing the technical hurdles will instantly fix the problem, we are optimistic that the problem is solvable if we address these hurdles.

To summarize some of the discussions we have had about stovepipes in prior sections: Stovepipes exist primarily because the service provider needs many people with specialized skills to work on specialized systems. The organization is divided along functional lines with the activities being performed all but invisible to everyone else. Multiple layers of duplication seem to be a natural by-product as the work progresses through the disparate departments.

Because of poor communications between stovepipes, there is little visibility of workloads between the work centers and no consistent way to measure or forecast operational efficiency. There is also very little or no automated in-process tracking on the end-to-end work flow. The work flow itself is very convoluted and undocumented with little oversight of the overall process and the timing of delivery. In other words, there is no end-to-end accountability for work-flow performance.

Solutions

The ISLA framework provides a host of solutions to the underlying problems. The largest contributions to creating a smooth operator are made by the work-flow engine, Web and wireless portals, and integration server. These three ISLA components work together to practically eliminate the need for organizations to create stovepipes.

Service providers still need people with specialized skills, but the skill sets can be managed by the workforce management system within the work-flow domain. The specialized systems needs are still there, but the stovepipe aspect has been eliminated by new technology. This is accomplished by using the integrations server to provide interoperability between the systems and the Web portal to distribute visibility of the disparate systems to anyone who needs it.

NOTE The Web portal's *pages and channels* architecture allows legacy mainframe and client-server user interfaces to be *popped* into HTML Web pages through the use of a Citrix server or the equivalent. Alternatively, true HTML front ends can be built within the portal and overlaid on the underlying data structure via the integration server.

Yet the work-flow engine truly makes possible the elimination of stovepipes. This is because work-flow automation makes it possible, for the first time, to reliably model, deliver, measure, and optimize very complex business processes involving a large number of participants performing an equally large number of different activities.

Just as important, the work-flow engine through the presentation layer can make the end-to-end work-flow status visible to any or all work-flow community members. Universal access and visibility enable near-real-time status tracking and auditing capabilities at the task level. Every member of the work-flow community becomes accountable to everyone else. Communications between work-flow community members during the execution phase are simplified, as is shown in Figure 9.8.

By now, it should be obvious to the reader that the ISLA framework (through its ability to remove or reduce most of the reasons that stovepipe organizational structures are created) can be used as an agent for change within the large, established service provider and as a blueprint for smaller emerging carriers. We will be creating an example of such a blueprint in the following sections.

NOTE The organizational entities that we will address already exist in some form within most service providers; hence the following exercise in organizational engineering is intended to be a guideline for transition, as opposed to a complete overhaul or green fields approach.

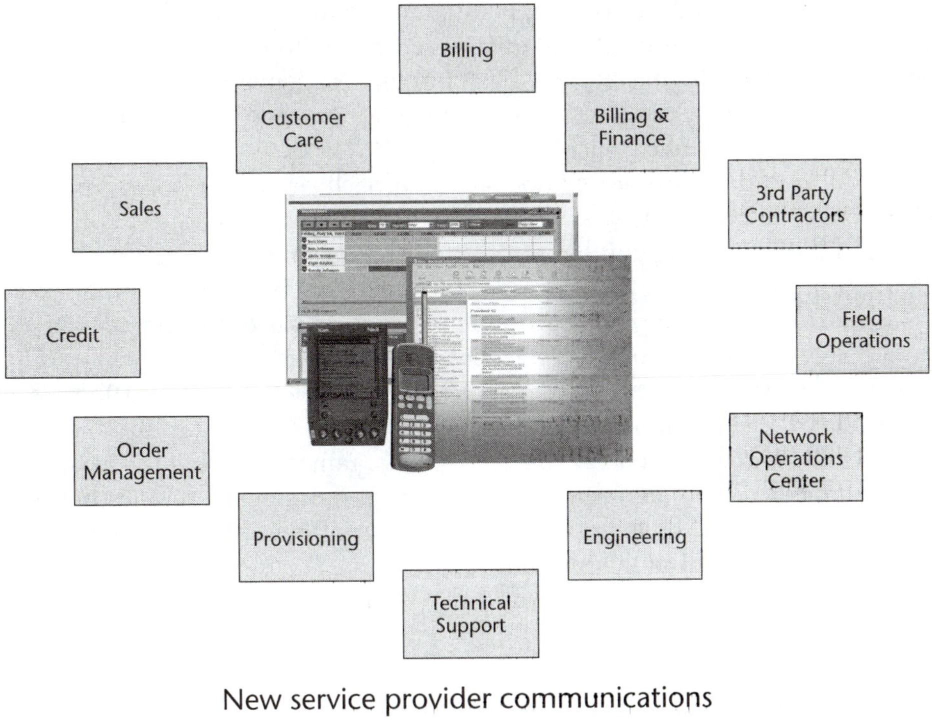

Figure 9.8 Communications between work-flow community members.

The Business Management Layer and Delivery Assurance

In some ways, the ISLA framework appears to be a very top-down, push-oriented concept because it appears that control of the entire service delivery environment is very centralized and is monitored at all levels of management. While top-down control certainly exists in some areas, the framework is actually based on a pull methodology. The entire sequence of activities is initiated by a generating event that is normally not a factor in internal management; that is, the generating event is a service order or trouble ticket. So the ISLA approach is a combination of the two methodologies and is neutral overall.

The ISLA framework, from a management theory perspective, is neither autocratic nor laissez-faire. It is instead an extremely participatory environment based on collaboration and collaborative inputs at all levels of the organization both during implementation of the ISLA framework and later during execution of the service delivery work flows.

The centralized, top-down aspects of the ISLA framework are all intended to do one thing: provide an organized, replicable, and measurable way to guarantee service delivery, efficiently manage resources, and effectively understand the financial implications of those activities. The end goal of all these activities is to ensure profitability within the service provider.

The ISLA framework, of course, is intended to meet the needs of the Business Management Layer (BML) within the TMN and to realize the potential in the Maslow model. To that end, the ISLA framework depends on the successful integration of people, processes, and systems, to manage tasks, time, people, parts, and other resources (such as money).

The integrated nature of our delivery approach drives the formation of a functional organization that is responsible for delivery assurance. Although we are possibly creating another entity, delivery assurance is not a stovepipe. On the contrary, delivery assurance should definitely be the most plugged-in organization within the service provider. This is because delivery assurance should oversee four groups: *organizational engineering*, *work-flow engineering*, *product engineering*, and *intelligence engineering*, as shown in Figure 9.9.

In Chapter 2, we defined several factors as being essential to SLA success relative to a product. In general, all four of the organizations underlying delivery assurance are intended to (1) satisfy these requirements, and (2) become the leading agents of change through business optimization. The factors we discussed mandated that the product(s) be:

- Definable end to end
- Successfully deliverable
- Meaningful in terms of entitlement metrics

- Measurable at the Service Access Point (SAP)
- Visible
- Financially reconcilable

The four groups that function under delivery assurance are responsible for delivering on the big picture. Their role initially is to define the product, its work flow and staffing support needs, and other delivery dependencies; then they will use performance metrics and actual performance measurement as the basis for optimizing (changing) any of the factors. Thus delivery assurance sets in motion a continual cycle of business optimization based on measured results.

The reason that they need to exist at the BML, that is, the corporate level, is that these groups will be responsible for making decisions and recommendations, on aspects such as budgets and staffing, that will affect a number of departments, and therefore these groups must be able to present as objective a viewpoint as possible to executive management.

The functions of the four groups are interdependent; that is, changes to products drive work flow, which could result in changes to staffing and organizations, and vice versa. The driver for recommending changes will be the optimization made possible by analysis of the business intelligence.

Because of this functional interdependence, collaboration between the groups is absolutely essential. Working together is made much easier because each of the groups uses the work-flow editor and work-flow monitor, as described in Chapter 8, to accomplish its tasks. A brief description of the primary responsibilities of each group follows.

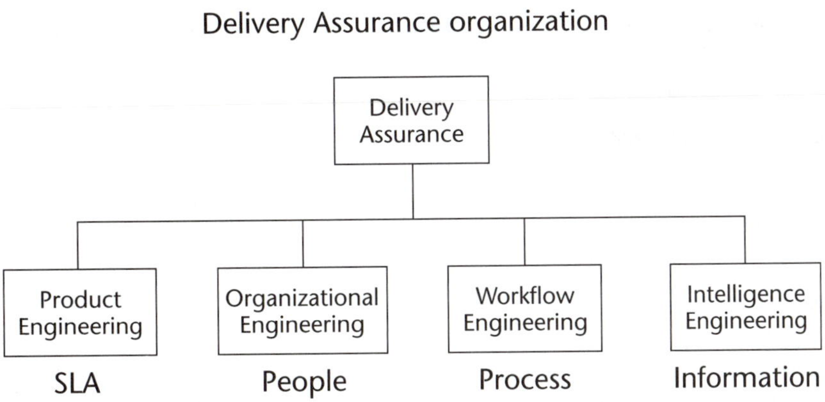

Figure 9.9 The four groups of the delivery assurance organization.

Product Engineering

Product engineering is responsible for the development, implementation, and profitability of products and services offered by the service provider. That means that this group is responsible for the contractual, financial, and delivery aspects of SLAs related to the core product.

Product engineering is extremely important to SLAs because the contract entitlements will be defined and managed within this group. The SLA entitlements will also need continual review and optimization based on the ability of the service provider to realistically deliver the product while maintaining profit margins.

Work-Flow Engineering

Work-flow engineering is responsible for the development, implementation, operation, and optimization of the end-to-end work flows that exist within the service provider. This is a cross-departmental function that requires that employees have a ground-level expertise in the day-to-day operations of the service provider's various departments. We recommend that the work-flow engineering group be made up of facilitators rather than of subject matter experts.

Organizational Engineering

Organizational engineering is responsible for optimizing the human resources available to support the work flow. Unlike conventional human resources organizations, organizational engineering is responsible for defining and understanding the roles played by external resources, such as third-party installers, temporary contractors, system integrators, and so on, as well as the cost implications of including these resources in the work flow (versus using internal employees).

Intelligence Engineering

Intelligence engineering is responsible for the development of KPIs, metrics, measurement procedures, and information management. The role of people in this group is to work with all levels of management within the service provider to optimize the measurement and reporting capabilities that are useful to managers at all levels.

The information management function manages the electronic and hard-copy repositories that contain archived reports, KPIs, standard operating procedures (SOPs), operator instructions, installation records, schematics, drawings, and/or other forms of documentation required to support the installation, operation, maintenance, and repair of the service provider communications network. These workers are tasked with maintaining current versions of all documentation as well as supporting the service provider training efforts.

NOTE We highly recommend that the groups within business assurance not be fully staffed by dedicated and permanent employees. Owing to the collaborative nature of the work requirements and the dynamic business environments that exist within the individual work centers, it is much more effective to pull resources from the individual departments to develop a product work flow than to create dedicated resources.

Championing Collaboration Forming teams around products rather than functions accomplishes a number of things. First, the work centers are directly involved in the work-flow definition, which should make for more accurate assumptions and more current information. Second, the handoffs can be understood and responsibilities defined prior to the product rollout. As we have often stated, the devil in delivery is in the handoffs. Third, as personnel rotate through these organizations, they will get a big-picture view of the service provider and their role within it. In addition, they will take the skills they learn back into the work center.

The last consideration is the most important. All the technical functionality in the world cannot make the stovepipe mentality disappear entirely. Empire building is intrinsic to human nature. For that mentality to disappear, service providers may have to create an entire generation of people who understand, practice, and champion collaboration. Temporary assignment to the big-picture project will help sow the seeds of collaboration throughout the organization.

The Service Management Layer

As we've discussed, the Service Management Layer (SML) starts out as much more of a pull environment than the BML owing to the event-driven nature of activities within the service management layer. This trend continues throughout the organization as the work flow pulls resources into the delivery cycle. We have again provided brief descriptions of some of the key organizations that exist at the SML.

Customer Care

Service providers almost always have established customer care organizations for front-line customer interface and advocacy. As the first level of quality assurance, customer service representatives (CSRs) provide users with support for billing and status inquiries. The CSR handles all initial inquiries and responds directly to customers during problem resolution, even after problems have been escalated. Customer service representatives will escalate outstanding issues to technical support (via a trouble ticket) that may cover a wide range of services such as fulfillment, service assurance, billing, SLA compliance, or other issues.

Order Management

Order management is responsible for accepting orders, tracking their status, and interacting with customers with regard to service requests/service orders (SR/SO). The order management group uses the Order Management System (OMS) to provide positive control of all service provider logical inventories (TNS, 800 numbers, available bandwidth capacity, and so on) and process customer or internal orders for new service, as well as adds, moves, and changes (A/M/C) to existing service.

In many cases, order management is the entry point where the customer begins a relationship with the service provider, with the initial service order becoming the generating event for a dynamic work-flow selection and dynamic work-flow community allocation. This implies that good work-flow knowledge is important in order management, because of the need for notifying and interacting with the customer.

Work-Flow Control

Work-flow control is the work-flow management function of both the service fulfillment (provisioning) and service assurance (trouble management) functional support responsibilities. Using the WMS, Network Management System (NMS), OMS, and other systems, work-flow controllers receive, administrate, input, update, and follow up on all SR/SO actions, trouble tickets generated, and other service actions.

Work-flow controllers are responsible for prioritizing resources and attempting to optimize restoral times, provisioning, and maintenance status through proper personnel assignment, scheduling, and logistics control. Work-flow controllers work closely with order management, technical support, the Network Operations Center (NOC), and logistics personnel at all times to ensure customer satisfaction and that high levels of QoS are delivered throughout the service provider.

Technical Support

The technical support group delivers tier 2 support to the service provider and its customers. The technical support responsibilities differ from those of the NOC in that tech support will support logical (normally software-driven application, configuration, or database) problems, provisioning, and Operation and Maintenance (O&M) actions, as compared to the NOC and field operations groups, which handle the virtual and physical layers of the network.

Logical functions are classified as tier 2 actions and include functions such as account and password maintenance, adds, moves, and changes, user-specific software application support, translation, routing, and configuration support, report generation, order and trouble status tracking, and other duties, as needed.

Any actions that require or are performed more effectively by a physical change in configuration, inventory, equipment, or systems, or are deemed to be exceptional owing to complexity, level of access required, logistics, or physical proximity will be escalated to the NOC for further action.

The Network Management Layer

In Chapter 4, we discussed a number of functional and semantic gaps that exist within the service provider's environment and the difficulties that are being experienced as the TeleManagement Forum (TMF) tries to lead the way to full plug-and-play interoperability. In Chapter 6, we addressed (although we did not entirely solve) some of the semantic issues through the use of domain masters for product, work flow, and workforce, among others.

The Network Management Layer (NML) sits at the crux of the semantic gap issue. As we have discussed, the Service Management Layer above it (from a TMN perspective) is primarily a logical entity, while the Network Element Layer below it (again, from a TMN perspective) is primarily made up of physical entities.

The bridge between the two layers is the virtual entity known as network management. Network management must be able to span all domains in order to understand the impact to customers, service providers, and networks of each activity that is performed. It is with good reason that the best technical people, in most service provider organizations, are found in the NOC. Descriptions of the work that goes on in the NOC follow.

The Network Operations Center

The Network Operations Center (NOC) delivers tier 3 level support within the service provider escalation plan. The people who work in the NOC are responsible for the critical function of providing service assurance, optimizing network performance, and maintaining the highest level of operational communications services and support. The NOC provides a centralized command and control location for the provisioning of user services, network management, operations, maintenance, repair, and associated requirements. Network Operations Center personnel perform fault management, configuration management, accounting, performance management, and security management (FCAPS), to which we also add contingency planning.

Trouble desk functions are also performed by the NOC group. The specific tasks may vary greatly, but, in general, trouble desk functions can be classified as tasks performed remotely that result in virtual (as opposed to physical) state, database, or configuration changes that restore functionality; assist customers in performing actions; enhance network performance, personnel efficiency, or a combination thereof.

Network Engineering

Network engineering is responsible for the technical architecture, operation, and maintenance of the service provider network. The responsibilities include tasks such as capacity planning, load balancing, traffic engineering, performance optimization, and a host of other technology-specific tasks. The engineering group will be as diverse as the technologies that are in the network, as each technology brings its own challenges and idiosyncrasies.

Network engineering will also normally be responsible for any network build-out, capacity enhancements, and network construction projects, as well as technology review, selection, and procurement. This department will also serve as the escalation point for the NOC and provide interface between the operations groups and the network technology vendors.

The Network Element Layer

The Network Element Layer (NEL) or physical layer is an absolutely critical element in the SLA equation. As we stated in Chapter 4, the NEL is where the customer lives, breathes, and operates. For that reason, the majority of optimization efforts should be concentrated on creating efficiency and effectiveness at the NEL—whether through getting the jobs to the NEL more quickly, making parts more available, training staff so they have better skills, and so on. It is very important that the organizations in the NEL have what they need.

During the work-flow execution phase, the work almost always ends up being pushed down to the NML at some point in time. That is not to say that all service orders and trouble tickets have a physical component to them. Many service orders are completed without human intervention or physical changes to the network element. The same is true for many trouble tickets.

In fact, the authors' experience suggests that it is more often configuration or software incompatibilities rather than hardware failure that are the root cause of the majority of trouble tickets and provisioning difficulties. Following is a description of the organizational responsibilities that exist at the NEL.

Field Operations

The field operations group is responsible for the essential function of providing the hands-on installation, administration, operations, maintenance, and repair capability to the facilities, cable plant, electronic systems, and other network elements that reside within the physical network, including fiber optic, switch, data, and wireless networks. Field operations should be designed to be able to provide quick response to network outages ranging from routine preventive maintenance to full-scale network outages that may be caused by natural disasters or catastrophic failures.

Logistics

The logistics group is responsible for all activities related to asset tracking. Since logistics management is the most physical part of the entire service provider, most service providers have some form of logistics and/or maintenance center. This center provides the managers, supervisors, technicians, and administrative personnel within a defined geographic area with a facility for the management, shipping, receiving, accounting, secure storage, issuance, and relinquishment of spares, bench stock, tools, test equipment, vehicles, and other items or materials related to the operations and maintenance of the network. Some of the key functions and definitions of the asset management function are defined in the following sections.

Network Asset Management

Network asset management is responsible for providing positive physical control, status accounting, and financial accounting for deployed network assets, regardless of location (that is, customer premises, and so on). In general, network assets include ancillary equipment positioned in deployed locations, such as communications cabinets, uninterruptible power supply (ups) systems, generators, and relay racks that belong to the service provider, as well as any forward-deployed spares.

Shipping and Receiving

Shipping and receiving provides positive control, tracking, and financial accountability for all incoming and outgoing material shipments. It is the initial point of inventory management, property accountability, quality control, and other program materials functions.

Fleet/Tools/Test Equipment Management

The equipment issue area provides a secure area and consolidated issuance point for controlling vehicles, tools, test equipment, high-value spares, and other essential items. Access to the area is severely limited, and all issued items are closely tracked and accounted for individually.

Spares Inventory

The spares inventory area contains accountable, critical, and/or unique electronic or electro-mechanical items that are necessary for carrying out maintenance and/or repair to the service provider's telecommunications network in the event of an outage, malfunction, or failure. Spares must not be classified as bench stock.

Bench Stock (or Expendables)

Bench stock consists of critical or noncritical items that are normally disposable, have high usage rates, low unit costs, are multipurpose, nonaccountable, and cannot be classified as property items. Examples include certain types of wires, cables, connectors, diodes, light bulbs, terminal blocks, nuts, bolts, and so on. The items may be electronic, mechanical, electro-mechanical, or hardware in nature.

Organizational Summary

As we have said, most of the organizational entities that we have described already exist in some form, and organizational example we have provided in this chapter is more of a blueprint for transition as opposed to a suggestion that current organizations need a complete overhaul. But there are many reasons for some of the differences between current practices and our future-state example, which we will be discussing in this section. Here is a list of the work centers that we have outlined in our example:

Business management

- Business finance
  - Revenue assurance
  - Delivery assurance
    - Operations Support System engineering
    - Product engineering
    - Organizational engineering
    - Process engineering
    - Intelligence engineering

Service management

- Customer care
  - Billing
  - Order management
  - Trouble management
- Work-flow control
- Technical support

Network management

- Network Operations Center
- Network engineering

Element management

- Field operations
- Logistics/asset management

Although this list of work centers may appear to be rather conventional, there are a number of significant differences in the overall structure and accompanying relationships that can best be shown in Table 9.1

As you can see in Table 9.1, the consolidated view of the organization has been overlaid with a number of important considerations that have already been discussed throughout the preceding chapters, including

- Recognition of the importance of the physical layer
- Recognition of the functional gaps
- Recognition of the semantic issues
- Leveraging workforce management
- Leveraging work-flow automation
- Leveraging unified presentation

The end result of this alignment is that unified presentation, technical integration, and workforce management have removed many of the artificial stovepipe divisions, such as the need for specialized systems and skill set management. In addition, the robust work-flow automation coupled again with unified presentation and universal access accomplishes two extremely important things: It (1) provides visibility and status tracking of the end-to-end process flow, which (2) makes every work-flow community member accountable to the others for timely completion of the tasks.

Table 9.1 Integrated Service Level Agreement-Aware Organizational Structure

FINANCIAL		LOGICAL				VIRTUAL		PHYSICAL
BUSINESS MANAGEMENT		SERVICE MANAGEMENT				NETWORK MANAGEMENT		ELEMENT MANAGEMENT
Business Finance	Revenue assurance	Customer Care	Billing	Workflow Control	Technical Support	NOC	Network Engineering	Logistics
	Delivery assurance		Order Management					Field operations
			Trouble Management					
Workforce management								
Workflow automation								
Unified presentation								

It is these attributes that will allow the ISLA framework to dynamically assign community members into and out of the work flow as it changes, based on the individual performance attained within the work flow itself. In effect, the work-flow automation has removed the stovepipe fences by making the entire community into one big labor pool. The system will then assign the best-qualified, most available, closest (and so on) community member to the assigned task.

Dynamic assignment means that organizational divisions that continue to exist can be purely functional in nature. This will allow managers at all levels to concentrate on building the skills and competencies of the personnel under them rather than their empires. Furthermore, the business intelligence that is available will make workforce management a much more objective science than the current environment allows.

Widespread SLA use will drive the industry toward an objective and replicable management approach. With many of the stovepipe organizational problems addressed, management of complex yet replicable work-flow processes can become a reality.

Summary

We have taken a hard look at some of the issues surrounding stovepipe organizations. By identifying some of the reasons that stovepipes have developed and bringing forward new technology and techniques to address some of those needs, we enable change to be introduced into the service provider.

We begin by changing the many organizations into one large labor pool that is flexible, dynamically allocated, and continually optimized. Dynamic community management and dynamic work-flow automation enable these attributes.

We have discussed new ways that users, groups, and organizations can be automatically related on a community-specific basis. These new relationships allow us to bring together diverse community members for a specific timeframe in order to achieve a specific objective. The objective is to deliver SLA-grade quality service to the customer.

Although the tendency for organizations to become isolated and proprietary cannot be totally eliminated overnight, by introducing open communications, end-to-end visibility, and an understanding of the role individuals play in contributing to the work flow, we can make much of the stovepipe mentality obsolete. Some of the techniques used to manage the dynamic work flow, optimize SLA delivery, and reconcile the results, both inside and outside the service provider, are discussed in Chapter 11.

As we have stated again and again during our discussions, it all starts with the entitlements and ends with the reconciliation of actual performance against those entitlements. Much of the ensuing chapters are predicated on a thorough understanding of these areas. So while we have been concentrating on enabling the successful delivery of SLAs, we now shift gears and in Chapter 10 focus on the importance of the structure of service contracts, penalty definitions, available recourse, and the underlying relationships.

CHAPTER

10

Contractual Commitments and Penalties

Service level agreements (SLAs) are put in place to protect the consumers of services. The service level agreement is a contract between the provider and the customer. As with any contract, an SLA defines the terms that the provider is committed to uphold. Contracts define commitments for both parties, and the consequences of failure to meet those commitments. Most business contracts define consequences in terms of financial repercussions, since money and profitability are the motivating factors behind business transactions. In this chapter we will explore the structure of service contracts in terms of the penalty definitions. Specifically, we will look at examples of how service entitlements or commitments are directly linked with penalty formulas and the various kinds of recourse available to consumers.

The focus of this chapter is primarily on the financial penalties defined in the SLAs. The definitions of these penalties are part of the contract and must be electronically defined in the contract's system for the integrated SLA architecture to function. Penalty definitions that are left on a paper contract are worthless because they cannot drive refunds in the billing process or make corrections in workload management needed to avoid incurring penalties. Therefore we will discuss not only the kinds of penalties and recourse that are commonly found, but also how contract systems can model terms and conditions in a way that can drive automated entitlement and billing adjustments. Automated entitlement and billing are very closely related to other topics we have already discussed and will discuss later in the book—in particular, in Chapter 12, in which we discuss measures, metrics, and performance assurance.

Customer Obligations

A contract is a bidirectional definition of responsibilities and repercussions. Not only does a contract define the commitments of the provider to the consumer; it also defines the commitments of the customer to the provider. Each of these commitments is then backed by penalties in the event that one of the parties to the contract does not meet the commitment. Examples of some commitments that a consumer may sign onto include contract lifetime, minimum number of Service Access Points (SAPs), and even minimum bandwidth.

Early Termination

When executing a contract, the customer commits to remain a customer under the terms of the contract for a minimum time period—this is the lifetime of the contract. Since the provider may have invested in infrastructure in order to support the service being provided under the terms of the agreement, the provider will typically want some guarantee that it will receive a return on its investment . Therefore the provider will want to make sure that if the customer wishes to discontinue the service, an early termination charge (or some other such recourse) can be applied. A customer termination clause is normally called a *termination liability agreement* (TLA), and it involves a penalty that is applied to the customer. A very common example of a TLA is the one that has become the norm within mobile services. In this market, providers have been known to offer the mobile phone for free or at a subsidized cost, as long as the consumer is willing to commit to a certain service period. If the customer later wishes to terminate the service before the specified service period is up, an early termination charge is applied to cover the cost of the actual phone.

Minimal Service Access Points

A second customer commitment may define the minimal number of SAPs. Since many services are rated based on the number of SAPs, providers will often provide preferable terms for customers who are willing to commit to some minimum number of access points. If a customer drops below this number of SAPs, the provider will always change the rate charged per access point (usually the number of access points is linked to an appropriate tariff). But providers may also apply an additional penalty in cases where additional equipment or infrastructure investments may have been made and need to be recouped.

Usage-Based Penalties

A third customer commitment is becoming more and more common within the Internet Protocol (IP) infrastructure. Since IP-based services are delivered based on tariffs that define bandwidth usage, providers need to build networks that deliver on bandwidth requirements with certain Quality of Service attributes. In order to do so, providers either need to build their own infrastructure, or, as is often the case in developed markets, they lease bandwidth. The modular bandwidth model is quickly becoming dominant because it ensures an efficient business paradigm, and it is therefore not surprising to find penalties associated with usage that fall under the agreed-upon bandwidth amounts. Obviously, one way to implement such a penalty is simply to charge the same amount even if the usage is low. While level usage pricing is dominant today, the industry is also moving to a model where usage patterns are becoming very dynamic and true penalties are applied to the consumer who is underutilizing resources. Usage-based pricing is similar to the pricing method that has been in place in other industries with very developed distribution networks, such as energy services—specifically gas and electric distribution networks.

Having briefly discussed the financial implications for the consumer, we now turn to the focus of this chapter—and the focus of SLA financial penalties: the penalties that may be applied to the provider (refunds to the customer).

The Effects of Regulation

Before we delve into financial penalties we need to understand why providers agree to pay such fines. After all, if a consumer has a contract with a provider and is unhappy with the service, common sense dictates that the consumer will discontinue and stop paying for the service. There are multiple problems with the service termination approach. Discontinuing service may invoke a termination charge, which is obviously unjustified when the provider is the one that failed to adhere to the contract terms. Once SLAs can be measured and tracked, it is easy to determine objectively and quickly which party is at fault. If the consumer invested time and money in selecting a service provider and the provider failed to deliver, a cost should be recouped from the provider in the form of penalties. More important, in many (if not most) telecommunication environments the consumer may not even have service provider alternatives. Many countries and regions have only a single provider, either because the provider is mandated by a regulatory agency or because the market is underdeveloped. In a monopoly environment the consumer has no termination recourse, and a service penalty is the only available protection for the consumer.

When it comes to SLAs, regulated and nonregulated environments are very different. In regulated environments, a central regulatory agency has a very important role to play in ensuring that providers do not misuse their position of strength. In such environments the regulatory agency often plays a protective role for the consumer by applying SLA reporting requirements and continuously monitoring the provider. In a regulated environment the provider builds an SLA model simply because it must.

In a nonregulated environment, on the other hand, SLAs often help a provider to differentiate itself from the competition on the basis of measurable performance. A nonregulated provider must use SLAs as a means of demonstrating customer satisfaction, not because some higher authority is enforcing the SLA, but simply because the market drivers require it. Unfortunately for consumers, market-driven use of SLAs is still somewhat limited today.

Deregulated Environments

Although the political landscape of SLAs is not the focus of this book, we need to comment on the complexities of deregulated environments. The turn of events around 2000 in the United States clearly showed that while market drivers and free competition are important, regulatory agencies have a role to play in the transition to a deregulated environment. The need for regulatory intervention has been proven in both the case of the meltdown of the competitive local exchange carrier (CLEC) market in the United States as well as the energy problems encountered by the deregulation of utilities in California, both of which have had a very negative impact on the economy as well as on many individuals—consumers and investors alike.

The good news (at least from the perspective of this book) is that the use of an integrated SLA model as the basis for building an Operations Support System (OSS) is of fundamental importance in both a regulated as well as a nonregulated environment. Most of the topics we discuss throughout the rest of this chapter do not need to address differences between regulated and nonregulated environments. We will conclude this section with a brief discussion about what distinguishes a nonregulated environment from a regulated environment.

Regulated Environments

Figure 10.1 shows the three relationships that are relevant in a regulated environment: the subscriber relationship, the regulatory relationship, and the representational relationship.

The *subscriber* relationship is the normal relationship that exists between the service provider and the customer in both regulated and nonregulated environments. A provider establishes service commitments, publishes performance reports, and manages the billing and refund process. The subscriber relationship and billing and/or refund processes exist in both regulated and nonregulated environments, and these are the focus of this chapter.

The two other relationships shown in Figure 10.1 exist only in regulated environments. A *regulatory* relationship exists between the regulatory agency and the provider. In regulated environments, the regulatory agency can grant and revoke the provider's license; the licensing power is often the basis for the provider-regulator relationship. Licensing control allows the regulatory agency to require that the provider publish certain performance reports, implement certain audit procedures, and implement penalty policies (on itself). Underlying all of this is the threat that the provider's license may be revoked or (much more likely) that regulatory penalties may be applied to the provider.

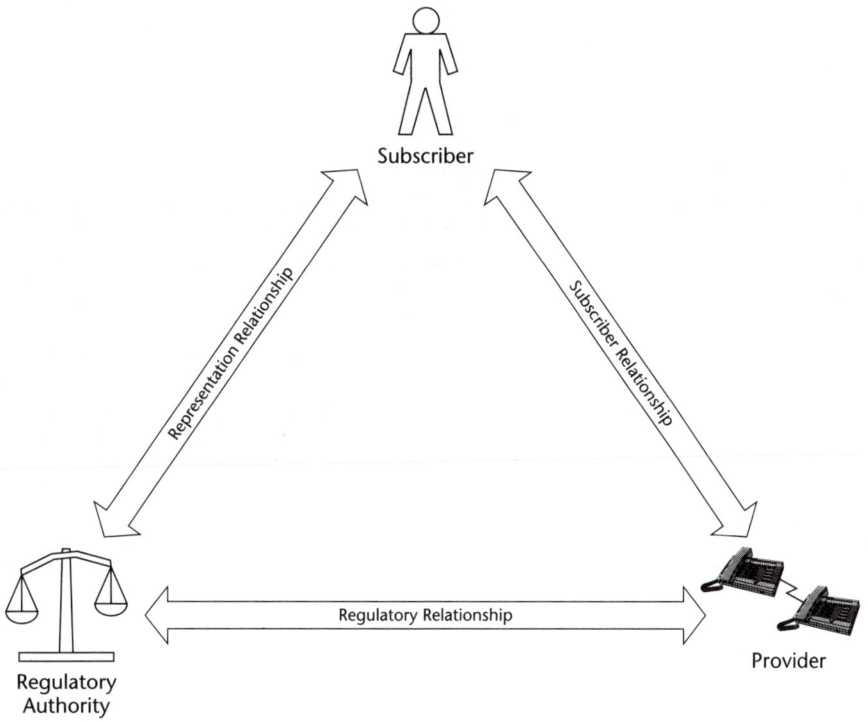

Figure 10.1 The three relationships in a regulated environment.

The final relationship is between the regulatory agency and the consumer. The *representational* relationship between these two parties defines the environment in which the consumers can be represented as a unified entity, and that relationship can drive various improvements that will be carried out within the provider through the regulatory agency.

The subscriber, regulatory, and representational relationships share three important mechanisms that affect the SLA framework—*SLA commitments, measurement information,* and *recourse*. Each of the three relationships may have different implementations in each of the three categories. For example, one form of performance report may be delivered from the provider to the customer, while another set of reports (usually with a different level of detail as well as a different delivery schedule) may be required to be prepared by the provider for the regulatory agency. The same differences hold true for commitments. A provider will have commitments for each of its customers, but the provider can also have statistical commitments defined by the regulatory agency. Table 10.1 shows an example breakdown of these categories by relationship and mechanism.

Penalties and recourse options are very interesting in the context of this chapter. In a regulated environment there are a variety of penalty structures. Because a regulatory agency is normally a higher authority than the provider,

Table 10.1 Relationship Attributes in a Regulated Environment

RELATIONSHIP	INFORMATION	COMMITMENT	RECOURSE
Subscriber relationship	Performance information Processing information in case of malfunction	Commitments set by Service Level Agreements in contract Clear conditions set in termination agreement	Automated crediting and refunding as defined by Serivce Level Agreement Multiple dispute resolution methods
Representation relationship	Publications by regulatory authority		Involved in dispute resolution
Regulatory relationship	Collection and analysis of performance measurements	Targets set in license (optional)	Court resolution

compensation may be awarded not only at an individual level (that is, to a single consumer) but also at a collective level (such as through a class action suit), all the way to suspension of the provider's license. Obviously, different regulated environments resort to different penalty schemes and recourse paths. Table 10.2 maps the penalty schemes in a few European countries, and Table 10.3 maps the dispute resolution procedures available in these countries.

Example Service Level Agreements and Penalties

Service Level Agreements and penalties are defined within a contract. The contract is a legal document and is as legal as it gets, so to speak. The SLA contract is built by lawyers and has all the parts you would expect from a contract (including the fine print). The purpose of the contract is to define in a detailed manner the commitments as well as the penalties and recourse available to both parties to the contract should one party not live up to the agreed-upon terms. Since we are not lawyers, and we assume that most readers of this book are not lawyers, we will try to keep this section as brief as possible and provide two very simple examples instead.

Service Level Agreement Contract for Internet Protocol Virtual Private Network: Sample 1

Security Services

1. Performance Objectives

The provider will use reasonable effort to meet the following criteria.

Software Problem: Diagnose and resolve a software failure or malfunction within 4 hours after the provider opens a trouble ticket

Hardware Problem: Correct a hardware problem within 10 hours after the provider opens a trouble ticket

Security Rule Change: Implement an information change request required for changing security options within 4 hours after receipt of all of the information the provider needs to proceed with the change

Table 10.2 Penalty Schemes in Sample European Countries

PENALTIES	BELGIUM	DENMARK	FINLAND	FRANCE	GERMANY	ITALY	LUXEMBURG	NETHERLANDS	PORTUGAL	SPAIN	UK
Refund to subscriber	Y	Y	Y	Y	Y	Y		Y	Y	Y	
Collective refund									Y		
Fine to regulatory authority	Y	Y	Y	Y	Y	Y	Y	Y	Y	Y	
Suspension of license	Y	Y	Y	Y	Y		Y		Y		

Table 10.3 Recourse Schemes in Sample European Countries

DISPUTE RESOLUTION	BELGIUM	DENMARK	FINLAND	FRANCE	GERMANY	ITALY	LUXEMBURG	NETHERLANDS	PORTUGAL	SPAIN	UK
By operator	Y	Y	Y	Y	Y	Y	Y	Y	Y	Y	Y
By user association				Y	Y	Y		Y	Y	Y	
By mediator			Y	Y		Y				Y	
By regulatory authority	Y	Y	Y	Y	Y	Y	Y	Y	Y		Y
By other government office		Y		Y		Y				Y	
By court	Y	Y	Y	Y	Y	Y		Y	Y	Y	Y
Other						Y		Y			

2. Performance Commitments

2.1 Scope of Coverage

SLA commitment for each Security Service are as follows:

	SOFTWARE PROBLEM	HARDWARE PROBLEM	SECURITY RULE CHANGE
Managed firewall access	Y	Y	Y
Managed firewall hosting	Y	Y	
Internet Protocol Virtual Private Network–internet firewall-based	Y	Y	Y
Internet Protocol Virtual Private Network–Internet router-based	Y	Y	Y

2.2 Customer Credits

The provider will issue a credit equal to 15 percent of the provider's monthly charges for Managed Firewall Service and IP VPN-Internet Service if one or more of the performance objectives are not met for that month.

No more than one credit will be issued for a given monthly billing period.

2.3 Credit Procedures

Should the specified levels of service fail to be achieved, the customer will be entitled to the credits and required to fill in and submit a credit application form within two (2) weeks of the fault occurrence. Credit will normally be provided in the next billing cycle but may be carried over until a later billing cycle depending on the nature of the customer contract and the timing of the fault occurrence.

2.4 Other

The performance objectives do not apply to and no credits will be issued for:

1. Outages or failures related to the provider's Internet Access Services
2. Testing or other operations requested by the customer
3. All work for maintenance or support as part of planned outages
4. Any problems caused by events beyond the provider's reasonable control

Access Services

1. Performance Objectives

1.1 Network Availability

The network availability objective is 100 percent as calculated by the following formula:

$$\text{Availability} = \frac{\text{Required clicks to first purchase}}{\text{Actual clicks to first purchase}}$$

MTTR is the average downtime within a one-year period.

1.2 Packet Loss

The packet loss objective between all Network Operations Centers (NOC) is less than 1 percent.

1.3 Backbone Latency

Below are the objectives for the average monthly round-trip latency for traffic within the provider's Internet network:

Domestic Backbone Network: The objectives for round-trip latency between all domestic NOCs is less than 35 milliseconds (ms) as averaged monthly.

Japan-U.S. Backbone Network: The objective for round-trip latency is less than 180 ms as averaged monthly.

1.4 Outage Notification Time

The objective for the length of time between the service outage occurrence and notifying the customer about the trouble is less than 30 minutes.

2. Performance Commitments

2.1 Scope of Coverage

The Internet access SLA sets forth the following guarantees:

1. Internet Protocol transmission between the router located at the provider's NOC and the router located on the customer's premises is possible at all times.
2. The router located at the provider's NOC to connect the customer's leased lines is available for use at all times.

   Internet Protocol transmission is possible at all times between the router defined in (2) and the provider's backbone.

Customer credits wouldn't be issued in a case where the service outages were caused by customer premises equipment or leased lines used to support the service. This equipment includes routers or terminal adapters (TAs).

2.2 Customer Credits

LENGTH OF SERVICE OUTAGE	AMOUNT OF SERVICE CREDIT
Less than 10 minutes	None
10 minutes to 180 minutes	One-day's prorated portion of the monthly recurring port charge
More than 180 minutes	Three-day's prorated portion of monthly recurring port charge

2.3 Maximum Credit Allowance

A customer may receive no more than one service credit for the 24-hour period beginning with the opening of the trouble ticket, even if more than one outage occurs during that period (refer to section 2.4 for the credit procedures). In addition, a customer's total credit in any contract year shall not exceed a 30-day prorated portion of the monthly recurring port charge within a contract year.

2.4 Credit Procedures

In the event of credits resulting from outages exceeding 10 minutes as specified above, the customer is required to fill in and submit a credit application form within two weeks of the fault occurrence.

Credits will normally be provided in the next billing cycle but may be carried over until a later billing cycle depending on the nature of the customer contract and the timing of the fault occurrence.

2.5 Other

Under no circumstances will credits be given for outages involving:

1. Customer premises equipment such as TAs and rental routers
2. The customer's leased line used for the provider's Internet access services
3. Outages associated with service installations
4. Testing or other operations requested by the customer
5. System partially down—partial access router or port failure
6. All work for maintenance or support as part of planned outages

Service Level Agreement Contract for Internet Protocol Virtual Private Network: Sample 2

Internet Protocol Virtual Private Network–Dedicated Access Service Level Agreement

Network Availability Guarantee

The Network Availability Guarantee will apply to each dedicated Internet access connection in the contiguous United States ordered as part of IP VPN service, provided that references in that Network Availability Guarantee to credits calculated on the basis of a monthly fee shall mean the monthly fee for the dedicated Internet access connection for which that Network Availability Guarantee was not met—not the entire monthly fee for the IP VPN service.

Network Latency Guarantee

The U.S. Network Latency Guarantee will apply to each dedicated Internet access connection in the contiguous United States ordered as part of IP VPN service, provided that references in that Network Latency Guarantee to credits calculated on the basis of a monthly fee shall mean the monthly fee for the dedicated Internet access connection for which that Network Latency Guarantee was not met, not the entire monthly fee for the IP VPN service.

Outage Reporting Guarantee

The Outage Reporting Guarantee will apply to each dedicated Internet access connection in the contiguous United States ordered as part of the IP VPN service, provided that references in that Outage Reporting Guarantee to credits calculated on the basis of a monthly fee shall mean the monthly fee for the dedicated Internet access connection for which that Outage Reporting Guarantee was not met, not the entire monthly fee for the IP VPN service.

Circuit Install Guarantee

The U.S. Circuit Install Guarantee will apply to each dedicated Internet access connection in the contiguous United States ordered as part of the IP VPN service, provided that references in that Circuit Install Guarantee to credits calculated on the basis of a startup charge shall mean the startup charge for the dedicated Internet access connection for which that Circuit Install Guarantee was not met, not the entire start-up charge for the IP VPN service.

Internet Protocol Virtual Private Network Latency Guarantee

Scope

The IP VPN Latency Guarantee is set as an average round-trip transmission of:

- 120 milliseconds (ms) or less between the customer premises routers for an IP VPN with all of its sites in North America,

- 120 ms or less between the customer premises routers for an IP VPN with all of its sites within Europe, or
- 300 ms or less between the customer premises routers for an IP VPN if sites are located in both North America and Europe.

Process

Beginning in the first full calendar month after site installation, VPN latency shall be measured by averaging sample measurements taken during the calendar month between IP VPN sites. The customer's IP VPN must include three or more sites to qualify for the Latency Guarantee. Only sites meeting the SLA eligibility requirements set forth in the IP VPN Site Order Form for the country in which the site is located will be included in this calculation. Sites outside North America or Europe shall not be included in this calculation. This IP VPN Latency Guarantee is only applicable if the customer's sustained use level for each dedicated Internet access connection (as measured by the provider) is less than or equal to 50 percent of the total capacity of that customer's dedicated Internet access connection. If the customer's sustained use level exceeds 50 percent of the total capacity of any customer dedicated Internet access connection during any two consecutive months, the customer must place an order for a capacity upgrade within the 30 days following notice that the 50 percent sustained use level has been exceeded. If the upgrade is not ordered within the 30-day period, the site with the connection that exceeded the 50 percent sustained use level and all other IP VPN sites connected to that site shall be ineligible for this IP VPN Latency Guarantee for the remainder of the service term.

Remedy

At the customer's request, directed to the provider's designated point of contact in the 30 days following the end of the month in which the provider failed to meet this IP VPN Latency Guarantee, the customer's account shall be credited the prorated charges for five days of the dedicated access portion of the IP VPN's monthly fee for the month in which this IP VPN Latency Guarantee was not met. No credits will be made if failure to meet this IP VPN Latency Guarantee is attributable to reasons of force majeure (as defined in the applicable service agreement).

Internet Protocol Virtual Private Network Dedicated Availability Guarantee

Scope

The IP VPN Dedicated Access Availability Guarantee is to have the dedicated access portion of the IP VPN Total Access Service available 99.9 percent of the time, averaged over all eligible sites, for customers with ten or more IP VPN sites and 99.8 percent of the time, averaged over all eligible sites, for customers with three to nine IP VPN sites.

Process

Beginning in the first full calendar month after site installation, and at the customer's request, the provider will calculate the IP VPN unavailability in a calendar month. The IP VPN unavailability consists of the number of minutes that the dedicated access portion of the IP VPN service, provider-ordered telco line, or the provider's network (as defined in the applicable service agreement) was unavailable to the customer through the customer's dedicated access connection, but will not include scheduled maintenance or any unavailability resulting from the following:

- Any customer-ordered telco circuits
- Customer equipment, applications, or facilities
- Acts or omissions of the customer or any use or user of the service authorized by the customer
- Reasons of force majeure (as defined in the applicable service agreement)

Only sites meeting the SLA eligibility requirements set forth in the IP VPN Site Order Form for the country in which the site is located will be included in this calculation. Sites outside North America or Europe shall not be included in this calculation. This Availability Guarantee is only applicable if the customer's sustained use level for each dedicated Internet access connection (as measured by the provider) is less than or equal to 50 percent of the total capacity of that customer connection. If the customer's sustained use level exceeds 50 percent of the total capacity of the customer's dedicated Internet access connection during any two consecutive months, the customer must place an order for a capacity upgrade within the 30 days following notice that the 50 percent sustained use level has been exceeded. If the upgrade is not ordered within such 30 day period, the connection that exceeded the 50 percent sustained use level and all other IP VPN sites connected to that site shall be ineligible for this IP VPN Dedicated Access Availability Guarantee for the remainder of the service term.

Remedy

At the customer's request, directed to the provider's designated point of contact in the 30 days following the end of the month in which the provider failed to meet this IP VPN Availability Guarantee, the customer's account shall be credited the prorated charges for five days of the dedicated access portion of the IP VPN's monthly fee for the month in which this IP VPN Availability Guarantee was not met. No credits will be made if failure to meet this IP VPN Availability Guarantee is attributable to reasons of force majeure (as defined in the applicable service agreement).

Network Latency Guarantees

North American Network Latency Guarantee Scope

The provider's North American Network Latency Guarantee is average round-trip transmissions of 65 ms or less between provider-designated inter-regional transit backbone network routers ("Hub Routers") in North America.

European Network Latency Guarantee Scope

The provider's European Network Latency Guarantee is average round-trip transmissions of 65 ms or less between provider-designated Hub Routers within Europe.

Transatlantic Network Latency Guarantee Scope

The provider's Transatlantic Network Latency Guarantee is average round-trip transmissions of 120 ms or less between a provider-designated Hub Router in the New York metropolitan area and a provider-designated Hub Router in the London metropolitan area.

Process

Latency shall be measured by averaging sample measurements taken during a calendar month between Hub Routers. Each month's network performance statistics relating to the Network Latency Guarantees shall be posted on the Web site. No credits will be made if failure to meet a Network Latency Guarantee is attributable to reasons of force majeure (as defined in the applicable service agreement).

Remedy

If the provider fails to meet any Network Latency Guarantee in any calendar month, the customer's account shall be automatically credited for that month for the prorated charges for one day of the provider's monthly fee for the service with respect to which a Network Latency Guarantee has not been met.

Network Packet Delivery Guarantee

North American Network Packet Delivery Guarantee Scope

The provider's North American Network Packet Delivery Guarantee is packet delivery of 99 percent or greater between provider-designated Hub Routers in North America.

European Network Packet Delivery Guarantee Scope

Provider's European Network Packet Delivery Guarantee is packet delivery of 99 percent or greater between provider-designated Hub Routers within Europe.

Transatlantic Network Packet Delivery Guarantee Scope

Provider's Transatlantic Network Packet Delivery Guarantee is packet delivery of 99 percent or greater between a provider-designated Hub Router in the New York metropolitan area and a provider-designated Hub Router in the London metropolitan area.

Process

Packet delivery shall be measured by averaging sample measurements taken during a calendar month between Hub Routers. Each month's network performance statistics relating to the Network Packet Delivery Guarantees shall be posted on a Web site. No credits will be made if failure to meet a Network Packet Delivery Guarantee is attributable to reasons of force majeure (as defined in the applicable service agreement).

Remedy

If the provider fails to meet any Network Packet Delivery Guarantee in a calendar month, the customer's account shall be automatically credited for that month for the prorated charges for one day of the provider's monthly fee for the service with respect to which a Network Packet Delivery Guarantee has not been met.

Service Quality—100 Percent Service Availability Guarantee

Service Availability Guarantee Scope

The provider's Service Availability Guarantee is to have the provider network (as defined in the applicable service agreement) available 100 percent of the time.

Scheduled Maintenance Scope

Scheduled Maintenance shall mean any maintenance at the provider hub to which the customer's circuit is connected (a) of which the customer is notified 48 hours in advance, and (b) that is performed during a standard maintenance window on Tuesdays and Thursdays from 3 A.M. to 6 A.M. local time of the provider hub to which the customer's circuit is connected. Notice of Scheduled Maintenance will be provided to the customer's designated point of contact by a method elected by provider (telephone, email, fax, or pager).

Service Availability Guarantee

Process

At the customer's request, the provider will calculate the customer's "Network Unavailability" in a calendar month. "Network Unavailability" consists of the number of minutes that the provider network or a provider-ordered telephone company circuit in the contiguous United States was not available to the customer, and includes unavailability associated with any maintenance at the provider hub to which the customer's circuit is connected other than Scheduled Maintenance. Outages will be counted as Network Unavailability only if the provider notifies the customer of the outage in accordance with the Outage Reporting Guarantee set forth below or if the customer opens a trouble ticket with customer support within five days of the outage. Network Unavailability will not include Scheduled Maintenance or any unavailability resulting from the following:

- Any customer-ordered telephone company circuits
- The customer's applications, equipment, or facilities
- Acts or omissions of the customer, or any use or user of the service authorized by the customer
- Reasons of force majeure (as defined in the applicable service agreement)

Remedy

For each cumulative hour of Network Unavailability or fraction thereof in any calendar month, at the customer's request the customer's account shall be credited for the prorated charges for one day of the provider's monthly fee and one day's telephone company line charges for the service with respect to which a Service Availability Guarantee has not been met.

Customer Care Quality

Outage Reporting Guarantee Scope

The provider's Outage Reporting Guarantee is to notify the customer within 15 minutes after the provider's determination that the customer's service is unavailable. The provider's standard procedure is to ping the customer's router every five minutes. If the customer's router does not respond after two consecutive five-minute ping cycles, the provider will deem the service unavailable and will contact the customer's designated point of contact by a method elected by the provider (telephone, email, fax, or pager).

Process

The Outage Reporting Guarantee is applicable only to service provided in the contiguous United States and is applicable only if the customer completes the provider's Customer Information Form in its entirety. The customer is solely responsible for providing the provider with accurate and current contact information regarding the customer's designated points of contact. The provider will be relieved of its obligations under this Outage Reporting Guarantee if the provider's contact information for the customer is out of date or inaccurate owing to the customer's action or omission or if the provider's failure is owing to reasons of force majeure (as defined in the applicable service agreement).

Remedy

If the provider fails to meet the Outage Reporting Guarantee, at the customer's request the customer's account shall be credited the prorated charges for one day of the provider's monthly fee for the service with respect to which this Guarantee has not been met—provided that the customer may obtain no more than one credit per day, irrespective of how often in that day the provider failed to meet the Outage Reporting Guarantee.

Circuit Install Guarantee Scope

The provider's Circuit Install Guarantee is to have installation of a provider-ordered telephone company circuit and activation of a provider port completed within 40 business days for frame relay, 56K, and T1 services; 60 business days for T3 services; and within the scheduled installation date provided in writing by a provider Sales Manager for OC-3 or OC-12 services.

Process

These dates shall be counted from the date the provider has received all of the following from the customer: signed service agreement, signed price quotation or authorized purchase order, completed Customer Information Form, and (if requested by the provider) completed credit application. The Circuit Install Guarantee is not available for customer-ordered telephone company circuits, provider-ordered telephone company circuits outside the contiguous United States, or if installation delay is attributable to the customer's equipment; the customer's facility; acts or missions of the customer, its employees, or agents; the customer not passing the provider's credit check; or reasons of force majeure (as defined in the applicable service agreement).

Remedy

If the provider determines in its reasonable commercial judgment that the provider has failed to meet this Circuit Install Guarantee, the customer's account shall be credited 50 percent of the provider's standard Startup Charge for the service with respect to which this Guarantee has not been met.

Example Service Level Agreements and Penalties Summary

The preceding sample contracts defining SLAs and penalties in the IP VPN arena are merely examples; each product and each provider will have its own unique, typical contract structure, SLA definitions, and specific financial impact definitions. We have chosen to omit the actual provider names and have drastically scaled down the legalese (each one of these contracts can easily take up 30 pages). Although the contract is the basis for SLA management, the number of parameters that are of direct interest is small. For example, Table 10.4 shows the important parameters that need to flow into the integrated SLA model—two of the columns shown in this table are extractions from the contracts shown in Samples 1 and 2. These parameters form the basis for defining terms which model these parameters in a way that is later accessible to both the SLA assurance systems as well as the billing systems when refunds and penalties are to be applied.

Table 10.4 Sample Service Level Agreement and Penalties from Real Internet Protocol Virtual Private Network Providers

SERVICE LEVEL AGREEMENT TERMS	SAMPLE 1	SAMPLE 2	SAMPLE 3
Network availability	99 percent	100 percent for enhanced access 99.9 percent for traditional access	99.9 percent for customers with 10 or more sites 99.8 percent for customers with 3-9 sites
Packet Loss	1 percent or less on backbone		1 percent or less
Average backbone latency	85 ms (in North America and Europe) 120 ms (transatlantic) 180 ms (Asia Pacific to North America)	70 ms	65 ms (in North America and Europe) 120 ms (transatlantic)
Virtual Private Network Latency			120 ms (within North America and within Europe) 100 ms (transatlantic)

(continues)

Table 10.4 Sample Service Level Agreement and Penalties from Real Internet Protocol Virtual Private Network Providers *(Continued)*

SERVICE LEVEL AGREEMENT TERMS	SAMPLE 1	SAMPLE 2	SAMPLE 3
Busy-free dial access		99.0 percent	
Outage Notification			Outage reported within 15 minutes of occurrence
Penalties	1 day per consecutive hour of unavailability, up to 7 days' credit 1 day credit if packet loss not met for 2 consecutive months, plus 1 day credit for each continuous subsequent month 1 day credit if latencies not met for 2 consecutive months plus 1 day of credit for each continuous subsequent month	3 day port charge for outages less than an hour additional day of credit for each hour beyond the first, up to 100 of monthly port charge 10 percent of monthly port charge if busy-free access not met	5 days for failure to meet VPN availability commitment 1 day for failure to meet packet loss commitment 5 days for failure to meet VPN latency commitment

Terms

Terms and conditions are crucial to the correct modeling of SLAs and the financial liabilities inherent to the contract. Terms describe the relationship between the provider and its customers. They define the conditions that must be met to satisfy the customer's requirements. Terms affect both the price of the service as well as the liability assumed by the provider, in that terms are primarily a financial instrument and should be viewed as such. In fact, we believe that in the not too distant future, SLA architectures and contract management systems will share many properties with financial engineering systems, including the hedging of terms, support for back-to-back terms, and risk management.

Terms in the integrated SLA model are used primarily in three areas:

Contract creation. Where the SLAs and the terms are defined and contracted and where the customer gets billed for not only the service but also the terms.

Service assurance. Where entitlement is computed based on the terms and where the terms can be used to effect efficient assurance processes that are driven not by coincidence but rather by the financial impact on the provider. Service assurance includes monitoring of SLAs, escalation, and correct scheduling.

Billing. Including penalty calculations and refunds.

Telecommunications products and services are provided to all kinds of customers—businesses and residential. A provider with many markets and many offerings can have quite complex contracts with medium and large business customers. While residential products and simple contracts typically have few terms with which the product is defined, complex contracts have many terms. Specifically, terms can be defined at multiple levels of what we call the service hierarchy.

A Multisite Contract Example

Let's look at a contract between a provider and a large financial institution. There are typically two sides of a financial house—private banking and capital markets. Private banking supports many distributed branches with account managers and brokers. Each such office has a few people in it, and the telecommunications services used can include a PBX, a T1 or partial T1, a frame relay, and so on. Many of these offices will have similar terms, so, at the site level, all these branches will have the same terms. Since there could be hundreds and even thousands of such sites, we would probably not want to define terms at every such site. Among financial institution branches there may be four branches (perhaps in the large cities) that have many more products on the contract and different service terms than the smaller branches. After all, if a major branch goes down, the implication to the entire company can be disastrous. The capital markets side is even more crucial—it includes trading floors and investment banking, and the terms defined in these offices will be very different than in the banking institution branches.

In order to support a complex yet flexible architecture that does not require an infinite number of repetitive definitions, terms must be defined within a hierarchical structure. For example, we must be able to define the most common terms at the customer level (or at the departmental level). Using a hierarchical structure we can drastically reduce the number of terms we need to define. We can define the general terms and then define only the exceptions to the general rule.

Suppose that the customer in question has 1,000 sites (named SITE1 to SITE1000) in the private banking side and that SITE11 through SITE14 are the large branches. Also assume that there are three trading floors (in New York, London, and Tokyo) that are part of the capital markets area, and that there are 50 more consumers of services in the capital markets side that all have common needs and common service terms (call them SITE1001 through SITE1050). Also assume that in our example the SLAs consist of terms such as *availability*, *resolution time*, and *latency*. If we organize the hierarchy in the way shown in Figure 10.2, then we can define all contractual obligations using only nine sets

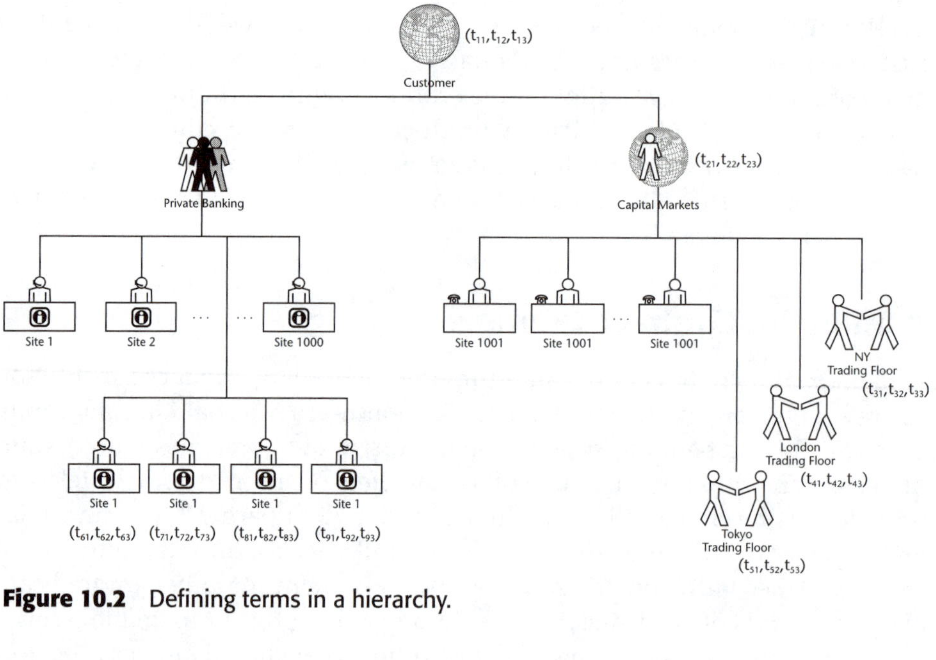

Figure 10.2 Defining terms in a hierarchy.

of terms. Note that in this scheme not only have we managed to create a manageable framework for defining terms we have also ensured that any time a new product is sold it will automatically inherit the terms and no work will be needed, unless different terms are required.

Figure 10.3 shows the definition of a service-level commitment using a new term. In addition to defining the value ranges and penalty parameters, we can define various alerting and monitoring intervals. In addition, Figure 10.4 allows the SLA administrator to define a term that can be used for multiple service levels. In this screen we can define not only the penalty code (which points at the penalty conditions and parameters) but also the various service levels (or fault grades) that this term can apply to. This example shows how a single term can actually be applied to multiple service levels—once more in the interest of saving effort when defining the SLAs. Finally, atomic terms may be aggregated, as shown in Figure 10.5, to create term sets (or packages of terms) that aid even further in simple management of the electronic contract.

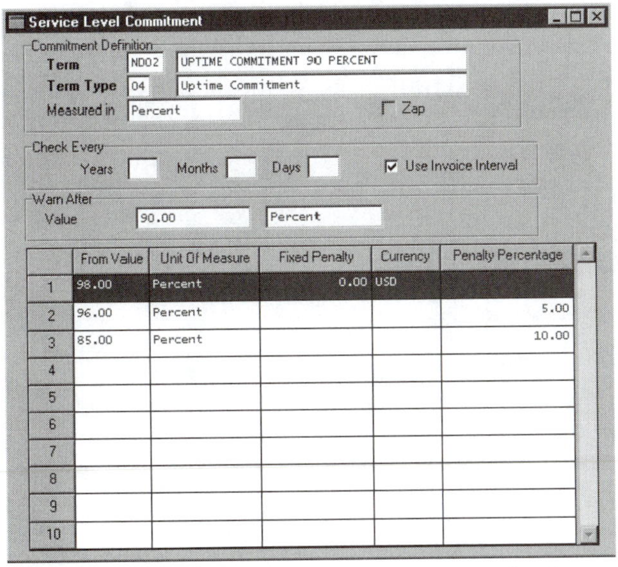

Figure 10.3 Defining the service commitment level.

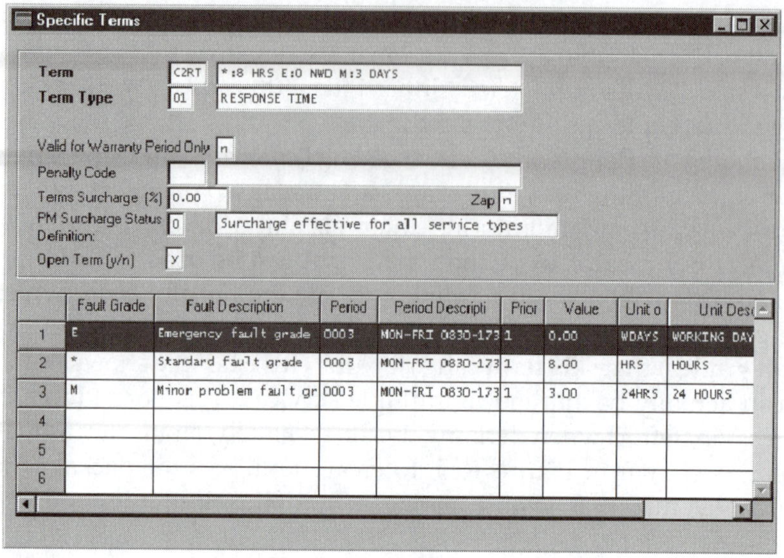

Figure 10.4 Defining a term for multiple service levels.

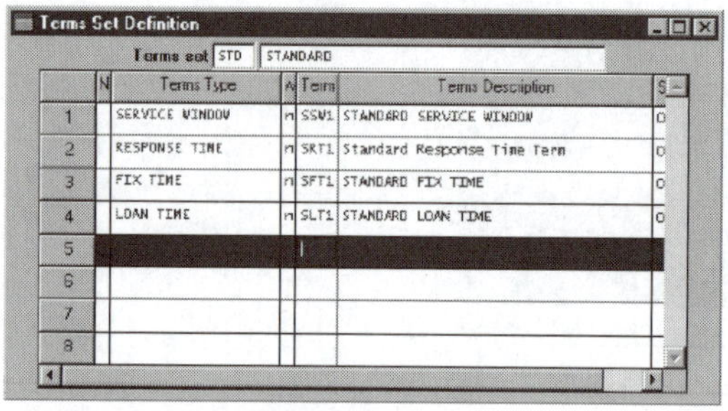

Figure 10.5 Creating term sets.

Summary

Terms and conditions define commitments on each side of the contract. These definitions are the service-level commitments. The contract aggregates these service levels and the financial implications in an agreement—the SLA. The fines and penalties incorporated into the SLAs help to stabilize the telecommunications market by providing a form of *insurance*—making sure that each party upholds its commitments as well as defining how the other party is compensated in case the commitment is not met.

The financial implications that are defined in the contract must be the drivers of all activities in the OSS; after all, money is the motivating factor for all activities in a company. In Chapter 11 we will describe the processes that service providers can use to minimize financial penalties.

CHAPTER

11

Operational Process, Work Flow, Notification, and Alerts

In Chapter 9, we discussed how organizational stovepipes have affected the service provider's delivery capability. We also discussed ways to overcome the stovepipe tendencies, including innovative ways to promote interoperability between the service provider and its customers, suppliers, and trading partners, using a number of capabilities provided by the ISLA framework. The concept of dynamic work-flow communities allows service providers to optimize their organizational structure based on the true business needs.

This chapter will continue to build on the foundation of dynamic community management that we established in Chapter 9. We will discuss the advantages of using real-time work-flow automation and unified presentation to proactively drive the delivery of service to the Service Access Point (SAP) based on the SLA Quality of Service (QoS) entitlements in the concept we call dynamic work flow.

NOTE Because services covered by SLAs are delivered to the customer premises, and not from behind a desk, in much of this chapter we will concentrate on modeling operational processes in such a way that SLA compliance activities inherently create effective field service operations.

Traditional workforce management methods have significant disadvantages when it comes to addressing the issues posed by SLAs. For example, SLA entitlements are not usually available in the Order Management System (OMS),

Network Management System (NMS), Element Management System (EMS), or any other Operations Support System (OSS) that most operations people have access to. So SLAs are invisible at the most critical places: the Network Operations Center (NOC) and the SAP.

The reality is that many SLAs consist of merely a few subparagraphs in a contract document that is buried deep within the recesses of a file cabinet. They have absolutely no meaning within the context of the day-to-day activities of the people and systems delivering service to the customer.

Owing to the lack of SLA entitlement visibility, service providers most often rely on the NOC, service dispatchers, and operations managers to identify and prioritize service orders and trouble tickets on a service affecting and/or non-service-affecting basis, hoping that with their wide net they can catch all the jobs that involve SLAs.

Even in the rare cases where SLA entitlement information is available, other problems arise, such as volume. When the number of SLAs is small, it may be relatively easy for the dispatcher to track them. But as the number of agreements with varying levels of penalties increases, it becomes humanly impossible to try to balance the resulting conflicts in order of priority.

It is easy for calls involving SLAs to be assigned the wrong priority or even to slip through the cracks and go into the queue with ordinary assignments. Even when the SLA entitlement is immediately recognized, it's often difficult to determine what actions should be taken.

Many times dispatchers have difficulty in determining where each community member is, what he or she is doing, and whether the worker has the skills and parts needed to address the high-priority job. In some cases, the only way to determine the location of a community member or the status of his or her assignments is by calling him or her on a cellular phone. Manually tracking down community members one by one via cell phone is a very time-consuming process, especially when the order volume and number of field personnel are high.

Dynamic Work Flow

The ISLA framework concept of *dynamic work flow* offers the service provider the tools needed to overcome these problems. Dynamic work flow is enabled by creating an environment in which critical pieces of information (such as SLA entitlements) are inserted into an intelligent work-flow automation system at certain predefined times or occurrences during task performance related to a core work flow.

The work-flow engine can then use those information updates to decide what effect those updates have on the core work flow and what further actions need to be taken based on predefined business rules and parameters.

A simple example of automated work flow is a scenario in which an on-site technician determines that a power supply is bad. Using a wireless Personal Digital Assistant (PDA), the technician opens a trouble ticket and orders the part through the work-flow engine, which is connected to the logistics system. The system searches for the part and discovers that one is available in another technician's van across town and another is in the warehouse. The system checks the SLA entitlement and finds that there is no service impact and automatically requisitions the part from the warehouse for 2-day delivery.

Alternatively, the system might find that the outage caused a critical operations failure within the network. The critical failure will cause a number of platinum SLA violations if it is not corrected within the next 2 hours. In this case, the work-flow engine system immediately notifies the operations manager, preempts the second technician's current call, and dispatches him or her, again via wireless notification, to deliver the power supply and assist in restoring the critical circuit.

In this example, the work flow was changed based on several pieces of information: (1) the circuit outage had caused a critical operations failure, (2) the operations failure was covered by an SLA entitlement that mandated circuit restoral within 2 hours, (3) business rules dictated that any jeopardy to platinum SLAs must result in notification of the operations manager, and (4) the second technician's existing call was not as high a priority and could be preempted. Figure 11.1 illustrates the work flow for the example we've provided.

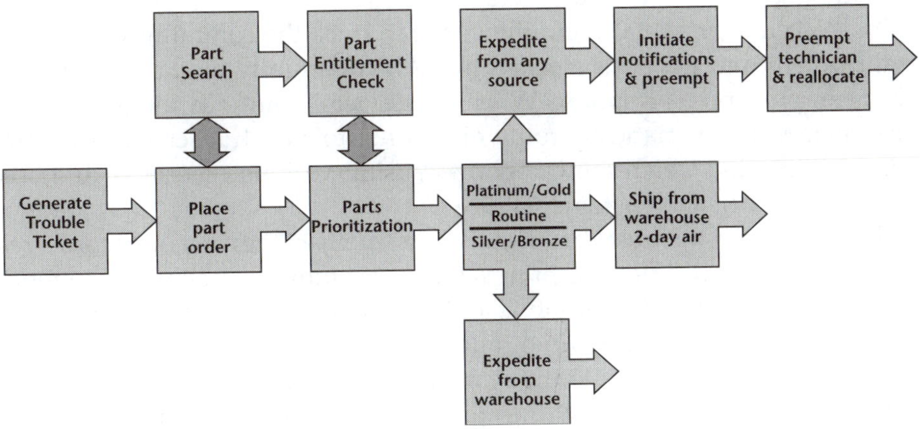

Figure 11.1 An example of dynamic work flow.

Relating the product, workforce, and work-flow domains in a certain way enables dynamic work flow. These relationships are created within the ISLA framework. The roles played by several ISLA capabilities in enabling these relationships are discussed in the following section. These capabilities include the following:

- Unified presentation
- Work-flow automation
- Business intelligence

Universal Presentation

Universal presentation is critical to the capability to proactively manage SLAs. Universal presentation can provide near real-time, bidirectional communications with service community members by enabling distributed communications in the field service environment (that is, the SAP). Community members can be equipped with commercial wireless devices such as PDAs or Internet-capable wireless phones. These capabilities are discussed in Chapter 14.

The significance of universal presentation in the ISLA environment is that it makes the entire fulfillment, assurance, and billing (FAB) work-flow environment near real time. The entire community, especially the work-flow engine, can monitor or affect the activities as they happen. Real-time communication makes it easy to change the technician's work-flow process or task assignments. The PDA used by the community member can provide an immediate notification through an alarm that the community member needs to interrupt the current job and move to a different one.

The universal presentation framework can track the community member's qualifications and the parts stocked by each community member in order to ensure an appropriate response. When the service community member logs in, the system will automatically route him or her to a central screen displaying outstanding calls, which are categorized using various criteria such as call type, call number, and customer site.

The community member can acknowledge or reject the call and record a reason for the rejection. After accepting a call, the community member can report work against it such as travel, labor, and wait times. The system automatically tracks arrival and departure times and downtime. Service community members enter each milestone into the system, such as arriving at a new job, completing the job, going to lunch, using a part, and so on. Figure 11.2 shows examples of the technician's view on the Palm Operating System (OS) platform.

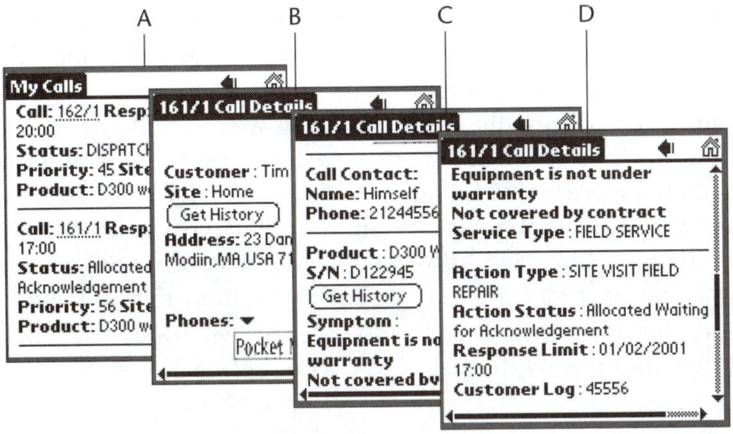

Figure 11.2 A technician's graphical user interface on the Palm Operating System.

At any point in time, the system can track the location of each community member, how long he or she has been working on a particular job, when he or she is expected to finish, and what parts he or she has on the truck. Having this information available to the work-flow engine on a real-time basis makes it possible to use business logic to automatically assign community members and resources for addressing SLAs.

For example, a trouble ticket covered by a platinum SLA may come in at midday. The work-flow engine would work in conjunction with the Workforce Management (WFM) and other systems to determine that truck 12 may have the closest qualified field engineer but does not have the part needed to restore service. Truck 13, on the other hand, may have the right part but is 15 miles away. Under these circumstances, the dispatcher operating the system may decide to send both trucks to a customer site—one to immediately start work on the assignment and the other to deliver the part.

Work-Flow Automation

Work-flow management is the key to successfully delivering SLAs. Implementing the advanced work-flow automation espoused in the ISLA framework greatly improves the service provider's ability to fulfill SLAs. Automating the process of delivering on SLAs ensures that resources are prioritized with the goal of avoiding financial penalties or other criteria specified by the user. Business rules are employed to ensure a more efficient response that prioritizes the service orders or trouble tickets relative to their SLAs.

By linking the information stored in the product domain (such as SLA entitlements) and the workforce domain (such as technician qualifications), the work-flow engine can match the customer entitlements against the location, capabilities, and status of each member of the work-flow community.

The work-flow engine then searches for, identifies, and dispatches community members based on the predefined criteria within the work flow. It can also automatically generate application program interface (API) calls through the data domain or provide notification to managers under predefined criteria, such as when a field engineer has not been dispatched within 15 minutes to a customer holding a platinum SLA. The technology and techniques of work-flow automation were thoroughly discussed in Chapter 8.

Business Intelligence

Perhaps the most important advantage of the ISLA framework is the business intelligence that it provides on work-flow performance. Especially critical is the ability of the service provider to correlate service activities with their financial impacts to the organizations. All costs incurred in performing a task for a customer, whether internal or external, are captured. The correlative cost accounting enables accurate monitoring of the financial implications of all actions, relationships, and performance measures.

The service provider can, for example, track the productivity of individual community members in performing specific types of assignments and more accurately determine the type and location of inventory. The dynamic work-flow engine monitors the cost efficiency of all processes and generates bills or accumulates cross charges accurately.

The community member may also generate a new assignment in response to a request by a customer while he or she is performing another job. The system will access the entitlements database to determine if the job is billable and, if so, include the new assignment on the customer's bill. Cost, margin, and other financial types of analysis can be applied directly to the service activity.

The types and amounts of data that can be captured, queried, massaged, and reported is limited only by the imagination of service managers or executives. With an almost endless variety of Key Performance Indicators (KPIs) available in near real time, increased personnel utilization, more efficient logistics, and continual optimized work flows seem almost automatic. Creating and optimizing reporting is discussed in Chapter 12.

Dynamic Work-Flow Processes

The work-flow engine manages the dynamic work-flow process. There are actually two processes that, in the beginning, run simultaneously. The core process is the set of predefined tasks that have been identified and sequenced by the service provider as being required to deliver a product or service to the customer. This process may be known by various names such as the order flow, provisioning plan, or turn-up and test. We use the term *delivery work flow*.

NOTE These techniques can also be applied to work-flow processes that are developed to perform internal tasks, such as the hiring process by human resources.

The second process is the Integrated Service Level Agreement Compliance (ISLAC) work flow described in Chapter 6. The ISLAC work flow is a set of processes specifically sequenced to provide real-time monitoring of the delivery work flow. Real-time monitoring allows the work-flow engine to identify, detect, and take appropriate actions related to potential or actual SLA violations that may occur in the performance of the delivery work flow.

The Delivery Work Flow

The delivery work flow must be developed from an end-to-end perspective. In many cases, the disparate departmental processes must be mapped into a single work-flow entity that can be managed and monitored by the work-flow engine and ISLAC work flow. The single work flow includes the mapping of both human and electronic (API) interfaces relative to the work flow.

The starting point for mapping the work flow from end to end is understanding the need for a core flow of defined task milestones. The core work flow is necessary to allow multiple task types to be brought to a common ground so that they can be related.

For example, service orders may be sent to the work-flow engine by the provisioning system while trouble tickets may come from the trouble management system, yet in an efficient organization they may both be worked on by the same technician. For the work-flow engine to address SLA entitlements correctly, trouble tickets cannot be addressed on a first come, first served basis. They must be prioritized relative to the provider's business needs.

The core flow is designed to be flexible enough to handle almost any situation, yet replicable enough to ensure quality delivery of services. It consists of a number of key actions that will allow the service provider to use a common methodology for defining and overlaying the delivery tasks, thereby most effectively managing the delivery work flow's task allocation, assignment, and status tracking relative to the assigned community resources.

The core flow, along with the specific delivery tasks and interfaces that make up the end-to-end delivery work-flow processes, are formalized as the product's work-flow template. Templates can be developed for every process within the service provider and form the baseline for all measurement and metrics that are to follow. Templates are stored for reuse on a per instance basis.

As discussed in Chapter 8, the work-flow editor provides a graphical user interface for all work-flow modeling, as well as customization, revision, and configuration management of the work-flow templates. In the end, there may be hundreds, perhaps thousands, of work-flow process templates stored in the work-flow repository.

The core flow includes the following steps, as shown in Figure 11.3:

- Generation
- Assignment
- Prioritization/escalation
- Allocation
- Execution
- Updating/evaluating
- Closure
- Reporting/reconciliation

Generation

A generating event, such as a service order, trouble ticket, or internal work order, initiates the process. Within the ISLA framework, the generating event will normally be an electronic interface from the specific OSS that is responsible for the task type; that is, service orders come from the OMS, while trouble tickets come from the Trouble Management System (TMS). Activities within the departments can be conducted on portal screen pops of the vendor-specific GUI.

For example, the service provider maintains an around-the-clock trouble reporting procedure. Customers, other service providers, Local Exchange Carriers (LECs), as well as the provider's administrative, technical, and support personnel can report a problem to a customer service representative (CSR). The CSR can open this ticket in the Remedy trouble ticket system. Upon saving or committing the remedy trouble ticket, an electronic notification is sent to the work-flow engine. The work-flow engine creates a generating event, which initiates the work-flow instance. The creation of the work-flow instance sets the stage for all work to be performed.

Assignment

The work-flow engine must validate that all information related to the work-flow instance is properly received and normalized by the system. The work-flow engine then selects the appropriate work-flow template(s), validates tasks, and generates the ISLAC work flow and other tracking procedures.

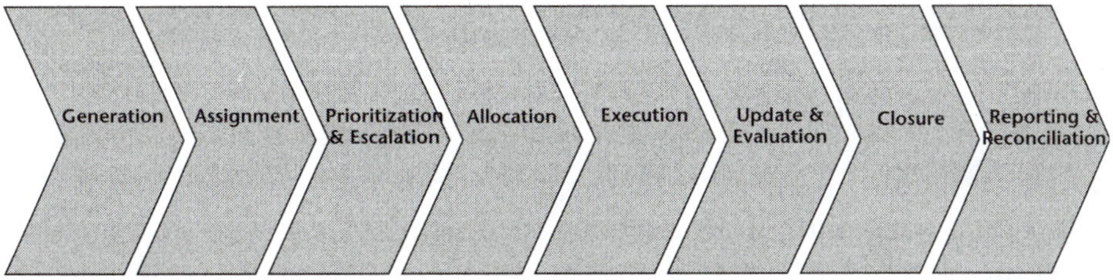

Figure 11.3 An example of the Integrated Service Level Agreement core work flow.

For example, when the trouble ticket call is generated by a CSR, the CSR will create a trouble ticket number for tracking the action. The trouble ticket tracking numbers will be provided to users or other points of contact at the time of task generation and may be used to reference the appropriate response, actions taken or in progress, procurement, task status, or other follow-up actions.

When the work-flow engine creates the work-flow instance, it must normalize the ticket number and validate certain information from the ticket, such as type of equipment affected, to properly select the delivery work-flow tasks related to this instance from the template library. Information such as configuration data and key fields of the trouble ticket will be automatically populated based on unique circuit IDs or equipment identifiers.

The work-flow engine will then select the appropriate delivery template(s) from the library (and overlay them onto the work-flow instance. The template will relate the baseline tasks to be performed by all community members with the work-flow instance and trouble ticket number.

The work-flow engine will also generate (or update) the ISLAC work-flow instance, associating the current work-flow instance to the service. An existing ISLAC work-flow instance may already be running on the same circuit ID, which could have been put in place during the service fulfillment or on a prior trouble ticket for this circuit. Whether or not an existing ISLAC work flow is already in place will depend on the SLA entitlements.

Prioritization and/or Escalation

The work-flow engine will prioritize and/or escalate the delivery work-flow instance based on SLA entitlement, criticality, and service impact. In general, a work-flow instance is prioritized the first time through the process and escalated (that is, reprioritized) on following passes. Escalation is normally done in response to a perceived need or triggering event, such as an imminent SLA violation or an actual threshold violation.

For example, the trouble ticket will be evaluated for prioritization based on the SLA entitlements, scope, type, and impact of the trouble. It will then be placed in the queue in priority order.

Besides SLA entitlements, other parameters such as service impact and current status can also be used to determine prioritization. Service providers should set up a common prioritization schedule that bases response to work flow on the criticality of the entitlements and the impact of the trouble on the service provider and/or customer, rather than on a first in, first out approach.

Prioritization Schedule

The prioritization schedule allows for establishing priorities among different types of tasks to ensure that equipment, tools, worker-hours, funds, and other resources are directed to the higher-priority requirements.

Using this system, the mean response and repair time for each level of priority and the service provider's support infrastructure, as a whole, can be determined. Work-flow instances may be expedited or lowered in priority as needs, resource availability, and/or schedules change.

The system also provides for excellent management reporting capabilities as well as efficient utilization of workers and equipment, visibility, and resource accountability. This data will serve as the basis for technical analysis of the efficiency of the operational support being provided. Any necessary adjustments can be made in work flow, planning, technical manpower, training, prepositioning of spares, or in an almost unlimited number of other factors to achieve the most rapid, effective, and efficient QoS possible. Following is an example of how to develop a common schedule based on service impact.

Service Impact

The service impact is a general statement made about the effect that a failure, outage, incident, or action has on the total service provider network and its capability to support service provider and other government agencies. The service impact consists of three key areas (fields): (1) priority, (2) type, and (3) action. Predefined impacts for critical circuits are determined by their location within the service provider network, by the customer SLA, network capacities, and other factors.

The standard designations within each field provide further definition and together provide instantaneous information to the technicians, engineers, or managers. These personnel can understand the importance of that particular task in relation to the overall telecommunications network, equipment, or capability. Table 11.1 lists areas and field selection options by importance.

Table 11.1 Prioritization Schedule

PRIORITY	TYPE	ACTION
CRITICAL	Operations	Failure
GOLD	Provisioning	Outage
MAJOR	Engineering	Jeopardy
SILVER	Quality	Incident
BRONZE	Service	Order
MINOR	Maintenance	Action
ROUTINE		Request
SCHEDULED		
PREVENTIVE		

Possible Service Impact Examples:

- Critical operations failure (highest priority)
- Routine service order (standard priority)
- Preventive maintenance request (lowest priority)

Sample Definitions

Critical. An outage or failure of a critical operational system resulting in the total or near total loss of the service provider's overall service support capability, or the loss of any system or subsystem that results in a real and immediate threat to life and/or safety. The response is immediate and will be ongoing until restoration of the system is achieved using whatever means necessary.

Gold. An outage or failure of a system resulting in the total or near total loss of the customer's service capability on a defined circuit or service, or the loss of any system or subsystem that results in such loss. The response target is 1 hour, and the restoral target is 2 hours. Restoral efforts will continue until restoration of the system is achieved, regardless of time of day, using whatever means available.

Major. An outage or failure of a critical operational system that results in a partial loss of overall service provider service support capability, total loss of an operational subsystem's service support or redundant capability, or loss of any system or subsystem responsible for ensuring life and/or safety. The response is immediate and will not exceed 4 hours. Restoral will continue until restoration of the system is achieved or all immediate means have been exhausted.

Silver. An outage or failure of a system resulting in the total or near total loss of the customer's service capability on a defined circuit or service, or the loss of any system or subsystem that results in such loss. The response target is 4 hours, and the restoral target is 8 hours. Restoral efforts will continue until restoration of the system is achieved regardless of time of day, using whatever means available.

Bronze. An outage or failure of a system resulting in the total or near total loss of the customer's service capability on a defined circuit or service, or the loss of any system or subsystem that results in such loss. The response target is 8 hours, and the restoral target is 24 hours. Restoral efforts will continue until restoration of the system is achieved during the hours of between 8:00 A.M. and 6:00 P.M., Monday through Friday, using whatever means appropriate.

Minor. An outage or failure that results in the partial loss of an operational system or subsystem's service support capability, the partial loss of redundancy for an operational system affecting the overall service provider's service support capability, or other loss of support capabilities. The response is as soon as possible, not to exceed 24 hours, and will continue on an as-available basis until restoration is achieved.

Failure. An unscheduled and unanticipated system or subsystem loss of function that occurred or was discovered during actual use, operational conditions, pre-op tests, maintenance, or other applicable activities.

Outage. A system or subsystem loss of function that is made to occur, occurred, or was discovered during installation, upgrade, change, maintenance, repair, or other applicable activities. All scheduled downtimes are classified as outages.

Incident. An event that takes place or that is observed but presents no immediately noticeable loss of function to any system or subsystem. An incident is noteworthy for the purposes of reference, tracking, historical significance, or technical indications or implications. Examples include tests, studies, lightning strikes, power fluctuations, and so on.

Allocation

Now that the delivery work flow has been identified and related to the trouble ticket instance, the process of allocating tasks to the work-flow community can commence.

Allocation is usually done both up front and dynamically throughout the life of the work flow because real-time events such as schedule slips can affect personnel availability. The allocation will be based on a large number of factors that reside across several domains. Some of these factors include the following:

- SLA entitlements
- Task requirements
- Timing requirements (due dates and firm order commitments)
- Availability of personnel
- Scheduling (calendars and diaries) procedures
- Skill requirements
- Geography
- Availability of parts

Task allocation begins with the work-flow engine creating a number of work orders or *calls*, as shown in Figure 11.4. The work-flow template is replicated by creating work orders for each instance of human intervention within the end-to-end work flow. These work order instances are directly related to the service order or trouble ticket number.

The work orders will then be allocated to the various organizational queues identified on the template. The next level of allocation is done at the organizational level and, depending on the process within the service provider, can be done through any combination of automatic, semiautomatic, or manual allocation methods.

Using manual allocation, the work orders will be electronically forwarded to the departmental queue where an assigned individual, such as a dispatcher, job controller, or work center coordinator, will review it. The dispatcher will make an initial determination as to the nature of the outage then manually assign a community member to complete the work. The community member, on receipt of the work order, must manually acknowledge the work order via the system.

In semiautomatic allocation, the work order is still sent to the departmental queue, but the system makes an initial determination of the most suitable (as determined by skills, geography, availability, and so on) community member and provides a list of these candidates in rank order. The dispatcher selects one

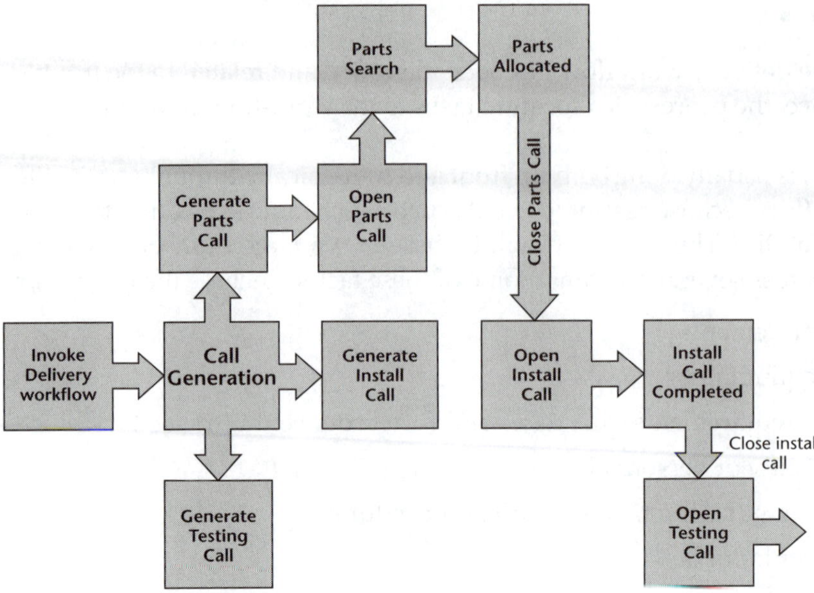

Figure 11.4 The work-flow engine creates multiple calls.

of the community members from the list or can manually assign a different member. Acknowledgment of the work order is optional, depending on the service provider's policies.

In automatic allocation, the work order is sent to the departmental queue. The system then automatically identifies the most suitable community member within the department and assigns the work order. No acknowledgment is required, and the assigned member must complete the work as assigned. No human intervention is required to complete the allocation process. Figure 11.5 depicts the three allocation options.

Execution

Once allocated, task execution by the assigned community member(s) is initiated and actions are performed in accordance with service delivery work flow. Throughout the execution phase the NOC, job controllers, technicians, engineers, and other supporting personnel update the database with regard to actions taken, status changes, parts being ordered, and so on.

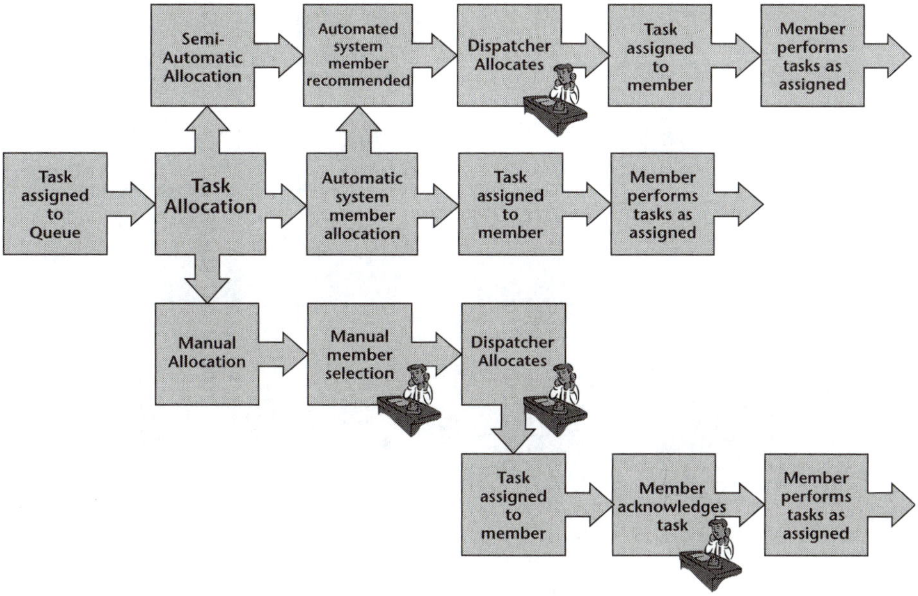

Figure 11.5 The three options for task allocation.

Specific activities are performed in accordance with departmental procedures. These lower-level processes can also be modeled in the work-flow editor to ensure replicability and compliance within the department.

For example, if a trouble ticket is the result of a switch fault, the on-duty tech support or NOC technician can use the predefined restoration procedures that have been modeled in the work-flow editor as a sub-work flow. The sub-work flow may require that the technician run a number of real-time tests using built-in diagnostics or schedule them for execution during the night.

The fault restoration work flow may also include provisions to use direct online access to the network element to interface directly with the network element to determine the cause of failure. Test results can be entered directly into the system and used to make dynamic work-flow decisions as well as stored for historical purposes. The dynamic work-flow options are shown in Figure 11.6.

Updating/Evaluating

During execution, the community members will update status information about the nature of the outage and each action taken to resolve the problem in real time, or as soon as possible thereafter, and electronically forward the status back to the work-flow engine.

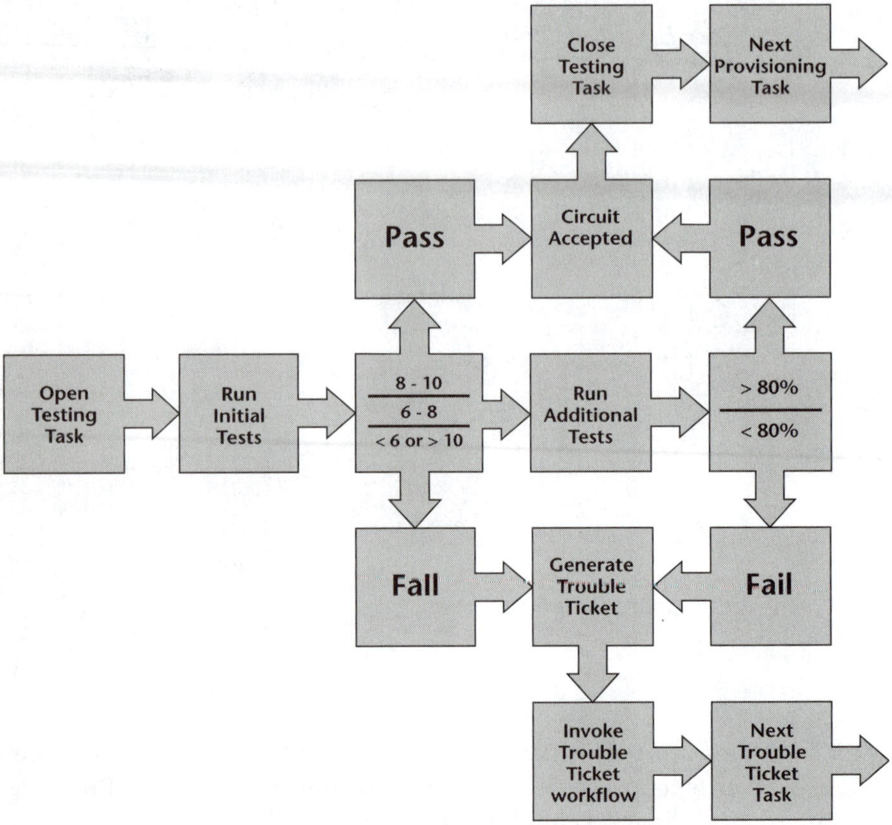

Figure 11.6 Test results can determine dynamic work flow.

Visibility of these actions can be provided through universal presentation. The call center, technician, and/or customer can view activities in near real time and historically. Customer care should do a follow-up with the user each time there is a scheduling change, closure, or other significant event related to the service order or trouble ticket. Follow-up can also be automated and done electronically.

Status updates are accomplished and evaluated continually for further actions. The ISLAC work flow, running in the background, will continually compare activity updates for SLA compliance. In most cases it will find no cause for alarm. When there is cause, the ISLAC work flow will prompt the work-flow engine to take appropriate actions. In this case, the actions can include the following:

- Notifications
- Alerts
- Escalations

Notifications

Notifications can be delivered within the system, by email, pager, telephone, or by any number of other means. Notification can be construed as normal updates made during the course of the execution phase. The work-flow engine can automate the notification as part of the work flow.

For example, the work-flow engine might be configured to send out an email reminder to the customer 7 days, 2 days, and 1 day prior to a scheduled installation that requires a confirmation from the customer. Sending reminders would likely reduce drastically the times when a technician shows up only to find no customer at home.

Similarly, the work-flow engine could be configured to send out a notification to a technician that an SLA entitlement related to provisioning a circuit with a silver SLA will be violated within 3 days if no action is taken.

Alerts

Alerts are high-priority notifications that something (normally negative) is about to happen or has happened that requires immediate action. Alert generation from the ISLAC work flow makes the ISLA framework valuable to service providers.

For example, if the technician did not correct the problem we told him or her about 3 days ago (prior example), the work-flow engine might be configured to send alerts out to him or her, his or her manager, and the regional manager, that a silver SLA violation is imminent and will occur within the next 24 hours.

Escalation

Escalation is the process by which additional technical capabilities are allocated or the work is reprioritized in order to ensure completion. Escalation is usually much more associated with service assurance and trouble ticket response than with fulfillment.

In Chapter 9, we outlined four distinct levels of trouble response support in the escalation process:

1. Customer support
2. Technical support
3. Network Operations Center (NOC)
4. Engineering support and/or analysis

In general, each level will perform trouble resolution and corrective actions to the limits of its abilities. Once the problem has been identified as not resolvable at the current level, the trouble will be progressively escalated to the next level until restoral or closure has been attained. Service Level Agreements may also be used to drive the escalation process to ensure compliance. Figure 11.7 shows the escalation of a trouble ticket.

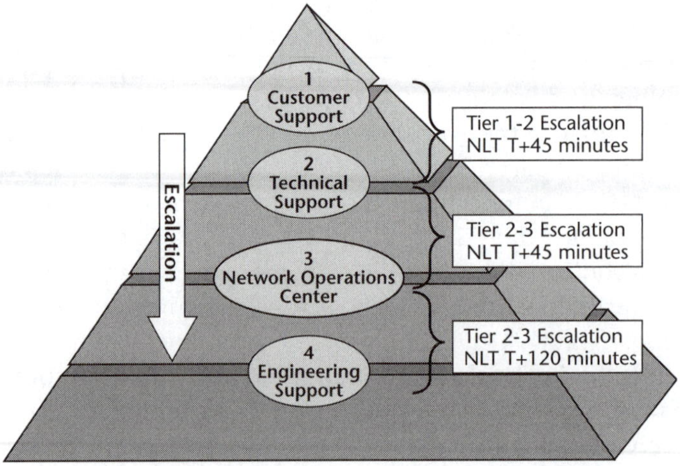

Figure 11.7 An example of the escalation of a trouble ticket.

On a case-by-case basis, the service provider (NOC or management) may also determine that a trouble ticket is more time critical or more liable to affect service and may require expedited servicing and response. In this case, the service provider may request that the normal process for both escalation and prioritization be bypassed, that a higher priority be established for addressing that ticket. The ticket is then reprioritized and reallocated with the higher priority.

Continuing with our last example, if neither the technician nor his or her managers has taken corrective action, the work-flow engine might be configured to auto-escalate. The auto-escalate work flow, in this case, may be to generate a trouble ticket with a "silver provisioning jeopardy" impact statement and to route the ticket to the NOC for action, 12 hours prior to the violation. The NOC would then be expected to correct the condition.

Closure

After all the work-flow tasks have been completed successfully, the delivery work flow can be closed. Depending on the type of product and the SLA entitlements, the ISLAC work flow may also be closed or could remain open for ongoing monitoring. All work-flow activity and updates will be stored to provide for an audit trail, historical reporting, and later analysis. The CSR will then contact the user and verify that service has been restored, and provide the user with information about the cause of the outage and resolution of the trouble ticket. On-line visibility of the status of individual service orders and trouble tickets is also available throughout the process.

Reporting/Reconciliation

As we have discussed, reporting on the delivery work flow is available in real time throughout the process and is stored historically. Managers within the various internal departments, as well as external community members, can view the service provider's performance through Key Performance Indicators (KPIs) and be updated on important events through notifications, alerts, and escalations.

Over the longer term, the stored historical information can be used as the basis for further optimizing the work-flow template, the organization, or to identify shortcomings within the systems support area. By collecting and quantifying the performance information, the service provider can create the continual optimization loop we have previously discussed.

Reconciliation of the SLA component of the delivery work flow will be addressed in the section on ISLAC work flow. Chapter 12 covers the technical aspects of reporting and developing KPIs that will enable continual optimization.

The Integrated Service Level Agreement Compliance Work Flow

Once an instance of the end-to-end delivery work flow has been invoked, an instance of the ISLAC work flow we discussed in Chapter 6 is overlaid on it. As mentioned earlier, the purpose of the ISLAC work flow is specifically to enable in-process and ongoing SLA compliance monitoring and reporting on the QoS levels of the products and services delivered by the service provider.

But, unlike the delivery work flow, the ISLAC work flow is an almost totally automated background process that continues to run well past the closure date of the delivery work flow. The ISLAC work flow is intended to remain in place and run in the background as long as the product or service is being delivered.

In Chapter 6, we identified the task within the ISLAC work flow. In this section, we will break these tasks down further and discuss some of the concepts, issues, and challenges of implementing real-time SLA monitoring and notification. The ISLAC work-flow tasks can be listed as follows:

- Define entitlements
- Event generation
- Identify provisioning and/or troubleshooting work flows

- Extract performance data
  - Work-flow activity
  - Network statistics
- Analyze Performance
  - Real-time
  - Historical
- Identify exceptions
- Respond
- Calculate financial impact
- Reconcile

Define Entitlements

Throughout our prior discussions, we have stressed the importance of good product and SLA definitions. One of the primary reasons that SLAs have not been properly managed is that until recently there were no available contract entitlement platforms that possessed the required functionality.

A key requirement for any SLA management tool is the ability to define and set entitlement thresholds for a contracted deliverable. Along with listing the terms and conditions, an important system requirement is the ability to set entitlements and thresholds that can be read by other modules or systems.

Within the telco space, the deliverable entails managing service entitlements and thresholds for a circuit, line, or associated service (such as the 2-hour restoral required on an OC-3 circuit). In the contractual sense, these circuit IDs, telephone numbers, Common Language Location Identification (CLLI) codes, and so on, would appear as the product master with the SLA entitlements appearing as line items bundled into the contract.

Because SLA entitlements are normally line items bundled onto a product during the ordering process or after the fact, they should be construed as a product option—so SLAs must appear in the product catalog.

As we discussed earlier, service providers must consider a number of semantic issues within their organizations when they are creating a universal understanding of product catalogs within the different OSSs. We have specifically addressed these issues by creating a semantic master-slave domain within the ISLA framework.

In other words, the ISLA framework would be the semantic master for the other OSSs, with technical and semantic integration enabled by the integration server. The product domain therefore serves as the master repository for entitlements.

Event Generation

Event generation for the ISLAC work flow should be automatic upon generation of the delivery work flow. The work-flow template of every delivery work flow must have an auto-generate task that will invoke the ISLAC work flow as a subprocess. Figure 11.8 shows the auto-generated ISLAC work flow.

Identify Provisioning and/or Troubleshooting Work Flows

The ISLAC work flow must validate the product or service that it monitors. Validation will be accomplished by first extracting the product, customer, and order information residing within the delivery work flow, ascertaining which work-flow template is in use, then accessing the entitlement information stored in the product domain to determine the SLA entitlements. When the initial entitlement check is completed, these entitlements will be the basis for any notification, alert, or escalation generated by the ISLAC work flow.

Extract Performance Data

The system must be able to periodically extract a statistical representation of the performance that is directly related to the commitments made in the SLAs. In general, these stats fall into one of two categories: (1) work-flow activity and (2) network statistics.

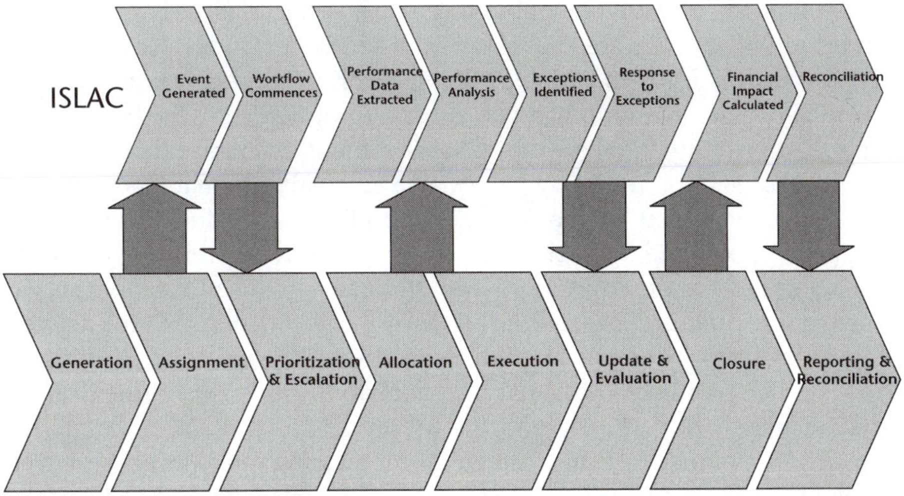

Figure 11.8 A delivery work flow auto-generates the Integrated Service Level Agreement Compliance.

Work-Flow Activity

The ISLAC work-flow monitors and reports on tasks and activities surrounding the performance of the service provider in satisfying the service fulfillment and service assurance portions of the delivery work flow. The data that can be found in the provisioning and trouble-ticketing systems may be acceptable as a source for reports; but in general the workforce management systems are preferable because they maintain activity data at a finer level of granularity.

Network Statistics

The majority of network statistics that are pertinent to SLAs are based on the availability and reliability of the contracted service. In most cases, these attributes will be reflected in statistical analysis related to downtime as measured within the network.

The most readily available source of information on network statistics is obviously the Network Management System (NMS). As we have discussed, the amount and quality of the information are generally very good, and NMS vendors have been making concerted efforts to support SLAs within their offerings. They are also starting to provide entitlement management and including customer impact analysis in their products.

No matter how good the NMS may be at gathering the statistical data provided by the network, a basic problem within service providers makes SLA compliance measurement a problem: As we have said before, there are few, if any, service providers that have NMS visibility over their entire networks end to end.

Competition once again creates a problem with QoS because multiple service providers are involved in delivering end-to-end service. Large parts of many end-to-end circuits are invisible to the service provider. Not only does invisibility create a problem with QoS; it makes provisioning, troubleshooting, and even day-to-day operations much more complex.

The lack of visibility and control makes it difficult to ensure that SLA compliance measurements are being taken at a relevant point in the network. Obviously, the most accurate measurement point would be directly at the SAP. Unfortunately, accessing the SAP is not always an option because of the dumb (unmanaged) devices deployed on many customer premises. As more service offerings require manageable customer premise equipment (CPE) for delivery (such as premises routers, Digital Subscriber Line Access Multiplexer [DSLAMs], and premises modems), the availability of measurement at the SAP will increase.

Both activity monitoring and network monitoring play important roles within the ISLA framework. The information is extracted from the operational database or disparate OSS and stored in the datamart. Figure 11.9 shows how a service provider can extract performance data.

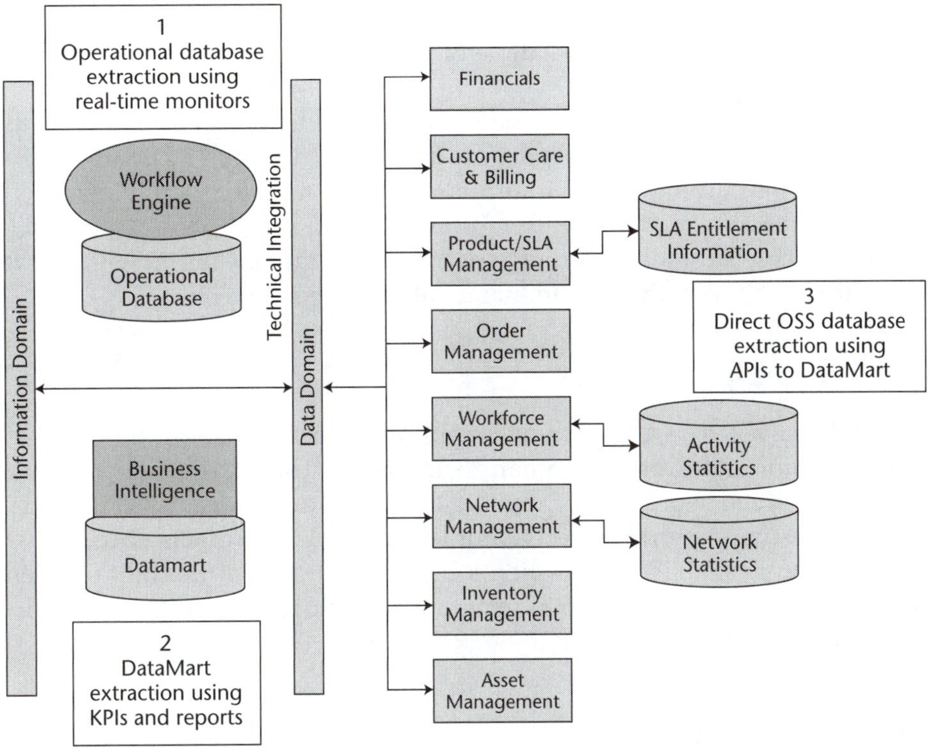

Figure 11.9 Options for extracting performance data.

Monitors, KPIs, and reports can then be developed to provide further information for the analysis process. These developments are detailed in Chapter 12.

Performance Analysis

Analysis can also be loosely termed *entitlement checking*. The work-flow engine working with the contract master within the product domain will execute comparisons between the performance information and the entitlements within the contract. Entitlement checks can be done continuously, periodically, or on an ad hoc basis. There are two types of analysis: real-time analysis and historical analysis.

Real-Time Analysis

Service monitors usually handle real-time analysis and exception identification. Service monitors can be configured to monitor the information held in the datamart or on the operational database. In most cases, the factor determining which configuration to use will depend on the refresh requirement of the information.

For example, *near real-time* may be defined within the service provider as 15 minutes. In this case, the datamart can be refreshed every 15 minutes without affecting the currency of the information, so the monitor would be placed on the datamart.

In other cases, the information may need to be instantaneous, in which case placing the monitor on the operational database is more effective.

Historical Analysis

Historical analysis is rarely done on a continuous basis. Instead, this type of reporting is normally periodic in nature and presented as KPIs, reports, or a combination of the two. Many types of entitlements do not readily lend themselves to real-time reporting. For example, many SLA contracts specify that compliance to availability entitlements be reconciled on a monthly or even annual basis. The best solution is to generate periodic reports or KPIs that mirror the entitlement requirements.

Identify Exceptions

Exceptions are identified as the analysis takes place. The disposition of exceptions will fall into one of two categories: (1) open and (2) closed. Open exceptions will usually result in response generation. Closed exceptions are either closed work orders (that may have been responded to earlier but still resulted in SLA violations) or are related to cumulative SLA entitlements that do not require real-time response (such as annual availability), but are important as KPIs.

In either case, the work-flow engine will generate the appropriate action, such as a response notification or simply a refreshing of the datamart with the most current information. For example, the engine might add the most recent downtime attributed to a circuit outage to the downtime already aggregated from other outages to come up with a total downtime. Total downtime is a contributing statistic needed to calculate percentage of availability. Figure 11.10 shows aggregated downtime.

Respond

The work-flow engine generates a real-time response when exceptions or potential exceptions are identified. As we outlined in our discussion on the

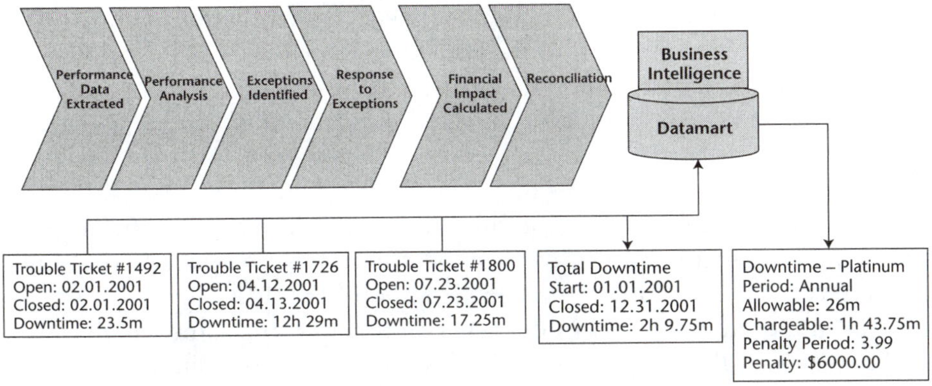

Figure 11.10 Aggregated circuit downtime for periodic reconciliation.

delivery work flow, the response can be a notification, alert, or escalation depending on the severity of the violation. A response will usually be a notification or an alert to the delivery work flow that would trigger a dynamic work-flow change or escalation. The ISLAC work flow rarely performs an escalation, although this is possible.

Community response is not part of the ISLAC work flow. Task reprioritization, reallocation, escalation, or dynamic work flow changes are all performed within the delivery work flow. If there is no current instance of work flow running, the response of the work-flow engine to the ISLAC notification may be to generate a work flow, such as opening a trouble ticket.

Calculate Financial Impact

Financial impact is calculated by invoking a very specific automated work flow that consists of a number of tasks. These tasks invoke API calls to the disparate OSSs to populate the correct fields with the most current data. Once the data is refreshed, the work-flow engine then invokes the KPI engine that calculates the financial impact. The tasks include the following:

- Aggregating the activity and network statistical data
- Verifying that SLA violations did occur
- Establishing the type and duration of the violation
- Extracting the specific remedy for the violation

As we discussed in Chapter 6, a number of sources within the OSS are called upon to contribute to the work flow. For convenience, we have reprinted the table we used in Chapter 6, shown here as Table 11.2.

Reconcile

A number of SLA violations may occur within a single work-flow instance, as well as on a number of work-flow instances that may be opened on a single service. Every violation must be reconciled appropriately.

For example, an outage may occur several times on the same circuit owing to what was thought to be a bad batch of circuit cards. Each outage takes only approximately 30 minutes to fix, but the allowable downtime is only 11 minutes a year (99.95 availability). So each time the circuit goes down, there is at least one SLA violation (availability). If the response takes longer than 2 hours, another SLA violation occurs on the same ticket.

Table 11.2 Operations Support System Sources Contributing to Work Flow

DATA TYPE	OPERATIONS SUPPORT SYSTEM MASTER	METHOD	OPERATIONS SUPPORT SYSTEM SLAVES
Penalties	Financials	Calculated	
Rating	Billing	Extracted	Financials
Entitlement	Product catalog	Core	Billing, Order Management System, Workforce Management
Customer	Customer Relationship Management	Extracted	All
Activity	Work flow	Core	All
Network	Network Management System	Extracted	Element Management System
Network configuration	Network inventory	Extracted	OMS, Geographic Information System (GIS)
Asset inventory stock	Supply chain	Extracted	GIS, ERP, WM, financials

Core: stored internally
Extracted: data provided to datamart via integration
Calculated: formulated by Business Intelligence from two or more sources

The downtime entitlement, in this case, is specified for reconciliation annually, while the response reconciliation may be a 30-day period. The definition of when and how reconciliation is to occur is very important because of the relationship between reconciliation and financial reporting. The reconciliation definition is a critical part of the overall SLA definition.

Financial reconciliation can be automated. Once the financial impact is known, automated invocation of an API will export the information to a billing system as a credit or to accounts payable as a request for payment. This information can also be sent to the financial system for tracking and reporting purposes, or as a notification of the liability and the need to set aside reserves for the annual reconciliation.

Summary

As you can see, the combination of the service delivery work flow and the ISLAC work flow makes the ISLA framework a compelling solution to managing SLA-compliant delivery. The SLA entitlement drives the work flow from end to end when the ISLAC work flow, generating alerts and escalations, dynamically affects the prioritization and escalation of the work being performed.

By dynamically reallocating community members in response to changing priorities and slipping schedules, the ISLA framework ensures optimal utilization of all members within the work-flow community. Data domain integration and business intelligence enable the service provider to develop monitors, KPIs, and reports that will allow for full end-to-end visibility and, more important, accountability for the performance being delivered by the work-flow community members. These same techniques are then used to calculate financial impacts and finally provide a commonly accepted method for reconciliation.

Finally, visibility and accountability can be used to drive change. The work-flow monitor and work-flow editor enable the service provider to continually optimize operations. They provide the information necessary to make decisions about the actions that will drive better performance.

Optimization is critical to delivering on SLAs. While we have shown you how dynamic work-flow automation can help service providers become more effective and efficient, the success of efforts to optimize the environment will depend on how the service provider reacts to the feedback that the ISLA framework makes available as business intelligence.

The volume and type of information that can be harvested from a fully functional ISLA environment is truly unprecedented. Successful business optimization will only be limited by the ability of the users to design relevant monitors, KPIs, or reports that will measure exactly what the user intended. In Chapter 12, we will discuss how to create the monitors, KPIs, and reports that are relevant to SLA-compliant delivery and are also important to the optimization process.

CHAPTER

12

Metrics and Performance Reporting

We have talked quite a bit about service performance management, maintaining quality of service on behalf of the customer, defining and delivering on Service Level Agreements (SLA)s, and so on. All that we have spoken about is and must be quantitative. Even when we speak (and will speak further) about the differences between quality of service and *perceived* quality of service we must be able to measure these qualities in some quantitative manner. We will focus on metrics (or measures) in this chapter. Note that while we place great emphasis on making the SLA framework quantitative, we do not try to claim that it is objective. While it is true that metrics tend to elevate the discussions to a more civilized level (and possibly reduce disputes), quality of service is not objective at all. Metrics aid in making the discussion semi-objective simply because people have more respect for numbers and statistics and tend to accept quantitative analysis more than they accept qualitative reports and reviews.

Metrics and Measures

Metrics are a central component in the delivery of SLAs—there cannot be a notion of SLAs or quality of service without metrics. The metrics are derived from the SLA and the contract itself. They reflect the commitments made in the contract and the SLAs, and they allow continuous tracking of the service being delivered and gauging whether service delivery conforms to the agreed-upon SLA.

Metrics and measures need to quantify something that is in principle qualitative. Measuring delivery on SLAs requires a long thought process because if done wrong it may actually do more harm than good. Making business decisions based on incorrect interpretations of data is unfortunately not too uncommon. Therefore it is not enough to just define Key Performance Indicators (KPIs) and produce nice graphs and hard numbers;the equations must be validated, tuned, and a feedback loop put in place. In terms of what these metrics need to give us, the TeleManagement Foundation's (TMF's) work on performance reporting identifies a set of criteria to which a performance metric within an SLA must adhere.

It must provide concrete and repeatable measurements in a well-defined unit of measure without subjective interpretation. It is clear why this criterium is important. But sometimes perceived quality of service is more important than real quality of service. It is also not always clear whether a truth with no subjective interpretation even exists. In the life of a provider everything is relative to some business context, and subjective interpretation always exists (after all, every system and database does some data massaging before passing the data on to the level on top of it). Still, subjective quantification is important and should be a guiding principle.Subjective criteria should:

- Be easy to understand by users.
- Have as little bias as possible between different technologies used.
- Be agreed upon at least by the provider and its customers, and preferably by a third party as well.
- Be derived from a formal specification that is the basis of the contractual commitment (for example, the notion of making the KPI a part of the product catalog as shown in Chapter 6).
- Be part of a community process and not owned or biased by the provider.
- Be useful for diagnosis, forecasting, and what-if scenarios.

When we talk about SLAs and performance management, we are talking primarily about two categories and frameworks: Key Performance Indicators (KPIs) and performance reports.

In many ways both frameworks are the same. Both report on the service delivery performance and the quality of service. The main difference is in how they present information. Key Performance Indicators are by nature very concise and provide the user with a very focused and summarized view of a single metric or small number of metrics that represent the core measurement that is of interest to the user. The big advantage of KPIs is that they provide a small and very summarized information set and thus are easy to follow, easy to understand, and can be monitored continuously without much overhead. It is conceivable to think of a customer or manager who monitors a set of KPIs daily—it may take only 30 seconds a day. Performance reports, on the other hand, can consist of a lengthy set of reports that provide much more detailed information about the SLAs and Quality of Service (QoS) being delivered. Performance reports do not take a backseat to KPIs; in fact, the two frameworks complement each other. They will typically be used together. Key Performance Indicators afford the high-level summarized view, and the performance reports are the next level of drill-down from the KPIs. Typically users will monitor the KPIs continuously. If they see a metric that seems suspicious, they will want to investigate and drill down to see more details and more information in the reports from which the KPI measures were derived; these details are available in the performance reports.

The way in which KPIs are used varies among different providers and different countries because different regulators enforce different requirements. Providers do not adhere to performance indicators because they want to elevate customer service but rather because they are forced to by regulatory authorities. Table 12.1 illustrates the different performance indicators used in different countries (primarily within the European Union (EC)). Table 12.1 also shows what kind of policies providers adhere to. Differences in indicators are not only owing to different regulatory measures; they are also dependent on the type of provider, as shown in Table 12.2.

Table 12.1 Performance Indicators and Adherence Policy by Country

CRITERIA	BEL	DEN	FIN	FRA	GER	ITA	LUX	NED	POR	SPA	UK
Service											
Mobile coverage	Y	Y	Y	Y	Y	Y	Y	Y	Y	Y	Y
Pay phone availability	Y			Y	Y	Y	Y		Y	Y	Y
First connection time	Y	Y	Y	Y	Y	Y	Y	Y	Y	Y	Y
Completion percentage before due date	Y										Y
Operator response time	Y			Y	Y	Y	Y	Y	Y		Y
Directory services response time		Y	Y		Y	Y	Y	Y	Y		Y

(continues)

Table 12.1 Performance Indicators and Adherence Policy by Country *(Continued)*

CRITERIA	BEL	DEN	FIN	FRA	GER	ITA	LUX	NED	POR	SPA	UK
Fault rate per access line	Y	Y	Y	Y	Y	Y	Y	Y	Y		Y
Service restoration before confirmed date											Y
Fault repair time	Y	Y	Y	Y	Y	Y	Y	Y	Y		Y
Network											
Call failure		Y	Y	Y	Y	Y	Y	Y	Y		Y
Mobile calls dropped	Y			Y			Y				Y
Call setup time	Y	Y		Y	Y	Y	Y	Y	Y		Y
Speech transmission quality									Y		
Billing											
Accuracy	Y	Y	Y	Y	Y	Y	Y				Y
Correctness complaints	Y				Y					Y	
Reporting obligations											
Reporting to regulatory authority	Y		Y	Y	Y	Y	Y	Y	Y	Y	
Publication to users by operator				Y	Y	Y	Y			Y	Y
Publication to users by regulatory authority	Y		Y	Y	Y			Y		Y	

Table 12.2 Performance Indicators Used by Providers of Fixed, Mobile, and Internet Telephony

CRITERIA	FIXED TELEPHONY	MOBILE TELEPHONY	INTERNET TELEPHONY
Service			
Mobile coverage		Y	
Availability of pay phones	Y		
First connection time	Y	Y	

Table 12.2 Performance Indicators Used by Providers of Fixed, Mobile, and Internet Telephony *(Continued)*

CRITERIA	FIXED TELEPHONY	MOBILE TELEPHONY	INTERNET TELEPHONY
Completion percentage before due date	Y		
Operator response time	Y	Optional	
Directory services response time	Y	Optional	
Fault rate per access line	Y	Y	
Service restoration before confirmed date	Y		
Fault repair time	Y	Y	
Network			
Call failure	Y	Y	
Calls dropped	Y	Y	
Call setup time	Y	Y	
Speech transmission quality	Y	Y	
Billing			
Accuracy	Y	Y	Y
Correctness complaints	Y	Y	Y

The General Information Framework

Before going into the details of KPIs and reporting, we should discuss the general information framework that must exist in order for KPIs and performance reports to be readily available for use by customers, service providers, and network providers. Key Performance Indicators and performance reports by their nature need to be built on top of fairly large and robust data stores—data stores that aggregate information from multiple sources in the Operations Support System/Business Support System (OSS/BSS), and data stores that maintain historical as well as current information. Figure 12.1 illustrates a simple scheme that is used as the basis for the framework that must be put in place for KPIs and performance reports to be possible.

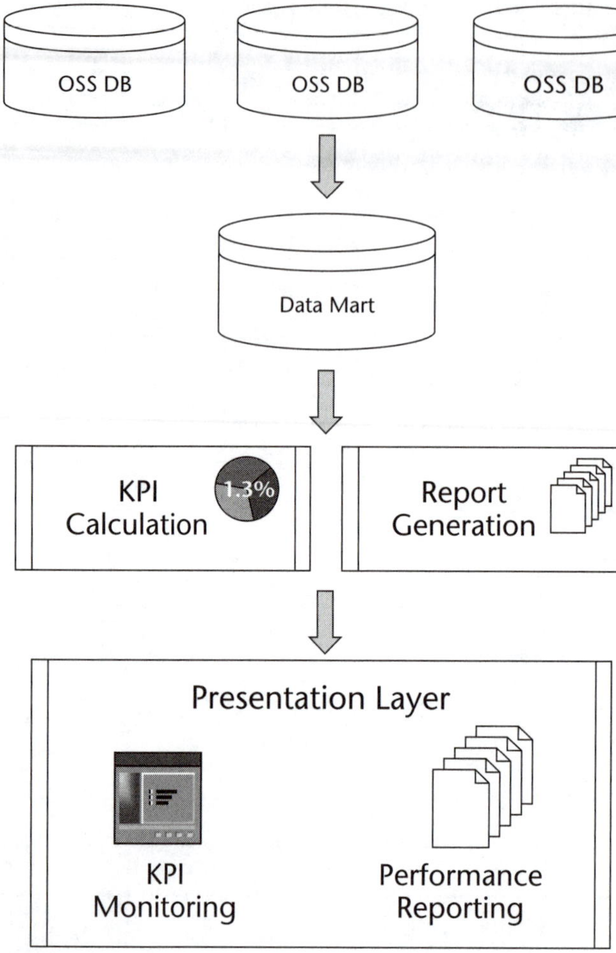

Figure 12.1 The data scheme that serves as the basis for Key Performance Indicators and performance reports.

The Data Mart

The main repository in Figure 12.1 is the data mart. Different SLA frameworks call this data store by different names—some call it the *active SLA repository*, some call it the *performance database*. In fact, every vendor with a fully functional OSS/BSS has some name for it, and unfortunately there is no consensus. We have chosen therefore to stick with a generic name—one that reflects what the data store is used for and how it is organized. The *data mart* aggregates information from multiple OSSs and maintains information in such a way that it is readily available for KPIs and performance reports. It also maintains a lot of historical information. It is therefore a data mart of sorts. We have been careful not to call it a data warehouse because this term brings with it too many overloaded meanings; a data mart seems to be a much more neutral and accepted term.

As we will see later in this chapter, KPIs and performance reports are merely encapsulations of some query. But the queries tend to be very complex and tend to be based on data that comes from more than one OSS. The scheme shown in Figure 12.1 allows the query to be performed quickly enough to be useful. If the underlying queries had to access multiple (and disparate) OSSs with differing models and structures, the query process would not only take much too long to access the data, but it would also be too sensitive to any change in any system—the uptime of the metrics framework would be close to zero. Instead, the framework defines a data mart that represents a stable information model that is used for delivering the query results. Data from multiple OSSs is extracted on some periodic basis from the various OSSs such as network management, trouble ticketing, and provisioning systems and is injected into the data mart.

Not only do the extraction routines move the data from one data store to another; they modify the form in which the data is maintained rather than leave it in the same form in which it exists in the OSSs. Operations Support System databases are usually operational databases and are optimized for very fast transactions and very high throughput. Simple queries, updates, and inserts must be lightning fast since the response time and throughput requirements of these operational systems can be rather extreme. At the same time, schemas that are optimized for updates, inserts, and relatively simple queries do not perform all that well when complex (and sometimes very complex) queries are run.

The data mart is a database that is optimized for these complex queries. Its role within the OSS is to ensure that the complex queries necessary to manage a KPI framework and a performance report framework can be computed fast enough and in a way that does not compromise the operational systems. If performance reports and KPIs were computed using the operational databases, then not only would the response time for the KPIs and performance reports be unbearable, but the operational databases would incur so much additional work that their real task (running the OSS) would be compromised.

That the data mart is optimized for KPI and performance report frameworks can mean one of two things. One option is to use a data management system that is itself especially suited for this task. The most common instance of such a solution is to use a cube within an Online Analytical Processing (OLAP) system rather than a more traditional relational database system. The other possibility is to stick with a traditional data management system but use a design that is suited to support the KPI and performance report frameworks. The common example is the use of a Relational Database Management System (RDBMS) for implementing a data mart using a star schema.

Extraction Routines

The routines that populate the data mart from the operational systems usually do more than transform the data and move it to a form that is useful for the queries. The extraction routines usually perform a lot of computations. An example includes various time interval calculations. Operational systems often keep data in its raw form. Many systems will maintain data about events, timestamps for systems going down and then coming back up, and so on. Service Level Agreement information by its nature is a much higher level of data. For example, the following equation is often used to calculate the service availability value (SA = Service Availability as a percentage):

$$100 \times \left(1 - \frac{\sum_{t} OI(t) \times DF(t)}{TotalTime} \right)$$

where OI = Outage interval
DF = Degradation factor

The equation should be intuitive. Looking at a certain time window we run through the full interval and look for outage intervals. Outages may be complete or partial—the degradation factor is a number between 0 and 1 and serves as a grading factor. The ratio of the outage interval to the total time reflects which portion of the full time window the service was provided with the given degradation factor. This equation is a simple example. In real life the equations used will often be more complex. For example, usually the customer attaches a different level of importance to each Service Access Point (SAP). This is usually represented by the terms attached to the various contract lines in the contract. It can get even more complicated; the customer may wish to attach different levels of importance to different times of day. All this can be implemented through the terms in the contract. The equations for service availability in this case quickly become complex and hard to compute. For example, the equation may look something like this:

$$100 \times \left(1 - \left(\sum_{\lambda} \frac{\left[\sum_{i} \left(SAPweight(i,\lambda) \times \sum_{\tau \subseteq \lambda} SAPOI(i,\tau) \times SAPDF(i,\tau) \right) \right]}{\sum_{i} SAPweight(i,\lambda) \times |\lambda|} \right) \right)$$

(Where λ runs over all time in intervals defined in the contract terms and τ runs on the uptime/downtime intervals within such an interval λ)

The operational systems do not always keep the outage interval time as raw data. If this is the case, then these interval values need to be computed. Depending on the actual equations being used, these interval values may require a lot of computations. For example, in order to be able to use the second equation for service availability, it is not enough to look at various alerts and trouble ticketing information. We need to look at these as well as the time intervals used within all contract lines and create time intervals that are the intersections of the various alerts and trouble ticketing information with the time intervals specified in the contract. This is required because in the equation we have just seen, we have multipliers that pertain to the contract term intervals as well as multipliers that are related to the service performance. The option of running the query when computing the KPI is certainly not feasible. It is also wasteful because the query will be computed again and again.

Star Schema

Figure 12.2 best illustrates the essence of what a star schema is all about. In a *star schema,* data is organized according to a hub-and-spoke architecture. A star schema is a set of tables that hold the data that is of most interest and that is the subject of the queries. These data elements are maintained within very large tables that are called FACT tables. In Figure 12.2 the DM_CALL table is an example of a FACT table.

The FACT tables maintain the data that will be used as the measures (the actual elements that the KPI metrics will be based on) and the values that will be reported. In addition to the actual values that will be of interest, the FACT tables maintain the codes and identifiers that the queries will search on. The FACT tables are de-normalized in the sense that they maintain an explosion of information. The records in the FACT tables are maintained for many permutations of the keys that represent the entities for which the FACT data values relate. For example, information in the FACT table may be queried for a certain customer, a certain product, a certain geographical area, a contract, and so on. The FACT table in this case maintains relevant data for many of these permutations. In addition, the data is maintained for many date ranges including quite a bit of historical information. The goal of all this is that when a complex query runs against this kind of database, the answer can be computed quickly because most of the work has already been done in populating the FACT tables. When the actual KPI values are computed or the report is generated, the only work left is usually some simple aggregation or even just the extraction of a single value. The keys in the FACT table are then used along with the small tables surrounding the FACT table (hence the name star schema) to extract the descriptions or other attributes that are necessary to complete the display of the KPI or report. In any case, what is required is usually a sequence of very small joins (each one usually involving two or three tables) that are very fast—especially since the Relational Database Management System (RDBMS) optimizer will implement the join as a SELECT out of the large table (indexed in a way that it brings the few records back very quickly) and then a SELECT out of the peripheral table.

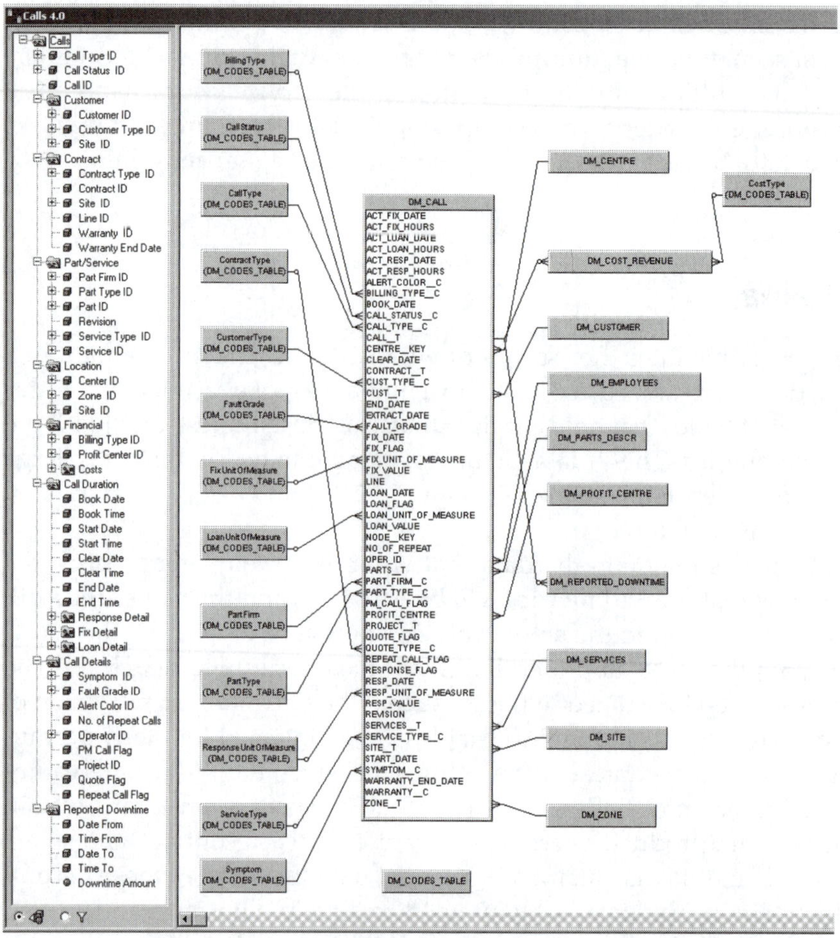

Figure 12.2 An example of a FACT table from a data mart organized as a star schema.

Implementing Key Performance Indicators

Key Performance Indicators are informational elements that have deep business meaning and consequences. The term *Key Performance Indicator* represents what it is (a performance indicator) and an adjective (key). A KPI is of fundamental importance to someone—a service manager, a customer, a CFO. Therefore, although a KPI is fundamentally a query that fetches information from the data mart, it needs to be displayed and viewed in the simplest and most natural manner. In fact, KPI values may need to be delivered to a customer or a manager in a mobile environment and therefore these values need to be easily accessible over the Web and/or via a wireless device.

Since a KPI bridges the back end (the data mart) with the front end (for example, Web access for customers), implementing KPIs requires multiple layers of software. This is especially true owing to the fact that although KPIs often need to be modified, enhanced, or even created by the IT department of the provider; KPIs are normally provided by SLA frameworks purchased from vendors in the OSS space. Yet service providers often need to add their own KPIs or customize existing KPIs to fit a certain need. This need for customization means that tools for manipulating KPIs and documentation about standard KPIs are very important. Tools ensure a quick turnaround time, and good documentation means that service providers will be able to base their extensions on well-structured and tested software. As an example, Figure 12.3 shows an example of well-documented KPI specifications for some KPIs including contract renewal rate, SLA percentage of late fixes, nearly missed response time, and fixes that did fall within the entitlement defined by the SLAs (it is also good to look at something done right once in a while).

Note that the specification defining nearly missed response time is defined as a Monitor (look at the subtitle of the KPI shown in Figure 12.3 in the lower left-hand corner). A Monitor differs from a KPI only in the rate at which it is calculated and refreshed. A KPI normally shows values that are updated monthly, weekly, or sometimes daily. Monitors show real-time, up-to-the-minute information that may be crucial in order for service providers to take immediate actions to ensure that SLAs are met. For example, if allocation decisions can be triggered when this value goes up, then perhaps resources can be reshuffled and commitments met. This is a very central theme in the concept of integrated SLAs; the SLA information *must* be used as important input at an operational level.

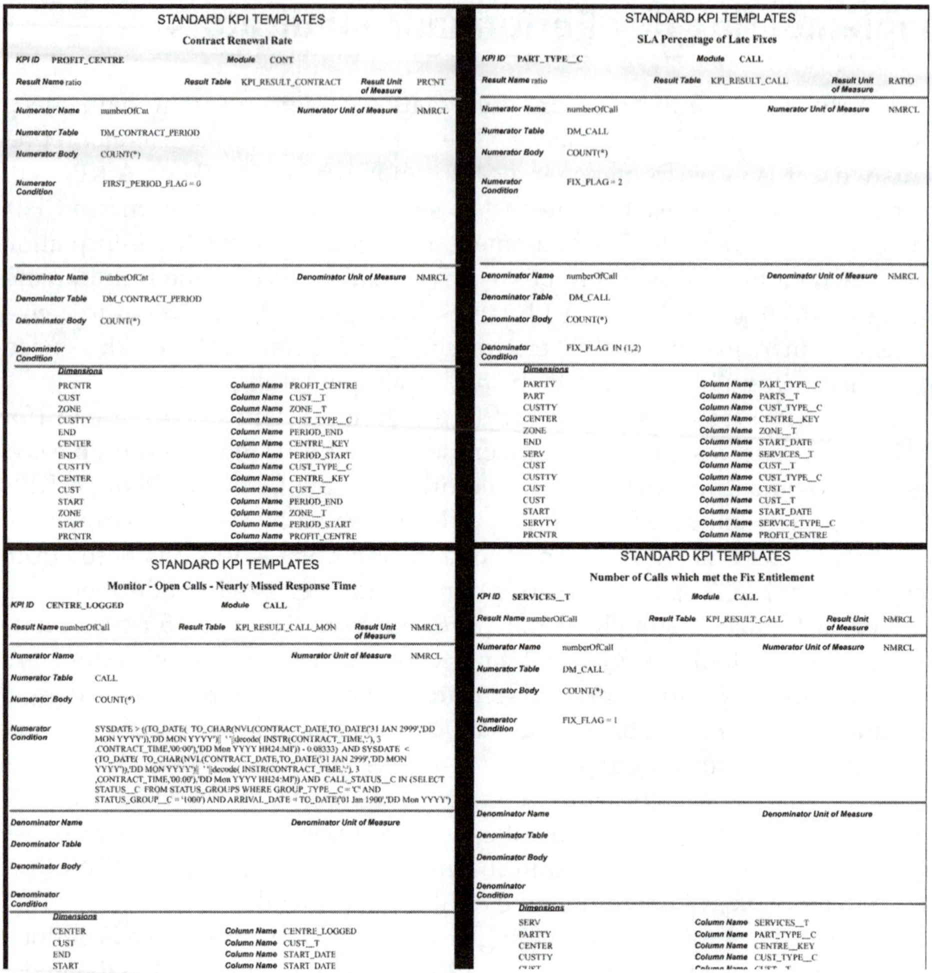

STANDARD KPI TEMPLATES

Contract Renewal Rate

KPI ID PROFIT_CENTRE Module CONT

Result Name ratio Result Table KPI_RESULT_CONTRACT Result Unit of Measure PRCNT

Numerator Name numberOfCnt Numerator Unit of Measure NMRCL

Numerator Table DM_CONTRACT_PERIOD

Numerator Body COUNT(*)

Numerator Condition FIRST_PERIOD_FLAG = 0

Denominator Name numberOfCnt Denominator Unit of Measure NMRCL

Denominator Table DM_CONTRACT_PERIOD

Denominator Body COUNT(*)

Denominator Condition

Dimensions

Dimension		Column Name
PRCNTR	Column Name	PROFIT_CENTRE
CUST	Column Name	CUST__T
ZONE	Column Name	ZONE__T
CUSTTY	Column Name	CUST_TYPE__C
END	Column Name	PERIOD_END
CENTER	Column Name	CENTRE__KEY
END	Column Name	PERIOD_START
CUSTTY	Column Name	CUST_TYPE__C
CENTER	Column Name	CENTRE__KEY
CUST	Column Name	CUST__T
START	Column Name	PERIOD_END
ZONE	Column Name	ZONE__T
START	Column Name	PERIOD_START
PRCNTR	Column Name	PROFIT_CENTRE

STANDARD KPI TEMPLATES

SLA Percentage of Late Fixes

KPI ID PART_TYPE__C Module CALL

Result Name ratio Result Table KPI_RESULT_CALL Result Unit of Measure RATIO

Numerator Name numberOfCall Numerator Unit of Measure NMRCL

Numerator Table DM_CALL

Numerator Body COUNT(*)

Numerator Condition FIX_FLAG = 2

Denominator Name numberOfCall Denominator Unit of Measure NMRCL

Denominator Table DM_CALL

Denominator Body COUNT(*)

Denominator Condition FIX_FLAG IN (1,2)

Dimensions

Dimension		Column Name
PARTTY	Column Name	PART_TYPE__C
PART	Column Name	PARTS__T
CUSTTY	Column Name	CUST_TYPE__C
CENTER	Column Name	CENTRE__KEY
ZONE	Column Name	ZONE__T
END	Column Name	START_DATE
SERV	Column Name	SERVICES__T
CUST	Column Name	CUST__T
CUSTTY	Column Name	CUST_TYPE__C
CUST	Column Name	CUST__T
CUST	Column Name	CUST__T
START	Column Name	START_DATE
SERVTY	Column Name	SERVICE_TYPE__C
PRCNTR	Column Name	PROFIT_CENTRE

STANDARD KPI TEMPLATES

Monitor - Open Calls - Nearly Missed Response Time

KPI ID CENTRE_LOGGED Module CALL

Result Name numberOfCall Result Table KPI_RESULT_CALL_MON Result Unit of Measure NMRCL

Numerator Name Numerator Unit of Measure NMRCL

Numerator Table CALL

Numerator Body COUNT(*)

Numerator Condition SYSDATE > ((TO_DATE(TO_CHAR(NVL(CONTRACT_DATE,TO_DATE('31 JAN 2999','DD MON YYYY')),'DD MON YYYY')|| ' '||decode(INSTR(CONTRACT_TIME,':'), 3 ,CONTRACT_TIME,'00:00'),'DD Mon YYYY HH24:MI')) - 0.08333) AND SYSDATE < (TO_DATE(TO_CHAR(NVL(CONTRACT_DATE,TO_DATE('31 JAN 2999','DD MON YYYY')),'DD MON YYYY')|| ' '||decode(INSTR(CONTRACT_TIME,':'), 3 ,CONTRACT_TIME,'00:00'),'DD Mon YYYY HH24:MI')) AND CALL_STATUS__C IN (SELECT STATUS__C FROM STATUS_GROUPS WHERE GROUP_TYPE__C = 'C' AND STATUS_GROUP__C = '1000') AND ARRIVAL_DATE = TO_DATE('01 Jan 1900','DD Mon YYYY')

Denominator Name Denominator Unit of Measure

Denominator Table

Denominator Body

Denominator Condition

Dimensions

Dimension		Column Name
CENTER	Column Name	CENTRE_LOGGED
CUST	Column Name	CUST__T
END	Column Name	START_DATE
START	Column Name	START DATE

STANDARD KPI TEMPLATES

Number of Calls which met the Fix Entitlement

KPI ID SERVICES__T Module CALL

Result Name numberOfCall Result Table KPI_RESULT_CALL Result Unit of Measure NMRCL

Numerator Name numberOfCall Numerator Unit of Measure NMRCL

Numerator Table DM_CALL

Numerator Body COUNT(*)

Numerator Condition FIX_FLAG = 1

Denominator Name Denominator Unit of Measure

Denominator Table

Denominator Body

Denominator Condition

Dimensions

Dimension		Column Name
SERV	Column Name	SERVICES__T
PARTTY	Column Name	PART_TYPE__C
CENTER	Column Name	CENTRE__KEY
CUSTTY	Column Name	CUST_TYPE__C

Figure 12.3 An example of documented standard Key Performance Indicator specifications.

The software layers in the KPI framework include meta-data components as well as runtime components. The software layers required to implement a full KPI framework are as follows:

Data mart. The data mart stores the information in a semiprocessed manner (that is, it stores the results of the extraction process).

Key Performance Indicator templates. Key Performance Indicator templates define the structure of the KPIs. These elements are primarily the meta-data components used to create KPI instances.

Key Performance Indicator instances. Key Performance Indicator instances include meta data as well as run time components. As a meta-data component, a KPI instance relies on a KPI template for the general structure but adds some additional data that is specific to what a certain user needs to track. The KPI instance may also hold meta data such as a target definition as well as possible alerts and notification methods that should be used when the target is not met. As a runtime component, the KPI instance holds the computed values.

Key Performance Indicator displays. Key Performance Indicator displays maintain meta data that defines how the values computed by the KPI instances should be displayed to the user.

An Example of Installation Follow-ups

In order to understand better what the framework for KPIs and performance reports contains as well as gain more insight into the structures that need to be put in place to support KPIs, we will use an example in which we will address the issue of follow-up calls after an installation. For example, assume a scenario in which a provider has too many trouble tickets that all follow a firewall/Virtual Private Network (VPN) installation. The provider is introducing a different process that aims at lowering the number of trouble tickets and wishes to monitor this value continuously. This issue has become very critical to the provider; not only is the service provider losing money through increased costs; it is also not meeting its SLAs for its business customers in terms of timely installations. The issue has become so critical that it has bubbled up all the way to the CFO. Over the next three months the CFO (as well as various other managers in the organization) want to see this KPI on their desk every morning to make sure that improvements are indeed being made. By the way, this example can also illustrate why it is important that a KPI solution have a set of tools so that the IT department can build its own KPIs. While it is very likely that any SLA solution has sets of KPIs that can be deployed, it is not expected that such a focused KPI can be pulled right out of the box.

Data Availability

First we need to make sure that data exists in our data mart. Indeed, the information needed by the managers in our example does exist within the data mart that we are using, and specifically within the DM_CALL FACT table already shown in Figure 12.2. Figure 12.4 shows the FACT table fields and the ones that we will focus on when building the required KPI. Specifically, in this example we need to identify that this is a firewall/VPN call (using the SERVICES__T fields), that this is a trouble ticket opened as a follow-up to a recent installation (REPEAT_CALL_FLAG), that the ticket has a certain symptom that we wish to track (SYMPTOM__T), and that it is related to a business customer (CUST_TYPE__C).

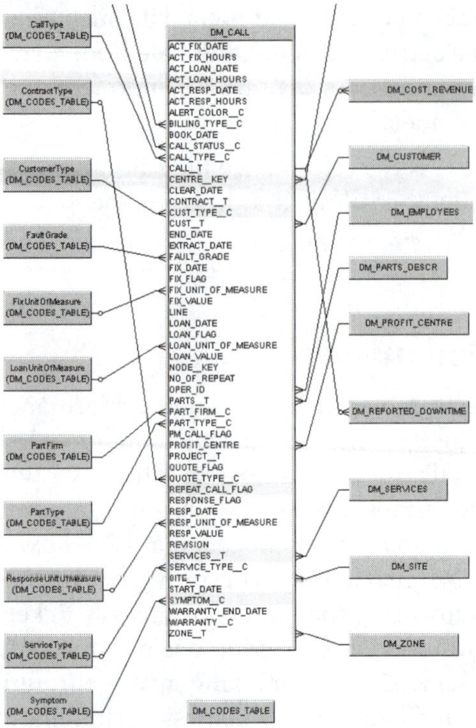

Figure 12.4 Fields in the FACT table that are necessary for creating the example Key Performance Indicator.

Building the Template

Next we need to define the KPI template. In doing so we need to define the meta data that will be true to every KPI instance generated based on this template. Such meta data includes how the KPI will be calculated (the actual Structured Query Language [SQL] for the KPI calculation to be performed), what access restrictions are placed on the KPI, and the dimensions that are available to the KPI. The access restrictions allow the provider to decide which roles in which business units are allowed to view this information (and, for advanced providers, whether the providers also want to provide this information to their customers). The dimensions define the data elements that could be used to build focused values. For example, the CFO may care about the value for the entire company, while a regional manager may care about the specific value in only his or her region.

One last definition that is often very useful is a pointer to a comprehensive report. Key Performance Indicators are great in that they summarize a lot of information into a single value that may be displayed in a graphical format and easily understood by a person. But a KPI does not tell the full story. It is therefore useful to define a performance report to back up the information displayed by the KPI. This report is typically used in a drill-down scenario—for example, the CFO will look at the value, see that there is no improvement, drill down into a report, and see that three regions have a significant improvement while two have actually gotten worse; then heads will roll.

In terms of the actual formula that we need to compute for this example, it is fairly simple:

$$100 \times \frac{\text{tickets with SYMPTOM xyz and REPEAT\_CALL\_FLAG} = 1}{\text{all tickets}}$$

This is the measure that forms the KPI. The rest of the fields comprising the query defined by the template are used to limit the domain that we are counting—so that we count only firewall/VPN tickets for business customers.

Dimensions

The dimensions provide the slice-and-dice feature as it is sometimes called. If we allow a certain dimension within the template, then that dimension can be used to create a KPI instance from the template. Figures 12.5a and 12.5b show how we would go about defining the dimensions for the KPI template in our example. A template will typically have many dimensions. Each one is added by pressing the Add button on the screen, as shown in Figure 12.5a; pressing Add will bring up the screen shown in Figure 12.5b. Each dimension has a name that appears later in the tools for building the KPI instance and a column name in the FACT table that defines the key. If a certain key does not exist in the FACT table, we cannot select values based on that data element. Note that there are two types of dimensions defined at this stage, identified by whether the dimension is marked to be mandatory or not (in both Figures 12.5a and 12.5b). The dimensions are the elements that can be added to the eventual SELECT statement that is performed when the KPI value is computed. For example, if we allow the region as a dimension, then the SELECT for the eastern region will differ from the SELECT for all regions by the addition to the WHERE clause of the delimiter form WHERE ZONE_T = ... This type of dimension is not mandatory, but the part in the WHERE clause that limits the aggregation to the SYMPTOM we are looking for is mandatory—it is the essence of the KPI, and regardless of what kind of slicing and dicing we wish to perform, the SYMPTOM must always exist in the calculation.

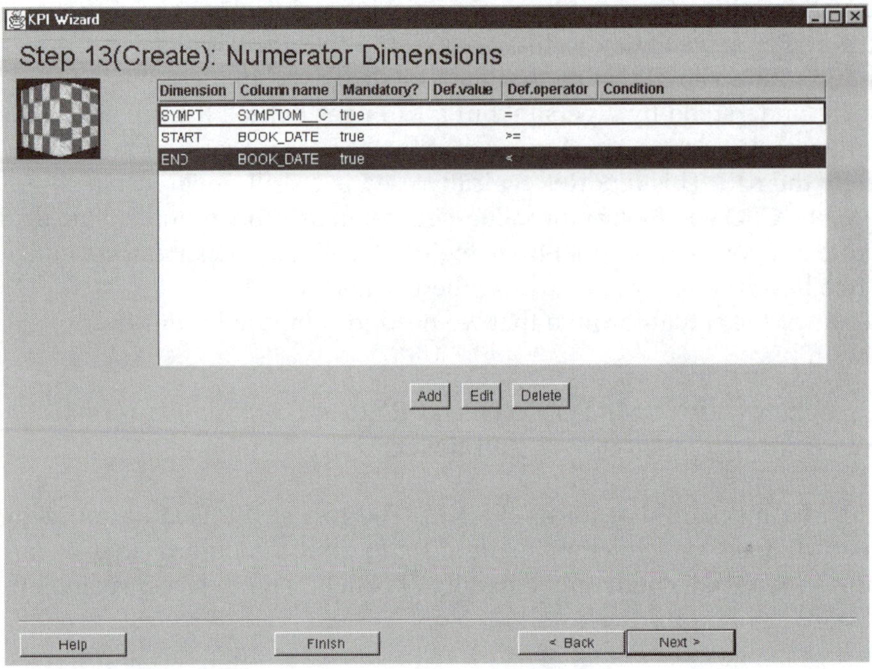

Figure 12.5a Creating the template's dimensions.

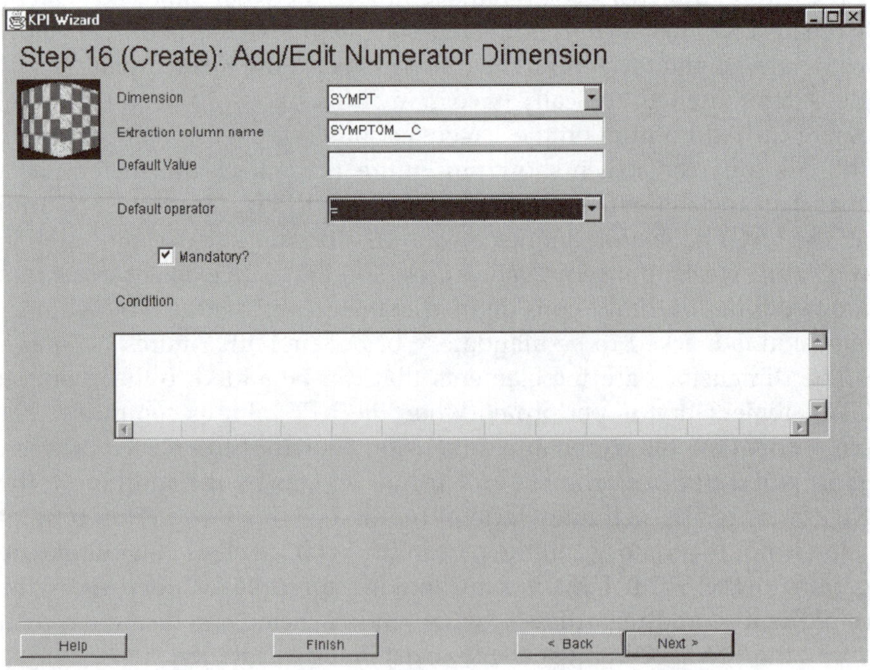

Figure 12.5b Creating a single dimension.

Defining the Instance

Now that we have defined a KPI template for our example, we will move on to define a KPI instance based on this template definition. In doing so, we first assume all the attributes that were defined at the template level. Then we define additional attributes such as:

- Calculation timing attributes defining how often the KPI value should be recomputed (every day, every week, and so on) and what periods that calculation is to compute (for example daily, months-to-date, quarterly, and so on)
- Dimension information
- Target, threshold, and alert information
- Additional attributes such as currency if the KPI has a monetary amount related to it

Dimension values defined for the KPI are based on the dimension definitions for the template. When selecting dimension values for the KPI, one can select among those dimensions allowed at the template level minus the mandatory ones. For example, if the template allowed slicing by product, customer type, region, and center (and had three mandatory dimensions for symptom, start date, and end date), then users can create KPI instances with any combination of values for product, customer type, region, and center. They will be able to create a KPI to track the value for a certain customer type, for a certain product, in a certain region, for a product in a certain region, for a product in a certain region, for a certain customer type, and any of the permutations on the four dimensions (hence the name dimension). But no KPI based on this template will allow computing the value for a certain contract type since that dimension was not allowed at the KPI template level.

Defining the Target

The target definition is helpful in supporting management through exception scenarios. While it is true that the KPI in itself may be something that the user wants to see all the time (it was so in our example), this is not always the case. Often the assumption is that most of the time service is provided in a business-as-usual mode and the user should not be bothered with all details constantly; that much reporting just requires too much overhead. Instead what the KPI should allow is a definition of a target. For example, the outage time should be less than *X*, and time to repair or time to restore service should be less than *Y*. In addition, one may want to define thresholds—either below or above the target value. These thresholds go hand in hand with a notification, alert, or some other process that should be spawned when the threshold is crossed. As mentioned before, it is crucial to allow thresholds to be defined so that alerting and process flows can be started before the SLA is missed, so as to avoid potential financial repercussions.

The KPI also has a runtime component. The meta data tells the KPI engine which values to compute. These values are stored as part of the KPI framework either inside the data mart or within its own database schema.

Defining the Display Properties

Finally, KPIs need to be displayed. Key Performance Indicators may be displayed using a client-server tool as shown in Figure 12.6 or as a Web display as in Figure 12.7. Both options are valid, and in many cases both may be available

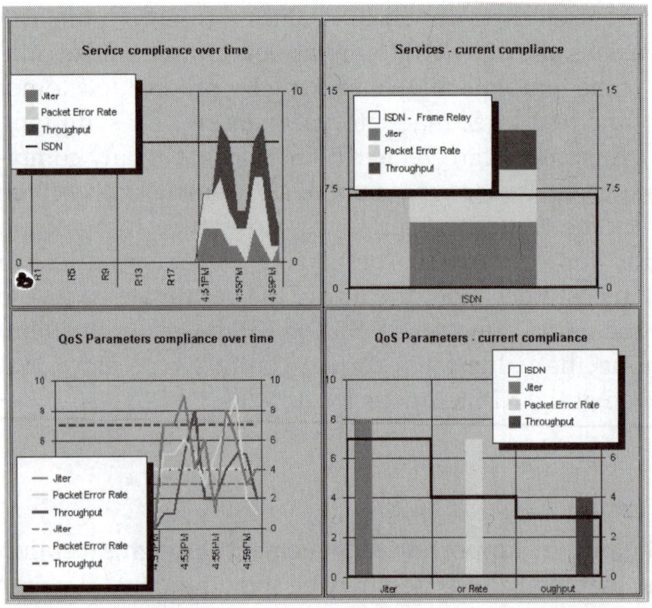

Figure 12.6 Client/server Key Performance Indicator display tools.

simultaneously. The advantage of a client/server set of tools is that usually the display characteristics will be superior to a Web-based display, while the big advantage of a Web display is that it can be viewed from any place and by anyone—including people outside the company's intranet. A Web-based display allows for delivering KPI displays to customers and business partners and supports an ebusiness implementation. In addition, KPI values may be pushed all the way out to a mobile device as shown in Figure 12.8.

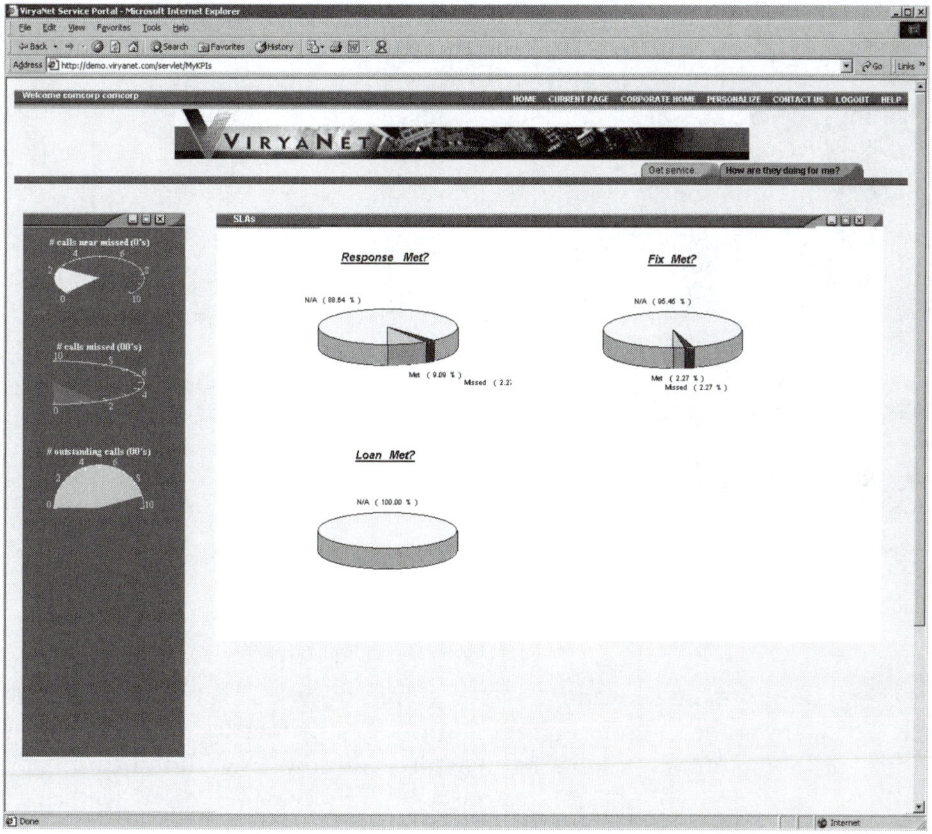

Figure 12.7 Key Performance Indicator values displayed on the Web.

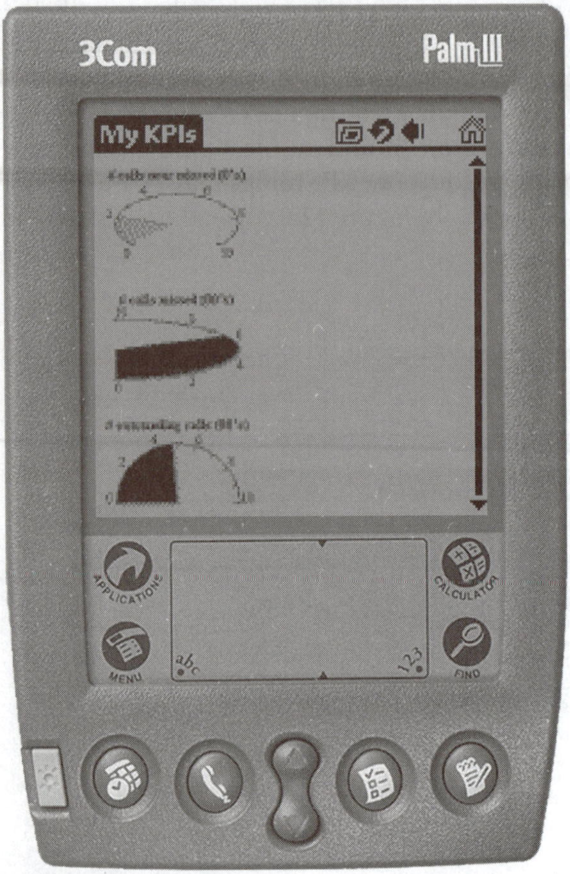

Figure 12.8 Key Performance Indicator values on a mobile device.

Display formats are secondary to the actual measure. Yet since a picture is worth a thousand words, getting the display properties right is just as important. Therefore tools must be provided for adjusting and customizing the display properties of the KPI displays—both by IT personnel as well as by the users themselves. Display attributes include the type of display (graph or tabular), the type of graph (for example, pie, bar chart, or line chart, as shown in Figure 12.9), general preferences as shown in Figure 12.10, and drill-down preferences as shown in Figure 12.11.

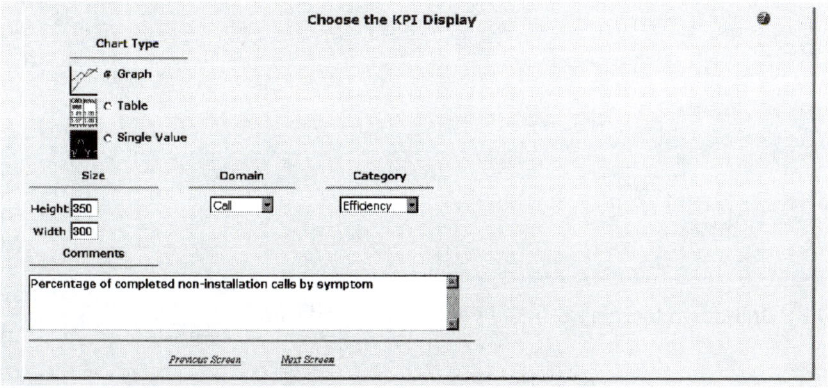

Figure 12.9 Selecting the graph type.

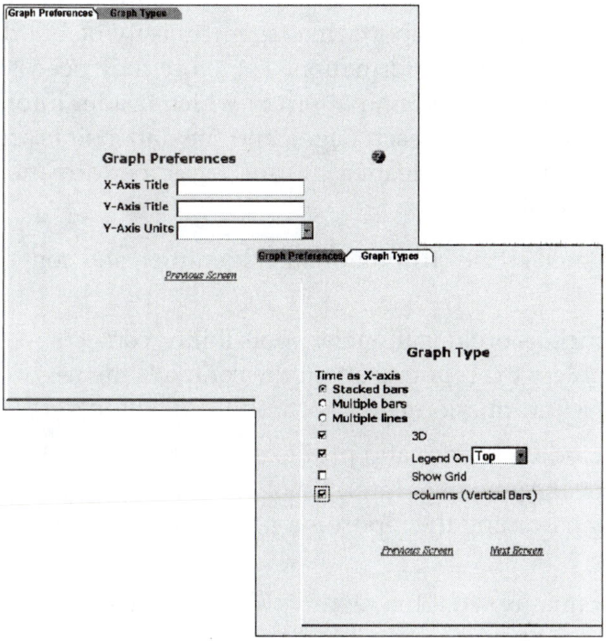

Figure 12.10 General graph properties.

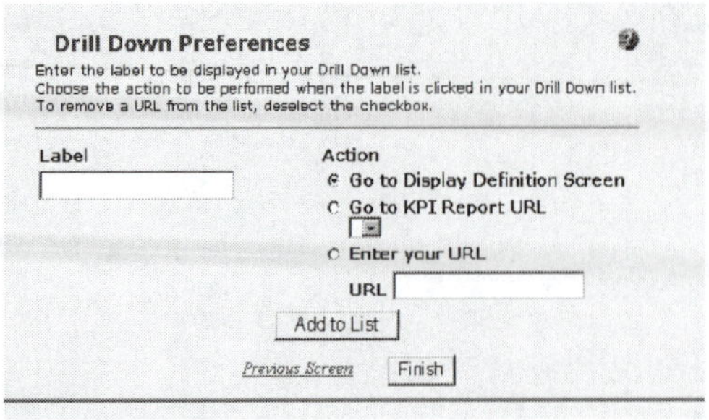

Figure 12.11 Drill-down targets from Key Performance Indicator.

Performance Reports

Reports are both the most boring and the most interesting elements in the OSS. For the IT department and the solution providers, reports are often viewed as a necessary evil. For business managers, reports are the lifeline of the business and the essence of the operation. Without reports, management is flying blind.

Reports present information—a lot of information. Therefore they need to be organized. Reports usually follow a certain pattern in which header information appears at the top (or at the top of each page), and the data points are presented in the details (or data) section. Header information in performance reports will usually include the following:

- Customer information such as the customer name, identifier, and contact information.
- Provider information such as organizational responsibility, contacts, contract information (unless the report is about the contracts themselves, in which case this information will appear in the data section).
- Service information including service and profile descriptors and SAP information. Service Level Agreement information is also typically presented in the header assuming the report is a performance report related to certain SLAs.
- Report descriptors that qualify what the report is about and what it represents.

The data section in the report depends on the specific performance report. The format will also differ depending on the information that needs to be presented. In cases where service availability is the topic of the report, the report will contain information about outage intervals, time-to-restore values, and so on. Service attribute reports will inform managers about bit error rates, error ratios, unavailability seconds, and so on.

An important part of any report is the summation area. Summation segments can include averages, sums, counts, and various other aggregation operators. These sections are very important because they represent the bottom line of the report and thus they are first to be viewed. In many ways this part of the report is the bridge between the KPI and the detailed report area.

Summations are always about grouping, and grouping is done based on dimensions. Performance information and SLA information can be requested for the provider level, at a customer level, or according to any dimension. Each data element will sometimes appear in the header (for example, when the whole report is about a certain SAP) or in the data area (when, for example, the report details all SAPs for a customer).

The number of dimensions for which performance reports are required is quite large. The problem is that on a theoretical basis this number is the number of possible permutations on the full set of dimensions—and this is a very large number. The very unfortunate thing is that reports are sometimes associated with printed volumes. These reports are often generated, printed, and distributed (at great cost to the provider and our environment), regardless of whether or not they are used.

Paperless Reporting

In the past 5 years a new set of technologies has appeared that can be used to eliminate the need for paper reporting (or at least delay the printing of the report until there is someone who really needs the report on paper). This development is based on a set of tools often termed business intelligence tools, as well as the ubiquitous access to the Web and email. The tools bring with them intuitive user interfaces that allow ordinary users to change dimension information and various other report parameters without the need for IT personnel to be involved. This means that a user can easily get precisely the right information needed within a report before it goes to the printer. Some of these tools even support a feature called ad hoc reporting, which provides the ultimate flexibility in allowing users to create their own queries and reports.

The more important evolutions in technology are the dominance of the Web browser as an application desktop and the spread of email as a primary (if not *the* primary) information distribution channel. These trends allow reports to be easily viewed by anyone from any desktop, and make possible the distribution of electronic versions of reports easily through email. The dominance of the Internet as an application platform, along with document and application de facto standards—such as Adobe Acrobat and PDF, Microsoft Word, and Microsoft Excel—provide a technology and application platform that can support simple design, generation, distribution, and viewing of performance reports by provider personnel as well as customers. The two trends (business intelligence tools and Web technology) are certainly not mutually exclusive.

All of the major business intelligence vendors have released versions that make use of Web technologies providing one-stop shopping for a reporting and distribution environment (for a hefty price, of course).

Reporting Solutions

Reporting solutions for the provider can come in one of three forms:

1. A full business intelligence solution that is used for all reporting purposes
2. Sets of reporting solutions, each one being an add-on to one of the operational or customer-care systems used by the provider
3. A set of infrastructure tools used by IT to develop a reporting solution

The first category involves solutions from business intelligence vendors such as Business Objects, Cognos, Actuate, Hyperion, Brio, Microstrategy, and many, many others. These programs are perhaps the simplest solution for the provider and usually the most expensive. The second category is very common since many of the systems that are used for SLA management have some form of reporting capabilities. This approach is seemingly the easiest one and the one that should involve the least amount of work. There are unfortunately a number of problems with this approach. One is that each product has its own reporting solution, and these solutions are often different from one another. The reports they produce, therefore, tend to look dissimilar, and it is very hard to acquire the very diverse skill sets to customize and add reports as well as manage the reporting operation on a daily basis. Therefore when a solution in this category is employed it is often mixed within a larger framework that is itself either of the first category or the third category.

The third category is one in which infrastructure tools are used to generate, manage, and distribute reports. These infrastructure tools belong to classes of tools such as portals, document managers, and application servers, and they tend to be used where report generation is viewed as a job that needs to be scheduled and reports are seen as documents that need to be managed in a document repository and/or distributed to community members by email. The actual definition of the reports is still usually done using a commercial report generator, but in this case the tool used may cost a lot less and have fewer capabilities. For example, Crystal Reports is often used because of its simplicity, ease of use, large installation base, and low cost.

Within this last category there is another approach that bears mentioning. Microsoft Office tools have become very dominant and well known. Even Microsoft bashers must admit that these are excellent tools. In fact, they are so good and so full of various goodies that they have become to many a reporting and document management infrastructure. One possible approach for report management is to be able to fire off queries and get the results back in a comma delimited format (or any other format that Excel can read) and present the reports and graphs using Excel itself. Since Excel, Word, and the use of HTML are so well integrated (and getting better with each release of the Office suite), this approach provides a very low cost and user-accepted entry point. One excellent example is the pivot table feature in Excel. A pivot table report can be used to analyze related information that depends on many dimensions. A pivot table report is interactive and supports ad hoc-like features allowing the user to change the view of the data to see more details or calculate different summaries, such as counts or averages. In a pivot table report, each column in the spreadsheet (or external data source) can become a field that summarizes multiple rows of information. Building pivot table reports uses a wizard metaphor—creating a very short learning curve. In the wizard, the user selects the source data from the spreadsheet after which the wizard builds the report and a list of the available fields. The user may then drag the fields from the list window to the outlined areas (see Figure 12.12), and Excel then summarizes and calculates the report automatically.

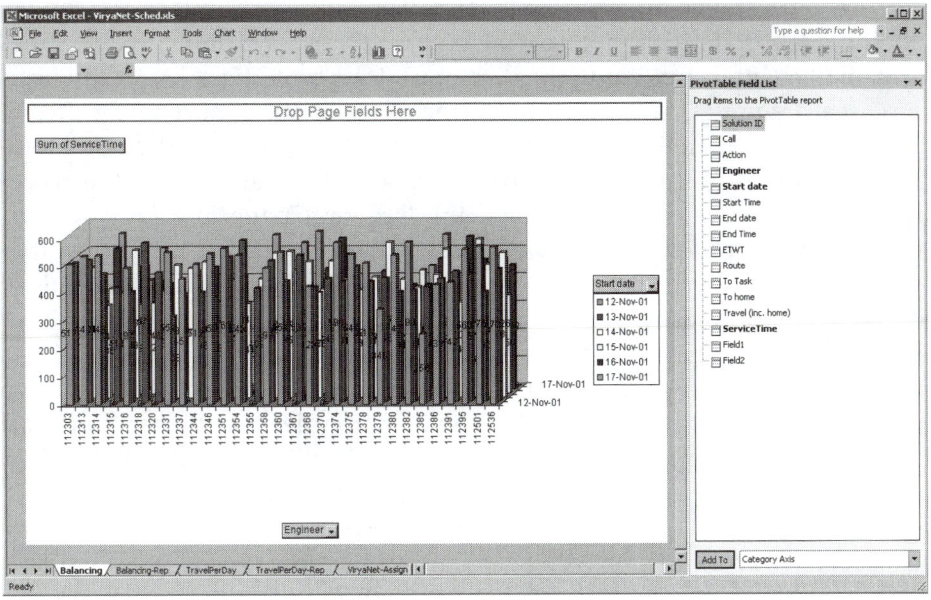

Figure 12.12 Using the Excel pivot table feature.

Designing Reports

Any reporting framework must address the three stages of the reporting life cycle:

1. Report design
2. Report generation
3. Report distribution and viewing

Building (or designing) a report is almost always done using a report builder. The business intelligence vendors have all grown out of the report builder world and have very robust and intuitive report builders. Other vendors offer a report builder only as a development tool as opposed to offering a complete OLAP solution.

Report design is usually done by the implementation team or the IT department. Building reports usually requires good knowledge of the data mart's data model or some high-level abstraction of that schema. For example, Business Objects has a concept called universes, which supports data abstractions that are useful for users who want to build their own reports (it is kind of like the data mart's schema in a business owner's language). The design of the reports is then done using a visual tool that displays the available data entities and allows the report designer to pick the report elements, the groupings, and all other attributes of the reports.

Figure 12.13 shows an example session using a report builder. As shown, building a report does not necessarily require any programming. If all entities are available and computed in the data mart, then building a report can be as simple as dragging the entities to be included in the report to the Result Objects panel and defining the conditions for the query by dragging-and-dropping entities and conditional operators. Note, for example, that the downtime amount entity at the bottom of the left-hand pane in Figure 12.13 is shown as a computed entity—the round ball—as opposed to data entities shown as a cube; hence the more complete the data mart is the easier it is to build good reports easily.

Once the query is defined (the resulting query can always be validated through inspection as shown in Figure 12.14), one can run the report as shown in Figure 12.15. The default layout is seldom the desired output, but most report generators follow a What You See Is What You Get (WYSIWYG) metaphor and allow users to complete the report design through in-place editing and drag-and-drop properties. Some of these tools (Business Objects is an example) have an ad hoc reporting capability that allows users (usually power users as opposed to ordinary users) to create their own reports, drill-downs, and more—all within a set of access restrictions so that they cannot view

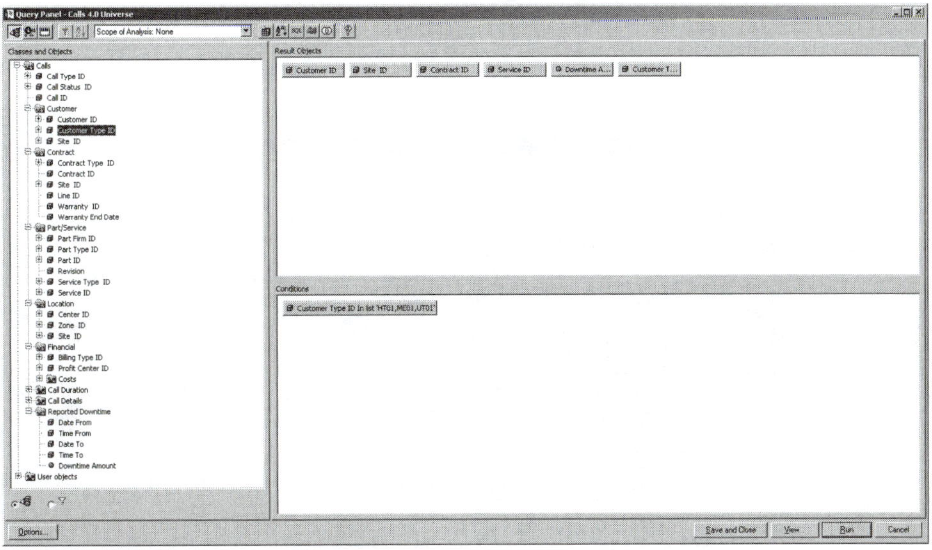

Figure 12.13 Using a report builder.

data that they are not entitled to see. This issue of data access is probably the most complex one to manage; the notion of data-level security is not only hard to support from a tool perspective but also hard to define as a business-level requirement. Therefore, although ad hoc reporting sounds like a good idea, it is often abandoned in favor of a predefined set of performance reports and drill-downs.

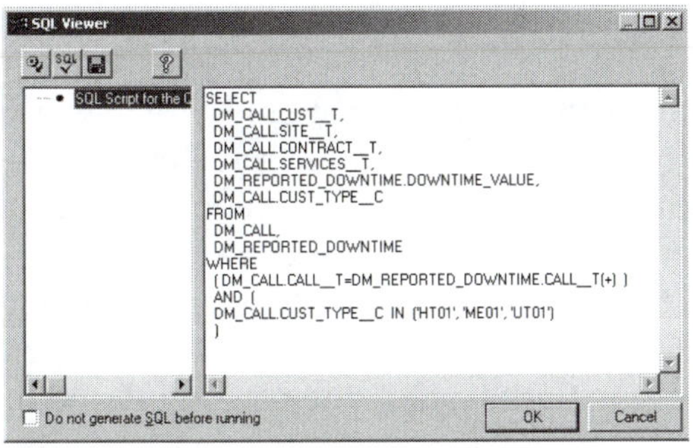

Figure 12.14 Implied Structured Query Language generated by the report builder.

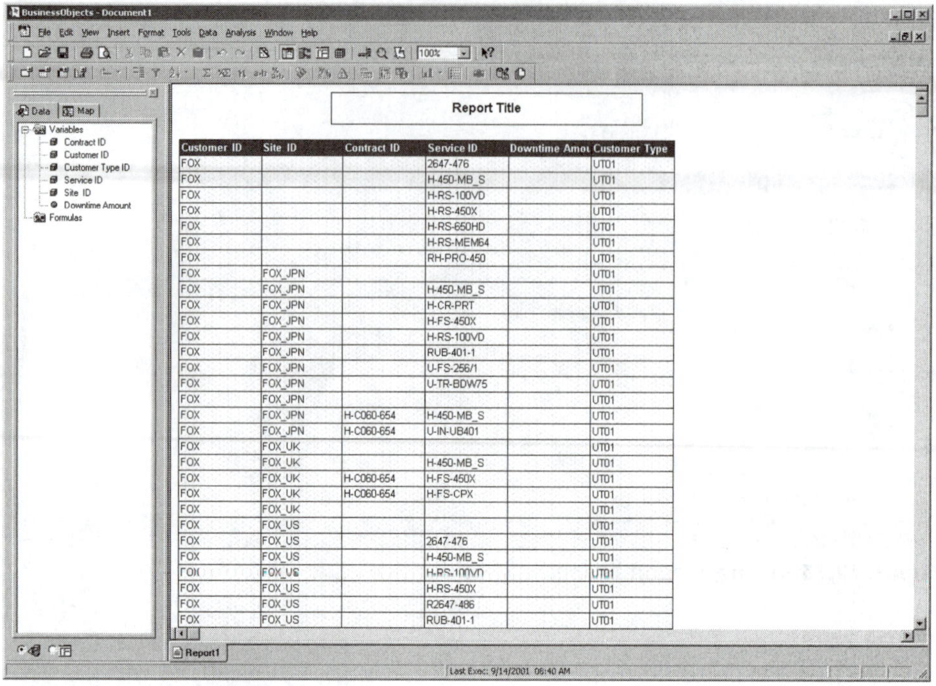

Figure 12.15 Running the report.

Web Delivery

What is definitely of major importance in report functionality is the use of the Internet for report distribution. This includes the use of Web portals for posting reports for on-line viewing as well as the use of email for delivering reports. The actual formats of the reports will almost certainly be in HTML PDFs, or Office documents. Therefore all users—regardless of whether they are employees of the provider, customers, or business partners—will have the tools necessary to view the reports (and usually from within the Web browser or an email server). Figure 12.16 shows an example HTML report delivered within a channel in a portal-type display. Note that the set of reports that are available to the user logged into the portal is shown in a channel on the left-hand side. By clicking on one of the entries in this list, users can see the report displayed in the main channel. Once users find the data they are interested in, they may click on the Download button and retrieve the data in a format that can be edited and further displayed by Excel (typically a Comma Separated Value [CSV] file).

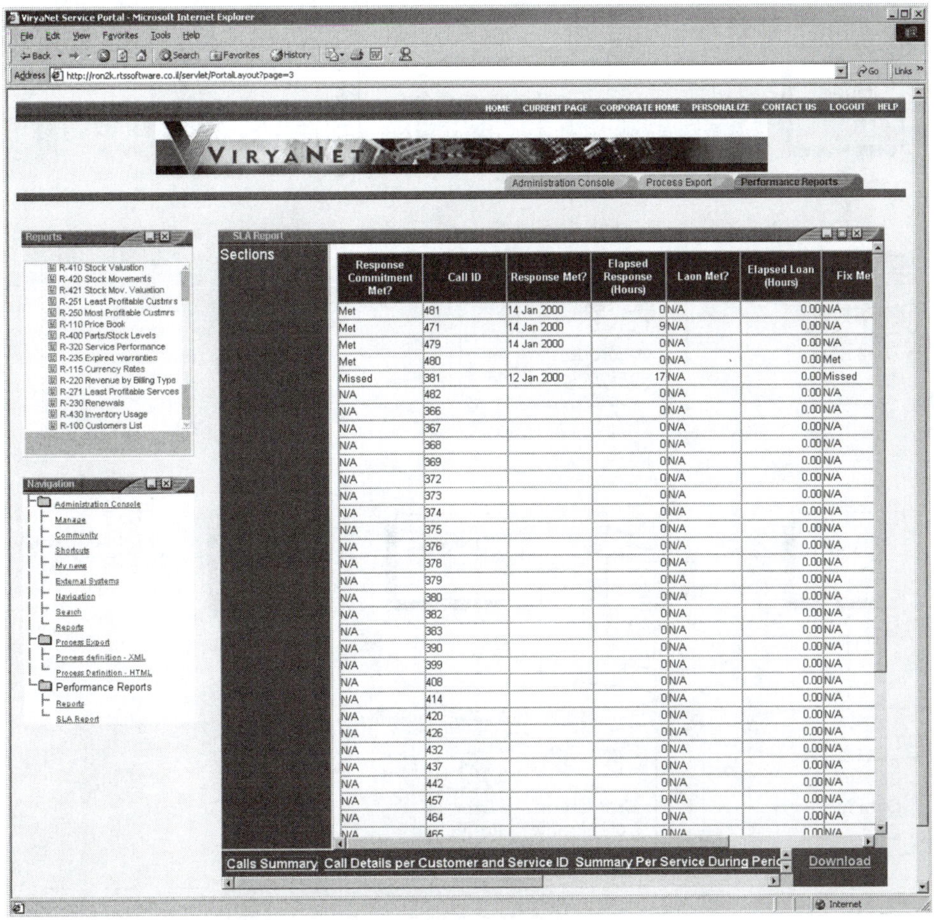

Figure 12.16 A report viewed from within a portal.

Figure 12.17 shows the three primary Web delivery paradigms. In the first one, reports are statically defined and generated. Given the report definitions, a report server runs periodically and computes the reports. Each report becomes a document and is placed within a document repository. The organization of the reports is usually hierarchical and depends on organizations and roles. When a user logs on to the system (usually through some form of enterprise portal), the profile defined for that user and for the user groups that he or she belongs to determines which of the reports may be accessed. In effect, the profiles filter the document repository and define a subset of the full report set that the user has access to. The second scheme shown in Figure 12.17 is similar except that in this case the delivery server periodically extracts a report or a set of reports and sends them by email to the user.

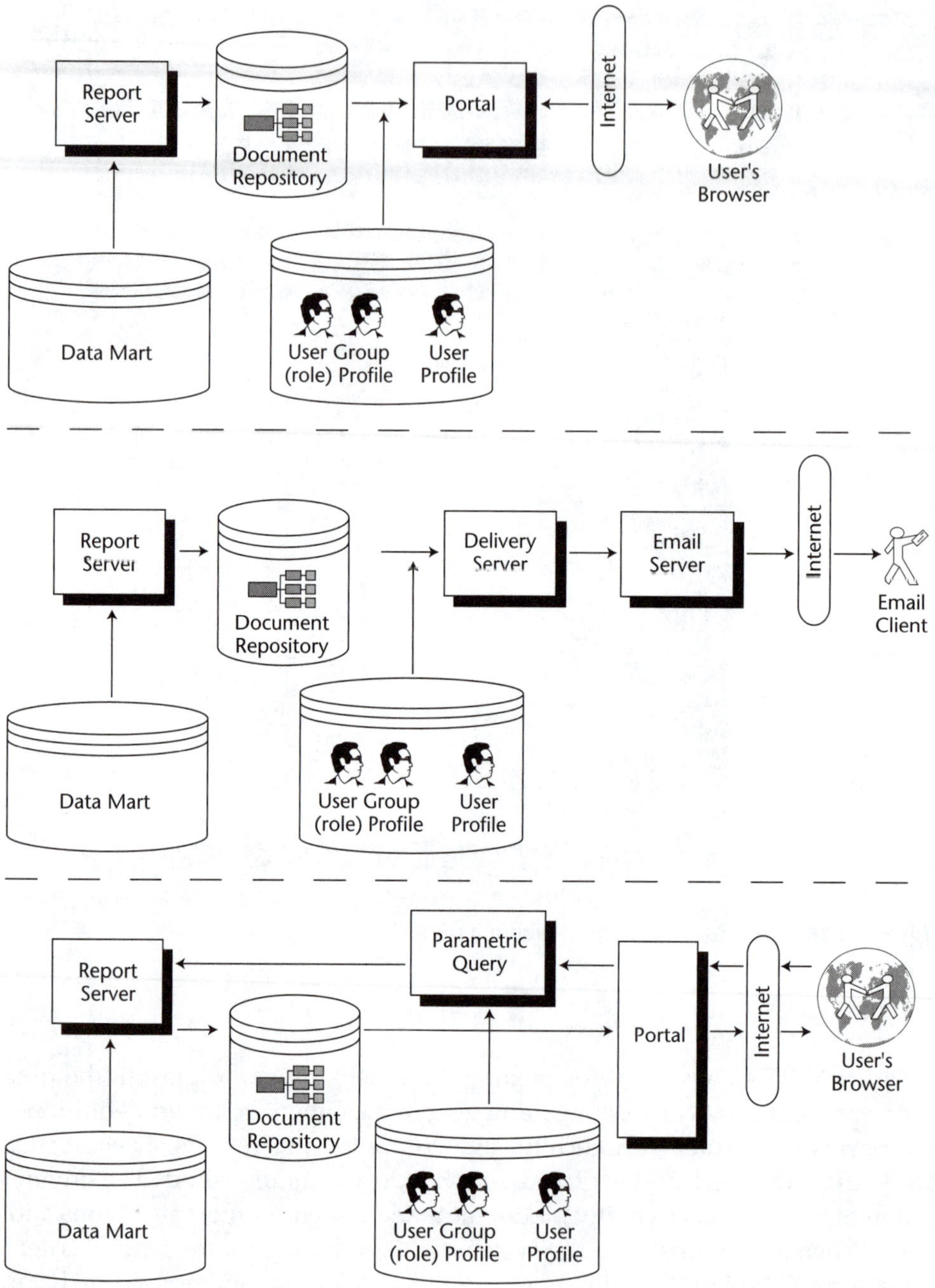

Figure 12.17 Internet delivery of reports.

The third scheme shown in Figure 12.17 is slightly more complex but more realistic. Reports are often parametric—implying that information in the user profile is used as part of the query. For example, the customer's identifier can be part of the query if we display SLA information for the customer, and a report of all missed SLAs for a manager will certainly have the manager's domain of responsibility as a parameter (that is as part of the WHERE clause). The scheme is therefore shown to take the arguments from the user and role profiles, pass them to the report server to compute the report (if it hasn't done so already), and then proceed to cache the report in the document repository before delivering it to the user. The cache in the repository ensures that the relatively long wait entailed while the report is computing only occurs once in every reporting period (for example, once a week for a weekly report). The question of whether it is better to pre-compute a lot of the reports for all the possible profiles and store them in the repository or wait until one is asked for is an instance of the classic space versus time trade-off that is so common in computer science. What is normally done is a mix—the really important people have batches that pre-compute their reports while the rest of us wait (typically less than a minute) for our reports to be computed.

Summary

Since SLAs define the service levels that a provider commits to, it must be easy to measure whether or not these levels have been achieved. Without the ability to measure and report on what happened in the real world, the SLA is nothing more than a piece of paper. Therefore a framework through which customers can easily review the performance of the service provider is central to the concept of an integrated SLA model. For the provider, these measures are also important. By alerts that are based on the measures, a provider can more easily manage exceptional conditions and ensure that service does not fall below a certain committed level.

In our discussion of KPIs and reports, we mentioned the use of Web access and a portal display for viewing performance information. This is an important part of the subject of the next chapter—that of delivering all information in a unified presentation model.

CHAPTER

13

Service Level Agreement Portals: A Unified Presentation Layer

Users are strange. They like consistent data, usable interfaces, intuitive navigation of applications and data—and they actually want their information tools to reflect their business needs (gee whiz, where did these people acquire such ideas anyway?). Unfortunately for IT, these same strange people are also the ones who bring in the money to pay the salaries; so these annoying requests need to be accommodated.

Users and business owners do not see back-end systems, and they typically do not care about the back end (as long as it runs the business). What users see are user interfaces. The Operations Support System (OSS) is a complex (sometimes overly complex) collection of systems that are themselves not simple. As long as the back-end system blueprint follows the integrated SLA architecture, these systems will be tied together based on the various principles of integration and automation that have already been discussed in Chapters 7 and 8. The purpose of the blueprint is to make the combination of the systems managing SLAs behave and look to business users like a single system that deals with SLAs throughout their life cycle. But even when uniformity is accomplished on the back end, it is not enough since users view information systems through their user interfaces. Therefore, in order to ensure that an integrated architecture is actually usable as an integrated solution, we need to unify the presentation layer in a consistent way through which users can do their work.

Unified Presentation

When discussing unified presentation, our goal is not to unify the user interfaces (UIs) of all the relevant systems into a single UI. First, this would be very difficult to do (or impossible, more likely). Second, there is no good reason to integrate all UIs (except that if we could pull it off it would be really cool—precisely because it is so hard—but that's not really a good business reason).

We do think two things are important. First, all user interfaces should follow a common UI metaphor. We believe that while the business applications have embedded within them the data models and application functions specific to that part of the life cycle, all these models and functions should be exposed to the user within a common UI framework that allows users to easily manage and personalize their SLA desktop. This common metaphor should be one that is familiar to users from other application environments so they will feel as comfortable as possible working within it.

The second element we believe to be important is a consistent presentation model for a single individual who is using more than one application. We see no special value in trying to unify all systems involved in the integrated SLA architecture if these applications are used by different roles within an organization. But, if we find a role within the chain that needs to use more than one of these applications simultaneously, then these applications should have similar presentation models if not a common presentation model. The unified presentation model is required only when an individual needs to use more than one application at the same time in order to complete his or her work. If the UI is inconsistent, then using various applications will be very difficult since that individual will have to continuously mentally translate what he or she is viewing in one application into the semantic model of the other application. For applications that are common to one user it is necessary to create a higher-level view that aggregates the two semantic models, or select one as the primary model and find a way to extract data from one application and inject it into the other. This unified interface approach is certainly at the leading edge and far from commonplace. Yet unified presentation is so important that we have chosen to describe it with the hope that with time it will become ever more possible.

Information Portals

Over the past few years, portals have become an important category within information systems. Internet portals such as Yahoo, Lycos, AOL, and MSN have led the way. *Internet portals* create entry points into the Internet through which one can organize and manage access to the entire Internet. The primary tool for the Internet portal is the search engine—it is of vast importance for Internet portals since the Internet is so large and accessing focused information is very difficult. The Internet portal has also created a new user interface metaphor that we will call the *Web desktop*. This interface metaphor allows users to organize the content they view on the Web. It involves Web pages that organize channels of content and access to other Web sites. The portal UI metaphor is fairly standard, and there are few differences from a presentation point of view between myYahoo, myLycos, and so on.

But Internet portals are just the beginning. After Web portals illustrated the value of a single point of entry and the aggregation of content, two important portal categories emerged—*vertical portals* (sometimes called *vortals*) and *enterprise information portals*. Vertical portals focus on a single domain and provide applications and content for a specific user group (or set of user groups). The key point in vertical portals is that since the use of the portal is much less generic and members of the user community using the portal share some common attributes, the functionalities and capabilities built into the portal can be far richer than those built into a generic portal. As an example, a software developer portal can offer code libraries, shared project areas, and reviews.

Enterprise Information Portals

The other important category is enterprise information portals. Instead of looking at a user community in a focused area of interest, this category of solutions looks at a user community belonging to or interacting with a certain corporation. Within an enterprise there is commonality among the users, and this commonality can be used to build better support in terms of applications and content. As an example, in enterprise information portals a company can support its employees with human resources (HR) applications, its customers with self-service applications, and its business partners with sourcing applications.

Both vertical portals and enterprise information portals follow a common thread—that of focusing on a more specific area—and through concentrating on a much higher common denominator among the users, creating much better support for these users. The two categories of portals are, of course, not mutually exclusive; it is very common to find an enterprise portal that branches out into a sales portal, a service portal, and an HR portal.

The Service Level Agreement Portal

We're sure you already see where we're going with all this—to an SLA portal. We believe that in the life of a provider, SLAs are important enough to merit creating a specialized information portal that will aggregate applications and data for all parties (employees, customers, regulatory authorities, and so on).

All the applications and information elements in such a portal should focus on the SLA life cycle and be a part of the provider's larger enterprise information portal strategy. The SLA portal will be used by customers who wish to track their SLA metrics, view bills, and consult refund reports. Regulatory authorities may also view their reports on the Web through the SLA portal.

The SLA portal is not just a reporting tool; it also aggregates and provides controlled access to applications. The applications on the SLA portal will be used primarily by employees but will span the entire organization all the way from the contract term creation process through to SLA assurance and monitoring, and into the billing and penalty processes.

In terms of the user interface metaphor, the SLA portal should follow the portal metaphor. The familiarity of the two metaphors lowers the effort that a user needs to commit to in order to start using such a portal. Since most users are already familiar with portal metaphors, the natural hesitation to try a new UI metaphor can be alleviated. Also it should by now be very clear that the new application model that has become dominant is the Web application model. The application model that has won the battle is the application front end that is delivered as Web pages that run within the Web browser without the need for plug-ins, applets, or ActiveX. The presentation layers are dynamic HTML pages, which are generated by a server component and run with no need to install the applications within the user's browser.

A portal display featuring SLA information and OSS applications is shown in Figures 13.1 through 13.3. Portal displays are organized as pages. Each page has a tab and usually aggregates a set of applications and informational elements that have to do with a certain role, task, or process. One possible organization of the SLA portal for an account manager could have one tab set for contract management applications and reports, one tab for assurance applications and Key Performance Indicators (KPIs), and one for refund reviews.

Alternatively, an account manager may choose to organize his or her SLA desktop so that there is a single page per account with all the relevant data and applications pertaining to that account appearing on that page. This user-controlled organization is probably simpler to navigate from a user perspective, but not all applications support this metaphor. In order for such a

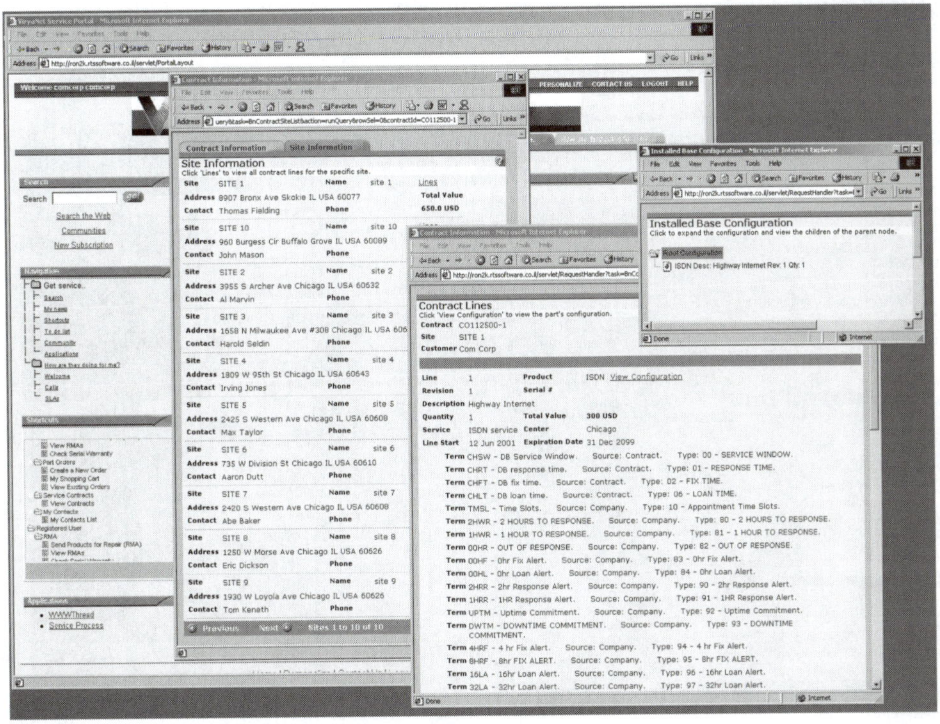

Figure 13.1 A portal view including contract applications.

presentation layer to exist, applications must allow external control (sometimes called *scripting* or *automation*); that is, an external definition must be able to control directly how an application is opened and navigated. This control is enabled either through a set of windowing system capabilities, or, when the application is Web-based, through parameters passed over the Uniform Resource Locator (URL) or as part of an HTTP request.

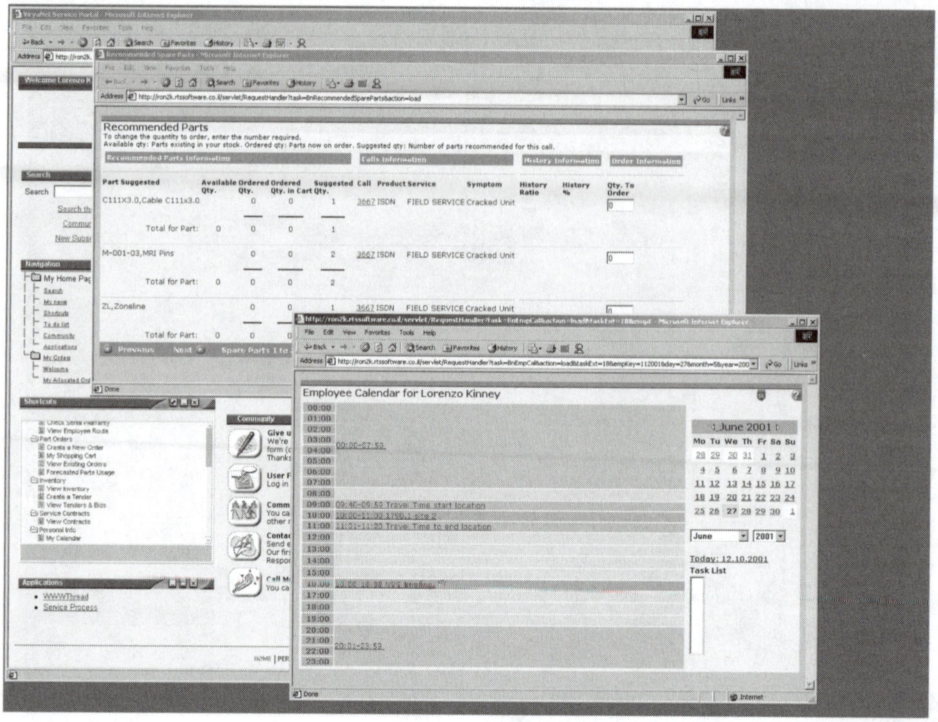

Figure 13.2 A portal view including time management and inventory management applications.

Uniform Resource Locator Automation and Scripting

The ability to automatically drive an application through a set of Hypertext Transfer Protocol (HTTP) requests is an added bonus that is available in the Web application model. A Web application is usually deployed on application servers that get requests through a Web server. Requests come over an HTTP connection and follow a request-response paradigm. Each request has a target, which is the URL, as well as a set of arguments that are embedded within the HTTP request either on the URL (if the request is of the type GET) or within the body of the request (if the request is of the type POST). These arguments are normally used within the activation of a business function. As an example, these arguments may be used as parameters used by a dynamic query. Each

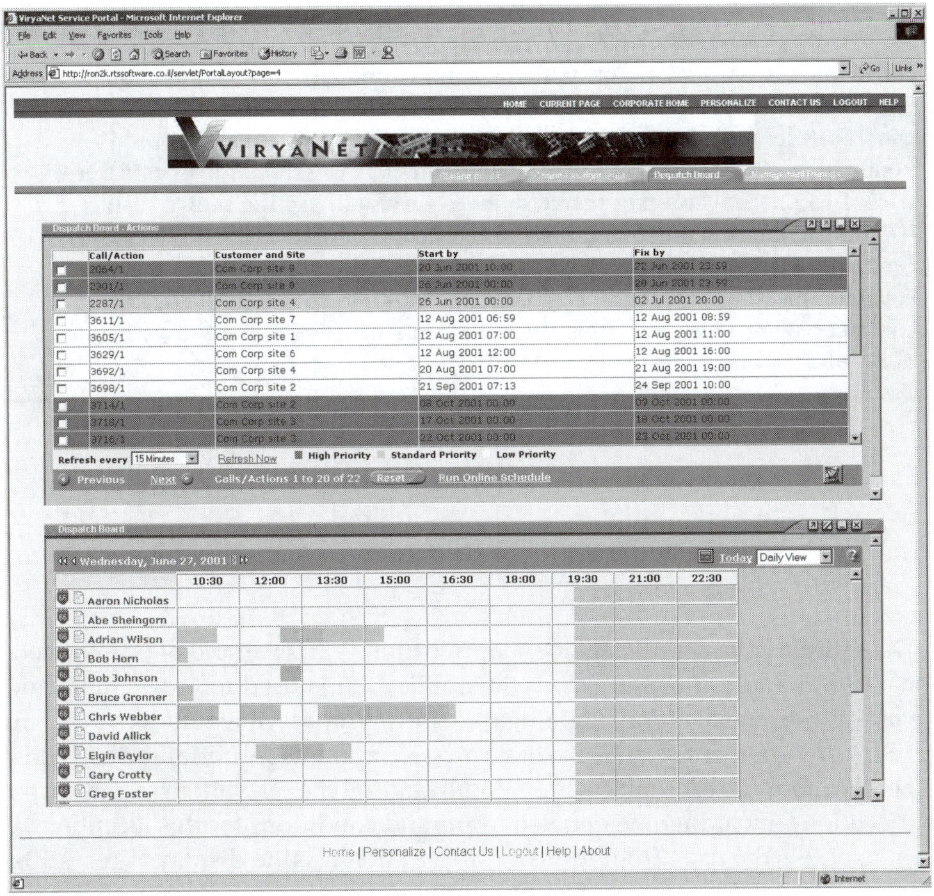

Figure 13.3 A portal view including workforce management application.

function in an application may be thought of as a single HTTP request/response pair. Activating the function is done through the HTTP request, and the answer is returned within the response. A full application session is then made possible by chaining together such HTTP requests and controlling the arguments passed on along these connections.

The really great thing is that the Web application model has become dominant and is truly a de facto standard among business applications in general (and OSS applications in our context). Therefore the notion of Web automation and URL scripting is a great enabler of unified presentation—as long as the applications to be unified are Web-enabled and can be activated by HTTP requests.

EXAMPLE 1: CONTRACT NAVIGATION

Let's look at a navigation flow within a contract management application. We will take the simple example in which we would like to view the terms and conditions for an existing contract. The first application screen we would normally use is a query screen that would allow us to search for a customer (Figure 13.4). After entering search criteria, we would use the search result (Figure 13.5) to drill down and view general contract details for a certain customer (Figure 13.6). We could then look at contract information per customer location in case the customer has multiple sites covered by the contract (Figure 13.7), and from there we could drill down into the particular terms and conditions as in Figure 13.8.

The sample contract management application is an example of one conventional use of applications in which the application is used to access data, and the user is responsible for navigating this flow. What if we would like to set up our SLA environment so that we have a page on our SLA portal for each customer location? On each such page we will have all the relevant information for this location—including the detailed terms and conditions for this location. We want to access the page from the same application used to display Figures 13.4 through 13.8 (that is, we don't want a customer report to be built). Using the

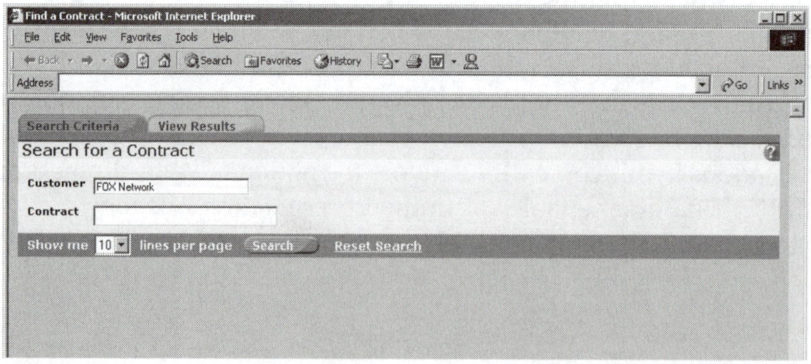

Figure 13.4 An application screen showing a search for a customer.

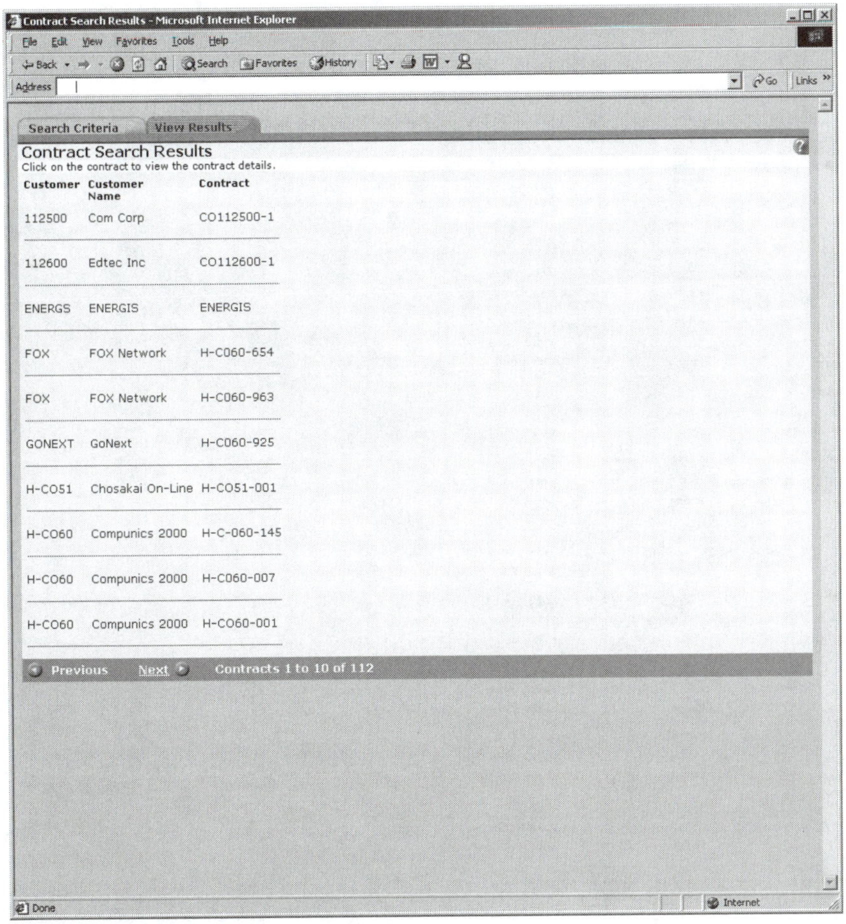

Figure 13.5 Customer search results.

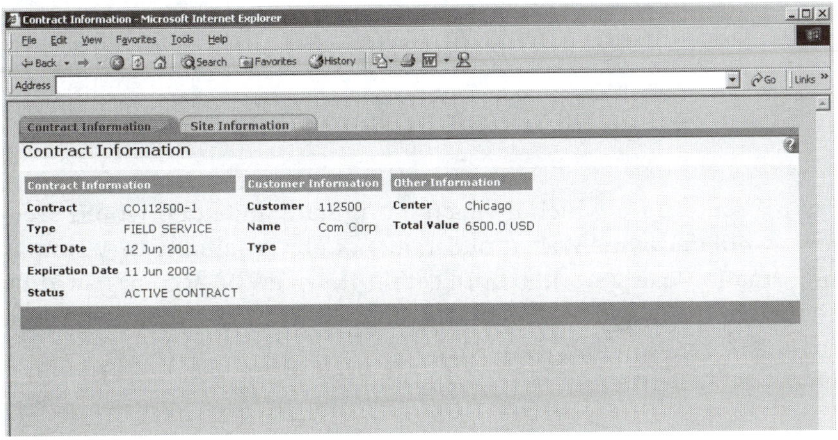

Figure 13.6 General contract information.

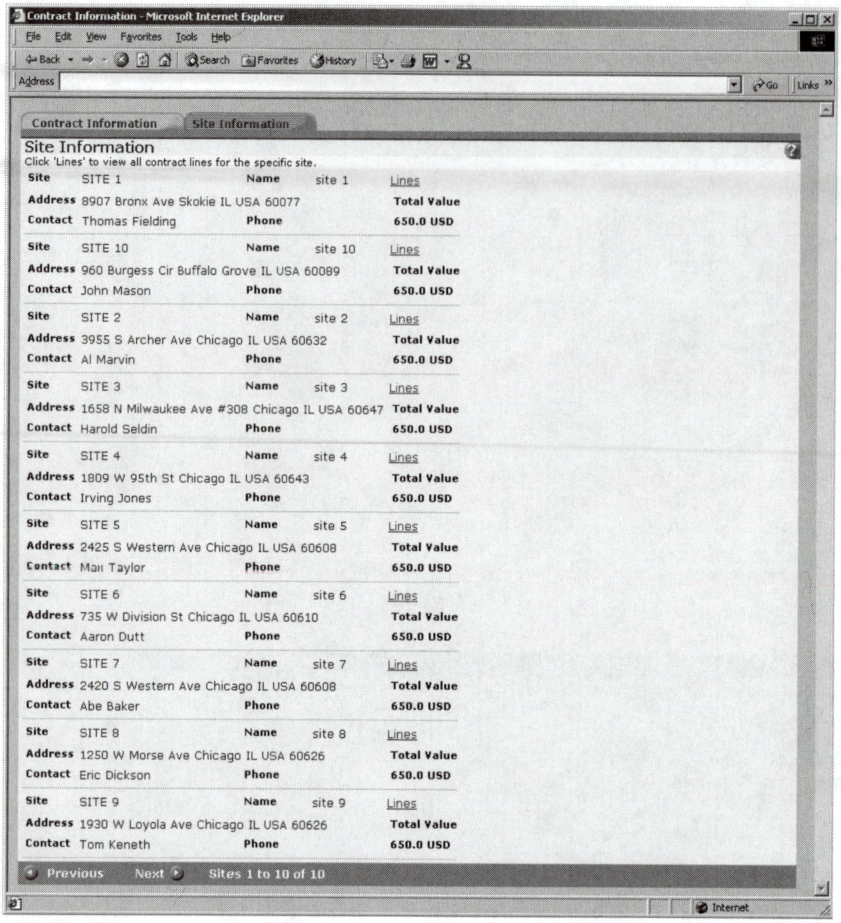

Figure 13.7 Contract information per customer location.

application in a pattern for which it was not originally intended would seem difficult to do—but under the Web application model it is actually very simple. Merging information using normal application flow can be accomplished by looking under the covers and understanding that URL automation can be used for building the navigation into the URLs.

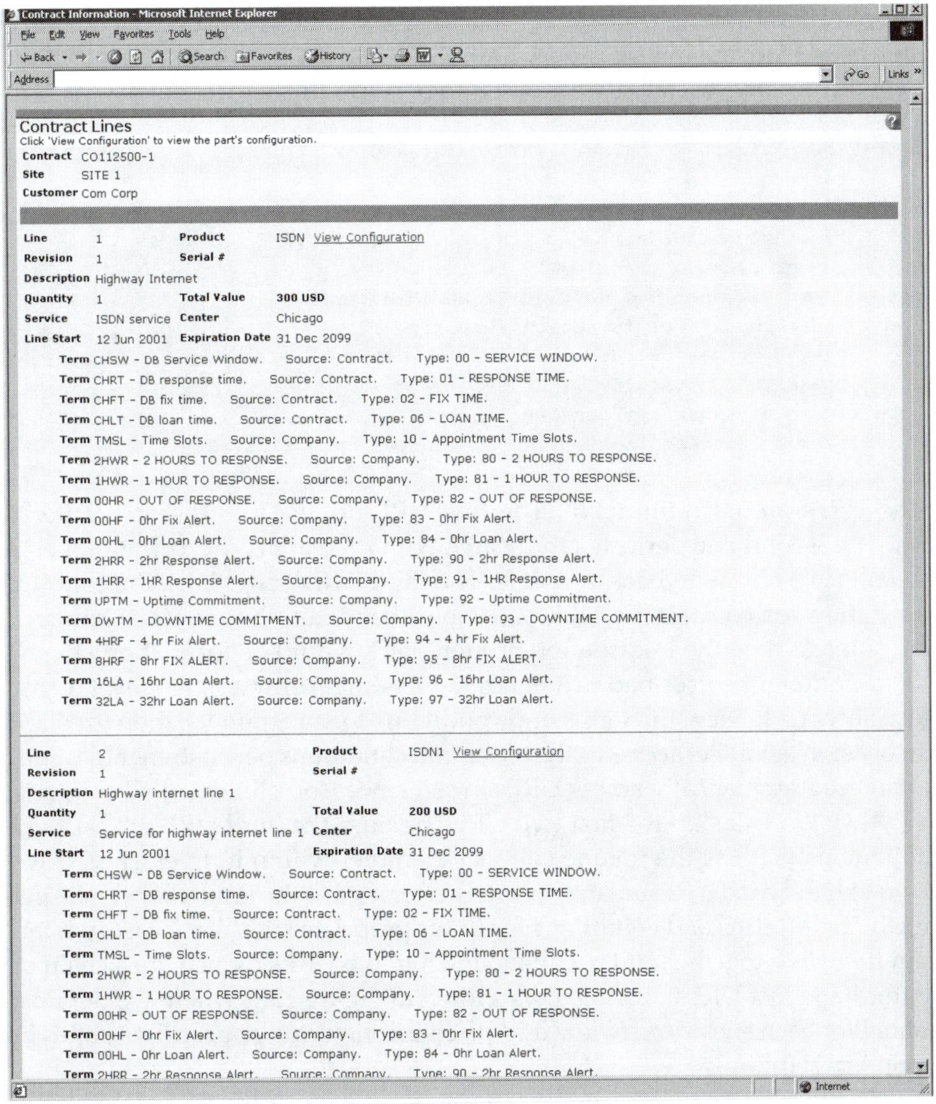

Figure 13.8 Terms and conditions (contract lines) per sample location.

Automating the Flow

If we inspect the HTTP requests used to navigate Figures 13.4 through 13.8, we find that we can automate the flow using Uniform Resource Locators (URLs) and arguments placed on the URL. This ability to automate is retained even if the application running uses HTTP POST requests; the back-end functionality more often than not will support both GET and POST. Based on the flow shown, the following URLs can be used to perform this very same navigation:

```
http://demo.viryanet.com/servlet/RequestHandler?
      task=BnContractSearch&action=runQuery
http://demo.viryanet.com/servlet/RequestHandler?
      task=BnContractSearchResults&action=runQuery&
      customerId=&contractId=&blockSize=10
http://demo.viryanet.com/servlet/RequestHandler?
      task=BnContractInfo&action=runQuery&
      task=BnContractSiteList&action=runQuery&
      rowSel=0&contractId=CO112500-1
http://demo.viryanet.com/servlet/RequestHandler?
      task=BnContractLines&action=runQuery&siteId=SITE%201
```

The URLs are fairly intuitive. The first URL brings up the search criteria form. The second one performs the search with no search criteria but requests 10 results to be brought back at a time. The third URL brings back the contract information for contract CO112500-1. Note that if another contract number were entered, then the information brought back would be for that other contract (assuming the user had privileges to view that contract). Finally, the last URL allows us to view the terms and conditions for a certain location (or site).

In order to get direct access to the terms and conditions per customer location, we can programmatically access URLs in sequence (sometimes called scripting the URLs). We will skip the first two URLs because the third URL can be used autonomously; it has the unique contract identifier within it. In essence, if we can go to the second URL and immediately after it go to the last URL, we will get directly to the terms and conditions for the appropriate site. In our case, we can chain these two together and use the following two URLs (which are a chain of the third and last URLs); the result is shown in Figure 13.9, where we define a channel for each such direct view and place the views on appropriate pages in our SLA portal):

```
http://demo.viryanet.com/servlet/RequestHandler?
   task=BnContractInfo&action=runQuery&
   task=BnContractSiteList&action=runQuery&
   rowSel=0&contractId=CO112500-1&
   task=BnContractLines&action=runQuery&
   siteId=SITE%201
http://demo.viryanet.com/servlet/RequestHandler?
   task=BnContractInfo&action=runQuery&
   task=BnContractSiteList&action=runQuery&
   rowSel=0&contractId=CO112500-1&
   task=BnContractLines&action=runQuery&siteId=SITE%202
```

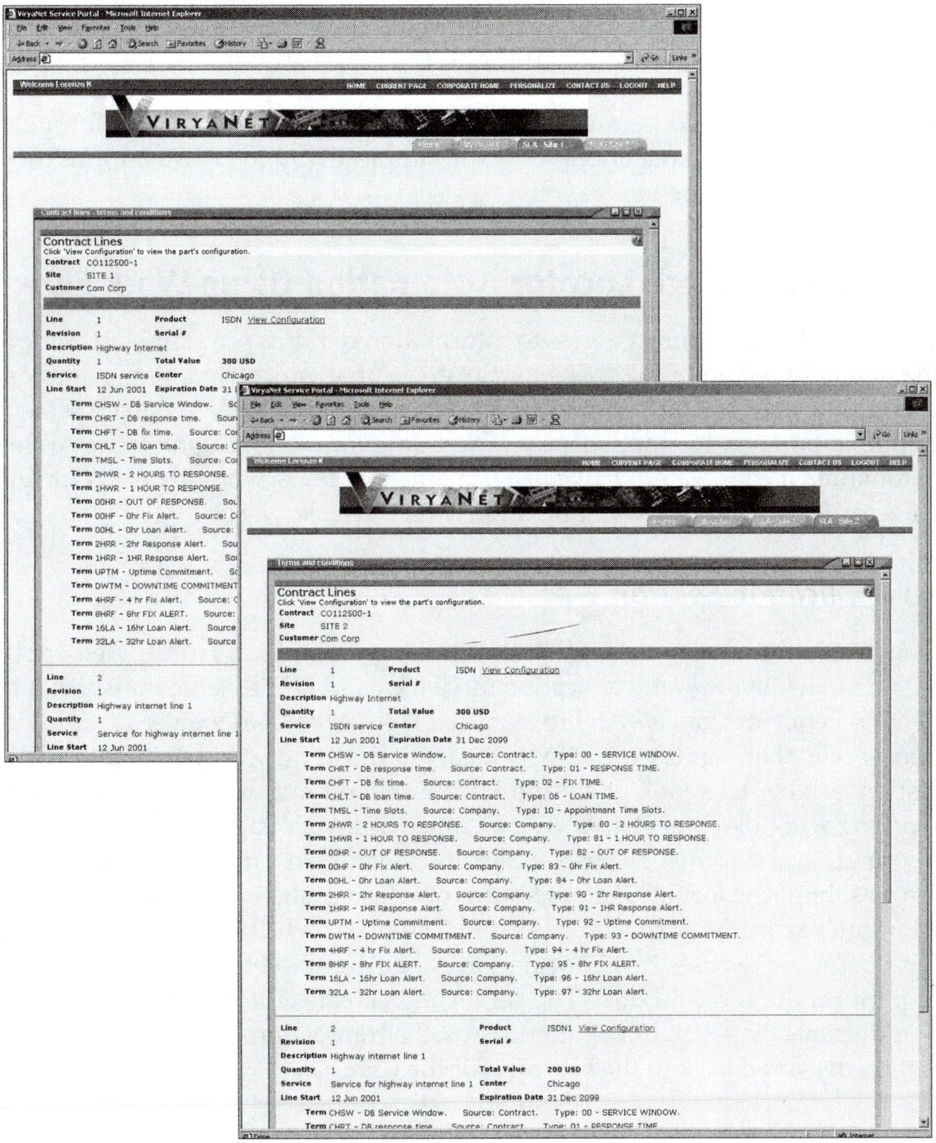

Figure 13.9 Using uniform resource locators for direct access.

Such chaining depends on the application infrastructure, and it is not always applicable. In the examples shown above the RequestHandler servlet manages the application flow. Unless the software was specifically built to allow this, another type of infrastructure is needed. As another example, if the application uses Apache's Struts framework, then such scripting is easy. Infrastructure support is necessary for mimicking navigation among Web pages. Mimicking is required because application context is often built up throughout the application navigation—and the simplest way to capture application context is to mimic the navigation.

Uniform Resource Locator Automation Using Work Flow

The general case for direct access to information requires programmatic scripting and automation of the URLs for the pages that are created by the application. Uniform Resource Locator automation means that a Web-enabled system can be automated by another program. Using a process engine to drive this automation means we can make use of all the functions exposed by all our systems to create "meta -flows," and all in a very generic way.

An Application Session

Once more, the assumption is that the application conforms to the Web application model. In the Web application model, we use HTTP as the transport that delivers requests from a Web browser to a Web server and we use an application server that creates an HTML page that is returned within the HTTP response. Now let's look at an application session in this model. The user is working with a Web page in a Web browser. The Web page displays business information and forms. The user enters information in a form and clicks a button to submit the form. When the button is clicked, the browser packages the data entered in the form into the HTTP request, which is delivered to the server. The server uses this information either to complete the transactions or to perform queries (or both). The server then creates the resulting Web page that displays the result of the queries and the transactions. The resulting page is then delivered back to the browser for the user.

Web "Scraping"

Web page form submissions are triggered by clicks on a button in a form, and information can then be viewed and used for making business decisions. But submits really produce HTTP requests, and the data used for making business decisions can be *scraped* from Web pages. Screen scraping for mainframe applications is a well-known method for using features available within legacy applications without making changes to the application. Sometimes it is just impossible to make changes, and scraping is the only option outside of rewriting the functionality. Uniform Resource Locator automation can in many ways be viewed as a modern scraping technology, with the benefit that we can make use of application functionality in a very broad category of applications—that of Web applications.

Chaining Requests

It is not enough to be able to create HTTP requests and make use of HTTP responses. We must be able to chain together such cycles in steps and (for example) make use of the information we extract from one HTTP response to create input to be used in a later HTTP request.

In addition, data elements embedded within the response can be used to create a display; a good example is scripting multiple applications and collecting data elements from all of them to create a *meta user-interface* that aggregates these data elements and creates a higher-level display that is very helpful to the user. Such unification and aggregation of user interfaces has huge value to end users.

Enter Work Flow

We can make up an infrastructure for the chaining of these scripting steps—but in fact we don't have to. In Chapter 8 we described the importance of work-flow automation and introduced the model of the state machine in which functions may be chained together using transition rules. Work-flow automation and transition rules form the exact infrastructure we require in order to perform generic Web application automation and scripting.

Using the Work-Flow Token

Recall from the section in Chapter 8, *Process Templates and Tokens,* that a token is a data structure that forms the common context for a process instance. The solution we are describing makes use of the work flow as a meta flow that makes use of existing application functions through URL scripting. The common information that flows through this meta flow can be stored in the token. Technically, we can use the token as the context through which we pass data structures from one scripting step to the next, and we can define steps in the process that hit the application server. In such a step we can define the URL that will be the basis for the HTTP request as well as the parameters that this HTTP request will include. The data elements forming the arguments need to come from the token. An example of such a step definition is shown in Figure 13.10.

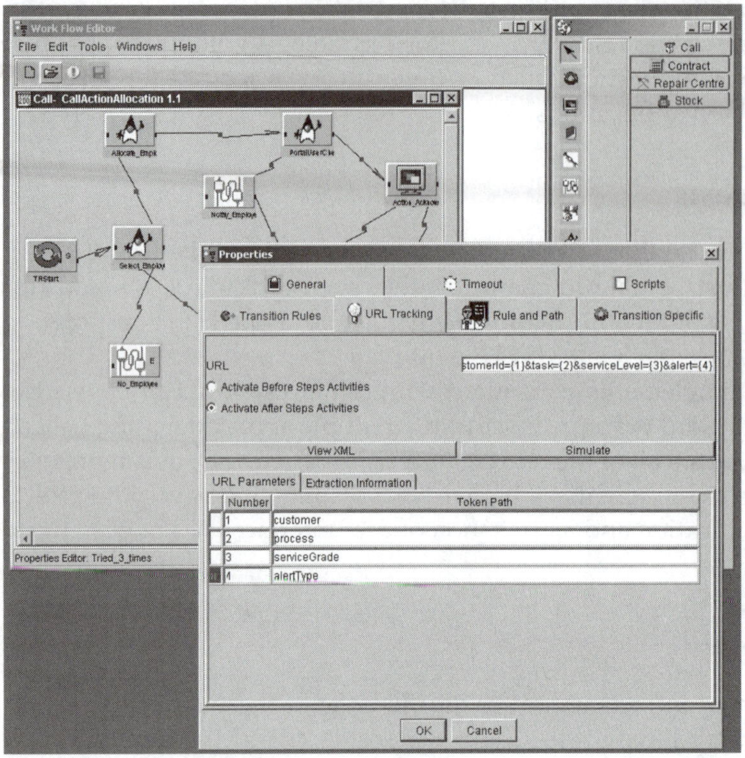

Figure 13.10 A work-flow step scripting Hypertext transfer protocol.

Extracting Data from Scraped Pages

Once the HTTP request has come back, we need to extract information from the resulting page for use later in the process flow. We can use this data in transition rules (to determine what the next application step should be) or as data that will be used in other HTTP requests. In any case, we put the information extracted from the response into the token. Here, too, we make use of standards; HTML is a subset of Standard Generalized Markup Language (SGML) as well as a subset of eXtensible Markup Language (XML). Unfortunately, not all HTML is well-structured XML, but luckily we do have some utilities that will clean up HTML and generate well-formed XML from the page content within the HTTP response. We then use eXtensible Query Language (XQL), the XML query language, to pull information from the generated XML. What we need to do is define XQL expressions that determine which information we pull out of the XML (which is really the resulting page). We then define which token entry each such extraction is injected into—as shown by Figure 13.11. The result is a generic and powerful infrastructure for creating dynamic and unified user interfaces—something that is certainly a first in our industry.

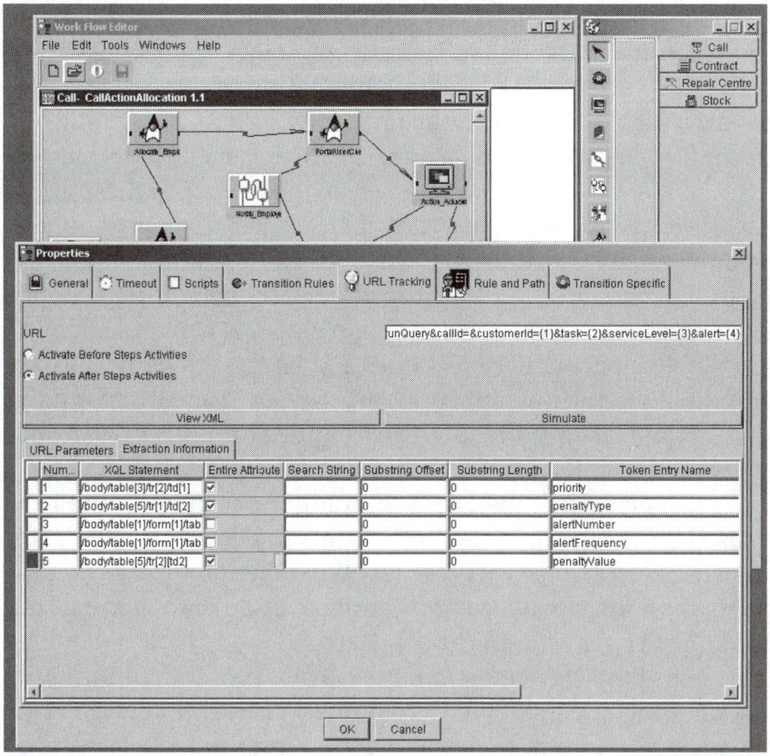

Figure 13.11 Extracting data from the Hypertext Transfer Protocol response using eXtensible Query Language.

Security, Access Control, and Profiles

Integrating the security and access models is critical when a service provider seeks to unify presentations into a single portal. By default, every application has its own security mechanism. All applications maintain user information that includes at least a username and a password, and more likely additional profile information that is used to drive the application presentation as well as the access permissions. Most applications also maintain user group information that defines a set of user groups (or roles) and mappings that circumscribe to which user groups each user in the application belongs. Finally, applications tend to maintain security rules made up of access control lists for various functions as well as (possibly) advanced data security rules that can help limit what data a user has access to and which operations on the data each user may perform.

While it may be true that all applications have some form of security mechanisms, it is also unfortunately true that each such system handles security in a different way. This disparity makes the implementation of a unified presentation layer very difficult. The difficulty lies not only in security but also in profile management. When constructing a meta UI we are, in effect, using multiple applications, and we must be logged into each one. If each of these applications has its own user control infrastructure, then we need a many-to-many mapping between the security entities. Since we cannot assume that we will require the user to log in multiple times (once per application that we are unifying), we must support some notion of a single logon. When a user logs on to the master portal, we must, behind the scenes, log on to each of the applications we are unifying. In order to unify logon, we must create mappings between each user of the master portal and user entities (or *principals*) in each of the other systems.

Unfortunately, the logon issue is only the beginning. Since many of the security policies are based on user groups and profiles (attributes maintained at the user level, at the user group level, or at other levels in a hierarchical structure), we must also create mappings between such entities. But even mapping user entities is not enough. The real complications start when we look not only at creating these mappings but also at managing these mappings. Creating a unified presentation layer means, by default, that all administration happens in one place. For example, if we wish to provide more access to a set of users by making them part of additional user groups, then we must flow the access requirements into all of the applications using the mapping defined. Furthermore, all password maintenance must be done centrally through the master portal.

The security and access issue is fairly complex, and we cannot begin to describe solutions in the context of this chapter. What we do want to impress upon readers is that security and access rights is an issue that can be (and has been) resolved. We also want to offer an overview of the two major access management solutions that are available.

Integrating Interface Layers

The first solution requires a lot of integration work. Integration involves managing interface layers that hook into the master portal. For each system we need to manage within the master portal we must implement a set of routines that are called when a user logs on to the portal, logs out of the portal, changes password, changes profile, and so on. These routines are called by the portal software for each of the applications being managed in a sequence defined by the portal infrastructure. An integration project in this case involves taking this Application Program Interface (API) set and implementing it once for every application that needs to be deployed within the portal.

Directory Services and the Lightweight Directory Access Protocol

The second approach to unified security and access is one that is based on directory services. The reasoning behind a directory services approach is that the integration approach requires too much up-front work, requires too much work continuously throughout the lifetime of the system, and is too unstable owing to additions and changes that are made. Changes and additions are a common and frequent fact of life when you are managing so many disparate systems. The directory services approach is based on the premise that security and profile services are important enough to require distinct handling. In effect, we are saying that there should be a separate system to manage user and profile information. All other systems then link into this system to access user and profile information. Instead of creating mappings between different systems, all security related information is maintained in one place and used by all systems.

The directory services approach uses a standard that has emerged as both the formal and the de facto standard for directory services—the Lightweight Directory Access Protocol (LDAP). The Lightweight Directory Access Protocol is an open industry standard that defines a method for accessing and updating information in a directory. The protocol got a boost partly because of the Internet; it is often used as a directory access method on the Internet and is also being used strategically within corporate intranets. The LDAP is being supported by many software vendors and is incorporated into many applications.

A *directory* is a collection of information about objects arranged in some order that gives details about each object. Examples from real life include telephone directories and library catalogs. From an IT perspective, directories are databases or data repositories that list information for keyed objects. The main difference between a generic database and a directory is that directories tend to have a great number of lookup requests but relatively few update requests as compared with a generic database. This lack of update requests in a directory means that there is opportunity to specialize and optimize—precisely what directory servers do.

Directories allow users or applications to find resources that have the characteristics needed to carry out a particular task. For example, a directory of users can be used to look up a person's email address or fax number. A directory can be searched to find a user group to which a user belongs, and then the directory can be queried about the attributes possessed by this user group or this individual. Other types of directories allow the publishing and discovery of a service. As an example a Universal Description Discovery and Integration (UDDI) registry allows creators of services to publish their service and consumers to find services based on search criteria. In the rest of this section our focus is on the use of directories to merge and lookup user information.

Directory services are APIs exposed by the directory serve that are used to access information in a directory—services (or APIs) such as looking up information attributed to a managed entity (for example, the profile maintained for a user), updating that information (which occurs much less often), and finding an entity given some selection criteria. Directory services are provided by directory servers—software components that manage the directories and implement the services. Applications access directory services by using a directory client as shown in Figure 13.12.

Lightweight Directory Access Protocol is, as its name implies, a protocol. But it is also associated with an API set and a family of directory servers. At this point in time, LDAP is the only standard in the arena of directory services—and it is quickly becoming dominant. It allows multiple applications to have simple standardized access to security-related information, user profiles, user group attributes, and so on. By integrating the applications involved in SLA management with an LDAP server and having all user information and profiles stored in such a directory service, it is much simpler to manage the implementation of a unified presentation framework in the long run.

Summary

The integrated SLA model focuses on integrating systems in the OSS and automating processes common to service providers. This chapter has focused on integrating systems and automating processes at the front end of the systems. Although an integrated SLA solution can work only if the back ends of the systems are integrated and being managed within a work-flow management framework, users care only about the front end of systems. It is therefore imperative that a unified presentation layer exist in order for the users to efficiently participate in the automated processes.

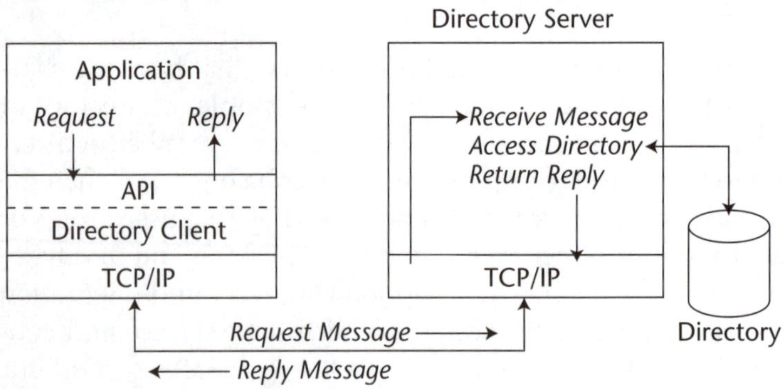

Figure 13.12 An application accessing directory services.

Many of the users in a provider's operation work in centralized environments and can use an information portal. But many of the employees of a communications provider work in the field. In order for end-to-end automation to occur, we must ensure that remote workers are serviced by the OSSs when these workers are out in the field—the topic of Chapter 14.

CHAPTER

14

Notification, Mobile Computing, and Wireless Access

Operations Support Systems and Business Support Systems (OSS/BSS) are large systems deployed in a data center serving users who are mostly internal employees. Architecturally, they are traditionally server-centric systems with very robust database servers, application servers that are accessed over networks (mostly local area networks [LANs]) by client software running on users' desktops. Systems dealing with SLAs include contract management systems, SLA monitoring systems, and network management and service assurance systems. All of these are centralized systems that manage and correlate large databases. Most of the components we have been describing as part of the integrated SLA architecture run on desktop computers or servers. Yet the personnel involved in operations that ensure adherence to SLA terms also include people working in the field.

Another typical characteristic of the integrated SLA model is that the components and systems interact with a large number of data sources in order to manage the SLA information. It is necessary to correlate contract information with network information with financial information with trouble ticket information. We have touched upon much of the required infrastructure to deliver such correlated information (using automation and integration), but there is one aspect we have yet to cover. We have not yet described how workforce management and field workers using mobile devices can be integrated into the ISLA framework.

Service Level Agreements are often used to define response times when problems occur, as well as turn-up and installation times. These SLAs affect (or need to affect) the way that the workforce is utilized, managed, and dispatched in terms of how resources are prioritized. If the link between the SLAs and the workforce management application is broken, it is almost certain that SLAs will be missed, incurring high penalties for the provider.

Dealing with a distributed workforce out in the field requires a new kind of infrastructure. A mobile computing and notification infrastructure is required in order to ensure that the workforce has real-time information on work orders and in order for the central dispatch role to have up-to-date information on resources and work. Such real-time information is required in order to correctly prioritize the workforce and resources and ensure that real-time re-prioritization can be done if need be in order to meet SLAs. This information delivery infrastructure is complex and requires a set of technologies that are often overlooked. It is our belief that technologies like wireless gateways and mobile devices are essential for making efficient use of the workforce in order to adhere to SLAs.

Notification

Notification is a general concept that is vital to SLA management and is relevant to almost every system in the OSS that is part of the integrated SLA model. Notifications include messages sent to Network Operations Center (NOC) personnel when a network alert occurs, notifications sent to managers and account managers when an SLA at a customer level is in jeopardy, notifications sent to contract administrators when a contract has not been renewed, and so on. Notifications are merely a convenient way to manage a huge installed base. Rules define conditions that require other activities to be performed. Instead of having personnel that continuously monitor and poll data from systems within an OSS, a proactive rule-based approach can be used. A rule has a set of inputs that are extracted from systems in the OSS. A rule also has a set of computational elements that determine when a notification or action needs to occur. By using such an approach labor-intensive activities can be reduced and human intervention is required only to deal with exceptions. When a rule is activated, a notification is sent to a person. In effect this is a *management by exception* paradigm, and it is vital to the operations of any provider. Service Level Agreement management requires this kind of paradigm, and if anything it is the primary case that demands an exception-based framework.

The events that precipitate a notification request are many, and they can come from any of the systems we have discussed within the integrated SLA architecture. What we have yet to describe are the notification methods and the infrastructure required to make various notification modes possible. Since many of the OSSs require notification infrastructures, many service providers have duplicate or redundant sets of services used for notification. The duplication of notification infrastructure creates a management nightmare for OSS managers. Notification and mobile computing are required building blocks in an integrated SLA architecture. If providers use a common set of notification and wireless access services, they will create a much more manageable environment.

Synchronous and Asynchronous Notification

There are two categories of notifications. Synchronous notification occurs when both the sender and the receiver of the message need to be online for the message to be delivered. An example is a phone call. Asynchronous notification (more commonly known as store-and-forward) involves an intermediary that stores messages. The sender delivers the message to the intermediary, and the intermediary is then responsible for delivering the message to the recipient. Most notification methods (including email, voice mail, paging, and so on) fall into this category. Store-and-forward technology is central to efficient business operation since it is very likely that the sender and receiver will not be online at the same time.

Internet-Based Notification

The most common form of notification is email, which uses the Internet infrastructure. Most companies and users have access to the Internet. Other forms of Internet-based notification schemes include instant messaging and portal alerts.

Email is so ubiquitous that it has become the backbone for many other notification schemes. Notification schemes now often add an email server that functions as a gateway. Notification requests from a paging system, for example, can be posted for delivery over the email infrastructure. In fact, email has become a de facto standard when it comes to store-and-forward notification types.

The Simple Mail Transfer Protocol (SMTP) is the basis for using email servers as an infrastructure component. Using SMTP, applications can send email to users—a common notification method used by applications in the OSS. In fact, SMTP has become an integration layer in the OSS—a natural development given that most systems have email capability, and can extract data from email. Simple Mail Transfer Protocol is not that difficult to write to, and writing to SMTP is not required. Since SMTP has become dominant, libraries for sending email messages exist in every conceivable programming environment on earth. As an example, Figure 14.1 shows a Java program sending an email message. Note that the libraries encapsulate all of the SMTP specifics as shown by the use of the `Transport object` in Figure 14.1.

```
public char sendMail(
            String mailType,
            String address,
            Object[] params,
            boolean sendAsHtml) {
      MailTemplate template = (MailTemplate)templates.get(mailType);
      if(template == null) {
            RTSTracker.displayError(
                  getProcessName() + ": template is not defined for "
                  + mailType);
            return STATUS_FAILURE;
      }

      try {
            Session session =
                Session.getInstance(mailServerHost, null);
            MimeMessage msg = new MimeMessage(session);
            msg.setFrom(new InternetAddress(sender));
            msg.setRecipient(
                  Message.RecipientType.TO,
                  new InternetAddress(address));
            msg.setSubject(template.subject,encoding);
            String body = MessageFormat.format(template.body,params);

            if(sendAsHtml) {
                  msg.setHeader("Mime-Version","1.0");
                  msg.setHeader("Content-Transfer-Encoding","quoted-
printable");
                  msg.setHeader("X-Mailer","sendhtml");
                  msg.setHeader("Content-Type","text/text");
                  msg.setDataHandler(new DataHandler(
                      new DataSource(body,"text/text",encoding)));
            } else {
                  msg.setText(body,encoding);
            }

            Transport.send(msg);
      } catch (Exception e) {
            RTSTracker.handleException(getProcessName(),e);
            return STATUS_FAILURE;
      }
      RTSTracker.displayString(2,"Mail successfully sent");
      return STATUS_SUCCESS;
}
```

Figure 14.1 Sending an email message through a Java program.

Although email systems are very easy to use and are the most common form of notification schemes, they have certain limitations as a notification infrastructure. Four email characteristics should be taken into account. First, email is not a guaranteed messaging infrastructure. Email systems have become very reliable, but they do not *guarantee* delivery. If your message is returned, that is a good indication that it was not delivered. Returned mail may invoke a resend or an attempt to use another notification scheme. But even notification that a message was returned is not guaranteed, and such notification could take time to reach you, during which time you, as a service provider, could incur heavy penalties owing to a missed service level alert.

The second characteristic is that email is a send-and-forget technology. Any functionality that would require a reply or notification of receipt depends on the email client and/or the user; this functionality cannot be implemented at the infrastructure level. The third characteristic is that email systems do not guarantee how long it will take for a message to arrive at its destination. Once more, email systems have progressed a long way and have gotten to a point where mail delivery is, in general, very fast and reliable—but there are horror stories.

The final and most important characteristic is that users need to pull their email messages from the SMTP server. The *pulling* is done using a set of technologies such as point of presence (POP) and Internet Message Access Protocol (IMAP) that enable email clients to download or view email messages that are managed within the email server. In order for a user to see the email notification, he or she must pull messages from the server—mail is not proactively delivered to the user. Pull requirements, along with the lack of delivery guarantees, send and forget, and time delays, limit the use of email-based notification for the urgent and critical messaging that is sometimes required in SLA conformance management.

Paging

Pagers have traditionally been the most common form of instant notification among professionals. These devices are popular for a number of reasons. Pagers and paging services have been around for a very long time. Paging technology outdates most other notification mechanisms and has been in production for almost 20 years. Pagers are fairly inexpensive in terms of the cost of both the device and the monthly service charge. Finally, pagers have characteristics that make them very attractive as notification infrastructure, including very small message size (requiring little bandwidth), national coverage, real-time notifications, almost-instantaneous message delivery, and advanced features such as delivery acknowledgment, menu-driven responses, and more. Naturally, not all paging services support all of these capabilities, and different options affect the device and service prices. Finally, there are many paging service providers and paging services have become a commodity—meaning that differentiation is based on pricing.

There are four categories of pagers. *Numeric* pagers allow a page to be sent with a number that should be called back. These pagers are the most primitive of all devices and are very limited. They are not a good option for the notifications required to manage SLAs. The next level is the *alphanumeric* pager, as shown in Figure 14.2. Alphanumeric pagers allow a notification to include information that can be read by the person receiving the notification. Alphanumeric pagers are the minimal requirement for alerting people in an SLA assurance scenario.

The third and fourth pager types are more advanced and make use of the pager as a *mobile application terminal* (which we will discuss at length later in this chapter). The third category of paging services allows a message to be sent to the pager along with a menu of possible responses. When the recipient gets such a message, he or she reviews the content and then selects one of the options as a reply. For example, in an emergency situation, after the system registers the emergency, it dispatches a page to a responsible party to handle the emergency based on an SLA definition. The responsible party may either accept or reject the assignment—by selecting from among a fixed set of options. If the responsible party chooses to reject the assignment, the service assurance or workforce management system will go on to select an alternative to ensure that the service assignment is not missed.

The fourth paging category is a *true mobile terminal*. The most recognized of these advanced pagers is the Research In Motion (RIM) pager, shown in Figure 14.3. The RIM devices are true mobile terminals that can operate as a pager (if the user subscribes to a paging service), an email client, a Web browser, and a device upon which applications can run. These mobile terminal pagers normally come with a small but workable full keyboard and are extremely useful for mobile computing as well as notification services.

Most of us know how to page someone by using the phone. A phone call is the manual process that makes use of the infrastructure put in place by the paging service provider. What we need to discuss in the context of notification as a core capability required by the integrated SLA architecture is the infrastructure that needs to be put in place when implementing an automated paging system in the context of the OSS. After all—the goal of this infrastructure is to allow programmatic notification—that is, automation of the processes by which certain events recognized by systems within the OSS cause a notification to be sent to a responsible party.

Figure 14.2 An alphanumeric pager.

There are a number of technologies that support automated notification, including Telocator Alphanumeric Protocol (TAP), Simple Mail Transfer Protocol (SMTP), Simple Network Paging Protocol (SNPP), and Wireless Communications Transfer Protocol (WCTP)—listed in historical order.

Telocator Alphanumeric Protocol (TAP) is the dominant technology, having been in place for many years. It is also the most primitive one from a technological perspective. This protocol is used for sending alphanumeric pages using a modem dial-up connection. It allows only one-way notification and is supported by all pager carriers. Simple Mail Transfer Protocol (SMTP) is simply the use of an SMTP transport to deliver a message to the carrier—an example of the ubiquitous nature of SMPT. Simple Mail Transfer Protocol allows only one-way notification within the standard structures and is supported by most large carriers. Simple Network Paging Protocol (SNPP) uses a telnet protocol to deliver messages. It supports two-way notifications by allowing messages to include a set of optional responses, and it provides a way to query the subscriber response. This protocol is supported by most large carriers—but not all. Finally, Wireless Communications Transfer Protocol is a new two-way protocol that utilizes eXtensible Markup Language (XML) over HTTP (and is therefore our favorite). Wireless Communications Transfer Protocol (WCTP) has many goodies (including obviously two-way notifications). It is supported by a handful of carriers.

Figure 14.3 A Research In Motion pager.

Telocator Alphanumeric Protocol and Simple Mail Transfer Protocol

The Telocator Alphanumeric Protocol (TAP) is the dominant (or the incumbent) paging infrastructure. It was originally created to reduce the holding times on input lines to alphanumeric systems, and it allows paging information to be *dumped* to a central paging terminal using a dial-up modem. The central terminal is then responsible for delivering the message to its ultimate destination. Telocator Alphanumeric Protocol is an inelegant, low-level protocol. It is an American Standard Code for Information Interchange (ASCII) protocol with all the attributes we hate to remember (such as X ON, X OFF, start bits, even parity, and so on). A sample TAP session is shown in Figure 14.4. Luckily, TAP has been around long enough that higher-level libraries are available. As an example, jTap is a GNU Java package that encapsulates TAP in an RMI server to be used by Java applications (http://jtap.prominic.org). (GNU is a recursive acronym for ``GNU's Not Unix"; it is pronounced "guh-NEW".) Table 14.1 shows current TAP support in the United States, and Table 14.2 shows support for SMTP-based page message sends (that are eventually translated into TAP calls).

Table 14.1 Telocator Alphanumeric Protocol Providers

TELOCATOR ALPHANUMERIC PROTOCOL MESSAGING SERVICE	MODEM ACCESS NUMBER	RECEIVER ID
Arch (UVA 2400)	(800) 946-4644	10-digit pager -number
Arch (UVA 36000)	(800) 250-6325	10-digit pager number
AT&T PCS	(800) 841-8837	10-digit phone number
Nextel	(800) 201-2501	10-digit -phone -number
Satellink	(888) 237-5293	10-digit pager number
Skytel Pagers	(800) 679-2778	10-digit pager number
Sprint PCS	(888) 656-1727	10-digit phone number
Verizon PCS	(866) 823-0501	10-digit phone number

Table 14.2 Simple Mail Transfer Protocol Providers

SIMPLE MAIL TRANSFER PROTOCOL MESSAGING SERVICE	RECEIVER EMAIL
ALLTEL PCS	10-digit phone number @ message.alltel.com
Airtouch Pagers	10-digit pager number @ myairmail.com
Arch Pagers	PIN@archwireless.net (Only Nationwide and Universal Access subscribers)
AT&T PCS	10-digit phone number @ mobile.att.net
AT&T Pocketnet PCS	10-digit phone number @ dpcs.mobile.att.net
Carolina Mobile Communications	10-digit pager number @ cmcpaging.com
Digi-Page / Page Kansas	10-digit pager number @ page.hit.net

(continues)

Table 14.2 Simple Mail Transfer Protocol Providers *(Continued)*

SIMPLE MAIL TRANSFER PROTOCOL MESSAGING SERVICE	RECEIVER EMAIL
GrayLink/Porta-Phone	10-digit pager number @ epage.porta-phone.com
Infopage Systems	PIN @ page.infopagesystems.com
Metrocall	10-digit -pager number @ page.metrocall.com
Nextel	10-digit phone number @ messaging.nextel.com
PageMart Canada	10-digit pager number @ pmcl.net
PageMart/Weblink	PIN -@pagemart.net
PageMart/Weblink 2way	10-digit -pager number @ airmessage.net
PageNet Pagers	ModemNumber.PIN@pagenet.net
ProPage	7-digit pager number @ page.propage.net
Satellink	10-digit -pager number.pageme @ satellink.net
Skytel Pagers	7-digit PIN @ skytel.com
Sprint PCS	10-digit -phone number @ messaging.sprintpcs.com
Teletouch	10-digit pager number @ pageme.teletouch.com
Verizon Pagers	10-digit pager number @ myairmail.com
Verizon PCS	10-digit phone number @ myvzw.com
VoiceStream Wireless	10-digit -phone number @ voicestream.net

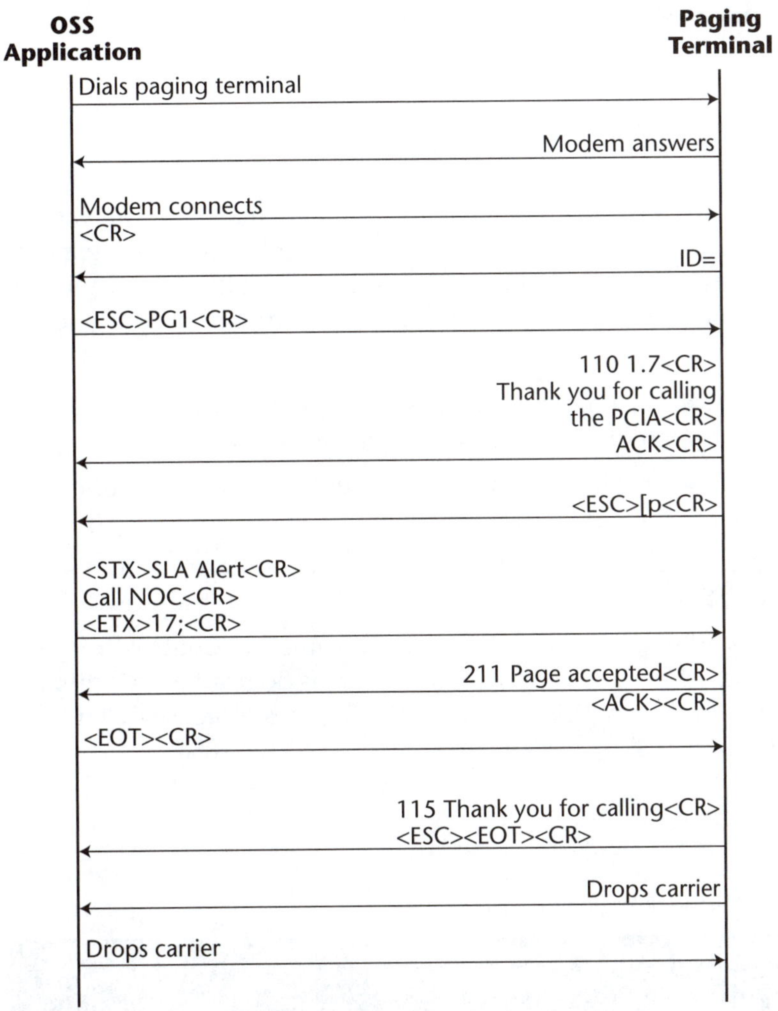

Figure 14.4 Sample Telocator Alphanumeric Protocol session.

Simple Network Paging Protocol

The Simple Network Paging Protocol (SNPP) defines a simple way for delivering wireless messages, both one-way and two-way, to appropriate receiving devices. Simple Network Paging Protocol is often used as a gateway to TAP servers, since it provides a much more elegant interfacing technique. In other cases SNPP stands on its own and delivers functionality that TAP gateways do not (such as two-way paging). Simple Network Paging Protocol uses telnet as its transport. An example of an SNPP session is shown in Figure 14.5, and current U.S. support is shown in Table 14.3. The main features of SNPP include the following:

- The ability to send, along with the message text, multiple response options from which the end user can select a response.
- At the end of the *send* transaction, SNPP issues a message identifier to be used when asking for status.
- Later the carrier can be polled for the server response using the message identifier.
- Simple Network Paging Protocol uses a Transmission Control Protocol/Internet Protocol (TCP/IP) connection—there is no need for a dial-up modem and thus the notification system integrates more easily into the OSS application.

Table 14.3 Simple Network Paging Protocol Providers

SIMPLE NETWORK PAGING PROTOCOL MESSAGING SERVICE	SIMPLE NETWORK PAGING PROTOCOL SERVER ADDRESS : PORT	RECEIVER ID
Advanced Paging	205.247.109.35 : 444	10-digit pager number
Airtouch Paging	snpp.airtouch.com : 444	10-digit pager number
Baystar	209.44.230.3 : 444	10-digit pager number
Digi-Page/Page Kansas	page.pageks.com : 444	10-digit pager number
GrayLink/Porta-Phone	epage.porta-phone.com : 444	10-digit pager number

Table 14.3 *(Continued)*

SIMPLE NETWORK PAGING PROTOCOL MESSAGING SERVICE	SIMPLE NETWORK PAGING PROTOCOL SERVER ADDRESS : PORT	RECEIVER ID
Infopage Systems	snpp.infopagesystems.com : 444	10-digit pager number
Metrocall	snpp.metrocall.com : 444	10-digit pager number
Nextel	pecos.nextel.com : 444	10-digit phone number
PageMart Canada	pmcl.net : 444	10-digit pager number
PageMart/Weblink	pagemart.net : 444	10-digit pager number
PageMart/Weblink 2way	airmessage.net : 444	10-digit pager number
ProPage	page.propage.net : 444	7-digit pager number
Satellink	snpp.satellink.net : 444	10-digit pager number
Skytel	snpp.skytel.com : 7777	10-digit pager number
Verizon Wireless	snpp.airtouch.com : 444	10-digit pager number

Wireless Communications Transfer Protocol

Finally, the Wireless Communications Transfer Protocol (WCTP) is the a standard that will dominate the other protocols in the long run (support in 2001 was limited, as shown in Table 14.4). Wireless Communications Transfer Protocol is a generic message protocol and is used not only by paging systems but also by other wireless technologies such as Personal Communications System (PCS), cellular, and Global System for Mobile Communication (GSM). Wireless Communications Transfer Protocol is a transfer protocol that makes use of an XML payload over an HTTP transport. It therefore fits well with other components in the integrated SLA architecture. We believe that all providers should implement WCTP as soon as possible.

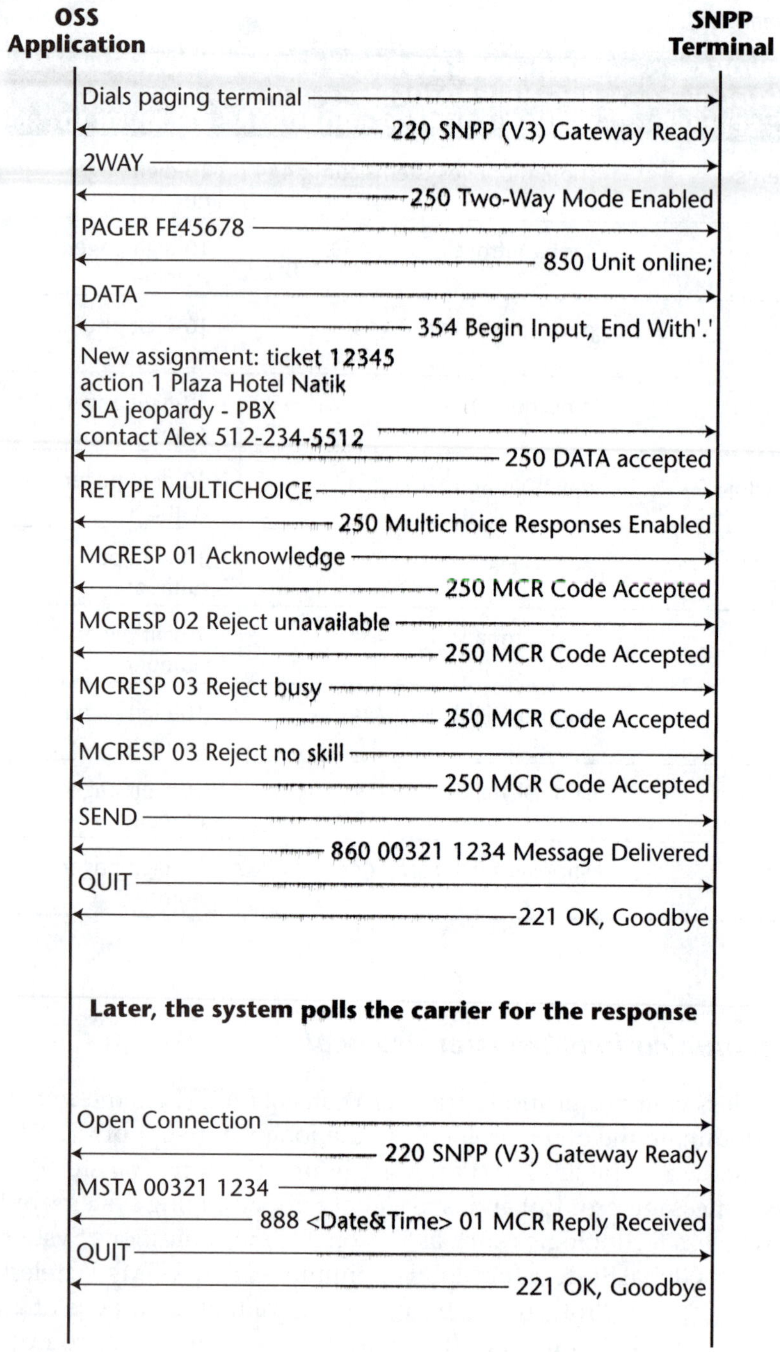
OSS Application
SNPP Terminal
Dials paging terminal
220 SNPP (V3) Gateway Ready
2WAY
250 Two-Way Mode Enabled
PAGER FE45678
850 Unit online;
DATA
354 Begin Input, End With'.'
New assignment: ticket 12345
action 1 Plaza Hotel Natik
SLA jeopardy - PBX
contact Alex 512-234-5512
250 DATA accepted
RETYPE MULTICHOICE
250 Multichoice Responses Enabled
MCRESP 01 Acknowledge
250 MCR Code Accepted
MCRESP 02 Reject unavailable
250 MCR Code Accepted
MCRESP 03 Reject busy
250 MCR Code Accepted
MCRESP 03 Reject no skill
250 MCR Code Accepted
SEND
860 00321 1234 Message Delivered
QUIT
221 OK, Goodbye
Later, the system polls the carrier for the response
Open Connection
220 SNPP (V3) Gateway Ready
MSTA 00321 1234
888 <Date&Time> 01 MCR Reply Received
QUIT
221 OK, Goodbye

Figure 14.5 A Sample Simple Network Paging Protocol session.

Table 14.4 Wireless Communications Transfer Protocol Providers in 2001

WIRELESS COMMUNICATIONS TRANSFER PROTOCOL MESSAGING SERVICE	WIRELESS COMMUNICATIONS TRANSFER PROTOCOL SERVER ADDRESS : PORT	RECEIVER ID
Arch Wireless	wctp.arch.com/wctp : 80	PIN or 10-digit pager number
Metrocall	wctp.my2way.com : 80	PIN or 10-digit pager number
Skytel	wctp.skytel.com/wctp : 80	7-digit -PIN
Weblink	wctp.airmessage.net : 80	PIN or 10-digit - pager number

Short Message Service

Another common notification method involves the use of mobile phones to deliver short text messages. Short Message Service (SMS) is most dominant in GSM and PCS networks where the short message service is very widely used. The short message service is a point-to-point narrow bandwidth transport mechanism that is available through most cellular, PCS, and GSM carriers. Different networks have similar services; for example, TETRA supports a service called SDS, a point-to-point short data service.

The reason SMS is so attractive is that most professionals have a mobile phone for use during work. Regardless of which wireless technology the phone uses (for example, iDEN, GSM, PCS, or CDMA), it is likely to support SMS. Therefore the mobile phone can function as both a voice terminal as well as a pager-data terminal of sorts. Although SMS is for the most part a one-way technology, some equivalent messaging service offerings (such as SDS in TETRA) have a two-way communication feature. The two-way communications allow the receiver of a message to select from among a set of options delivered with the message as a means of responding to the message. For example, if a message defining the assignment of a service order is sent to a technician, the message can include one option for the technician to accept the assignment and one option for the technician to reject the assignment. The technician can select one of the two options and send a reply with a single click.

Workforce Management

Having described various notification methods, it is time for us to move on to the application of these methods. While notification capabilities are important in many SLA management processes the most common use of notification is within the area of *workforce management*.

Workforce management is an application within the OSS that is responsible for making sure that the service provider's workforce is working efficiently in the field. This function manages the assignment of tasks to resources using an optimization engine and manages the flow of information to the field. It manages the life cycles of work orders from their initiation, through the dispatch process, and all the way through to closure.

Correctly managing the workforce is critical to adhering to SLAs. While many terms and conditions defined by the SLAs can be satisfied using self-correcting technologies, built-in redundancy, and other automated facilities, many other terms and conditions require human intervention. When human intervention is required, providers have the choice of managing their workforce manually or using an automated system. Manual management can go only so far; once the number of people in the workforce grows beyond a certain point, a workforce management system must be put in place; it has been our experience that the cutoff occurs in a workforce of around 50 to 100 technicians.

Our focus in discussing workforce management at this point is twofold. First, we need to explain the interactions between SLAs and the workforce management system. Then we need to describe what a real-time workforce management system requires in terms of mobile computing and notification.

Meeting Service Level Agreements through Efficient Use of the Workforce

A workforce management system manages the work order process in the field. It receives orders from trouble ticket systems, call center systems, network build-out schedules, planned maintenance, and so on. It then manages the flow of the work order including the assignment of resources (human and tools), the parts required for the work, scheduling, and appointment booking. Up-to-date data within the system is a fundamental requirement for the system to perform optimally. A workforce management system is measured in terms of whether it is lowering the costs of doing the work, whether it can drive higher throughput of work using the existing workforce (that is, can grow the subscriber base and services provided without growing the cost of labor), and whether it can increase customer satisfaction. Lowering costs may involve scheduling work for those in the field through the use of optimization algorithms that reduce driving time. Figure 14.6 plots two possible allocations of work to technicians. Notice the huge difference in driving distance between the two assignment schemes, and thus a huge difference in productivity. But all the functions of the workforce system have one primary goal—meeting SLAs.

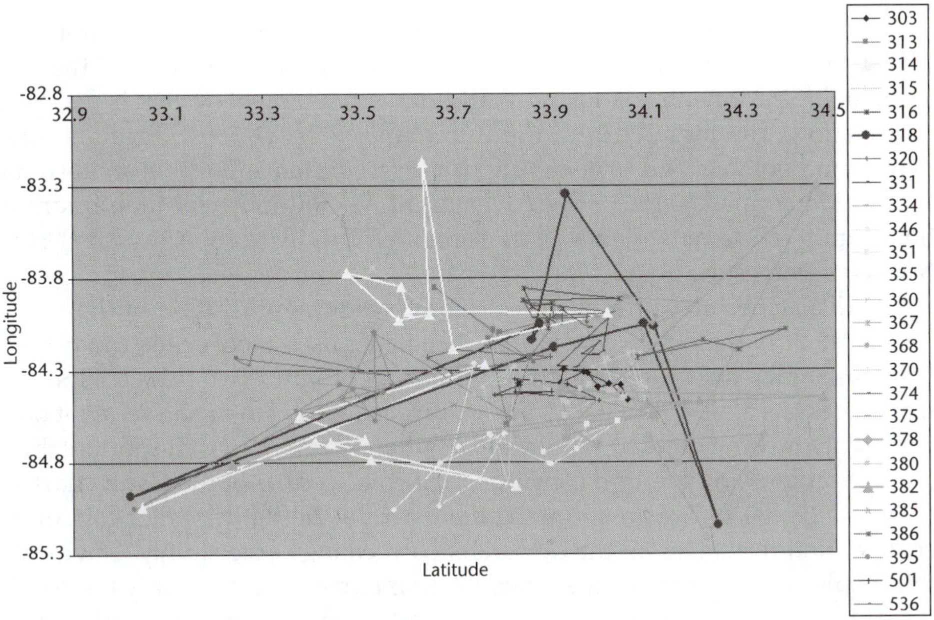

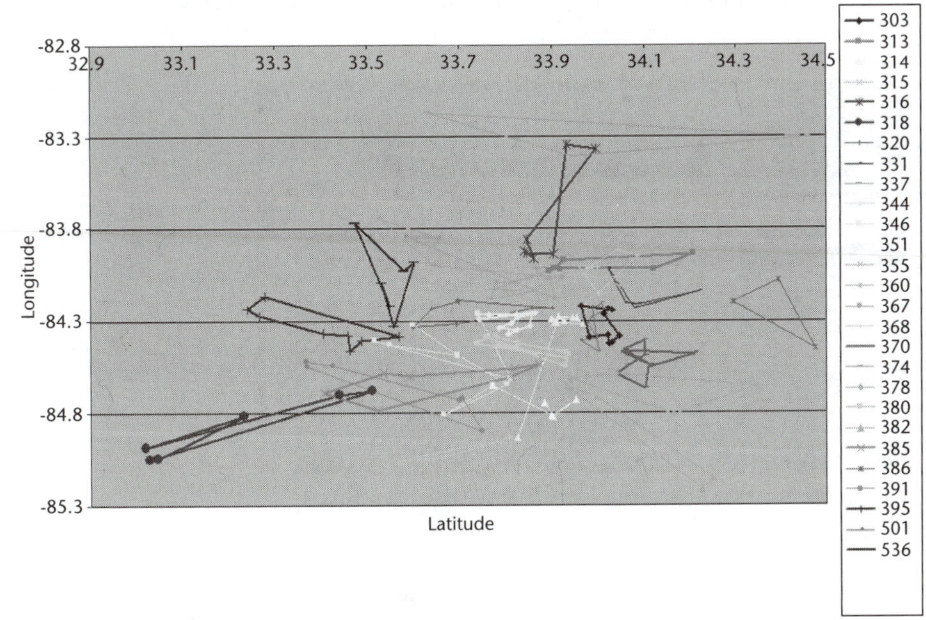

Figure 14.6 Driving routes based on two possible assignments.

For a workforce management system to function correctly it must be based on receiving full entitlement information from the SLA terms. The scheduling of resources must be done based on the financial impacts—the best assignment and work flow is one that will maximize revenue, lower costs, and reduce penalties. The workforce management system must be responsible for getting the SLA terms and applying them to scheduling phases, setting up appointments, organizing work flow, and the dispatcher workstation. One of the fundamental requirements for a good workforce management system is real-time information. The more current the information, the better the results—this may sound obvious and is generally true in all systems, but it is an absolute for workforce management to deliver on SLAs. Without real-time information from the field, emergency work cannot be handled properly, and *random behavior* becomes the norm.

The dispatcher plays a key role in monitoring the utilization of the workforce in an SLA assurance context. The dispatcher uses a tool called the *dispatch board,* as shown in Figure 14.7, to continuously monitor two things. First, the dispatcher has a view of what the workforce is doing. He or she sees not only what work is being done by whom and at what time, but, most important, how work is progressing through consulting the color coding of the Gantt chart, as shown in Figure 14.7. As real-time updates arrive, the status of the work order changes and the colors on the dispatch board change accordingly. Obviously, this display is only useful if the information is current—that is, only if the field workforce can continuously update the system in real time as work is progressing. The other view is the emergency task list that must be handled through a manual process or using automated procedures.

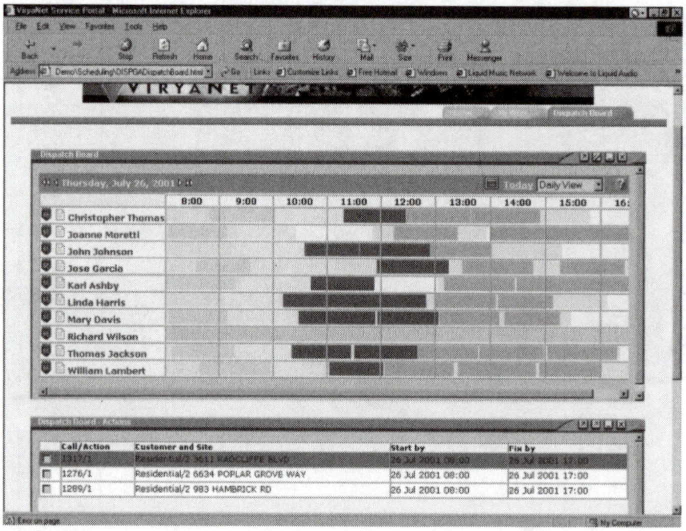

Figure 14.7 A Gantt chart on a dispatch board.

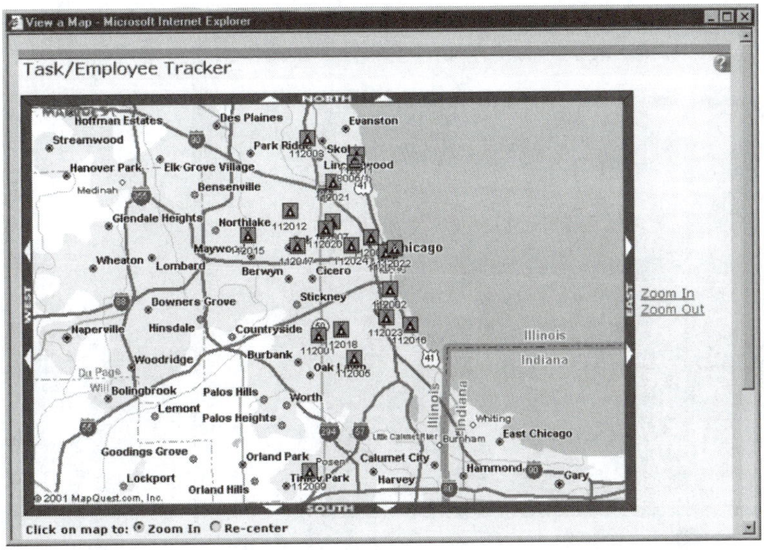

Figure 14.8 Locating the workforce.

If the system has the ability to use mobile devices for bidirectional real time updates (that is, both notifications to the field workforce as well as updates from the field workforce), then the dispatcher can easily have a full view of where the workforce is geographically at any given time (Figure 14.8), as well as routes being taken by the technicians (Figure 14.9). Depending on the investment in hardware, this data can be derived from either reports from the field (for example, a report sent upon arrival at a location) or the use of a GPS device attached to the mobile terminal.

Mobile Computing

Mobile computing is the key to fine control of the workforce, and using that control to adhere to SLAs. By arming the field workforce with mobile terminals on which workers can receive notifications and work orders, and on which they close out their work orders, we can assure that updates appear in real time. Real-time and continuous access is the key to keeping the entire workforce synchronized with the company's financial goals. This synchronization relies on scheduling and work-flow management, which are based on the entitlements information defined by the SLAs. There are many mobile terminals that may be used for a field workforce. Devices span the entire range from a simple alphanumeric pager through Wireless Application Protocol (WAP) phones and Personal Digital Assistant (PDA)-type devices, all the way to laptops. Terminals may have different-sized screens, different data entry facilities, and

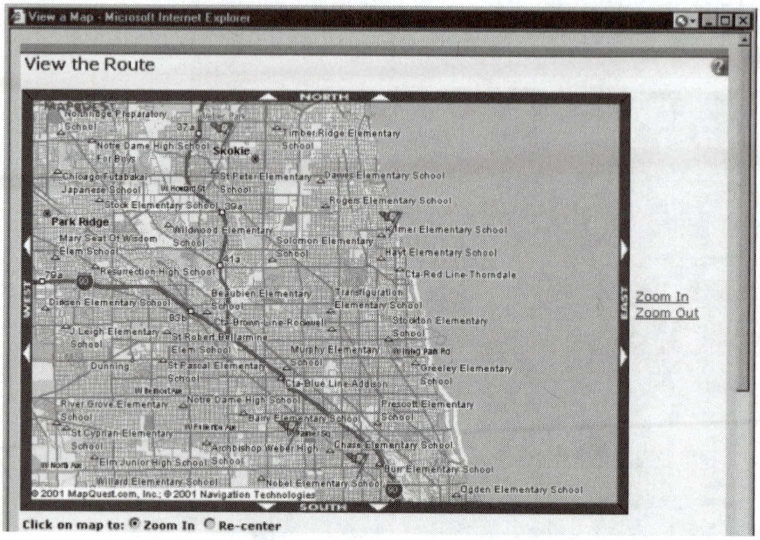

Figure 14.9 Drill-down to single resource.

different technical capabilities. But the terminals still share the same purpose: They serve to allow efficient, real-time, and bidirectional communication between management and the field workforce. Using these terminals, field workers can accept work orders, close orders, and modify their calendars. They can even order parts directly to their truck or as drop shipments to the site where the work will take place. These terminals can also be used for running additional support applications such as document viewing, Geographic Information System (GIS), diagnostics, and equipment testing.

Wireless Infrastructure for Mobile Computing

The most complex part of running an efficient distributed operation is the wireless infrastructure. The complexity is a direct result of the lack of standards (or the plethora of options) within the wireless world and especially in the United States. The United States has every conceivable wireless technology. Unfortunately, no one technology provides a good enough solution in terms of coverage. Since coverage is partial, large providers have no choice but to work with multiple wireless providers. The result is a wireless infrastructure that is difficult to procure and difficult to manage. In addition, some areas have no coverage at all, meaning that the providers need to either resort to satellite communications, forgo real-time communications, or build their own radio networks (a common solution in the past).

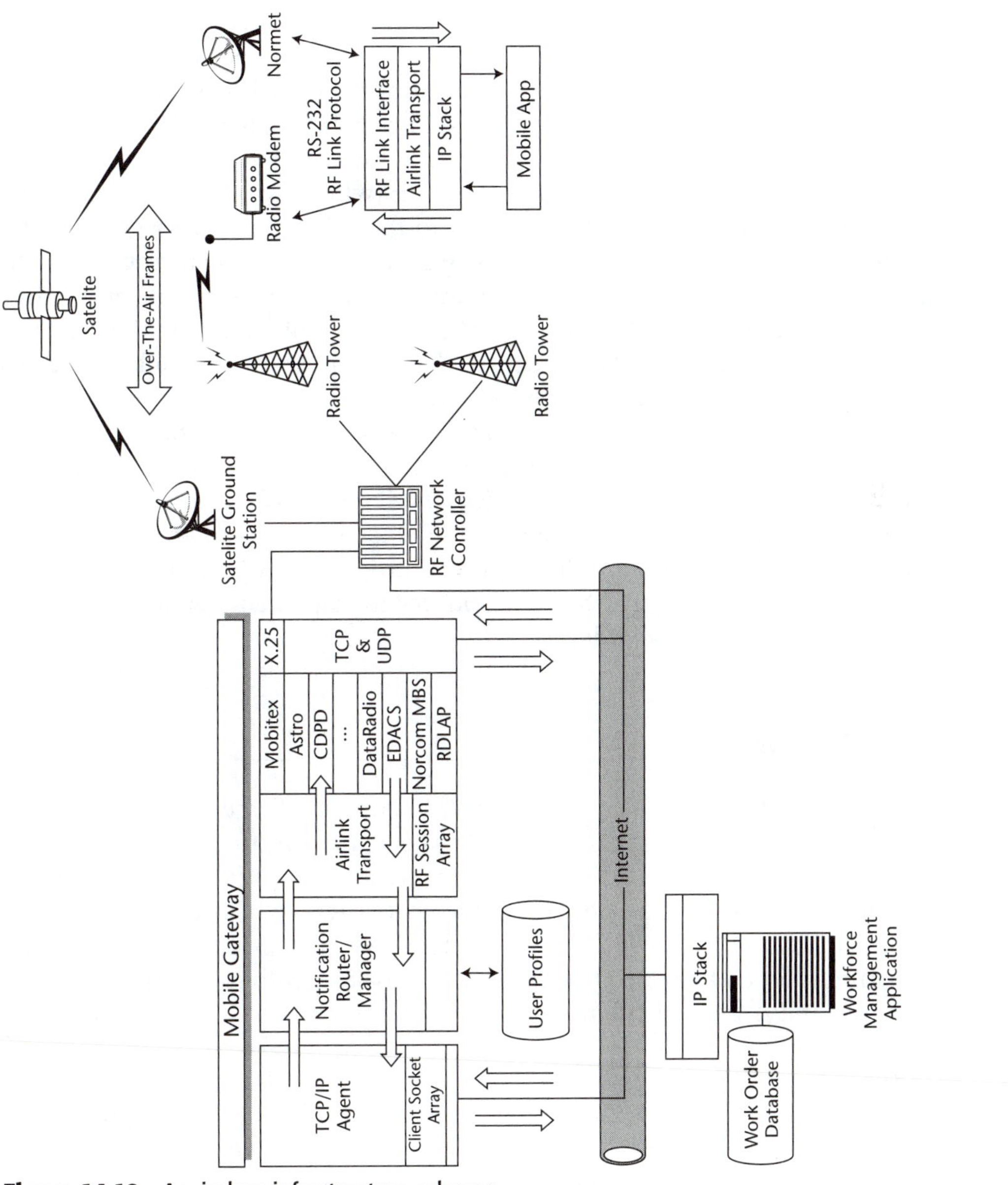

Figure 14.10 A wireless infrastructure scheme.

The result of the mixed infrastructure is complex and multiple gateways to different carriers as shown in Figure 14.10. The mobile gateway in this scheme is responsible for delivering information on the various air link transports using carrier gateways. The workforce management application communicates with the mobile gateway over IP, as does the mobile application on the mobile computing device. Runtime libraries (Data Link Libraries [DLLs]) installed on the mobile device are responsible for sending application data using the selected air link protocol. These runtime libraries usually convert IP packets to radio frequency (RF) packets. The mobile gateway converts these RF packets back to IP packets to be delivered to the application servers.

When a new order is allocated to a worker (who may be the only one close enough to respond in time for the SLA to be satisfied), a message with the work order information is sent from the workforce management application to the mobile gateway. The mobile gateway looks at the user profile and determines which transport this message should transmit over. The data is then packaged in a native packet structure depending on the air link transport, which is then communicated with the carrier's gateway.

When the message arrives at the mobile device (the assumption here is that coverage, indeed, is good), it is delivered to the work order application. The technician accepts the work and an acknowledgment (ACK) message is repackaged and sent over the RF network. The ACK is then received and delivered to the mobile gateway through the carrier's infrastructure. From the carrier, the message is finally delivered to the workforce management application, which updates the status of the order.

Summary

Full automation can be achieved only by looking at all users involved in service delivery. The focus in this chapter has been the workforce community. The workforce is the most problematic in service-level management owing to the distributed work environment of service providers, which has traditionally been difficult to support from an IT perspective. Fortunately, technology has caught up with the need, and it is now possible, both from a usability perspective and from a cost perspective, to close the loop in all service delivery processes.

With this chapter we conclude Part 2 of the book—the outline of the infrastructure components and the methods for achieving a highly integrated and automated OSS for managing SLA-centric service delivery. In the last two chapters of the book we will broaden the model by discussing other business models an integrated service-level architecture can support, and other industry verticals in which it can be applied.

CHAPTER 15

Service Marketplaces and Bandwidth Exchanges

Although only time will tell how the Integrated Service Level Agreement framework will fit into the future of telecommunications, the industry undoubtedly has changed in ways that were unimaginable back in 1984. Starting with the divestiture of AT&T and the development of the software-defined network (SDN) at about the same time, the number of service providers has grown steadily.

The Telecommunications Act of 1996 created the glut of CLECs, DLECs, ITCs, and other emerging service providers that eventually retrenched in 2000. The act also created an entirely new entity whose value has been questioned since day one and whose future is even less certain in the post-Enron economy—the bandwidth exchange. Certain forms of network capacity, that is, bandwidth, can and have been traded on the open market through exchanges. Ideally, a bandwidth exchange functions as an independent third-party facilitator, allowing players to buy, sell, swap, and trade excess bandwidth capacity, many times anonymously. We have depicted the many relationships in a bandwidth exchange in Figure 15.1.

The bandwidth exchange market is still in its infancy. The concept, like most Internet-based commodity exchanges, took off during the late-1990s heyday of the new economy. Enron, at the time one of the largest exchange owners, conducted the first over-the-counter (OTC) trade, between New York and Los Angeles in December 1999.

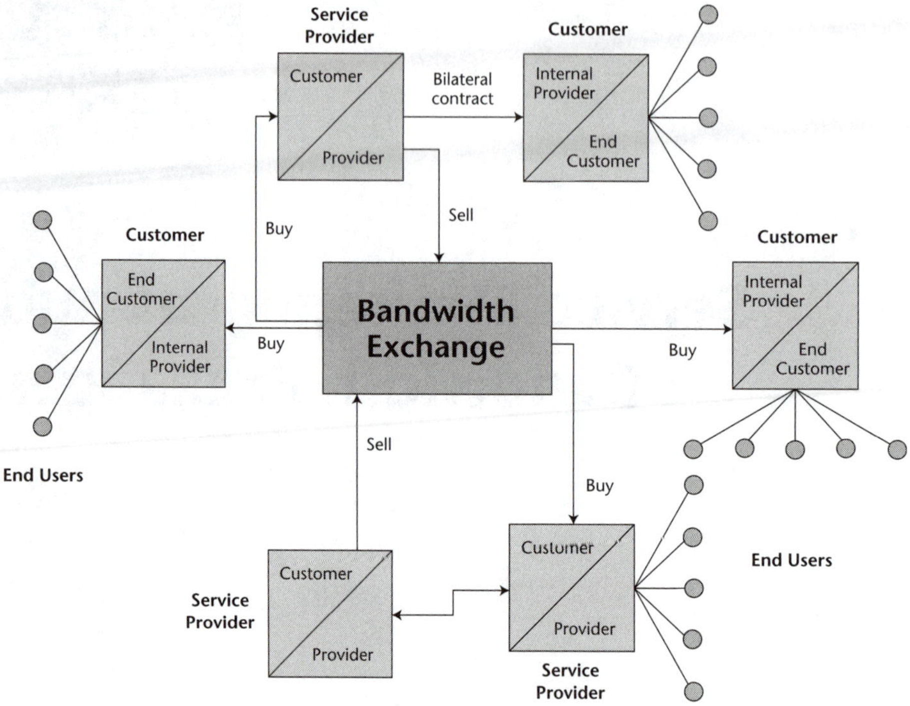

Figure 15.1 The relationships in a bandwidth exchange.

Can, and, more important, *should*, network capacity be traded in one or more large public exchanges? Apparently some people think so. Since 1997 a number of venture capitalists and some very large service providers have invested an immense amount of money in more than a dozen active exchanges, most of which trade exclusively in various forms of bandwidth.

Many exchanges have a long way to go; some are little more than electronic bulletin boards where buyers and sellers (mainly sellers) can congregate. These sites are expected to grow more sophisticated as time passes. Exchange sites must grow if there is to be any hope that these exchanges will achieve anywhere near expectations. Even after the communications downturn, studies and projections forecast steady growth in the trading of excess capacity. As recently as late 2001, new media and telecommunications consultant analysts projected that the bandwidth exchange market could see $18 billion traded by 2006.

But will the market *really* expand? In this chapter we examine what it will take for bandwidth exchanges to realize their potential. Then we will discuss whether the Integrated Service Level Agreement (ISLA) framework is the right platform to support bandwidth exchange efforts. Finally, we will attempt to answer the question, *where do we go from here*?

The Liquidity Issue

Thus far bandwidth trading has grown at a steady rate, but not quite as quickly as expected. Yet the growth rate may change. A 2001 study conducted by Arthur Andersen on the European bandwidth market found that over half of respondents had already participated in bandwidth trades and fully 85 percent expected to trade online within the next 18 months, as shown in Figure 15.2.

The most important component in creating a successful exchange of any type is liquidity, that is, buyers and sellers who are actually buying and selling. Creating the kind of vibrant and robust trading market that some people envision means that a lot of buyers have to buy.

The larger exchanges target the largest long-haul carriers as sellers and concentrate on attracting large private network owners, Internet Service Providers (ISPs), Application Service Providers (ASPs), global corporations, and the aforementioned content providers as buyers. The bursting of the dot-com and then the telecom bubbles obviously removed a lot of potential buyers from the marketplace. Many of the buyers who are left seem to have a wait-and-see attitude. Some of them probably do the same thing we do at home: use the online information to compare prices that are then taken into face-to-face negotiations as a point of leverage.

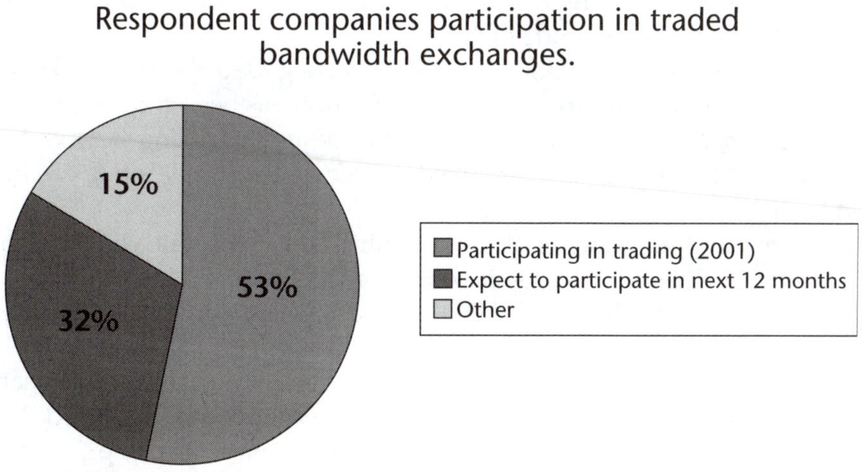

Source: Bandwidth Uncovered, Anderson, Technology, Media & Communications, 2001.

Figure 15.2 Expected participation in bandwidth trading.

Will there be enough buyers, sellers, and trades to bring liquidity to the bandwidth exchange marketplace? That will depend on whether the exchange market is able to provide sufficient incentive and motivation for the industry at large to participate. On the surface, the rationale for a bandwidth exchange appears to be quite convincing.

Apparently, the same market forces that created coöpetition could make bandwidth trading a rousing success. Participating service providers hope to increase network utilization and customer penetration, minimize risk, and increase return on the huge investments they've made in new network infrastructure over the last decade. Carriers have abundant excess capacity, with estimates ranging anywhere from 30 to 80 percent of their total network capacity, depending on the company.

On the other end, buyers can shop online for the most competitive pricing for their bandwidth needs. Once they've found the best deal, they can execute a contract and expect to receive quick and convenient service delivery. But is bandwidth trading as simple as that? As with everything else, it depends on whom you ask.

Both sides of the issue present compelling arguments. The proponents of bandwidth trading will tell you that the many buyers-many sellers approach to commodity trading will create market efficiencies that will result in faster transactions, lower prices to the consumer, and better utilization of resources by the service provider.

Advocates cite the inefficiency of the various forms of bilateral contracting, such as long-term leases, Indefeasible Rights-to-Use arrangements (IRUs), and other types of bulk bandwidth contracts. Bilateral contracting can be expensive and inefficient because a company needs to develop business relationships with each party the company trades with.

Contracts can take weeks or months to produce, negotiations add weeks or months into the equation, and by the time negotiation has been completed the price will have changed, putting both parties back at square one. This cumbersome process cannot adapt itself to the dynamic pricing models that can be expected in the future.

On the other hand, opponents of bandwidth trading will tell you that an exchange cannot deliver on its promises because it adds no value to the customer beyond what already exists. Carriers and resellers have been trading bandwidth for several years.

Large customers have become very good at negotiating large, multiyear contracts for bulk bandwidth or voice minutes, so why would they need the bandwidth exchange, which is, in reality, another middleman? Service providers traditionally take the reseller route when they are trying to increase market penetration and network utilization.

Sure, bandwidth trading is interesting to watch, but is anybody really buying anything? The answer appears to be: They're starting to. The most popular forms of bandwidth trading are the spot markets in voice minutes and transporting Internet traffic. Now that we know what companies are buying, we can learn a lot by examining why customers are starting to buy.

Success Factors

First we must understand why exchanges have begun trading voice minutes and IP traffic with some degree of success. We'll begin by identifying five major factors that will, in all likelihood, determine the viability of an exchange environment for any product. The five factors we will examine are as follows:

- Product
- Price
- Implementation
- Quality
- Settlement

Product

First, the product must truly be a commodity. To be a commodity the product must be available from many sources, and the quality of the product must be fairly equal across the board. This is certainly true in the case of voice minutes and IP traffic.

Price

Almost all bandwidth exchanges are set up so that buyers compete on price. Trades are most often anonymous, because many times service providers wish to avoid cannibalizing their regular network usage. The ability to choose from a variety of cost options is obviously a large advantage of exchanges, assuming that every other need has been satisfied. The decision on which route to use is made on a per call or per instance basis by the routing tables, to ensure that the customer gets the best deal on every call.

Implementation

Implementation refers to the ability of the buyer to quickly and easily realize the value of the product. In the telecommunication markets, implementation refers to the ubiquity and speed of connection. In the case of both voice minutes and IP traffic, the connections can be brought up and switched in real time by the exchange's switches.

Quality

The importance of Quality of Service (QoS) is elusive to quantify because perceived quality is most important to the customer, on both the requirement and the delivery sides of the equation. Interestingly, from a quality perspective, both voice minutes and IP traffic have relatively low perceived quality requirements. Voice quality is simply managed by hanging up and redialing (that is, bad connections are a way of life; just start over), and the Internet is considered too big to be controllable (there's no telling where the call went; it just got lost in cyberspace).

Settlement

Settlement refers to the financial reconciliation of activities conducted on the exchange. The complexity and accompanying difficulties of completing transactions is directly proportional to the technical difficulties in delivering the actual (as opposed to the perceived) QoS contracted for the product. If quality is not much of an issue, as it appears in this case, then billing and settlement are fairly straightforward.

Consolidating the Factors

To summarize, trading voice minutes and IP traffic through bandwidth exchanges has been reasonably successful because the products are commodities that are transparent to customers, the products can be implemented almost instantly, the exchange dynamically finds the lowest-cost supplier, QoS is not really an issue, so therefore the settlement is straightforward and easy to understand.

If we assume that these same factors will drive success or failure in other forms of bandwidth trading, we can start drilling down into the feasibility and practicality of trading other forms of bandwidth in an exchange environment. To examine other forms of bandwidth we will position the factors within a need hierarchy as shown in Figure 15.3.

The Vision

In the ideal world, as envisioned by the exchanges, a customer would be able to log on to an Internet bandwidth exchange and order up circuits for, say, streaming video on demand, Voice over Internet Protocol (VoIP), or interactive videoconferencing, in addition to bundling a platinum SLA provisioning package with their purchase. Very shortly thereafter the customer would be up and running well within the SLA timeframes, with no undue fuss, with complete transparency as to who the provider is, and at a very reasonable cost.

Figure 15.3 The bandwidth exchange hierarchy of needs.

Unfortunately, we don't yet live in an instant gratification world. Today we live in a far different world. We've briefly touched on some of the factors behind some of the early successes with trading voice minutes and Internet traffic in an exchange environment, but in some ways these may be poor examples. Voice minutes and Internet traffic are the low-hanging fruit, that is, the easy stuff. From here on, trading gets immensely harder.

Voice minutes and Internet traffic can be called low-hanging fruit because they are relatively mature technology, which makes trading simpler. Voice and Internet are simple to understand as products, are easily implemented, compete primarily on price, and have very low QoS expectations, which means very straightforward settlement. In short, they are truly commodity items that present no real issues from an execution standpoint.

Voice and Internet may also represent the only opportunities for successful trading for a while. We do not believe that voice minutes and Internet traffic are really what smaller carriers, emerging content providers, or large business customers would want to buy from an exchange. This is certainly not where the real money will be in the future.

The real progress will be made only when the exchanges are able to realistically trade circuits. Circuits in this case can be defined as bandwidth delivered between two or more physical locations. The bandwidth could come in various forms, sizes, and even colors (in the case of Dense Wavelength Division Multiplexing [DWDM] fiber optics). For example, a small local carrier may buy an OC-12 from a large national fiber company through an exchange.

Some early adopters have already started to experiment with such exchange models. One of the most vocal proponents and largest market makers to emerge in the late 1990s was Enron. Although Enron later became embroiled in the largest bankruptcy in U.S. history, the company did provide vision and legitimacy to the broadband exchange market during its formative period.

In December 1999, Enron Broadband Service (EBS) made what it called the first standardized bandwidth trade on a circuit from New York to Los Angeles. The company standardized a master agreement that laid out specific terms and conditions for delivery. The agreement stipulated the product, demarcation (demarc) points, and length of the contract. It also outlined QoS levels. This agreement was the very beginning of a disciplined approach to managing the process.

Enron Broadband Service defined the baseline product as a DS-3, OC-3, or OC-3(C) running from New York to Los Angeles. The contract template specified the length of the contracts as 1 month, 6 months, or 1 year. Implementation was addressed by providing pooling points in carrier hotels in each city that functioned as a traditional demarcation point, effectively relieving the company of last-mile responsibilities. Finally, EBS identified a Benchmark Quality of Service (BQoS) standard that it was willing to guarantee in the contract.

This benchmark appeared to address some of the product, implementation, and quality needs of successful exchange trading; price, of course, was the variable component. Although the Enron definitions were definitely a step in the right direction, they still left us a long way from the ideal world, as shown in Figure 15.4.

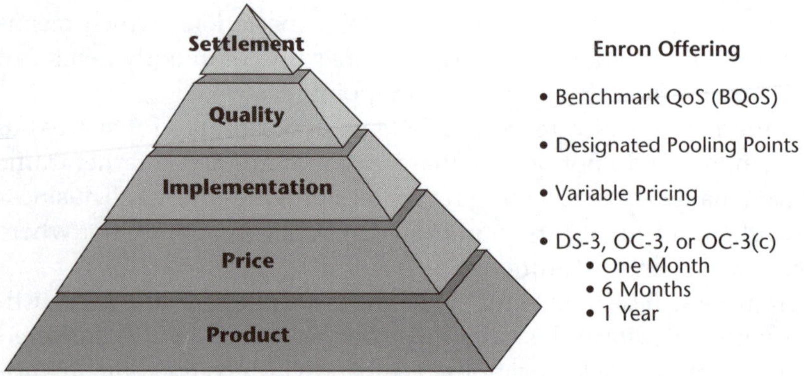

Figure 15.4 The exchange hierarchy and the Enron offering.

NOTE **There is some controversy over the model first seen with the Enron exchange. First of all, Enron was not truly a third-party entity, because it owned a large national fiber optic backbone of its own. Because the company owned a backbone, it was a direct competitor to the other service providers who joined the exchange as sellers. Dealing with the competition was obviously a cause of concern to potential sellers and perhaps added to the lack of liquidity.**

Second, Enron usually participated in trades directly. In other words, the company took the seller or buyer positions itself rather than merely facilitating the trade. The company was able to realize the profit margins of reselling the bandwidth in addition to taking a commission on the transaction itself.

The combination of Enron's backbone ownership and its direct participation in trades cast doubt on whether this was truly a public bandwidth exchange or simply a private exchange open to the public, and it generated many concerns over potential conflicts of interest.

The Need

While the Enron model of a standardized contract for ordering a baseline product offering was definitely progress, it effectively side stepped the real reasons most companies buy bandwidth on bilateral agreements in the first place: to ensure availability of mission-critical communications.

As we discussed in Chapter 3, the main reason today's businesses use SLAs is to assure availability of their bandwidth needs. The Andersen study found that 66 percent of respondents believed that bandwidth issues affected whether or not a company was successful *to a great degree*, while another 26 percent believed that the bandwidth issues *somewhat* affected the success of the company. This left only 8 percent who did not believe the bandwidth issue was relevant to a company's success.

The Andersen study can be interpreted to mean that 92 percent of the respondents felt that their telecommunications capability was at least *somewhat* mission-critical, including the 66 percent who felt that their telecommunications were directly responsible for enabling the success of their companies, as shown in Figure 15.5.

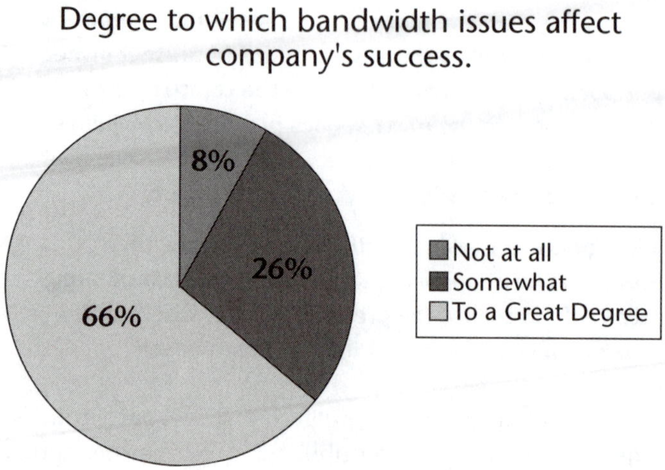

Source: Bandwidth Uncovered, Anderson, Technology, Media & Communications, 2001.

Figure 15.5 How bandwidth availability affects company success.

Mission-critical telecommunications are bought using bilateral agreements because bilateral agreements allow the customer to drive SLA entitlements, the majority of which revolve around availability. Availability is a longer-term service support issue, requiring the presence of a certain amount of trust (or credibility) between contracting parties, unlike anonymous exchange purchasing, which is based on finding the best available price using a quick ordering process and a very short decision cycle.

The lack of trust in the mechanics of anonymous exchange purchasing has kept a large portion of the potential participant base on the sidelines. If trust issues can be resolved, we believe that buyers will be much more inclined to enter the market, thereby creating the needed liquidity.

Today trust is built through a combination of relationship development and a history of successful execution. While the requirements for building trust may change, for the near term these two requirements do not lend themselves well to a system based on anonymity and competing solely on price. Instead, building trust in the mission-critical arena appears to be better served by long-term customer-centric relationships and products that can be differentiated contractually to support QoS levels that can be varied based on the needs of the business.

Product differentiation based on the customer's QoS needs is contrary to our earlier definition of a commodity, in that the quality is not relatively uniform across the board. The anonymity inherent to exchanges will make it particularly difficult for the buyer to perceive enforceability of the SLA entitlement when contracting through a third-party exchange. Bilateral agreements may continue to be the primary tool for buyers to purchase mission-critical telecommunications unless a solution can be found.

On the other hand, we believe that the development of a long and deep business relationship may not be a mandatory component of the trust equation, assuming that enough credibility in the form of historical proof of execution can be established.

Over the middle term the customer can be expected to adapt to the more impersonal type of relationship that is the norm for e-commerce. Simplified transaction is the underlying concept behind the tens of thousands of private exchanges that are being set up in the business-to-business (B2B) space, that is, *You know our name. You know our product. Let's reduce the customer acquisition, care, and retention costs through Internet trading, and pass the savings on to you.*

If the public bandwidth exchange is to present that same value proposition and still preserve anonymity for the seller, it must establish a level of credibility and buyer confidence that the exchange has the capability to deliver the mission-critical bandwidth at acceptable levels of QoS. Even if anonymity is not an issue, the exchange must perform an aggregation function to its customers or risk a perception that no value has been added.

These requirements mean that the exchanges will either have to (1) assume huge amounts of financial liabilities related to SLA penalties, (2) be able to manage the SLA compliance of the many sellers themselves, or (3) manage some combination of the two. Service Level Management is the single issue that will determine whether or not true bandwidth exchanges will ever succeed.

Solutions

Creating a true public bandwidth exchange means that every one of the product's attributes that we discussed as success factors has to become much simpler, all at the same time. Product, price, implementation, quality, and settlement must be bundled in such a way that potential buyers perceive that there exists enough credibility in the exchange to allow them to forgo the long relationship development that is normally a component of the bilateral contract scenario.

In order to accept this needed credibility, buyers will have to resort to the old adage Trust, but verify. Verification will come only when the problems related to quality and settlement are solved. Obviously, the complicated issues surrounding QoS and SLA compliance within the service provider are the same ones that will face exchange providers. Unfortunately, the difficulties associated with these issues are multiplied owing to the large number of service providers trading with exchanges.

Is the ISLA framework, and the way it manages the SLA environment, a possible solution to these problems? Let's further examine the ISLA framework relative to an exchange. Figure 15.6 depicts the exchange success factors we have been discussing in comparison to some of those we have used in developing the ISLA framework. The figure clearly shows a very interesting correlation between the needs of the bandwidth exchange, the roles we identified for SLAs in Chapter 1, and the factors we identified as being critical to SLA success in Chapter 2.

The obvious correlation between the needs of SLAs and those of the exchange further confirms that the major obstacle to both SLA delivery and exchange liquidity is the inability to manage QoS and reconcile the financial implications associated with it. The relationship implies that any solution found for SLAs could also be applied to solve some of the problems associated with creating a true bandwidth exchange that would be capable of trading mission-critical circuits.

To further test the theory that capabilities provided by the ISLA framework may address problems within bandwidth exchanges, we will step through the success factors once again, this time with the ISLA framework assumed to be in place to see what effect the ISLA framework may have on the exchange environment.

Product

In most cases, we expect the exchange to be the final guarantor to the customer. With the ISLA framework in place within the exchange, the product definition would be managed within the product domain. The feasibility of trading a product within the exchange environment would then be less

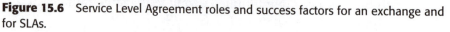

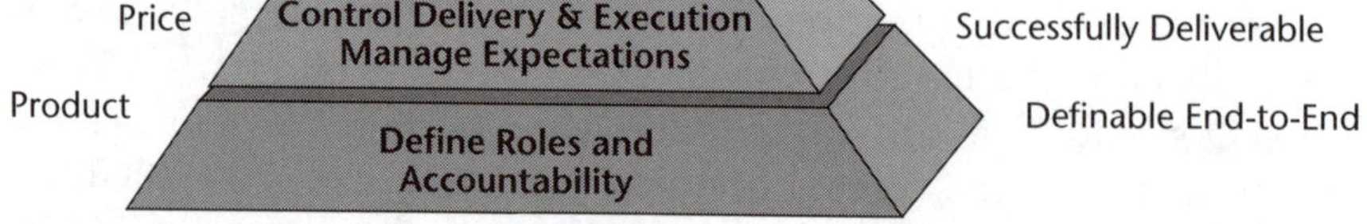

Figure 15.6 Service Level Agreement roles and success factors for an exchange and for SLAs.

dependent on the product (although the attributes we have discussed would still need to be satisfied), and become much more dependent on the exchange being able to aggregate and deliver the product under the right terms, conditions, and prices.

Yet the ability to successfully define the product entitlements, which will drive the product's delivery, is very important. Long term, this challenge will require the kinds of capabilities we've seen with the ISLA framework, that is, the entitlement engine residing in the product domain that can be linked to external product development, or contract management systems that reside within the seller's (service provider's) Operations Support System (OSS).

In the shorter term, we have seen exchange providers offering template product sheets that organize and establish some of the parameters around the product offerings. We believe that these are the first steps that may eventually lead to full integration of the product catalogs.

Technically, full integration can be accomplished through the integration server, most likely using an eXtensible Markup Language (XML) interface. Semantics will be handled within the exchange's product domain in what has been termed a business to exchange (B2X) connection. Exchange-driven aggregation of many products from many vendors is basically the same type of semantic aggregation we outlined in Chapter 6, where we discussed integrating multiple product catalog interpretations within the service provider's OSS environment. But the exchange aggregation would be on a much larger scale.

Price

In an exchange, price variability is an important factor in creating liquidity. After all, if prices are stable and relatively similar across the board, the exchange is relegated to a sales channel with little added value.

Once products are defined within the product domain, prices can be adjusted in near real time through interfaces made directly to the service provider's rating engine or billing system. The integration server can accommodate the billing interfaces.

Real-time adjustments would allow the portal to manage reverse auctions and the like with virtually no human intervention using Key Performance Indicators (KPIs) generated by business intelligence. The capability to manage such relationships at high volumes could be very valuable for both the exchange and its service providers.

For example, the service provider could set a floor price within the rating engine, and it would allow the system to automatically send out that price as a bid. This price might be based on actual delivery costs (plus a predefined margin) as represented by the KPIs used to track operational delivery within the service provider, or some other predefined method. A number of these automatic bids could then be rolled up into an aggregated end-to-end offering.

The concept of dynamic work flow and dynamic work-flow communities could then be used to create the temporary relationships between multiple buyers and multiple sellers based on criteria besides best price, such as geographic footprint, technology compatibility, SLA compliance, and so on.

Dynamic work flow would allow a bid on an end-to-end circuit to be aggregated within the exchange while presenting a number of possible combinations of service providers as options to the buyer. Hence buyers would be able to make buying decisions on an other-than-price basis.

For example, a buyer might wish to specifically avoid using a certain service provider in order to reduce his or her dependency on a single source, to specify diverse routes for redundancy, or he or she might need an IP network versus frame relay for a certain application even though frame might be cheaper. This kind of circuit aggregation and management capability, if provided by the exchange, would deliver immense value to the buyer.

Implementation

In the exchange environment, the holy grail seems to be the ability of the exchange to deliver end-to-end provisioning of circuits within a reasonable timeframe across multiple service providers. Unlike switched services, circuits take a longer time to bring up and usually stay up longer.

Ubiquity, speed, and ease of implementation are the critical factors that the ISLA framework must address. Those same attributes are, of course, some of the core competencies that the dynamic work flow and dynamic work-flow community concepts were developed to provide.

While effective implementation capabilities are primarily a factor of the service provider's operations, the ISLA has the potential to bring visibility to what the service provider is truly capable of delivering. The exchange obviously has a role within the work-flow community. To the service provider, the exchange would appear to be the customer. By automating the work flow involved in the ordering process, the exchange could reliably track service order progress through the service provider's organization.

In the best-case scenario, the service provider would have the capabilities necessary for visibility and reporting that are provided by the ISLA framework. In other cases, the interface might be via electronic bonding such as Access Service Requests (ASRs), Local Service Requests (LSRs), Electronic Data Interchange (EDI) transactions (such as 850s, 855s), or other such mechanisms. Although it is hard to imagine, in worst-case scenarios the service provider might even still receive its orders by fax.

Regardless of the type of interface, automated work flow could be developed within the exchange to manage transactions. This means that the exchange would automate and manage the different ordering requirements of the various service providers simply by developing various work flows that consisted primarily of electronic transactions.

Using the work-flow auditor and KPI engine, the exchange would then be able to track delivery both near-real-time and historically. Over time, this information could be displayed as performance or compliance information, similar to the on-time percentages that are tracked as key performance indicators by the airline and travel industries.

Quality

The ISLA framework, as we have discussed throughout this book, is specifically designed to enhance the ability of service providers to deliver SLA-compliant quality to the buyer. The capabilities we have been discussing are all available to the exchange as well.

The concepts of dynamic community management and unified presentation could provide differentiated levels of access to information or permissions to perform certain activities between the exchange, trading partners, and buyers. Likewise, service providers using ISLA concepts could decide how much access the exchange would be allowed, meaning that the exchange might have access to different levels of proprietary information from a number of service providers.

Differentiated levels of access would then allow the exchange to internally manage the end-to-end QoS that it delivers to the buyer without compromising provider anonymity or proprietary performance reporting. For example, a service provider might allow the exchange to access certain KPIs related to its ability to deliver SLA-compliant service across a number of markets. Yet, for competitive reasons, service provider A might not want this information visible to service provider B.

The exchange might need to access multiple (vendor) sources of proprietary QoS information to aggregate an offering that would meet a certain QoS level end-to-end or to manage its own liabilities to the buyer (by selecting certain providers over others), but it would not necessarily present the individual QoS to the buyer. Nor would it share provider A's QoS information with provider B.

The exchange might instead present an end-to-end guarantee that would reflect not only the abilities of the service providers within the offering, but also its tolerance for risk, its ability to monitor or affect in-process work flow, its ability to file and process violations, and its ability to receive financial settlements from its underlying providers.

The capability to securely manage the user community's individual information access levels is extremely important if the exchange is to be the final guarantor to the customer. Without such a capability, exchanges could not manage and mitigate the risks associated with having multiple anonymous sellers behind their offerings. Having access to the proprietary information of a number of vendor partners would require, of course, that an exchange be firmly established as an independent trusted third party with its partners.

Settlement

A large component of any trading environment is the concept of settlement. The telecommunications marketplace is no different. But the ability to manage settlement across the diverse community of trading partners will be critical to the long-term success of exchanges. We believe that the exchange proponents' version of the ideal world absolutely cannot be realized until settlement is addressed.

Our work suggests that to deliver added value, exchanges must become aggregators of both bandwidth and the financial aspects behind it. The customer will not buy anything that he or she cannot be reasonably sure will be delivered, regardless of price. As we said earlier, this means that the exchange must assume ultimate responsibility for huge amounts of financial liability.

The ISLA framework's inherent reporting capabilities and intelligent KPI engine would allow for in-depth compliance reporting based on the various financial aspects of settlement. In addition, the work-flow engine would be used to create work flow specifically designed to reconcile SLA violations. We discussed these capabilities within the service provider's environment in prior chapters.

As we have shown, the exchange success factors we have discussed make up a need hierarchy, meaning that each higher need is dependent on the ability to deliver the lower ones. Settlement is at the top of the pyramid. Delivery of a need hierarchy is built over time, as we have seen in examining different evolutions.

Long-term success will be determined by actions taken now. We have provided a possible roadmap for service providers. Exchanges must take these principles and implement them on a much larger scale. While the techniques and technology for creating these exchanges are known, the exchanges will face many of the same challenges that service providers face. Resolving these challenges will be much easier, of course, if the underlying service providers' OSSs have ISLA-type capabilities. Unfortunately, there is no way to predict whether or not service providers will adopt the ISLA concept.

The Outlook for Exchanges

The momentum behind bandwidth exchanges will likely continue to grow. An overwhelming percentage (94 percent) of respondents in the Andersen study believe that there will be a liquid bandwidth-trading environment emerging by 2004. Fully three-quarters of respondents have taken specific preparatory action to participate. While the Andersen study was released prior to the Enron debacle, we believe that the fundamentals are sound, as we discussed earlier in this chapter, and that respondents and others will continue to propel the growth of bandwidth exchanges.

We offer a caveat to those betting on the liquid environment appearing any time soon. As long as availability is a customer issue and SLAs are used to address availability, the viability of a large public exchange that is more than an electronic bulletin board will be directly related to the exchange's ability to manage the issues related to QoS, SLAs, and the accompanying settlement issues.

While trading in voice minutes and Internet traffic will continue to grow rapidly, it is very unlikely that any public bandwidth exchange will be able to generate sufficient liquidity within the marketplace for larger bandwidth (DS-3 and above) until a solution is found for quality and settlement.

Fully 80 percent of the respondents in the Andersen study cited the ability to reach agreement on liquidated damages (see Figure 15.7) and related penalty clauses for nonperformance as at least "somewhat of a constraint" to the formation of a liquid bandwidth-trading environment.

Larger bandwidths almost always require SLAs. As we discussed, the increased use of SLAs by end users will eventually drive flow-down SLAs from the customer all the way to the long-haul backbone. This flow-down movement infers that an exchange environment will potentially create a multiple layering of SLAs on an end-to-end circuit. As the end-to-end circuit may be made up of many service providers (with their backbone also potentially made up of a number of carriers), the final guarantor (that is, the one who sold the circuit to the customer) must be able to manage the financial implications of having so many players in the equation.

No service provider has been willing to assume the entire risk of financial penalties associated with this arrangement thus far, except through negotiated bilateral agreements.

The short- to medium-term outlook for exchanges is now clearer as a result of our examination of their needs. We project that two classes of bandwidth will emerge: true commodity and mission-critical. Trading in commodity bandwidth will continue to grow, and a liquid market will develop into a robust trading environment specifically for those products. Large and mission-critical bandwidth will continue to be procured on a bilateral basis, albeit through private exchanges owned by each service provider so that customers will perceive SLA accountability.

There is also a very good chance that the long-term outlook will actually resemble the ideal world we talked about earlier. In the ideal world, the problems associated with implementation, quality, and settlement will be addressed in such a way that all products can be perceived as commodities, including mission-critical circuits.

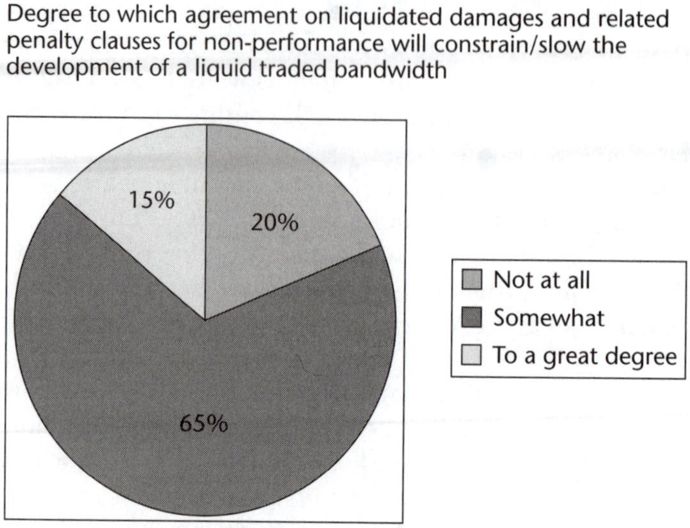

Source: Bandwidth Uncovered, Anderson, Technology, Media, & Communications, 2001.

Figure 15.7 Liquidated damages perceived as a constraint.

Having the issues addressed and communications (all of the possible products) truly perceived as a commodity will lead to an environment wherein a small number of large public exchanges will control the vast majority of trades. Buyers, sellers, and independent brokers will create liquidity in trading all bandwidth products under standard terms and conditions, regardless of size and criticality. The environment we have just described is not unlike the stock markets, where different derivatives such as spot and futures markets are also actively traded.

We cannot predict how long it will take to get to the ideal world that we have been discussing, but we do believe that the momentum and market forces will eventually overcome the obstacles. We do reiterate that, like the stock markets, the exchanges will need to be independent, trusted third-party entities.

Creating trust is essential to generating liquidity. A viable large bandwidth exchange means that the responsibility for identifying SLA violations and generating claims for nonperformance will become the responsibility of the service guarantor, not the customer. Otherwise, the *catch me if you can* mentality of today's market will prevail.

Key to the new exchange's success will be a settlement or reconciliation process that is based on compensation for liquidated damages using a business impact methodology as discussed in Chapter 2. Assuming we get this far, the systems used for monitoring and validation will also shed light on the potential financial liabilities associated with the SLA commitments made by service providers.

Someone will be forced to face the large potential liabilities that lie dormant within the service provider's SLA commitments. There are only a few candidates: the seller, the buyer, or the exchange. All three of these entities will have different views of its respective liabilities. Each will differ significantly from the customer's idea of who is responsible and for how much of the business impact.

Each entity will also be forced to somehow mitigate its risks. The need for risk mitigation of the huge liabilities associated with QoS in the exchange environment leads us to what is perhaps our boldest projection: By the time we get to the ideal bandwidth exchange world, if we ever do, the true enablers of independent, trusted third-party bandwidth exchanges will probably not be entities from the telecommunications arena at all. The enablers of bandwidth exchanges will be insurance companies.

The largest insurance companies have already established their trusted third-party reputations, but, more important, they understand the financial aspects of complicated risk mitigation, have the financial astuteness and expertise to develop the kinds of actuarial tables that the complicated bandwidth exchange environment will need, and have established relationships for underwriting large liabilities.

The need to mitigate the risks associated with SLA liabilities is not limited to bandwidth exchanges. Once the size and scope of these liabilities become visible, every service provider will be obligated to figure out a way to address them. Perhaps that's part of the reason there has been little real effort put forth by service providers to solve the problems associated with SLAs. They don't want to know because if they did they'd have to do something about it. Whatever they did about it, it would probably be expensive.

Summary

In this chapter, we have explored the relationships, issues, goals, and vision behind the notion of successful bandwidth exchanges. We have identified and defined the critical factors of product, price, implementation, quality, and settlement, as well as brought to the forefront the problems associated with creating the needed liquidity that is a requirement to the exchange concept taking off on a large scale.

What we have concluded is that the problems discussed in this chapter is typical of the discussion in earlier ones. As with other facets of implementing SLAs within the telecommunications industry, it appears that there is still much work to be done.

We don't believe that the problems we have discussed, the needs we have examined, or the solutions we have espoused are necessarily limited to the communications industry. Quite the contrary. We believe that the same problems exist in many industries. We think that the needs that drive customers to demand SLAs are probably fundamentally the same—to guarantee the availability of a perceived physiological business need—across many types of businesses both large and small.

We also think that the solutions we have developed and detailed in this book may be valuable to other entities within other businesses and other industries as they wrestle with their own SLA issues. In Chapter 16, we explain how the techniques, principles, and solutions we have been exploring through the last fifteen chapters can be used to address SLA issues in other industries.

CHAPTER

16

Applying the Model to Other Industries

Our focus throughout this book has been on driving the business of communications companies by basing it on Service Level Agreement (SLA) definitions and continuously monitoring these SLAs. We have defined and built the model in terms of the systems that form the Operations Support System/Business Support System(OSS/BSS).

The integrated SLA model can be applied to many other market segments. In fact, there are many other vertical markers where SLA-driven business practice is very well developed—sometimes even more developed than in the communications segment. One very good example is in IT infrastructure, and more recently in IT outsourcing. Another example, and the first segment in which SLAs were widely used, is third-party maintenance and service delivery.

In any vertical market, the concept of SLA-driven business practices follows the same patterns we have set forth throughout the second part of the book. The differences in industry applications of the integrated SLA model are in the types of systems that need to be integrated, and the types of processes that need to be automated. In this chapter we will talk about the role SLAs can play in the utility and field service industries, and how the business environment in each industry affects SLA management.

Utilities

The energy and utility industries share many traits with the communications industry. The businesses are structured in a similar fashion and have a similar service model and customer base. The similarities extend beyond the business structure. For example, with the deregulation occurring in the United States, traditional utility companies are starting to offer telecommunication services. While utility companies may initially operate communications services under a separate business arm, they will move to integrate the businesses to gain efficiencies and improve the customer experience.

From an OSS perspective, utilities have systems that are not too dissimilar from the communications providers. For example, the equivalent to the customer care and billing systems found in communications providers are the *customer information systems* (CISs). The equivalent to network monitoring and management systems such as Micromuse Netcool and HP OpenView are *supervisory control and data acquisition* (SCADA) systems such as Oasys by Metso.

There are, however, important differences between utilities and communications providers when it comes to SLAs. The most notable difference is on the service side of the business. Utilities differ very much from one another in the way they are organized. For example, different countries and regions have different regulatory agencies that govern what services a utility delivers. Electric utilities differ in many ways from gas utilities and generation based on fossil fuels differ from nuclear generation companies.

There are similarities in all utilities from a service and infrastructure perspective. If we look at utilities that provide customer service, we find that the field force falls into two categories—technicians who provide service to customers, and technicians who build out and maintain the utility's facilities and distribution network. The distribution network is the network of pipes (in the case of a gas utility) and wires (in the case of electric utilities).

If we look at the service side of the communications service provider, we find one very big difference in terms of SLAs. When a consumer calls in with a problem, a trouble ticket is opened. The ticket goes into the mix of tickets and is closed by the field technician when service is complete. Often in utilities, the root of a trouble ticket is not directly on the consumer's site. For example, if there is a downed electric line in a neighborhood, there can be typically tens, hundreds, and sometimes thousands of power outages. Each outage would be called in and have an associated ticket. But when a field employee is deployed, he or she will not visit each customer site. Instead the root cause of the problem will be discovered—either because the power company will get a call about the downed line, or the utility will correlate all tickets to pinpoint the real problem. This correlation may be done by the dispatcher or customer service representative who looks at the ticket locations and overlays them on the geographic information of the distribution network. The problem spot is located using common sense and experience. Alternatively, many large utilities employ outage management systems that do these overlays and correlations to identify root causes.

Once the utility worker identifies the most likely root cause, he or she opens a new ticket and associates all related tickets to the root ticket. Once the root cause is fixed, all tickets thought to be related are closed down. Tickets are closed without a callback to the customer. The assumption is that if the problem has not been fixed, the customer will call back and a new ticket will be opened! Consumers are seldom given precise information and restoration times. They are usually given very general times, which follow an incremental wait time.

Service Level Agreements on the service side start to have more meaning when one looks at big businesses. For example, when a hospital is connected to power, it must have some SLA guarantees. But even here, the concept of SLAs is not as well developed, and major healthcare facilities tend to own and maintain their own power generators.

The area in which SLAs are very well developed in the energy and utility practices is with regard to the transmission of energy among the power distribution companies. The energy industry is very advanced in terms of defining supply contracts and attaching SLAs to them. Distribution SLAs are mandatory because energy must pass through many hands before it gets to the consumer. The companies involved in the energy handoff have put in place a very complex network that must be continuously fed. It is very important that the energy flow be continuous and within very strict limits for problems to be avoided. Ensuring continuous energy flow is accomplished using sets of SLAs that are put in place between the energy companies, and that define precise delivery quantities, locations, and timetables. All requirements are defined in *tariffs* that must be published by the supplying company and approved by the regulatory authority.

EXAMPLE 1: THE NORTHERN NATURAL GAS COMPANY

Let's look at a tariff example for a gas company. Since tariff information must be public domain, all such tariffs and contract terms are published on the Web. The example we use is taken from a gas tariff published by the Northern Natural Gas Company and is accessible from the Enron Web site.

Northern Natural Gas Company is a corporation organized under the laws of the State of Delaware. Northern is authorized to do, and is doing, business in the states of Delaware, Texas, New Mexico, Oklahoma, Kansas, Colorado, Nebraska, Iowa, Missouri, Illinois, Minnesota, Michigan, Wyoming, Wisconsin, North Dakota, South Dakota, Montana, and Louisiana.

(continues)

EXAMPLE 1: THE NORTHERN NATURAL GAS COMPANY *(Continued)*

Northern, a *natural gas company*, is engaged in the purchase of natural gas and the transportation and sale thereof in interstate commerce. Northern currently obtains its supply of natural gas from producers in the Panhandle Field in the state of Texas; the Hugoton Field in the states of Texas, Oklahoma, and Kansas; the Permian Basin in the states of Texas and New Mexico; the Delaware Basin in the state of Texas; the Tiger Ridge and Sherard Areas in the state of Montana; the Federal offshore areas in the Gulf of Mexico; the Overthrust and Rocky Mountain Areas in the states of Colorado and Wyoming; and from numerous other gas producing areas in the states of Kansas, Oklahoma, and Texas.

The Delaware Basin gas is transported by Northern through its own facilities in a northeasterly direction into the states of Texas, Oklahoma, Kansas, Nebraska, Iowa, Illinois, Michigan, Wisconsin, South Dakota, and Minnesota. Offshore Gulf of Mexico gas, the Overthrust and Rocky Mountain Areas gas enters Northern's system via various transportation and exchange agreements with other natural gas pipeline companies.

The natural gas supplies purchased from the Tiger Ridge and Sherard Areas in the state of Montana are gathered by Northern and transported to a point on the Montana-Saskatchewan border where delivery of such gas is made to Many Islands Natural Gas, which has contractual arrangements for the transportation of these volumes across Canada and redelivery to Northern at the Minnesota-Manitoba border near Emerson, Manitoba. Great Lakes Gas Transmission Company (Great Lakes) receives such gas at Emerson for Northern's account and transports the gas for redelivery to Northern at Carlton, Minnesota.

A tariff describes the rates as well as the contractual obligations between the supplier (in this case, Northern Gas Company) and the companies to which it supplies energy. For example, this tariff defines precise rates and volumes that Northern supplies to the shipping companies as shown in Table 16.1.

One of the most important aspects of dealing with a distribution network is consistency. Gas flows through pipes, and the key to efficient distribution on a massive scale is a fixed and continuous flow. It is important that the agreement formed between the supplier and the shipper define throughput that is ensured by both sides. The supplier needs to continuously supply and the requester (shipper) needs to continuously consume. If supply falls short or is too great, then either the shipper will lack quantities or the shipper will levy storage and commodity charges. Therefore each party that contracts with Northern needs to set up a *firm throughput service* contract that clearly defines the thresholds for continuous supply and demand and the penalties for delivery that does not fall within set thresholds. Interruptions and excess are both

Table 16.1 Rates and Volumes in Northern's Tariff

SHIPPER NAME	RATE SCHEDULE	NEGOTIATED RATE	OTHER CHARGE	VOLUME	RECEIPT POINTS	DELIVERY POINTS
Barrett Resource	Schedule TI	$0.105/Dekatherm per day with adjustments based on Gross National Product	None	70,000	Matagorda 803	Any points on Matagorda Offshore Pipeline System
UtiliCorp United	Schedule TFX	$0.18/Dekatherm per day multiplied by the volumes transported	None	3,500 April through October, 7,000 November through March	Grlks/NNG Carlton and NNG Field/Mkt Demarcation (depending on time of year)	Zone EF - UtiliCorp UtiliCorp
Midwest Natural Gas	Schedule TFX	$4.498/Dekathern per month and many additional overhead and construction costs	Surcharges apply	314	NBPL/NNG Ventura, Glks/NNG Carlton or NNG Field/Mkt Demarcation (depending on time of year)	Zone EF - Midwest Natural
Great River Energy	Schedule TI	26 cents/MMBtu and an incremental schedule for storage costs	None	125,000	All receipt points	All Delivery Points

(continues)

Table 16.1 Rates and Volumes in Northern's Tariff *(Continued)*

SHIPPER NAME	RATE SCHEDULE	NEGOTIATED RATE	OTHER CHARGE	VOLUME	RECEIPT POINTS	DELIVERY POINTS
WPS Energy Services	Schedule TFX	$0.19/Dekatherm per day	None	5,000	NNG Field/Market Demarcation	Wisconsin Gas/NNG-Waukesha, Wisconsin Elect/NNG Waukesha Mukwanogo, Janesville Wisconsin Power and Light and Madison TBS #1

Rate schedules are defined elsewhere in the tariff document.
Source: F.E.R.C gas Tariff of Northern Natural Gas Company filed with the Federal Energy Regulatory Commission.

bad, and the supplier should avoid them so as not to incur penalties. The key word is *balancing*—and the firm throughput agreement defines consequences owing to volumetric as well as dollar valuation and dollar volume imbalances. The penalties are defined in terms of imbalances as shown in Table 16.2.

Given that balancing is the most important aspect of implementing SLAs in utilities, most of the emphasis in terms of systems supporting SLAs falls into two realms. One is the constant *measurement of flow* within the distribution network (not too different from systems that monitor the network in the OSS) and the second is on timely—and more important—preventive and *planned maintenance*. It is crucial for the distribution network to be well maintained and avoid problems rather than scramble when a problem does occur. Since the distribution networks at these levels of agreement are made up of very fat pipes, problems can be devastating (not to mention very hazardous).

Customer Service and Service Delivery

Another set of industry segments that are intimately familiar with SLAs (sometimes also called *service grades*, *fault grades*, and *service commitments*) include companies that provide field service on equipment. Service-intensive businesses include high-tech manufacturers that also provide customer service over the phone and on-site, medical equipment service providers, and third-party maintenance providers that do not manufacture the equipment but deliver service based on a contract that exists between the company and the customer.

Table 16.2 Gas Company Penalties Defined in Terms of Imbalances

IMBALANCE LEVEL	DUE NORTHERN	DUE SHIPPER
0 percent to 3 percent	MIP* × 1.00	MIP × 1.00
Greater than 3 percent up to 5 percent	MIP × 1.02	MIP × 0.98
Greater than 5 percent up to 10 percent	MIP × 1.10	MIP × 0.90
Greater than 10 percent up to 15 percent	MIP × 1.20	MIP × 0.80
Greater than 15 percent up to 20 percent	MIP × 1.30	MIP × 0.70
Greater than 20 percent	MIP × 1.40	MIP × 0.60

*MIP is the monthly index price.

The key to the service market segment is the contract and the SLA defined in this contract. Service is usually provided in one of two ways—remote or on-site. Remote service means that a customer can call into a support center where an engineer tries to resolve the problems over the phone. Problem resolution may take the form of phone assistance, remote diagnostics, or simply shipping a replacement for the faulty equipment. For example, if a computer keyboard is malfunctioning, it is simpler for the servicing company to ship a replacement than to dispatch a field technician. If the problem cannot be resolved over the phone, a field engineer is usually dispatched to the customer site. It is in the service company's best interest to try to resolve things over the phone since a call is by far cheaper than dispatching the engineer. Yet SLAs are defined in such a way that the clock starts ticking as soon as the problem is identified, so the process of routing the call through the support center and then possibly to the field must be very efficient.

The contract itself, as well as the terms and conditions agreed upon by the servicing company, can be very elaborate. The contract process starts by defining the term types themselves. Each term has a type, and the type defines the category for commitment as shown in Figures 16.1 and 16.2. There are different terms based on the conditions to which the servicing company commits. Once the term types are defined we can define the terms themselves as shown in Figure 16.3. Each term typically has a surcharge that affects the total contract price. Each term can also have different quantities associated with it depending on the fault grade. In the example shown in Figure 16.3, we have a 2-hour response time in a standard fault grade, but if the event being called in is defined as an emergency, then the response time is reduced to 1 hour. Obviously, such a definition can mean that the surcharge on the contract increases.

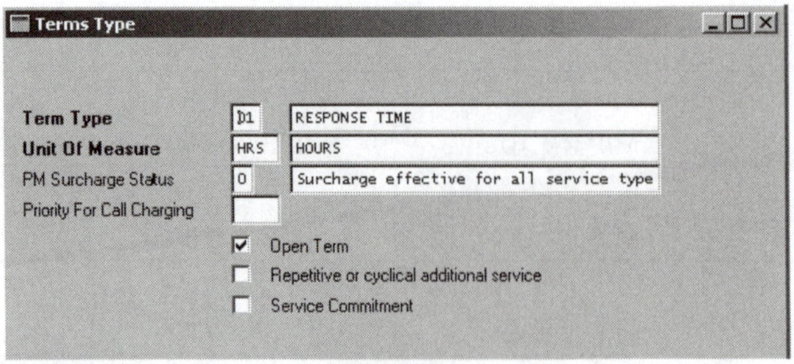

Figure 16.1 Defining a *response time* term type.

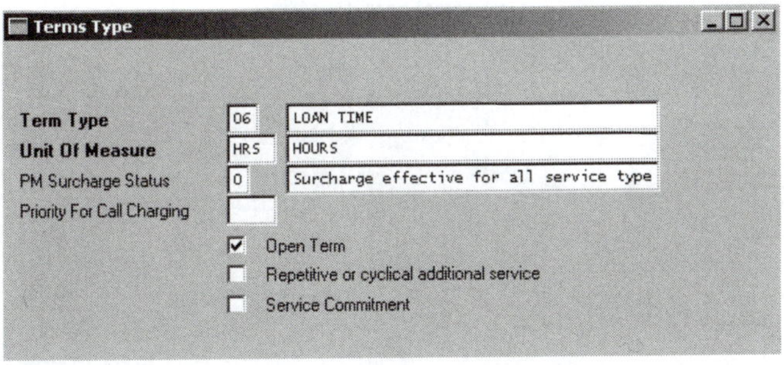

Figure 16.2 Defining a *loan* term type.

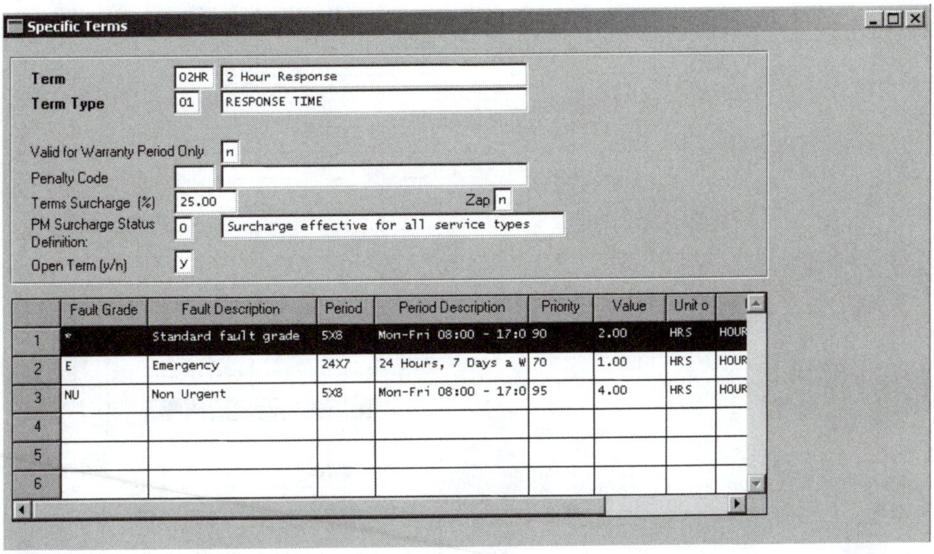

Figure 16.3 Defining a *term.*

Each servicing line per fault grade can also have different charging modifiers. It is possible, for example, that an SLA will stipulate a different charge for different terms and fault grades. Let's look at the example in Figure 16.4. Figure 16.4 shows that for the term and fault grade there is a charge for labor, but with a 10 percent discount. Travel time will not be charged, and there will be a flat rate for services. In effect, the customer has an incentive to use a *nonurgent* fault grade—the benefit for the servicing company is that the response time is 4 hours instead of 2 hours. All billing elements (for example, *parts*) are charged as per other definitions in the contract.

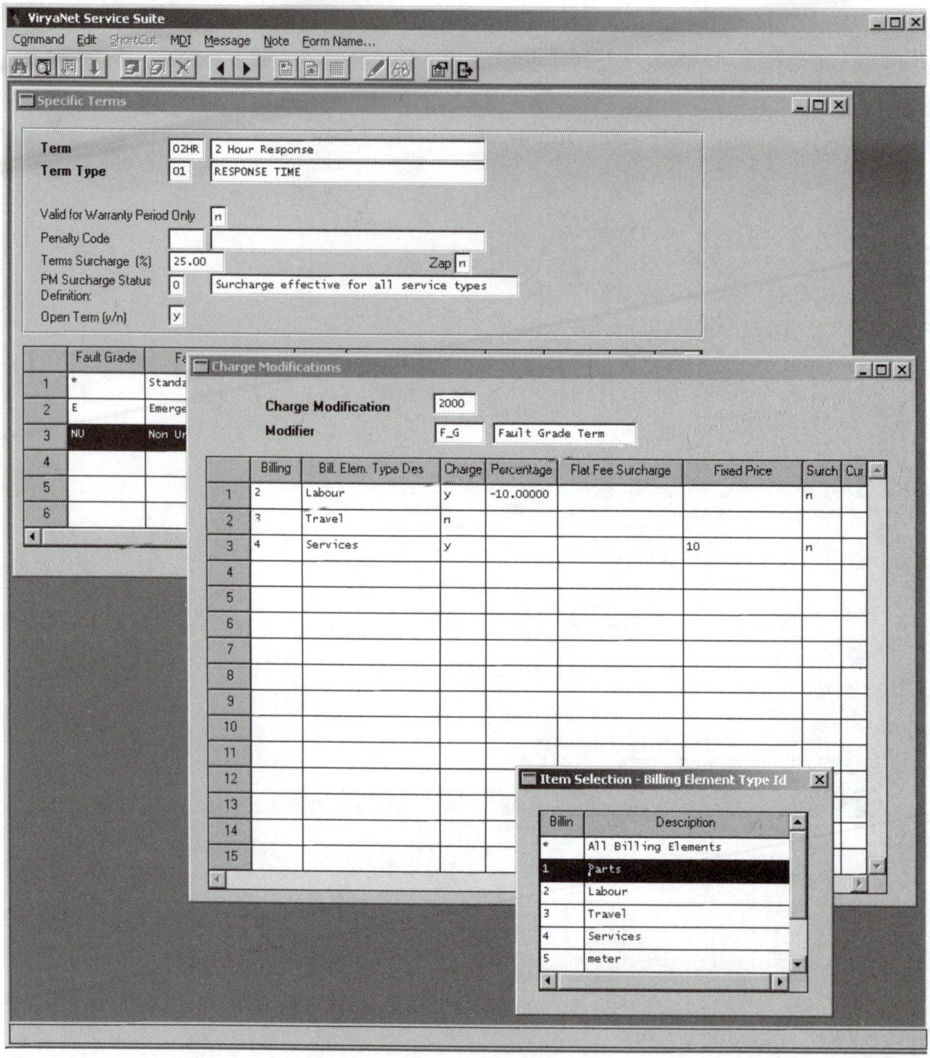

Figure 16.4 Term charge modifiers.

Once the terms are defined, they can be associated with the contract itself as shown in Figure 16.5. Finally, in addition to the terms themselves, which form the SLA, we can also define specific SLAs regarding our commitment for uptime for a certain piece of equipment. This commitment (shown in Figure 16.6) is often the only thing the customer requires, while in other cases the customer will require both overall uptime commitments as well as other servicing commitments.

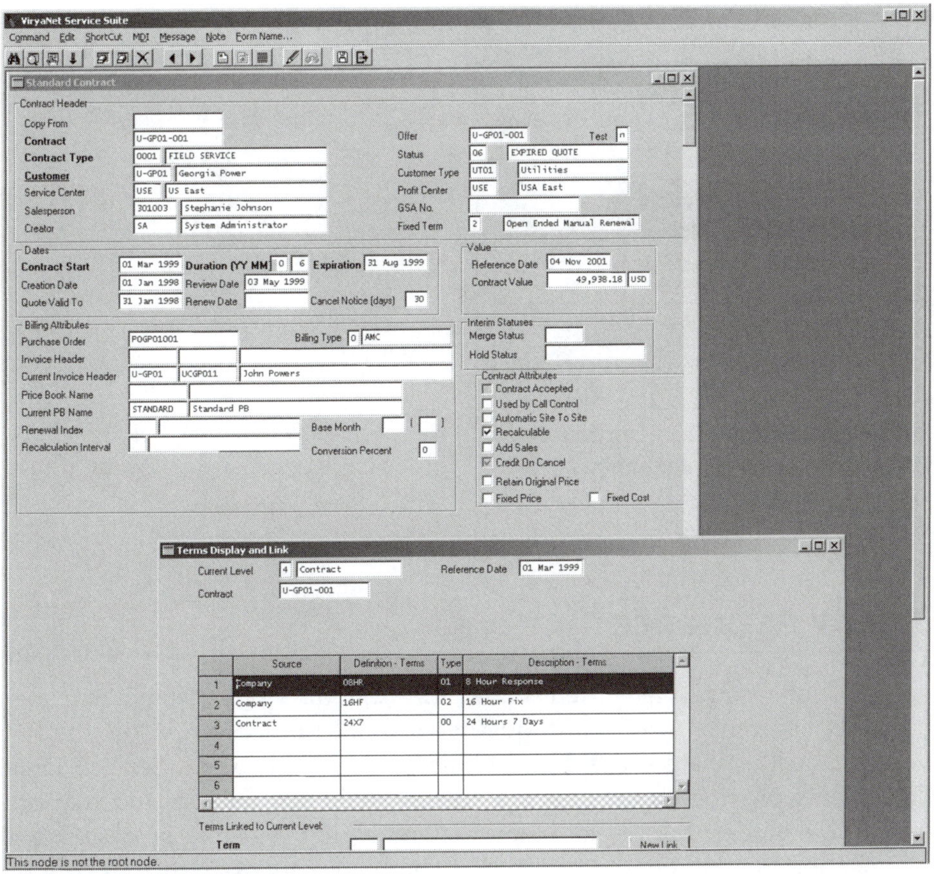

Figure 16.5 Terms on contract.

There are aspects in which the integrated SLA model differs for different service market segments. The first is that while these segments often manage the concept of equipment downtime, many of the terms relate directly to the servicing of the equipment. The second difference is that there are fewer monitoring facilities—although monitoring facilities are forecast to grow with the proliferation of smart sensors that continuously transmit uptime information from the equipment and its sensors to a central hub over the Internet (the so-called X Internet).

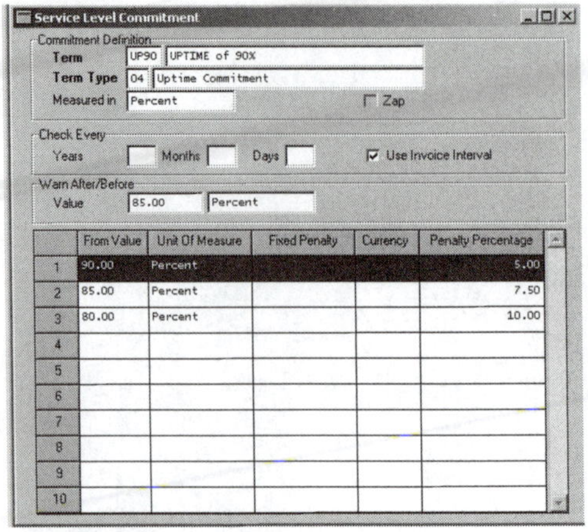

Figure 16.6 Uptime commitment.

Quality Assurance

One question we are often asked is how SLAs and SLA management is related to quality assurance metrics and quality assurance processes. While the two are not directly related, they are in many ways equivalent. Service Level Agreements provide metrics for measuring quality of service, and the integrated SLA model is a methodology for organizing systems, processes, and organizations so that quality of service is high. Quality assurance paradigms define metrics with which we can measure the quality of production, manufacturing, or other such activities as well as methodologies through which we can guarantee high levels of quality.

The industry is full of Quality Assurance (QA) and quality management processes, and it is outside the scope of this book to address QA. Still, we would like to mention two methodologies—mainly because they are also used in the communications industry as well as in other vertical markets for which the integrated SLA model can be applied. These two QA methods are the ISO 9000 family of standards and the six-sigma methodology.

ISO 9000

The ISO 9000 standard is the most widely known family of quality standards published by the ISO. ISO 9000 has become an international reference for quality requirements standards in business-to-business dealings.

The vast majority of ISO standards are highly specific to a particular product, material, or process. But the standards that have earned the ISO 9000 family a worldwide reputation are known as *generic management system standards*. By *generic* we mean that the same standards can be applied to any organization, large or small, whatever its product—including whether its *product* is actually a service—in any sector of activity—and whether the organization is a business enterprise, a public administration, or a government department. Management system refers to what the organization does to manage its processes or activities.

ISO 9000 is concerned with *quality management*. Quality management is what the organization does to enhance customer satisfaction by meeting customer and applicable regulatory requirements and continuously improving performance.

The standards, guidelines, and technical reports that make up the ISO 9000 family include the following (all of which define different aspects of the methodology for quality management systems):

ISO 9000: Fundamentals and vocabulary

ISO 9001: Requirements

ISO 9004: Guidelines for performance improvements

ISO 19011: Guidelines on auditing

ISO 10005: Guidelines for quality plans

ISO 10006: Guidelines for project management

ISO 10007: Guidelines for configuration management

ISO 10012: Guidelines for measuring equipment

ISO 10013: Guidelines for developing manuals

ISO 10014: Guidelines for managing the economics of quality

ISO 10015: Guidelines for training

Six Sigma

The term *six sigma* is a statistical term that comes from a measure based on a normal distribution (or Gauss distribution) in which defects can account for only a very small proportion in the sample. Conceptually, six sigma is a method used to improve quality in products and processes. The statistical foundation is not the important part of the methodology, but the methodology provides its proponents with a *mathematical foundation* (which seems to do wonders in making people feel that it is more than other quality methodologies).

For the mathematicians among you folks, the normal distribution is defined by the following formula:

$$N(x;\mu,\sigma) = \frac{1}{\sigma\sqrt{2\pi}} e^{-\left(\frac{(x-\mu)^2}{\sigma^2}\right)}$$

This formula gives the probability of a value x in a normal distribution with mean μ and standard distribution σ. If we apply the formula with $x = 6\sigma$ and mean 0, we get a very small probability, indeed. For the less analytic, recall from your third week in Statistics 101 that the normal distribution can be used to approximate very well any sample space when the sample size becomes very large—which is relevant for most production environments. Also recall that most of the samples fall within a single value of σ (sigma), and that the further away from the center you go the (exponentially) fewer samples you will find. In fact, when you look at the total sample points that fall more than six sigma (that is, six times the standard distribution) away from the average value (the expectation of the probability space), you get a probability that is very small—0.0000034 (3.4 in a million).

Six sigma at many organizations simply means a measure of quality that strives for near perfection. Six sigma is a disciplined, data-driven approach and methodology for eliminating defects (driving toward six sigma between lower and upper specification limits) in any process—from manufacturing to transaction and from product to service.

The statistical representation of six sigma describes quantitatively how a process is performing. To achieve six sigma, a process must not produce no more than 3.4 defects per million opportunities. A six-sigma defect is defined as anything outside customer specifications. A six-sigma opportunity is then the total quantity of chances for a defect. Process sigma can easily be calculated using a six-sigma calculator.

The fundamental objective of the six-sigma methodology is to implement a measurement-based strategy that focuses on process improvement and variation reduction through the application of six-sigma improvement projects. The strategy is implemented using two six-sigma submethodologies: define, measure, analyze, improve, control (DMAIC); and define, measure, analyze, design, verify (DMADV). The six-sigma DMAIC process is a system for improving existing processes that fall below specification and require incremental improvement. The six-sigma DMADV process is a system used to develop new processes or products at six-sigma quality levels. The DMADV process can also be employed if a current process requires more than just incremental improvement. Both six-sigma processes are executed by trained professionals known as six-sigma green belts and six-sigma black belts, and are overseen by six-sigma master black belts.

According to the Six Sigma Academy, black belts save companies approximately $230,000 per project and can complete four to six projects per year. General Electric, one of the companies that has been most successful in implementing six sigma, has estimated benefits on the order of $10 billion during the first 5 years of implementation. GE first began six sigma in 1995.

Summary

Service Level Agreements are perhaps most widely known within communications providers, but Service Level Management is a common thread throughout all companies involved in service delivery. The concepts introduced throughout this book, as well as the methods that we have outlined, are applicable to all service companies—regardless of industry. The differences will be in *which* systems need to be integrated and automated—but the crux of the methodology we have outlined in the book will not change. We hope that our methodology will help companies of all sorts to build an efficient service delivery operation and one that can guarantee financial success.

APPENDIX

Acronyms

ADSL: Asymmetrical Digital Subscriber Line

API: Application Program Interface

ASP: Application Service Provider

ASR: Access Service Request

ATM: Asynchronous Transfer Mode

B2B: Business to Business

B2C: Business to Consumer

B2X: Business to Exchange

BI: Business Intelligence

BLEC: Building Local Exchange Carriers

BML: Business Management Layer

BOB: Best-of-Breed

BSS: Business Support System

CABS: Carrier Access Billing System

CDN: Content Delivery Network

CDR: Call Detail Record or Common Data Representation

CFO: Chief Finance Officer

CIS: Customer Information System
CLEC: Competitive Local Exchange Carrier
CLLI: Common Language Location Identification
CLR: Circuit Layout Record
CMIP: Common Management Information Protocol
CO: Central Office
CORBA: Common Object Request Broker Architecture
COTS: Commercial Off The Shelf
CPE: Customer Premises Equipment
CRM: Customer Relationship Management
CSR: Customer Service Representative
CSU: Channel Service Unit
CSV: Comma Separated Value
DII: Dynamic Invocation Interface
DLEC: Data Local Exchange Carrier
DLL: Data Link Library
DLR: Design Layout Record
DMADV: Define, Measure, Analyze, Design, Verify
DMAIC: Define, Measure, Analyze, Improve, Control
DOM: Document Object Model
DSI: Dynamic Skeleton Interface
DSL: Digital Subscriber Line
DSLAM: DSL Access Multiplexer
DSS: Data Storage Service
DTD: Document Type Definition
DWDM: Dense Wavelength Division Multiplexing
EAI: Enterprise Application Integration
EBPP: Electronic Bill Presentation and Payment
EML: Element Management Layer
EMS: Element Management System
ERP: Enterprise Resource Planning
GIOP: General Inter-ORB Protocol
GIS: Geographic Information System

GSM: Global System for Mobile Communication

GUI: Graphical User Interface

HR: Human Resources

HTML: Hypertext Markup Language

HTTP: Hypertext Transfer Protocol

ICT: Information and Communication Technology

IDL: Interface Definition Language

IIOP: Internet Inter-ORB Protocol

ILEC: Incumbent Local Exchange Carrier

IMAP: Internet Message Access Protocol

IOR: Interoperable Object Reference

IP: Internet Protocol

IPDR: Internet Protocol Detail Record

IRU: Indefeasible Rights to Use

ISLA: Integrated Service Level Agreement

ISLAC: Integrated Service Level Agreement Compliance

ISO: International Organization for Standardization

ISP: Internet Service Provider

ISV: Independent Software Vendor

IT: Information Technology

ITC: Integrated Telecommunications Carriers

JSP: Java Server Pages

KPI: Key Performance Indicator

LDAP: Lightweight Directory Access Protocol

LEC: Local Exchange Carrier

LSR: Local Service Request

MIB: Management Information Base

MIP: Monthly Index Price

MOM: Manager of Managers or Message-Oriented Middleware

MPLS: Multi-protocol Layer Switching

MRC: Monthly Recurring Cost

MTBF: Mean Time Between Failures

MTTP: Mean Time to Provision

MTTR: Mean Time to Repair

NE: Network Element

NEL: Network Element Layer

NGOSS: New Generation Operations Support System

NMF: Network Management Forum

NML: Network Management Layer

NMS: Network Management System

NOC: Network Operations Center

NRC: Nonrecurring Charges

OMA: Object Management Architecture

OMG: Object Management Group

OMS: Order Management System

ONE: Open Network Environment

ORB: Object Request Broker

OSI: Open Systems Interconnection

OSS: Operations Support System

OTC: Over the Counter

OTS: Object Transaction Service

PKI: Public Key Infrastructure

PM: Preventive Maintenance

POP: Point of Presence or Post Office Protocol

POTS: Plain Old Telephone Service

PSN: Public Switched Network

PVC: Private Virtual Circuit

QA: Quality Assurance

QoS: Quality of Service

RBOC: Regional Bell Operating Company

RDBMS: Relational Database Management System

RF: Radio Frequency

RIM: Research in Motion

ROI: Return on Investment

RPC: Remote Procedure Call

SA: Service Availability

SAP: Service Access Point

SAX: Simple API for XML

SCADA: Supervisory Control and Data Acquisition

SDN: Software-Defined Network

SGML: Standard Generalized Markup Language

SI: Systems Integrator

SIM: Systems Integration Map

SLA: Service Level Agreement

SLM: Service Level Management

SML: Service Management Layer

SMS: Short Message Service

SMTP: Simple Mail Transfer Protocol

SNMP: Simple Network Management Protocol

SNPP: Simple Network Paging Protocol

SOAP: Simple Object Access Protocol

SOHO: Small Office/Home Office

SP: Service Provider

TAP: Telocator Alphanumeric Protocol

TCP/IP: Transmission Control Protocol/Internet Protocol

TLA: Termination Liability Agreement

TMF: TeleManagement Forum

TML: Telecommunication Markup Language

TMN: Telecommunications Management Network

TMS: Trouble Management System

TMW: TeleManagement World

TOM: Telecommunications Operations Map

UDDI: Universal Description Discovery and Integration

UI: User Interface

UMTS: Universal Mobile Telecommunications System

UNE: Unbundled Network Elements

URI: Universal Resource Identifier

URL: Uniform Resource Locator

URN: Universal Resource Name

VAR: Value Added Reseller

VAS: Value-Added Service

VC: Venture Capital

VPN: Virtual Private Network

WAN: wide area network

WAS: WebSphere Application Server

WCTP: Wireless Communication Transfer Protocol

WFM: Workforce Management

WSDL: Web Services Description Language

WYSIWYG: What You See Is What You Get

XLL: eXtensible Linking Language

XML: eXtensible Markup Language

XQL: eXtensible Query Language

XSL: eXtensible Stylesheet Language

XSLT: eXtensible Style Language Transformation

Bibliography

"Bandwidth Uncovered: A Survey of Current Views about a Traded Bandwidth Market in Europe," Arthur Anderson, Technology Media, and Communications 2001

"Break the OSS Logjam," Jack Codde, Telephony, 1999

"Goodbye to Build it, and They Will Come," Deborah C. Strong, Exchange, 1997

"Business Reinvented," Cap Gemini Ernst & Young, 2001

"Could the 1998 Telecom Executive Draft be Next?," X-Change, 1997

"A Closer Look at Customer Care and Billing," Jeffrey P. Cotrupe, Northern Business Information, tele.com, 1997

"Field Service Automation Applications Defined," B. Bivins, The Gartner Group, 2001

"Foundations of Service Level Management," Sturm, Morris, and Jander,

"Infrastructure upgrades ahead," Om Malik, Red Herring, August 2001

"It's All in the Process," Kathryn Weldon and David Porterfield, Telecommunications, 2001

"A Model of Telecommunications Consistency," Jeffrey P. Cotrupe, Jim Alsman, Northern Business Information, tele.com, 1997

OSS Essentials: Support Systems Solutions for Service Providers, Kornel Teraplan, John Wiley & Sons, 2000.

"OSS Market Report (GB 911)," TeleManagement Forum 2000

"The Right to be Human, A Biography of Abraham Maslow," Edward Hoffman

"Service Level Management - North American Survey 2000," www.nextslm.org, Price Waterhouse Coopers, Sun Microsystems, and BMC software, 2001

"SLA Management Handbook (GB 917)," TeleManagement Forum 2001

"Taking the Plunge," Michael Lafferty and Angela Langowski, CED, June 2001

"Telecommunications Operations Map (GB 910)," TeleManagement Forum

"A Theory on Human Motivation," Abraham Maslow, originally published in Psychological Review 1943

Websites

www.americasnetwork.com

www.bandwidth.com

www.band-x.com

www.comnews.com

www.colotraq.com

www.e-sax.com

www.fiberloops.com

www.globaloss.com

www.networkingnext.com

www.nextsla.org

www.telecoms-mag.com

www.thexchange.com

www.thegtx.com

www.tmforum.org

www.uu.net.com

www.ratexchange.com

www.rothstein.com

www.worldcom.com

Index

J

K

L

M

N

T

U

V

W

X–Y–Z

X

Z